RECOVERY AND RESTORATION IN AN ENGLISH COUNTY: DEVON LOCAL ADMINISTRATION 1646–1670

by

Stephen K. Roberts

UNIVERSITY OF EXETER
1985

First published 1985 by the University of Exeter

© 1985 Stephen K. Roberts

ISBN 0 85989 246 8

Typeset by P&M Typesetting Ltd, Bedford Street, Exeter

Printed in Great Britain by A. Wheaton & Co. Ltd, Exeter

FOR MY PARENTS

Contents

List of Maps,
Tables and Figures

Acknowledgements

This book is a revised version of a doctoral thesis, presented to the University of Exeter in 1980. The revision has in some places been light, in others heavier. The research on which the original thesis and this book both rest was begun late in 1976 and in the thesis I acknowledged the assistance given me by scholars, archivists, institutions and private individuals who helped my work. I am grateful still.

Since presenting my dissertation I have incurred more intellectual debts. Ivan Roots and Christopher Hill, supervisor and examiner respectively, have urged me to get on with revision and publication when lassitude and other pressures seemed to be blending dangerously. John Hatcher, for whom I worked on the NCB History of the British Coal Industry, has taken a generous interest in my work and has given me much useful advice. Conversations with Ann Hughes and other friends at the Institute of Historical Research have over several years kept seventeenth-century matters and London beer inseparably associated in my mind. A generous grant from the Twenty-Seven Foundation contributed to the costs of publishing this volume.

My greatest debts arc to my wife, in particular for her help in drawing the maps, and to other members of my family: the dedication records my oldest ones.

Salford Priors, Evesham, November 1984   STEPHEN K. ROBERTS

Abbreviations

BIHR	*Bulletin of the Institute of Historical Research*
BL	British Library
Bodl. Lib.	Bodleian Library
CCAM	*Calendar of the Committee for Advance of Money*
CCC	*Calendar of the Committee for Compounding with Delinquents*
CJ	*Commons' Journals*
CRO	Cornwall Record Office
CSPD	*Calendar of State Papers Domestic*
CTB	*Calendar of Treasury Books*
DCNQ	*Devon and Cornwall Notes and Queries*
DNB	*Dictionary of National Biography*
DQSOB	Devon Quarter Sessions Order Book
DRO	Devon Record Office
EHR	*English Historical Review*
F & R	CH Firth, RS Rait (eds.): *Acts and Ordinances of the Interregnum*
LJ	*Lords' Journals*
Lysons	D and S Lysons: *Magna Britannia VI: Devonshire*
PRO	Public Record Office
QS	Quarter Sessions
RO	Record Office
SRO	Somerset Record Office
TDA	*Transactions of the Devonshire Association*
TSP	*Thurloe State Papers*
Vivian	JL Vivian: *The Visitations of Devon*
WRO	Wiltshire Record Office

Spelling has been reproduced in the original but contractions and abbreviations have been extended and the 'thorn' has been replaced by 'th'. Dates are Old Style with the year beginning on 1 January.

Introduction

Yet another county study of the mid-seventeenth century needs some justification. The plethora of such local histories as a modern *genre* began in the 1930s with the work of Mary Coate and A. C. Wood on Cornwall and Nottingham respectively.[1] After 1945 the 'gentry controversy' provided further stimulus to historians who sought specific local evidence to confirm or to destroy the arguments of the original combatants, R. H. Tawney, H. R. Trevor-Roper and Lawrence Stone. 'The Gentry' flourishes still as a durable, if well-worn theme for local studies of the Civil War period.[2] As the interest in local approaches has developed, so historians have scrutinized other contexts in which to set the 'County community'. Alan Everitt's classic study of Kent resumed Mary Coate's theme of the peculiarity of each county. The interaction of national and local politics has been developed further by J. S. Morrill whose work draws more heavily on local manuscript sources now available in county record offices.[3] The study of local government in this period was pioneered by two Americans, W. B. Willcox and T. G. Barnes, writing twenty years apart but both on the period before the Civil War. Anthony Fletcher's examination of Sussex from 1600 to 1660 pulled the themes of government, community and county gentry together.[4]

More recently, the concept of the 'county community' has been critically reappraised by Clive Holmes and Ann Hughes[5] who have convincingly shown how allegiances and senses of identity could be focussed not on the county at all but on regional, economic and social realities which make county boundaries seem artificial conventions which hardly commanded loyalties for their own sakes. As Ann Hughes points out, 'a Lancashire Puritan might have more in common with a Warwickshire Puritan than either had with the Catholics of Lancashire and Warwickshire.'[6] But if we have to amend our estimate of England and Wales as a federation of semi-autonomous county communities taking up arms against the centralising government of Charles I, the primacy of the county as the principal local administrative unit *vis-à-vis* central government remains. I have tried to argue elsewhere that policies of 'centralisation' should more appropriately be viewed as rather unsystematic meddling and that seventeenth-century theorists and commentators lacked a cohesive concept of local as against central government,[7] but successive governments did deal with counties one by one, and this fact is sufficient justification for a local administrative study to continue to focus on the county. It is, of course, less of an argument to continue with county political studies. Here, regional considerations might well prove more promising. But relations between Whitehall and the provinces were mediated by the ancient practices of the courts of

MAP ONE   THE HUNDREDS OF DEVON

Key: 1. Axminster; 2. Bampton; 3. Braunton; 4. East Budleigh; 5. West Budleigh; 6. Clyston; 7. Coleridge; 8. Colyton;
9. Crediton; 10. Ermington; 11. Exminster; 12. Fremington; 13. Halberton; 14. Hartland; 15. Hayridge; 16. Haytor;
17. Hemyock; 18. Lifton; 19. South Molton; 20. Ottery St. Mary; 21. Plympton; 22. Roborough; 23. Shebbear;
24. Sherwill; 25. Stanborough; 26. Tavistock; 27. North Tawton; 28. Teignbridge; 29. Tiverton; 30. Black Torrington;
31. Winkleigh; 32. Witheridge; 33. Wonford.

Exchequer and Chancery—in which the county was an inescapable component.

Local studies have naturally been written within historiographical patterns, as contributions to specific debates. The gentry controversy was one such debate, the origins and character of the Civil War conflict another.[8] These works have, in general, been characterized by a focus on the Civil War itself and on the county gentry. Two consequences emerge. One is an almost invariable emphasis on the period 1625 to 1660 or 1600 to 1660 but with the latter as the decisive terminal date. Indeed, it is unusual to discover a county history which deals with the Interregnum in more than one or two chapters.[9] Furthermore county government is regarded solely as the interplay between central government and the county gentry in their administrative guise as magistrates. Quarter sessions is considered (with considerable justification, it should be admitted) as another expression of the power of the gentry. As a conclusion this identification is permissible but as a theme for discussion it gives less weight to the other local participants, who greatly outnumbered the presiding JPs, than is their due. The aims of this study have been to illuminate the sub-structure of local government and to shift the chronological perspective of study in order to discover to what extent conventional time-scales have influenced the conclusions of historians.

Devon was chosen as the area of study because apart from a rather superficial chronicle of the Civil War, and W. G. Hoskins's earliest works on the economic history of the county, it has been neglected by writers involved in the debates mentioned above.[10] Moreover, an admirable 'primary primary' source is available in the quarter sessions records of the county, plumbed only in a dated but still valuable selection illustrating the work of the magistrates, and in a modern short article with the same aim.[11] These uncatalogued and uncalendared manuscripts offer, with miscellaneous classes of records elsewhere, an insight into the structure of English county government at both its most exalted and most humble levels. But the work of the Webbs,[12] T. G. Barnes and W. B. Willcox, and the less instructive compilations of such records by local archivists[13] would make another descriptive essay on the organs of local government otiose and tedious. At the risk of skimping descriptions of the innumerable tasks to which local officials could be called, it was thought more important to try to discover how county administration moved, how it changed in a twenty year period, how it developed. Attention has been focussed on those organs of local government which commanded participation spread more widely than in the commissions of the peace. The jury system, universally acknowledged as a cornerstone of English justice, but never thoroughly studied, is one such institution; the office of head constable another.

Central and local government tensions should feature prominently in any study of this kind, as should an investigation into the social backgrounds of participants. But if this is not a study of the gentry, neither is it solely an inquiry into the social structure of the 'peasant', gentry and yeomanry. More weight is given here than has been common to the impact of patterns of participation on local administrative procedures. What was the impact of changes in the commission of the peace on attitudes to the tasks of government and on methods of completing those tasks? Were the characteristics of the jury system derived partly or entirely from the pattern of recruitment to it? What were the effects of political change in central government on minor officeholders in the county? How far down did political change percolate into local communities? Indeed, was the relationship between London and the county at its lowest social levels a simple one of cause and effect?

The concept of 'government' needs some defining. Here central government means Parliament and the key institutions of the executive,

Council of State or Privy Council. Local government is taken to mean primarily those institutions accountable to quarter sessions or derived from it, including petty sessions meetings. The welter of manorial courts has been ignored except where they impinged on the more effective organs of government. The work of the ecclesiastical courts and the wider, subtler but doubtless highly significant influence of the parochial clergy have been excluded, mainly because they have been the subject of an admirable study by Dr Anne Whiteman, and partly because the important effects of the so-called Clarendon Code have been a well-trodden theme in histories of the Restoration settlement.[14] The local results of the Corporation Act have only been studied where they have a particular bearing on the structure and performance of *county* government. On the other hand 'local government' here includes the outposts of customs, excise and post office; 'county' influences were brought to bear on appointments to these.

All commencing dates for historical investigation are to some extent arbitrary but 1649 is more so than most since it follows one of the most complex periods of political manoeuvre and exploration in English history. It would be misleading to ignore the high politics of 1646 to 1648 and their impact on Devon society, not least because they have never received the attention of historians. Chapter One is therefore a study of these years aimed at describing the events leading to the establishment of the Commonwealth and its cold reception in Devon. Chapters Two and Three deal with the achievements of government under the Rump Parliament of 1649 to 1653 and the pattern of appointments by central government during the rest of that decade. Chapters Four and Five are studies of the lower levels of county government: the officials and their work. Chapter Six considers the impact of the Restoration on local administration and Chapter Seven explores some developments and limitations of government over these two decades in case studies.

Devon, at its longest seventy-five miles from north to south, and at its widest seventy-three from east to west, was not a county where anyone could readily find ease and comfort. 'The soil of this county, being very uneven, full of hills and valleys, is very uneasy for travellers and their horses and gives a barren and unfruitful show to the beholders.' 'Be they never so well mounted upon horses out of other countries, when they have travelled one journey in these parts they can, in respect of ease of travel, forbear a second.'[15] On this the contemporary commentators were agreed. Both Westcote and Risdon offered their readers descriptions of the county which had been filched shamelessly from the pages of Hooker's *Synopsis Chorographical of Devonshire* of *circa* 1599, and blended with copious classical allusions, but endorsed this view of what was then the second largest county in England.[16] It was, moreover, a county of contrasts. The granite tableland of Dartmoor and the dividing line of the Highland and Lowland Zones running roughly along the course of the River Exe are the most imposing features of the topography of Devon. The east of the county has more affinity with Dorset and south-east England than with the county west of the Exe and in the north, which is typically Cornish in appearance.

Geological patterns imposed themselves on land use in Devon. Risdon speaks of the 'pasturing of beasts' in the east, the corn and pasture in the luxuriant South Hams around the Dartmouth hinterland and the comparatively barren landscapes of the north and west where 'many possess store of acres but little quantity of good land'.[17] In East Devon, manors were large and closes were small. A high degree of aristocratic landownership was giving way, by the mid-seventeenth century, to dominance by some of the most eminent gentry families: among them the Poles, the Drakes and the Youngs or Yonges.[18] Gentry hegemony was supported by the nucleated village settlement pattern typical of the east of the county.[19] The tenantry, by contrast, occupied scattered holdings of small closes and water-meadows in the river valleys: ideal conditions for stock-rearing. The pattern of enclosure into small fields following the boundaries of former common fields had been established in the early medieval period.[20] North and West Devon were regions of scattered communities and pastoral farming, except in the Barnstaple hinterland, a small arable district. Much of North Devon was poor quality land; in the more remote uplands the dominant settlement pattern of innumerable hamlets gave way to a more sparsely populated landscape of isolated homesteads, typical of upland regions.[21]

The South Hams was the most wealthy region of the county, where light, well-drained soils made ridge-and-furrow ploughing unnecessary. Arable farming was mixed with stock-raising and fruit-growing; South Hams and Dartmoor wool supplied the Ashburton and Totnes cloth trade. Settlement here, too, was in compact villages. The towns of the South Hams were, however, victims of changes in the cloth trade: Totnes and Dartmouth suffered during the contraction of the heavy broadcloth export trade.[22]

To the north of the South Hams lay the quasi-industrial communities of the Teign valley and beyond them Dartmoor. Despite the poverty of the soil on the moor a flourishing cattle-rearing and sheep-grazing trade existed on its edges. A contemporary view that commoners on Dartmoor were 'substantial' finds support in the movement of the land market in the west of the county, where in the mid-sixteenth century a supply of land had exceeded the demand for it and led to an invasion by outsiders. Furthermore, late settlement on the moor's edge had already produced a large freeholding class, and many moor farmers were enclosing large farms from the moor at nominal cost and then employing undertenants to herd the animals they could graze for other farmers.[23]

All who lived near the moor could use it as summer grazing and this use of waste was probably common on a smaller scale throughout the South West. Leland's comment on waste and improved land alternating in the Cornish landscape probably held good for much of the region but instead of waste being ploughed in a regular pattern of rotation as in the classic Midlands field systems, recent work on outfield cultivation in Devon suggests longterm fluctuations in waste tillage. During the seventeenth century outfield cultivation was declining after peaking with grain prices in the sixteenth century, for it seems that cultivation of wastes was undertaken for 'bonus cropping' when market prices were favourable, rather than as a regular pattern of husbandry. Outfields were used as pasture and for a source of gorse—'furze'—for animal bedding.[24]

This erratic use of waste as a means of augmenting regular income was paralleled by the development of the cloth trade in the region in accordance with Joan Thirsk's model of industries in the countryside.[25] For despite the early completion of enclosure in Devon the prevalence of waste alternating with enclosed cultivated fields restricted the size of holdings, encouraged pastoral rather than arable husbandry and left a surplus labour force available for subsidiary employment. The small scattered holdings of East Devon, with an average close size of three acres, were a brake on rapid agricultural change and by the sixteenth century the production of broadcloths, or 'Devon dozens' was established east of Exeter.[26]

Although 'proto-industrialization' thus came early to Devon, the East Devon cloth trade was experiencing considerable difficulty, before 1640, first as the local supply of wool failed to meet demand and then subsequently as the export trade in heavy cloths faltered. The opening-up of new markets in the Mediterranean for lighter finished cloths—the new draperies—saved the Devon cloth trade from total disaster. The new serge industry established itself in a large area stretching from the north-east of the county where it bordered on Somerset down to Tiverton, the Exe, Culme and Creedy valleys and across as far west as South Molton. Weaving was undertaken in the valleys, where water power was freely available, and finishing of cloth was concentrated in Exeter and Tiverton, prior to distribution and export. One contemporary estimate put the numbers engaged in the Devon cloth trade at 30,000 and by 1686 ulnage profits on Devon wool at the Exchequer amounted to £1,500, bettered only by Yorkshire and Lancashire.[27]

There can be no doubt, however, that despite the winning of new markets and the development of serge production the cloth industry in mid-seventeenth century Devon was in some turmoil. Not only was East Devon experiencing de-industrialization but the trade centred on the south-eastern slopes of Dartmoor was undergoing similar contraction. Dartmoor sheep provided the wool for weaving at Ashburton and Newton Abbot, and Dartmouth provided a natural port for the subsequent export trade, but again the new draperies were overtaking. The disruption of civil war was to throw an intolerable strain on the social fabric of an area already in recession: by 1648 the weavers and woolcombers of Newton Abbot were apparently totally dependent on poor relief. Weavers were the largest group among the sixty-nine poor people camped out at Alphington near Exeter in 1649.[28]

In West Devon a smaller woollen industry was based on the importation of Irish fleeces and the subsequent shipping of the spun wool via the Bristol Channel ports. Tavistock was the most important West Devon industrial town, in cloth and what remained of the tin-mining industry. Unlike the decayed cloth industry of East Devon, where weaving had been conducted as by-employment by those engaged primarily as husbandmen, the tin industry by the mid-seventeenth century had become concentrated in the hands of the gentry. The big family names in the mining towns on the fringes of Dartmoor—Plympton, Chagford, Ashburton, Tavistock—were those of Strode, Champernowne, Crocker, Drake, Elford and Speccott, all of them represented on the Bench of magistrates and all undeniably armigerous. Mining for metals was disrupted completely by the civil wars but was in any case a dwindling industry in Devon from 1600. When the Grand Duke of Tuscany visited Plympton in 1669 Sir William Strode 'shewed his highness different specimens in the mines of lead, tin and loadstone lately discovered by him in that neighbourhood'[29] but this was scarcely a revival. Strode had some sixteen tinworks which made him one of the largest producers, but involvement in the tin mining industry seems to have been confined to those living on Dartmoor and its south-western edges.[30] Lists of the wardens and jurats of the Stannary Courts in the 1680s tell us more about the invasion of these jurisdictions by the Tory gentry than about the condition of the tin industry. There was some revival of interest in the Combe Martin silver mines in the 1640s and 1650s, but despite Thomas Bushell's trumpetings the venture came to nought.[31] Apart from the expansion of the cloth trade, the industrial scene in mid-seventeenth-century Devon only served to confirm that the basis of county prosperity was land.

The third principal Devon industry, apart from agriculture, was fishing. All Devon ports engaged in the Newfoundland cod trade, which was particularly buoyant after 1660, but there were also the specialist fishing trades in herrings (Clovelly and Lynmouth) and pilchards (Plymouth and the Cornish ports). Although investment in the fishing trade came from beyond the fishing ports themselves, the industry presented closed ranks to the outside world: it was under the direction of the mercantile oligarchies which dominated the Devon maritime towns.[32]

The towns of Devonshire developed and declined with the fortunes of the cloth industry. Exeter was the centre for the export trade to France. Tiverton, Cullompton and Crediton flourished as never before, with a consequent expansion of population.[33] Totnes and Dartmouth suffered with the contracting market for heavy broadcloths, as did Ashburton, 'a poor little town' to Celia Fiennes in the sixteen-nineties. Of the northern ports, Bideford had overtaken Barnstaple in wealth and mercantile standing, again because of the accidents of geography—the River Taw was silting up.[34] Plymouth's prosperity depended on overseas trade but of course the town stimulated the agrarian economy in its hinterland by providing markets. The smaller towns changed hardly at all in this period. Many were like Okehampton, where 'a very few dared write themselves gent. let alone Esquire' and which to Cosmo III of Tuscany was 'a place of little account'.[35] The principal cattle markets of the county were at Barnstaple, Dodbrook, Modbury, Plymouth, Torrington and Totnes; corn markets were held at Crediton, Honiton, Tavistock and Totnes.[36]

Devon was a county of gentry, not of noble landowners, and among these baronets, knights and esquires 'landed property was divided in a remarkably uniform manner'.[37] The gentry displayed the same characteristics of solidarity before external pressures, a capacity for clinching crafty marriage alliances and an elitism based on length of pedigree in Devon as elsewhere. F. T. Colby listed some 430 families as pedigreed in the 1620 visitation. Westcote offered the descents of 300. When W. G. Hoskins considered the patterns of land occupation in 1938 he numbered the gentry of the status of esquire and above at about 350. He later estimated that on the information from feodaries' surveys and the records of the committee for compounding the figure should be 360 to 400.[38] If 'gentility' is used to include all who described themselves as 'gentlemen' the total should be expanded considerably. The Protestation Returns for Devon[39] cover thirty of the thirty-three hundreds and 590 men, apparently evenly spread through the hundreds, were described as gentlemen, esquires, knights or baronets. Over a hundred of the 'gentlemen' lived in the separate county of Exeter or were JPs and tax commissioners and perhaps were likely to be nearer 'esquire' status. Four hundred and eighty were plain gentlemen or esquires from the twenty-nine armigerous families whose members were excluded from county administration. The Protestation Returns offer a wider definition of 'gentility' than do the other sources partly because they include those resident in Devon but without estates, influence or ancestry there. Among these were Thomas Addington, Richard Belmayne, Richard Carwithiam and unknowns like John Hancock of Bradninch, Thomas Mark of Merton, John Hutchings of Petrockstow, George Chipleigh of Were Gifford and William Pagett of Tavistock, all esquires in the census but strangers to local politics and government. The returns also make frequent use of the title 'Mr', a designation vague enough to cover parochial prominence but ancestral and perhaps economic obscurity. It may be concluded that there was a nucleus of about 400 armigerous families in Devon, with a 'transition zone' of another 150 to 180 in which 'gentleman' could slide imperceptibly into 'yeoman' (and back again) and scarcely be noticed.

Not all the gentry took part in local government. Of the four hundred and thirty families listed by the 1620 Herald, one hundred and fifty-one participated by providing one or more magistrates or tax commissioners. This percentage of roughly thirty-three per cent is comparable with the ninety-eight out of three hundred families mentioned by Thomas Westcote who played some role in government between 1630 and 1670. About a third of the armigerous Devon gentry families provided JPs or were otherwise appointed to local office by successive central authorities. The wider group listed in the Protestation Returns includes those who served as constables, jurors, bailiffs or treasurers and among these the proportion participating would seem to be about twenty-five per cent or 119 out of 480, although the returns list individuals and not families. The group whose members described themselves as 'gent.' was large enough to defy the efforts of heralds and later historians to limit it to a definable sub-elite.

Ian Gowers has estimated the percentage of Puritans among the Devon gentry before the civil war to be five per cent at most,[40] but there can be little doubt that the policies of Archbishop Laud did much to stimulate Puritanism of a conservative, presbyterian kind among the Devon ruling class.[41] Furthermore, the upheavals of the civil war encouraged the emergence of a 'middling sort' and lower class nonconformity: Independent, Baptist and later Quaker groups. Puritanism and nonconformity in Devon were focussed firmly on the south and east of the county; indeed, Puritanism in the north may have been declining even before the civil war.[42] There were exceptions to this geographical pattern, of course: the fiery Thomas Larkham was Independent minister of Tavistock during the 1650s and William Morrice of Werrington, on the Devon/Cornwall border, who became Charles II's Secretary of State, was a part-time but prolix presbyterian theologian. The association between middle and lower class puritanism in Devon and the cloth areas is inescapable. Nonconformity in East Devon and the South Hams proved a bane of successive bishops of Exeter after 1660[43] and Baptist congregations sprang up in Exeter, Topsham, Clyst Honiton and Thorverton, with Baptist writers living in the Dartmouth/Totnes district. Quaker settlements showed the same geographical distribution.[44]

Catholic recusancy, by contrast, showed no signs of development, even during the 1650s, when the lot of Roman Catholics is generally considered to have been easier than in previous decades. The highest official estimate put the numbers of recusants at 148, including wives and children, and of these twelve per cent were gentlemen and esquires. When in 1655 two justices ordered all who appeared to be recusants to appear before them to abjure popery only thirty-three refused to attend.[45]

The relationship between nonconformity and the cloth trade in Devon has yet to be explored fully but it is remarkable how little of the zeal for religious self-determination was converted into civil action or political protest. As we shall see, the representative institutions of middling sort opinion were undeveloped and Devon, in the mid-seventeenth century, was not notorious for rural disorder.[46] This despite high levels of poverty in the cities,[47] dislocation in the cloth trade, slump in the tin industry, outbreaks of plague and some appalling harvests. The following pages attempt an explanation.

The most recent historian of the civil war in Devon shows that the issues exercising Devonians in the period leading to civil war were the general ones of ship money and Laudianism and the specifically local question of stannary reform.[48] Whether or not Archbishop Laud actively stimulated Puritan zeal in Devon there can be no doubt that the mood among the gentry early in 1641 was one of marked hostility to popery and episcopacy. In February a petition to Parliament from the county called for the removal of bishops; by November the Bench voted the details of a scheme to disarm recusants.[49]. Geography helped shape the Devon response to the crisis: its two long coastlines and its experiences as a point of embarkation for Ireland made its people rabidly anti-Irish and anti-Catholic and unusually susceptible to invasion scares, even in a period of *grand peur*. After other counties had moved beyond this, Devon was in 1642 still demanding the removal of papists from offices at ports—neatly illustrating the association in men's minds of popery and invasion.[50] Devon was one of the few counties to respond with enthusiasm to the proposal to fund the war in Ireland by land sales there.[51]

Musters were held in the county under the terms of the Militia Ordinance in August 1642; by contrast the attempts to implement the royalist commissions of array provoked hostility—and at South Molton and Cullompton near-riot—even though the royal agent was the Earl of Bath, the leading North Devonian.[52] The episode underscored the regional differences within the county; the commissioners enjoyed more success in the east and north. The hawkishly parliamentarian mood gave way early in 1642, despite the odd petition attacking popery, to a more conciliatory and fearful mood, in which both Parliament and King were urged to reconciliation.[53] Anthony Fletcher has described the 'naivety and bewilderment' of the Devon petition as an indication of the 'tragedy of a war that men hated but could see no way to prevent'.[54] Devon was one of at least seventeen counties to petition thus for an accommodation.

The course of the civil war itself can be treated summarily here. The parliamentary leaders were Sir John Northcote, Sir John Bampfield, Sir George Chudleigh and Sir Peter Prideaux. None of them were to survive in government during the 1650s.[55] The leading royalists were Edward, Viscount Chichester, Sir Hugh Pollard, Arthur Bassett of Heanton and John Gifford of Brightley, and this pattern of allegiances further exemplified the association between parliamentarianism and the cloth trade in the south and east and between older loyalties based on family hegemony and royalism in the isolated communities of the north. But the origins of the military leaders concealed a different pattern: of the 300 Devon men charged with royalist delinquency in the later 1640s, three quarters hailed from Exeter and the south and east of the county.[56] Numerically, royalism as well as parliamentarianism was rooted in the cloth-producing regions and, in fact, loyalties followed the spread of population very closely: there were, it seems, more parliamentarians *and* more royalists in the more heavily-populated districts of the county.

The military campaigns of the civil war followed a pattern of invasion and re-invasion of the south-western peninsula, in which Devon and its principal towns were targets *en route* to the goal of taking Cornwall from the east to establish total control. In 1643 the royalist army under Sir Ralph Hopton marched from Somerset into North Devon and down into north Cornwall. After taking Launceston they skirted south of Dartmoor, put Exeter under siege and by November had returned to Tavistock. By September 1643, Barnstaple, Bideford and Appledore had surrendered without struggle to the royalists and Exeter capitulated on 7 September. Dartmouth surrendered on 5 October but Plymouth, the bastion of south-western parliamentarianism, was better able to sustain a protracted defence and remained loyal to Parliament throughout the war. Chapter One of this study makes clear the significance of Plymouth as a seminary for military and civilian administrators: those who cut their teeth in the

Plymouth committees of 1643–44 became a cadre of county committeemen in 1646–47 and were in some quarters resented for it.

The siege of Plymouth lasted from January 1644 to January 1646 and the only serious parliamentary attempt to lift it by re-invasion disintegrated in ignominy in September 1644 with the Earl of Essex having to escape by boat from Fowey. The final parliamentary success was achieved in the aftermath of Naseby, when the royalist forces retreated into the west and were pursued by the New Model Army. Devon afforded Lord Goring's army some respite in 1645: it was a convenient resting-place and offered a chance to re-group.[57] The last campaign in the west was, however, a mopping-up operation for Fairfax. Dissensions among the royalists and a desire by Devonians to see an end to the war made his task easier than it might have been. By April 1646 most of the west had been secured for Parliament—Exeter surrendered on 13 April, Barnstaple on 14 April and Fort Charles, Salcombe, on 9 May. After Pendennis Castle, Cornwall, was secured on 18 August only Lundy Island, under Thomas Bushell, remained as a nominal outpost of royalism, to the embarrassment of a local administration anxious to meet the pressing needs of a war-ravaged county.

NOTES

1. Mary Coate: *Cornwall in the Great Civil War and Interregnum 1642–60* (1933, 2nd ed. 1963); A. C. Wood: *Nottinghamshire in the Civil War* (1937).
2. E.g., B. G. Blackwood: 'The Lancashire Gentry 1625–60' (Oxford DPhil 1973) published as *The Lancashire Gentry and the Great Rebellion* (Chetham Soc. 3rd series XXV, 1978); C. G. Durston: 'Berkshire and its County Gentry 1625–49' (Reading PhD 1977); C. B. Phillips: 'The Gentry in Cumberland and Westmorland' (Lancaster PhD 1974) and M. D. G. Wanklyn: 'Landed Society and Allegiance in Cheshire and Shropshire in the First Civil War' (Manchester PhD 1976).
3. Alan Everitt: *The Community of Kent and the Great Rebellion* (1966); J. S. Morrill: *Cheshire 1630–1660: County Government and Society during the English Revolution* (1974).
4. W. B. Willcox: *Gloucestershire: A study in Local Government 1590–1640* (1940); T. G. Barnes: *Somerset 1625–1640: A County's Government during the 'Personal Rule'* (1961); A. Fletcher: *A County Community in Peace and War: Sussex 1600–1660* (1975).
5. Clive Holmes: 'The County Community in Stuart Historiography', *Journal of British Studies* XIX (1980) pp. 54–73; Ann Hughes: 'Politics, Society and Civil War in Warwickshire 1620–1650' (Liverpool PhD 1980); idem: 'Militancy and Localism: Warwickshire Politics and Westminster Politics 1643–1647' *Trans. Roy. Hist. Soc.* 5th series, XXXI (1981) pp. 51–68; idem: 'Warwickshire on the Eve of the Civil War: A "County Community"?', *Midland History* VII (1982) pp. 42–72.
6. Hughes: 'The Civil War and the Provinces' in *The Revolution and its Impact*, Block 4 of *Seventeenth Century England: A Changing Culture* (Open University course A203, 1981) p. 15.
7. Stephen Roberts: 'Local Government Reform: A Survey' in Ivan Roots (ed): *Into Another Mould: Aspects of the Interregnum* (Exeter 1981) pp. 24–41.
8. The history of writing on the Civil War period is ably summarised in R. C. Richardson: *The Debate on the English Revolution* (1977).
9. Coate, *op. cit.*, Chapters 13, 14; Fletcher, *op. cit.*, Chapter 14; David Underdown: *Somerset in the Civil War and Interregnum* (1973), Chapters 9, 10; Everitt, *op. cit.*, Chapters 8, 9; E. Andriette: *Devon and Exeter in the Civil War* (1972), p. 174 describes the Interregnum and indeed the period after 1646 as 'a matter of waiting and hoping for better days and a return to constitutional government'.

10. Andriette, *op. cit.*, passim; W. G. Hoskins: 'The Ownership and Occupation of the Land in Devonshire 1650–1800' (London PhD 1938); 'The Estates of the Caroline Gentry' in H. P. R. Finberg and Hoskins: *Devonshire Studies* (1952), pp. 334–365.

11. A. H. A. Hamilton: *Quarter Sessions from Queen Elizabeth to Queen Anne* (1878), (and his short articles in *T.D.A.*); R. L. Taverner: 'The Administrative Work of the Devon Justices in the Seventeenth Century', *T.D.A.*, C (1968), pp. 55–84.

12. Especially Sidney and Beatrice Webb: *English Local Government from the Revolution to the Municipal Corporations Act: The Parish and the County* (1906) and *The Manor and the Borough* (1908).

13. E.g., E. H. Bates Harbin (ed.): *Quarter Sessions Records of the County of Somerset* Vol. 3 (1952); D. H. Allen (ed.): *Essex Quarter Sessions Order Book 1652–1661* (1974).

14. E. A. O. Whiteman: 'The Episcopate of Dr. Seth Ward, Bishop of Exeter (1662 to 1667) and Salisbury (1667 to 1668/9) . . .' (Oxford DPhil 1951). Cf. K. M. Beck: 'Recusancy and Nonconformity in Devon and Somerset 1660–1714' (Bristol MA 1961) and examples in I. M. Green: *The Re-establishment of the Church of England 1660–1663* (1978).

15. Thomas Westcote: *A View of Devonshire in 1630* (ed. G. Oliver, P. Jones 1845), p. 35; Tristram Risdon: *The Chorographical Description or Survey of the County of Devon* (1811), p. 4.

16. W. G. Hoskins: *Devon* (1954), p. 11 describes Devon as the third largest after Yorkshire and Lincolnshire, and Andriette *op. cit.*, p. 15 confuses this with the contemporary view. Westcote admitted only Yorkshire to be larger. The other seventeenth-century author on Devon was William Pole whose *Collections Towards a Description of the County of Devon* was published as late as 1791. His work is a catalogue of manorial descents, however, and offers no topographical introduction.

17. Risdon *op. cit.* pp. 4–7.

18. Hoskins: *Devon* pp. 14–21.

19. J. A. Yelling: *Common Field and Enclosure in England 1450–1850* (1977) p. 44; John Kew: 'Regional Variations in the Devon Land Market 1536–58' in M. A. Havinden, C. M. King (eds): *The South West and the Land* (Exeter 1969) pp. 32–36.

20. D. Levine: *Family Formation in an Age of Nascent Capitalism* (New York 1977) p. 105, quoting H. S. A. Fox: 'The Chronology of Enclosure and Economic Development in Medieval Devon' *Economic History Review* 2nd series XXVIII (1975) pp. 181–202.

21. Yelling *op. cit.* pp. 32, 44; Thirsk: *Agrarian History* IV pp. 72–73, 76–78; Kew *op. cit.* pp. 30–32.

22. Thirsk *op. cit.* pp. 72, 165; Hoskins: *Devon* pp. 115–16.

23. Thirsk *op. cit.* pp. 76–77, 169; Kew *op. cit.* pp. 31–32.

24. H. S. A. Fox: 'Outfield Cultivation in Devon and Cornwall: A Re-interpretation' in M. A. Havinden (ed.): *Husbandry and Marketing in the South-West 1500–1800* (Exeter 1973) pp. 19–38.

25. Outlined in Thirsk: 'Industries in the Countryside' in F. J. Fisher (ed.): *Essays in the Economic and Social History of Tudor and Stuart England* (Cambridge 1961).

26. Levine *op. cit.* pp. 105–07.

27. Hoskins: 'The Rise and Decline of the Serge Industry in the South West of England' (London MSc 1929) pp. 1–12; *idem: Devon* pp. 127–28; Levine *op. cit.* pp. 106–07; R. Pearse Chope (ed.): *Early Tours in Devon and Cornwall* (1918, reprinted Newton Abbot 1967) p. 107; J. de L. Mann: *The Cloth Industry in the West of England from 1640 to 1880* (1971) pp. 26–27.

28. Devon QS bundles loose Epiphany 1647–48; *ibid.* loose petition Midsummer 1649.

29. Pearse Chope, *op. cit.* pp. 98–99. I am grateful to Dr T. A. P. Greeves for information on Devon tin-mining.

30. Such as John Elford of Sheepstor, John Crocker of Lyneham, the Drakes of Buckland.

31. See Chapter One below.

32. H. E. S. Fisher: 'The South West and the Atlantic Trades 1660–1770' in Fisher (ed.): *The South West and the Sea* (Exeter 1968) pp 8–9; E. A. Andriette: *Devon and Exeter in the Civil War* (Newton Abbot 1972) p. 17.

33. Hoskins: *Devon* pp. 62, 66; M. Dunsford: *Historical Memoirs of the Town and Parish of Tiverton* (1790) p. 50; R. Pearse Chope *op. cit.* pp. 104, 107.

34. Hoskins: *Devon* pp. 115–16.

35. R. L. Taverner: 'The Corporation and Community of Okehampton 1623–1885' (London PhD 1969) p. 13; Pearse Chope *op. cit.* pp. 103, 110–11.
36. Thirsk (ed.): *Agrarian History* IV pp. 589–91.
37. Hoskins: 'Ownership and Occupation of the Land in Devonshire', *op. cit.*, p. 23.
38. Westcote, *op. cit.*; F. T. Colby (ed.): *The Visitation of the County of Devon in the year 1620* (1872); Hoskins: 'Estates of the Caroline Gentry', p. 334.
39. A. J. Howard (ed.): *The Devon Protestation Returns 1641* (2 vols., 1973).
40. I. W. Gowers: 'Puritanism in the County of Devon between 1570 and 1641' (Exeter MA 1970) p. 259. This is surely an underestimate.
41. Andriette *op. cit.* pp. 38, 42–43.
42. Gowers *op. cit.* p. 223.
43. J. Simmons: 'Some letters from Bishop Ward of Exeter' *Devon and Cornwall Notes and Queries* xxi (1940–41), xxii (1942–46); K. M. Beck: 'Recusancy and Nonconformity in Devon and Somerset 1660–1714' (Bristol MA 1961) p. 110.
44. Beck: *op. cit.* pp. 116, 156 and *passim*.
45. PRO E 377/61/5, 63/11.
46. See maps in Andrew Charlesworth (ed.): *An Atlas of Rural Protest in Britain 1548–1900* (1983).
47. Mary Griffiths: 'The Association between Mortality and Poverty in Exeter from the Seventeenth Century to the Present' in W. E. Minchinton: *Population and Marketing: Two Studies in the History of the South West* (Exeter 1976) pp. 32–36.
48. E. A. Andriette: *Devon and Exeter in the Civil War* pp. 42–43 and Chapters 2 and 3 *passim*.
49. Anthony Fletcher: *The Outbreak of the English Civil War* (1981) pp. 92, 211.
50. *Ibid.* p. 212.
51. *Ibid.* p. 250, Andriette *op. cit.* p. 48.
52. Fletcher *op. cit.* pp. 343, 364; Andriette *op. cit.* p. 63.
53. Fletcher pp. 217, 226, 268; *Lords Journals* V pp. 295–96; Andriette p. 54; J. S. Morrill: *The Revolt of the Provinces* (1976) p. 162.
54. Fletcher p. 270.
55. Andriette pp. 56, 61. What follows is derived from Chapter 5 *et seq.* of this account.
56. Analysis of delinquents mentioned in M. A. E. Green (ed.): *Calendar of the Committee for Compounding with Delinquents* (5 vols 1889–92).
57. R. Hutton: *The Royalist War Effort 1642–46* (1982) pp. 187–88.

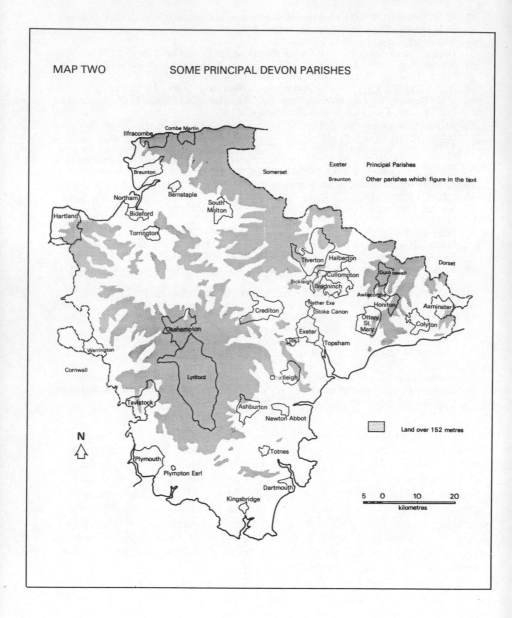

MAP TWO   SOME PRINCIPAL DEVON PARISHES

Chapter One

The Price of Victory, 1646-1649

The imposition of parliamentary rule upon the counties of the South West of England did not establish any political or administrative group in unchallenged authority in Devon, and the county, like the rest of England and Wales, was in the grip of military discontent and widespread social dislocation. Parliament was petitioned by at least twenty-five English counties for relief from punitive taxation imposed to finance the standing armies.[1] Subsistence crisis and disease made matters worse, as did a stop in trade and a widespread collapse of local civilian authority. The armies were seen as centralist intrusions into local domains. In these alarming circumstances strong local government in the counties was imperative. After the suspension of meetings in the first half of 1646 Devon quarter sessions met in that midsummer, to be followed by the first post-war Devon assizes.[2]

The first sessions meeting was held on 4 July at Crediton, not the customary Exeter, as a precaution against the plague besieging the city. The chief tasks were administrative, not judicial. Treasurers and mustermasters were appointed and constables found to be 'active for the Cavaliers and evill instruments to the State' were ordered to be dismissed by the justices acting out of sessions. Parishes visited by plague included those around Barnstaple and the smaller towns of mid and east Devon, and it fell to the justices to order collections, the keeping of watches and the movement of prison inmates to avoid further infection. After years of labouring on a 'fiscal treadmill',[3] the justices found that in raising the money to ward off the plague they were competing with a Parliament whose main aims were to prevent a revival of the royalist cause with Scots aid and to quell grumblings in its own armies. Plague treasurers were appointed, parishes were ordered to ensure that strangers ignoring the challenge of the watch were shot, but even so the local tax of £40 per week imposed on some East Devon parishes was not to be 'extended to lardgely thereby to debarr the countrey from paeing the weekly assessment imposed by ordinance of Parliament'.[4]

The army had come to recognise the value of the bureaucratic structure as a means of providing its two main requirements—arrears of pay and indemnity from legal proceedings arising from soldiers' actions.[5] These 'bread and butter questions' could be best resolved by working with administrators rather than by toying with the Agitators and Leveller ideology, perhaps, and such were the courses of action open to soldiers. For civilians in those areas not quite 'dark corners of the land' but at least dimly lit by a western sun there was no such choice. Plague and dearth made strong government a necessity. The JPs received complaints from

1

the rising North Devon seaport of Bideford and its larger neighbour, Barnstaple, that local officials were failing to collect taxes levied for plague relief. Other requests for help came from East Devon. The 'decay of trade' offered another reason to request aid. Strong government took the form of an order to JPs John Davy and John Drake (neither of them North Devonians) who were to be assisted by a 'partie of horse or foot soldiers'. The North Devon towns were therefore to be dragooned into paying extraordinary taxes by two magistrates, not carpet-baggers but without northern associations, assisted by the military. The soldiers were commanded by Lieutenant-Colonel Harris, ironically more sympathetic to the problem than the civilian justices. He was the governor of Ilfracombe garrison and a native of Barnstaple.[6]

The criminal side of quarter sessions business was neglected in the face of the wide range of administrative problems arising in 1646–47. The Indemnity Ordinance of 21 May 1647 was a response to the clamours of those 'sued, indicted, prosecuted or molested ... for such acts and things ... acted and done ... by authority of Parliament',[7] as well as to the agitation in the army. In Devon, several cases make it clear that the well-developed procedure of magistrates arbitrating in cases disputed between individuals was well-suited to resolving issues of indemnity. To save costs and time, such cases were referred to a committee of JPs sitting out of sessions. In one instance the committee examining the case against Captain Robert Yeo brought the issue back to sessions. In another, a widow was compensated for injuries suffered through 'the inhumane and Barbarous carriage of the Lord Paulett'.[8] The court was the only arbiter of complaints by the parishes, too. The JPs were caught between the demands of Parliament and the discontent of the Devonians who paid for its policies. Cautious arbitration[9] rather than outraged defence of the complaining parishes seemed the only realistic way in which quarter sessions could maintain its credibility as the government of the county.

The plague continued to spread. By Easter 1647 the infected areas included Barnstaple, Pilton, Bideford, Braunton, Honiton, Heavitree near Exeter, Colyford, Fremington, Totnes, Crediton, Tiverton and Ashburton.[10] To alleviate it hospitals were opened and watches maintained but money could only be procured by extraordinary levies. The first move came in the summer of 1646 when a special rate of £10.8s.4d. per week was imposed on Braunton parish. There was never a universally acceptable method of assessment, however, and when they had been granted relief the parishes fell to disputing their proportion of the tax. In response to complaints, the rates were continually adjusted and incremented. At the sessions of Epiphany 1647 a £100 weekly rate was levied on the south hundreds to relieve Totnes. At the next meeting the parishes of Ashburton and Buckland-in-the-Moor were exempted and £50 was added to the amount per week to cope with the spread of the contagion. Lifton hundred, after pleading poverty, was exempted from the collection. Such complaints were always taken seriously; one senses the JPs' concern that the hundreds should not become alienated through unduly heavy taxation.

Parliamentary taxes impeded local spending. Take the case of Barnstaple, which complained in 1647 against the sum imposed on it as a parish of Braunton hundred. Barnstaple had its own sessions and as the town was taxed by the county as a unit of a hundred, quarter sessions at Exeter appeared as the agent of a burdensome central government. The mayor and aldermen of Barnstaple regarded county quarter sessions as a body unfamiliar with their problems. Their petition formally reminded the county magistrates that Barnstaple was ruined 'partly by the late distractions of the kingdome, partly by decay of trade, partly by great losses sustayned partly by the death and departure of the ablest and men of best abilities of the town and partly by God's late visitacion with the plague and pestellence'. They were rated at one-fifth of the total assessment on the hundred but since there were twenty-one parishes, their rates 'should not bee the twelfth part'. They appealed not to natural justice nor to ancient county custom but to the Devon JPs' concern to prevent the obstruction of parliamentary ordinances. Inequality 'makes men unwilling and with many grudging thereunto who otherwise would strayne themselves to the utmost to bee conformable thereunto'.[11] Regular correspondents would not need to justify their complaint or to assert their loyalty to the victorious side. Here were two localisms, two local integrities, using central *diktat* to provide common ground for debate.

Parishes were not without initiative, either. Ministers and inhabitants of the better sort could act independently of quarter sessions to relieve poverty.[12] In North Petherwin in 1647 the fine from a discovered unlicensed alehousekeeper was employed to relieve 'such as were likely to charge the said parish hereafter ... with the well likeing and approbacion of the said parishioners'.[13] Sixteen inhabitants signed accounts to quarter sessions. Nevertheless parochial action alone could not resolve the grievances afflicting Devon society during 1646–48. Sweeping changes could only be initiated by petitioning Parliament. A petition signed by seventeen assize grand jurors was presented to the judges on 2 April, 1647.[14] It was conciliatory. The jurors doubted not that church government was being settled and godly ministers appointed to parishes and that these were the 'first and principal care' of the assize judges, but there was concern at the neglect in administering communion. Heavy taxes, the presence of soldiers, the lack of control over alehouses and corruption among sequestration officials were all singled out but the emphasis was on mismanagement not oppressive government. This was a 'country' petition with a strong presbyterian flavour in which criticisms of wrong-headed taxation merge not with demands for a return to old ways and less government but with requests for more government of a kind likely to produce benefits for local partisans. The signing jurors were mainly parochial gentlemen with a leavening of yeomen. They were minor scions of prominent Devon families who could expect no place on the commission of the peace.[15] Many of the petitioners did not participate in government in the 1640s but would do so in the 1650s.

Army occupation of Devon was a severe problem. The Trevelyan papers offer evidence of troop movements in the north and east of the county from 1646 to 1649. John Willoughby was unable to help his brother, a victim of the 1641 Irish rebellion, because he was 'undone by compositions, impositions, taxes, free-quartering of soldiers, plundering and other heavy burthens' late in 1647. As a sequestered royalist who paid a £500 fine, Willoughby had reason to grumble and possibly to exaggerate his sufferings,[16] but corroborating evidence for free quartering along the Devon-Somerset border came from his cousin John Turberville of Wiveliscombe who provided Willoughby with a vivid account of outrageous behaviour at his house. Two Halberton men complained to the Devon committee of the presence of one hundred soldiers *en route* for Ireland.[17] Parliament was fully aware of these grievances, and while planning disbandment as the ultimate solution, was sufficiently moved to remedy soldiers' complaints, too.[18] The indemnity ordinance passed the Lords on 21 May 1647, and was made more effective on 7 June when another ordinance offered a blanket indemnity to combatants on the parliamentary side. Not only did this abate agitation in the army but relieved some pressure on the over-burdened quarter sessions. The call for indemnity was made by the petitioning grand jury in the very month the ordinance was passed. Another presentment had demanded care for the dependents of war casualties, and twenty-three days later 'an ordinance for relief of Maimed Soldiers . . .' became law.[19]

There was no dichotomy between leadership of the Devon group in Parliament and activism at home. Men like Sir John Northcote and Sir Edmund Fowell were active both at Westminster and in the West Country. Sir John Bampfield, prominent in attempts to establish a local militia in the summer of 1648, sat for Penryn in Cornwall but was more deeply involved in Devon affairs. Orders for the relief of maimed soldiers appear in the sessions order book from April 1647; the ordinance appeared a month later and authorised the imposition of a weekly rate, in accordance with an Elizabethan statute. The 1601 act enjoined the appointment at sessions of *ad hoc* treasurers and at Easter 1648 three were appointed, among them Samuel Codnor of Ipplepen, one of the petitioning grand jurors at the assizes of May 1647. Unlike the provision for indemnity, the maimed soldiers' legislation was conservative, accorded with earlier Tudor and Stuart legislation and left administration wholly in local hands.

Indemnity and provision for the casualties of war could not remove the grievance of grievances, the army. The plan was to disband it and to ship some regiments to Ireland but apart from hostility from the army this led to localised unrest at the ports selected for the troops' despatch, one of which was Barnstaple. In early May 1647 it was reported variously that 300 Irish refugees were loose in the town and that many were soldiers.[20] In the early summer disturbances began in Plymouth, apparently caused by a failure to renew the excise ordinance by which the garrison there was provided. The unrest was a symptom of a much wider fiscal crisis in the country.

Since October 1645 Plymouth garrison had been under the command of Colonel Ralph Weldon. He was the son of Sir Anthony Weldon, an egregious local boss, head of the Kent Committee and political War Party man. Ralph Weldon had commanded a regiment since 1644, and had come to the West Country in 1645 to attend the relief of Taunton and the siege of Bristol in May and September. The formation of the New Model Army did not weaken Weldon's Kentish connections; as late as April 1645 troops at Plymouth were being paid by the Committee of Kent.[21] At the beginning of July 1647 lengthy correspondence began between Weldon and William Lenthall, Speaker of the House of Commons, on the problems of Plymouth garrison—or rather a series of anguished petitions from Weldon whose anxiety was compounded by what he considered as an unseemly reluctance of the Commons to reply to his letters let alone settle his troops' grievances. On 2 and 3 July, the House of Commons heard letters and petitions from Plymouth garrison and from the mayor and magistrates of the town on the severity of the garrison's arrears and the implications for poor relief in the town as a whole. £500 was ordered to be paid not to the garrison but to the poor stock of the town. This may suggest, with Weldon's prolonged laments, that Parliament was not acting swiftly enough to counter the unrest in the garrison, that part of the delay arose because Parliament had not yet decided which forces should be disbanded and which maintained. By 30 July, Weldon had had enough, and resigned his command, implying that his commission had never been more than a burden to him. His resignation was not accepted, however. The day after he penned his resignation letter, Plymouth was reassured that relief was at hand and local MP Edmund Fowell, the son of a Plymouth town clerk, wrote to the garrison. On 2 August the soldiers mutinied, supported by poor townswomen, here as elsewhere, a key group.

Military discipline could no longer be separated from civil unrest caused by plain poverty. Weldon had to take £500 from the Plymouth customs house to avert the immediate threat of riot, and Parliament, thinking along the same lines, authorised a £4,000 payment from excise receipts there.[22] Using national funds to meet local needs had once been a grand jury recommendation, but Weldon soon discovered the illusory nature of the panacea; by 6 August he wrote to Lenthall that there was nothing left in the coffers of either the customs house or the excise office.[23] A fortnight later Parliament ordered Sir Thomas Fairfax, the local committees and the parliamentary committee for Irish affairs to co-operate in reducing the strength of Plymouth garrison. Another £8,000 was ordered from local assessment monies, to be administered by the local committees. Weldon was under the impression, when he next wrote to Lenthall, on 17 August, that this money was being raised from the town of Plymouth and not from the county as a whole. On the 30th, Weldon was reported to have seven thousand men at his disposal in order to defend the West against royalists or the Irish.

This note of optimism accorded ill with events in Plymouth, where the soldiers were billeted on the town. The formerly sympathetic 'better sort' had now been alienated, and Weldon's jeremiads reached a zenith of recrimination against what he regarded as a perfidious Parliament.[24] In

September the Devon assessment committee told Lenthall how, in assize week at Exeter, a delegation of Plymouth soldiers had 'with high insolencyes disturbed us, imprisoned some and scattered others', thus bringing home to the commissioners their plight in the most effective way possible. The correspondence and unrest dragged on through the rest of 1647 and into the following year. Discussions between parliamentary committees and local bodies continued but no new proposals emerged. A grant from local assessment collections, although inadequate, became a fixed response.[25]

Violence erupted at Plymouth in the middle of February 1648 when a trooper attacked 'the governor with his sword but was prevented and killed'. Weldon shakily picked up his pen again and Parliament gave the garrison £6,000. A newspaper perceptively noted that the discontent was caused by friction between the soldiers and 'the country', a direct result of free-quarter. There followed a locally-supervised disbandment of supernumerary troops and the garrison was handed over to the supreme executive organ of Parliament, the Derby House committee.[26]

During the simmering summer of 1647 the troubles of the county were not confined to Plymouth. The assize grand jury petition in May had appealed to established local administrative procedures, but the army dominated the countryside and men came to regard it as a fourth estate to whose leaders appeals could be addressed. Fairfax's secretary, John Rushworth, recorded a petition from the 'well-affected in the county of Devon' on 2 August.[27] It was addressed to Fairfax as the commander of 'the only visible support the kingdom survives by' and was a comment on the wrestling for political power between the presbyterian 'moderates' backed by the oligarchy of the City of London and the Independent war party alliance who were looking to the army and the continuation of the county committees as the way to a decisive political settlement against the king.

Since 1645 the Independents had subsumed a numerically superior 'middle group' led by Oliver St John, Solicitor-General and MP for Totnes, which distanced the parliamentary alliance from army radicalism. The social and economic crisis of 1647 coupled with the burden of the army and the conspicuous affronts to county government by county gentry at quarter sessions hastened a peace party/presbyterian putsch in the City of London and Parliament. By December 1646 Holles's presbyterians dominated the House of Commons and by the early summer of 1647 controlled the most influential offices in the City. Encouraged by the shrill tones of Thomas Edwards's conspiracy theories, the presbyterians set about remodelling the militia with a view to creating a force to supplant the Independent New Model Army. These plans were backed by the self-interested hesitation of London aldermen, while in the Army the perfidy of the City could but foster radical ideology germinated by material grievances. These issues were resolved in June 1647 when the Army demanded the impeachment of eleven 'Presbyterian' MPs. These members withdrew but the City leaders connived at a counter-demonstrative show of mob violence at Westminster. Then came the flight to the Army of fifty-seven MPs and Speaker Lenthall, and the final exasperation of Fairfax's forces, which had been edging nearer London since June.[28]

The Devon petition was received by Fairfax four days before he entered London. It did not dwell on the tortuous struggles at Westminster nor with the ideological challenge confronting troopers of the New Model Army but on the ill-treatment offered the supporters of Parliament 'haled before magistrates and imprisoned' by a zeal 'little inferior if not exceeding the customary proceedings in the High Commission Court'. National issues, where they intruded in Devon, had clearly been unwelcome; local officials 'found a little differing in judgement about those outside controversies in the land, though blameless are thrust out'. This was a criticism of quarter sessions government itself, not a grand jury petition, and it appealed to the army as the only hope for men of integrity. That it was no 'Presbyterian' moderate attack on county committees (Underdown's phraseology) or a statement of 'Country' ideology concerned to defend 'traditional values and rights'[29] (Morrill's phrase) can be judged from the petitioners' submission that 'the root and spring from whence mostly our sorrow do arise' were the Cornish election results. The presbyterian propagandist, Thomas Edwards, was hinting darkly at an Independent patronage machine operating in the West Country recruiter elections.[30] His allegations that Hugh Peters personally organised the turn-out cannot be substantiated, but there is plenty of evidence that the War Party stalwart, Edmund Prideaux, was able to use his influence as a commissioner of the great seal, chairman of the parliamentary committee for the west and postmaster general to good effect in the earliest western elections in the autumn of 1645. Most of the Cornish elections were held in the autumn of 1646. Early in 1647 the parliamentary power balance shifted in favour of the moderates and Prideaux was superseded as local election manager by Anthony Nicholl, a nephew of John Pym and an officeholder whose local connections were as strong as those of Prideaux.[31] Both Prideaux and Nicholl held West Country seats; the former Lyme Regis, the latter, Bodmin, but the Westminster situation was decisive in ensuring that ten of the Cornwall seats were taken by men markedly 'Presbyterian' in outlook. Anthony Nicholl was one of the impeached eleven members named by the army on 16 June as having wielded undue electoral influence. The Devon petitioners mentioned this in their August complaint, at a time when the outrages of the Presbyterian-inspired physical assault on Parliament had still not been redressed.[32]

The Devon recruiter elections were held from April 1646 until February 1647 (with the exception of one county seat, taken by William Morrice as late as August 1648) so why were the petitioners not exercised by the results of contests in their own county? The answer would seem to be that for some Devonians what distinguished the elections in the two counties was that in Cornwall there was a high degree of outside manipulation and a strikingly high proportion of carpet-baggers returned. The Cornish elections were conducted with reference to issues other than local ones. Ten of the eighteen elected in 1646–7 were outsiders. By contrast only one of the representatives returned for Devon was not recognizably local, and he, Philip Skippon, owed his place to the influence peculiar to military occupation. Skippon was returned in Barnstaple in December 1646, his wife's connection with the Grenville family no doubt easing his passage.[33]

The victorious military leaders intended a greater impact on the Devon constituencies; from December 1645 to April 1646 there was a determined campaign to capture seats for War Party/Army members. Prideaux visited the West in September 1645. In December Thomas Fairfax asked his father to persuade the Commons to authorise writs for the Tiverton election with his brother-in-law, Sir William Selby, as his nominee. Selby was confidently expected to secure the place and the combined impact of military and political influence seemed likely to sweep the board. The writs did not appear. By April 1646 Fairfax had had to modify his aspirations in the West; sanguine confidence in his Tiverton's nominee's chances had given way to more guarded intentions to cleave it as a request with the western gentlemen that they will procure two that shall be named places there'.[34] The alliance of war party and moderates was disintegrating with every victorious move of the New Model Army. Once a peace had been forced on the country the imponderables of a political settlement to preserve that peace were large enough to shatter the coalition. Stalement at Westminster was followed by a palpable swing to the moderate Presbyterians and by late 1646 and early 1647 Nicholl's influence in Cornwall was proving decisive. The extent of Prideaux's local power is measurable by Nicholl's failure to gain a hold in Devonshire, and the defence against the outsider was stiffened by a tradition of local independence.

In many counties the recruiter elections were a test of specific local issues. In Somerset they became a measure of strength of John Pyne and the county committee, in Cornwall they offered a local officeholder a chance to build a party and in Cheshire Sir William Brereton intervened with a view to forcing through the local opposition a scheme of godly reformation.[35] In none of these counties was central government influence unchallenged or unlimited. Devon was no different. Samuel Clark (Exeter) and Charles Vaughan (Honiton) were conservative committeemen. Thomas Boone (Dartmouth) was a town grandee and businessman. John Elford, Robert Shapcote and Christopher Martin (the first two elected for Tiverton, the latter for Plympton) were probably placemen of Edmund Prideaux, *custos* and commissioner of the great seal.[36]

There was no 'party' organisation in Devon to be compared with that in neighbouring Somerset. The sequestration and assessment committees were never more powerful than quarter sessions, and the Devon politically active (except a knot of sequestered royalists) complied with committee government and quarter sessions rule to establish a settled administrative order and to limit the impact of plague and dearth. The inconsistency of complaining of 'new men in old places' at the same time as appealing to the army as the agent of reform is resolved when the provision of strong government is viewed as the aim of both appeals. This concern remained paramount from 1646, when Fairfax secured the county, to 1648 when in February an attempt was made to mobilize popular support for a protest against increasing central taxation. At the Michaelmas quarter sessions of 1647 the JPs conferred on a letter to be sent to Fairfax about a single troop of horse, taking free quarter, whose future was doubtless regarded as a test case. The justices were headed by the county leaders and MPs, Sir John Bampfield and Sir John Northcote, with Edmund Prideaux and nine other JPs including many of the still uncommitted. Major Perkins's troop was enough of a nuisance to provoke the normally quiescent quarter sessions grand jury into framing a presentment against it, despite the general sense of a year-old Commons' order that the soldiers should be disbanded, with arrears of pay. £375 had been borrowed to accomplish this, but the troop was with them still, as an affront to the jurisdiction of JPs and Parliament—five of the justices were MPs too—and as a mark of central intrusion and a psychological barrier to an already reluctant taxpaying populace.[37]

Why were the MPs present at quarter sessions in October 1647? When the Presbyterian-inspired violence broke on the House of Commons in July, Thomas Boone, Edmund Prideaux, Francis Rous and possibly Lawrence Whitaker were among the Devon men who fled to the army and subscribed the engagement to 'live and die' with Fairfax.[38] When the army entered London on 6 August the counter-revolution was clearly over but there remained some months of tight manoeuvring in the House of Commons to establish an Independent control there. Underdown describes these late summer months as a time of a middle-group/ Independent direction of events but there were moments of wavering, of spasmodic Presbyterian gestures. For example, on 9 August, only three days after Fairfax's entry to London, the House voted on whether the votes taken in the absence of the Speaker, who had fled to the army, were valid. This test of the legality of the brief Presbyterian rule proved a victory for the middle-group and radicals led by Evelyn and Haselrige, but by one vote only, and the vote turned to a Presbyterian majority by the appearance of three members who had not previously voted. Among these was John Rolle, London merchant and MP for Truro. His brother, Sir Samuel Rolle of Petrockstow in Shebbear, and Sir John Bampfield were regarded by John Rushworth as crypto-royalists or at best wavering neutrals.[39] After the second vote, Haselrige denounced the newcomers and attempted to force through a motion that all who had corresponded with the king should be disabled from voting. It was Edmund Prideaux who re-asserted the right of all MPs to vote. Prideaux, once a war-party leader who had signed the engagement to live and die with the army, began a course of uncommitted moderation as soon as the army reached London.[40]

Prideaux was among those whose absence from the House was noted and censured on 9 October, 1647. The very day that the Devon MPs wrote to Fairfax about the burden of the soldiery (to whose protection Prideaux and Bampfield were supposed to have fled) a Commons committee of mostly Independent and middle-group members introduced a measure to

fine those absent from the House without good reason. Lists were printed
in the journals and members were given a month to act. John Doddridge
and Sir Samuel Rolle (sick), Philip Skippon and Walter Young (excused)
were among the favoured seventy-nine, but sixteen Devon MPs appeared
in the list of 155 absent without leave. Only six Devon MPs were in the
House; twenty others were absent. A royalist newspaper spoke derisively
of the 'scattered Presbyters' but it is clear that the Devon MPs were
behaving as men who, for the moment at least, had lost their nerve.
Prideaux was back at Westminster by the 28th of the month but his trip to
Devon suggests that he had become an opportunist.[41] Bampfield was
another who had suddenly assumed the Independents' ways, but whose
real motive was probably a desire to be out of the controversy. As for the
quarter sessions complaint against the soldiers, it was acknowledged by
Fairfax, who was aware of the need to foster goodwill in an area sensitive
to the presence of troops moving to the embarkation port of Barnstaple,
and thence Ireland. He gave the JPs the responsibility of disbandment on
condition that some arrears of pay were cleared and that Exeter garrison
could be maintained from assessment collections. Fairfax's letter, from
Turnham Green, was copied into the Sessions order book; this seemed to
have been a victory.

But Fairfax's order related to one troop of horse only, and there could
be no escape from the drift of parliamentary events towards increasing
taxation to disband the army. Devon had extensive sea-coasts and when
disbandment plans included shipping soldiers to Ireland it would
inevitably suffer the presence of more, and not fewer, troops. The only
remedy would be to work for a re-adjustment of the assessment rate so that
Devon would pay a smaller proportion of the entire levy. This approach
was adopted by committeemen and magistrates in February 1648. A group
of twelve drew up a petition to the House of Commons and set about
obtaining mass signatures. Two of the JPs who helped frame the petition
had signed the letter to Fairfax in the previous November, but the group
of twelve was a much less distinguished body than the county leaders.
Four of the magistrates were not of the quorum and two were not JPs at
all. The petition is to be found in the quarter sessions bundles for
Midsummer 1647.[42] Internal evidence, however, suggests a misplace-
ment.

The petition mingled defensive, Leveller-like assertions of human
dignity with an apparently lively sense of Protestant outrage in its
demands that 'you will be pleased to impose no more on this exhausted
county beinge equally freeborne Englishmen then the equall and
proportionable parte therof; and we further humbly praye and begge for
religeons sake and for the cry of the martyred bloud of soe many thousand
protestants butchered and murthered by the cruell bloody and rebellious
Irish, only because protestants and Englishmen, to send thither speedy
and effectuall releife to our forces ...'. Resentful of taxation,[43] assertive of
the county's particular interests, volubly outraged at the Irish rebellion
and fearful of the social and political anarchy it threatened, the petitioners
expressed sentiments peculiar to the years 1642–48.

The assessment commissioners, charged with raising funds for a policy whose principles they endorsed but whose dependence on their pockets they deplored, met to word that protest carefully.[44] They were, in fact, trying to reconcile irreconcilable attitudes on policy and its financing. The middling sort supported them. Humphrey Dene, head constable of Black Torrington hundred, requested subordinate officials 'to excite every man to set their hand to ease that burden he is ready to sinke under'. The petition circulated in at least thirty-two parishes of Black Torrington, Hartland, Shebbear, Winkleigh and Witheridge hundreds, a substantial part of North West Devon, and doubtless reached areas nearer Exeter. The degree of assent in the parishes varied considerably, with the size of the parish and the zeal of the constables as varying influences. Nearly half the adult male population of Clovelly signed,[45] including the most prominent parish officers, but the proportion in Black Torrington parish was only just over eleven per cent. A sample of five parishes gives an average of about twenty-five per cent of the adult male population committing themselves to the sentiments of the petition. The 1648 petitioners were not as successful in obtaining popular assent as the parochial and hundredal officials who administered the Protestation of 1642 but, after all, in 1648 local government was in some disarray. Church services were normally an occasion when the parish should have been assembled together, but vacancies in benefices were a grievance of the assize grand jury. The smaller number of assenters may reflect inadequate administration rather than reluctance to sign. North west Devon was economically depressed and its natives were no strangers to petitioning in the hope of some economic relief.[46]

The popular petition was employed more frequently than the grand jury presentment to express grievances or to assert political commitment, yet despite the willingness of the yeomanry to 'set their hands ... to ease their burdens' this petition stayed among the quarter sessions records and was never presented to Parliament. It should have been given to the assize judges on 20 March but Sir Hardress Waller, in charge of the western forces in Fairfax's absence, may have been informed of the county-wide attempt to harness public opinion because on 3 March he issued a statement of the intentions of both Parliament and Army in order 'to prevent mistakes'.[47] He tried a frank explanation of how the Plymouth horse and foot regiments, the garrisons of Dartmouth and Exmouth and the county troop (employed in Devon as elsewhere by the sequestration committee) came to be lying on free quarter. The county assessment officials had failed to levy the rates to pay the troops, but Waller was diplomatic enough to pretend that 'by what occasion or defect this failure hath been I do not determine'. For the sake of political interests (Devon was not a natural recruiting ground for parliamentary Independents with whom the army was then enjoying a rapprochement) local officials could be exonerated. The taxpayers could be penalised without fear of repercussions. Waller declared that 'such as neglect or refuse to pay in their taxes must not only expect to have free quarter lie upon them but more than an ordinary number of soldiers sent unto them as the only obstructors of the present ease of these counties'. Grumbling continued through 1648; Barnstaple and Dartmouth appealed directly to the House of Commons.[48]

Confrontation between Devon and the army came on 8 May 1648, at Exeter. Waller was on his way to guard the Somerset/Devon border and quartered at Ide, two miles south west of the city. An army delegation was despatched to the city magistrate to convey their intention of entering Exeter.[49] Lieutenant-Colonel Salmon was received coldly and informed of the city fathers' need for two hours to consider the request to enter Exeter—regarded by the officers as a mere formality since the troops had already begun to move towards town. The mayor, Adam Bennett, and Alderman Christopher Clarke rounded on the officers with accusations that the army was 'not to be trusted' that it 'had done no service for the Parliament and that the additional ordinance touching billeting and quartering was not an ordinance of Parliament' and that it had wished to pull out Parliament 'by the ears' at Putney. This was the reporting of the soldiers, and the city act books avoided any mention of national politics but those in Exeter who led the attack on the army were exploiting general resentment at free quarter and taxation while taking a 'Presbyterian' stance on wider issues. Adam Bennett had been active in trying to establish a presbyterian church system in the city in 1646. Christopher Clarke was the brother of Samuel Clarke, the MP for Exeter. He, too, had been involved in earlier attacks on the army. The day after the soldiers entered the city the common council resolved not to provide quarters for the troops 'there being taverns, inns and alehouses sufficient for their entertaynment'. Parliament was informed of their decision, and the city saw the conflict as one between Parliament and Army. The common council resolved to abide by the judgement of Parliament. By 13 May the soldiers had taken quarters by force but after this all communications between the Army and the City were ordered by the sullen common council to be made on paper only.[50]

Against this background of military unrest at Exeter and Plymouth, Parliament grappled with plans to manage new county militias, which would replace the national armies. On 4 May, the day after yet another Devon complaint against free quarter was read in the Commons, Sir John Bampfield and Sir John Northcote were named to a committee on the settling of the militia.[51] Among radicals and the moderate Independents who had fled to the Army the plans were naturally received with considerable scepticism. On 16 May *Mercurius Pragmaticus* poured royalist scorn on the mixed nature of the national militia committee membership.[52] Discussion dragged on through the summer to reflect internal struggles. The Devon members were committing themselves to the waxing Presbyterian cause in the House of Commons. Sir John Bampfield, after being associated with the Army during the City of London apprentices' violence in July 1647 and after disappearing to Devon during the Army counter-moves in August was by 13 May 1648, a teller for a motion that the powers and numbers of militia commissioners be limited. His cautiousness and anti-militarism, formerly the characteristics of neutrality had now become the attributes of one who could be a fellow-traveller with the Presbyterians. (The aim of *positive* Presbyterianism was to conclude a settlement with the King, an aim which stood a chance of being realized with the Treaty of Newport later that year.) County unity, based on bitter experience of conditions at home, ensured that bills to establish local militia commissions stood more chance of success than the national plan.

On 22 May, Sir John Northcote and Sir Nicholas Martin, the two most prominent Devon JPs, of moderate/Presbyterian persuasion, were named as the first militia commissioners for the county and by 6 June the whole ordinance had passed the Commons and was ratified by the Lords the following day.[53] On the 19th, four Devonians, including Bampfield who sat for Penryn in Cornwall, and Thomas Earle, a Dorset MP with Devon family connections and a house at Axmouth,[54] were ordered to Devon to enforce the militia ordinance there. William Davy, the London barrister brother of the religious presbyterian John Davy of Creedy Park near Crediton, noted in a letter to his father-in-law, the moderate royalist John Willoughby, that a clause enforcing the Covenant on every commissioner had been defeated. This defeat would have been approved by the Devon MPs and gentry but by contrast the militia ordinance for Exeter ensured that the commissioners in that presbyterian city were of the same mind as its leaders.[55] Local conditions and opinion helped shape this essentially local variety of parliamentary politics. For the first time since the end of the civil war the Devon MPs were actively participating in Parliament.

Full power was given to the Devon militia committee to raise and deploy county troops when necessary; Parliament and the Derby House committee, the limited replacement of the privy council, were the only bodies to which it was accountable. Quarter sessions played no part in its frame of reference. Indemnity was offered its members (a *sine qua non* of new committees after the post-war epidemic of recriminations) who acted in meetings with a quorum of five. Individual members had no autonomous authority. Twenty-one of the thirty-three members were MPs and the only local members excluded were absentees and carpet-baggers Edmund Thomas and Laurence Whitaker (Okehampton), Samuel Browne and Hugh Potter, the last a crypto-royalist.[56] The other members were moderate but inexperienced. Six of the twelve had not been sufficiently trusted to be included in the quorum of the 1647 commissions of the peace. John Beare had not been a JP at all and was probably included because of his involvement in the siege of Plymouth. The commission brought with it its own Shibboleth by excluding all delinquents from its membership and supervision but the parliamentary drafters did not include all who had been active for Parliament in county government. Peter Bevis, John Bampfield junior (son of the MP), Rowland Whiddon, Henry Worth, John Quick, Henry Pollexfen and most importantly Edmund Davyes were all active at quarter sessions from their re-establishment in 1646 but none were militia commissioners.[57]

The absence of an effective county committee had allowed quarter sessions to revive with minimal interference from central government.

The prevalence of plague demanded a response in which administrative effectiveness was more significant than political commitment. Thus, Sir John Pole acted as a justice in the summer of 1646 and at the same time was fined over £1,000 for delinquency. At Michaelmas 1646 John Row of Crediton was named as an arbitrator in a case when he was not a magistrate at all.[58] 'Politics' and 'administration' had become separated in Devon after the civil war and it is not surprising that the first post-war attempt at a liaison between central and local government, a co-ordination accomplished notoriously well in other places by the county committees, should not reflect accurately the realities of local administrative power. The local militia commissioners were chosen with reliability and their likely dependence on the parliamentary majority in mind.

Why had the Devon committee not become as effective as the Dorset standing committee or the Stafford committee, or as notorious as its Kent or Somerset counterparts? A committee had been active at Plymouth since the winter of 1642, administering the garrison there.[59] Accounts from 1642 were audited in the visit of sub-commissioners for taking the accounts of the kingdom to Plymouth in May 1647 two months before the outbreak of unrest among Weldon's troops. It was at Plymouth that the sequestration committee for Devon had been formed, for the garrison there had never fallen to the royalists as the county had between the late summer of 1643 and April 1646. When full parliamentary control was resumed the Plymouth garrison was able to provide the county with a committed administrative corps. Richard Clapp, commissioner for sequestrations, had begun his career as a quartermaster in Plymouth in 1643, Stephen Revell was a clerk to a rudimentary sequestration body there in 1644 (its operations were confined to the town and its immediate suburbs) and Charles Vaughan and Giles Inglett, treasurer and deputy, were lawyers who doubled as clerk and deputy clerk of the peace. Vaughan was also MP for Honiton. Justinian Peard had been simultaneously mayor of Plymouth and treasurer of the garrison in 1645 and was a Barbados merchant before he became involved in the revival of sequestration business in 1648.[60] Sequestrations and compositions in Devon were thus in the hands of an urban and mercantile oligarchy and its clients rather than the county gentlemen who ran quarter sessions.

The military campaign of 1646 and the surrender of Exeter and Barnstaple to Fairfax determined the pattern of sequestration activity in Devonshire. The articles concluded on 9 April, in the names of Sir Thomas Fairfax and Sir John Berkeley, the surrendering royalist governor of Exeter, were conciliatory. Distance from London and a marked lack of enthusiasm for the cause of either Parliament or the King among the mass of Devon gentry were persuasive arguments for a moderate settlement. Among the Exeter articles was a provision that the maximum composition rate for those surrendering on these articles should be two years' value for land and exemption from penal taxation thereafter.[61] There were no 'notorious delinquents' of the kind active in the second civil war in South Wales, for example. The articles were favourable enough to entice the Devon gentry to seek composition at

Goldsmiths' Hall. Of the three hundred and forty cases, one hundred and twenty-seven came in in 1646 as a result of the Exeter surrender. By December of that year the number dwindled and during the whole of 1647 only thirteen cases were opened. The sudden drying-up of a promising flow of composition monies was not prevented by discovering and informing, the usual means by which delinquents were encouraged to compound. After 1646, the highest year for composition yields was 1652, when the Acts of Sale and the reform of the sequestration committee under closer supervision by central government showed how effective bureaucracy could depend on informing.[62]

The other tasks of the Devon committee included the disbandment of superfluous garrisons in the spring of 1647. In the face of continuous attacks on North Devon mercantile shipping by pirates and the guerilla-like marauding of the royalists or 'Gorings' as Devonians called them, the small Plymouth-based committee ventured as far as Torrington to supervise the closing of the Barnstaple and Ilfracombe military camps. The local-born governor of Barnstaple, Richard Harris, managed to set the town against the committee by assuring them that Parliament had promised that the townsmen, not the committee, would obtain the valuable materiel when the garrison was disbanded. The dispirited committee wrote a singularly depressed letter to the Devon presbyterian MPs, Bampfield, Rolle, Nicholl and Vaughan, reciting the problems of inadequate revenue and lack of information. More successful, it would seem, was their work from late 1646 in ejecting scandalous ministers and certifying the suitability of the godly for parochial livings, in liaison with the parliamentary committee for plundered ministers.[63]

When the second civil war erupted in May 1648, many entrusted with the settling of the militia and in Parliament thought that the security of Devon was threatened. To Cromwell, hurrying to South Wales, it seemed that the whole of the West was 'in a flame'. The Devon militia committee wrote to Lenthall of their fear that Prince Charles would land in Devon and that there would be an invasion by the Irish. Hardress Waller, who had been rebuffed at Exeter, wrote to the Derby House committee that the gentry of Devon and Cornwall were 'either for the king's party or (if possible) worse enemies' but a month later William Davy was telling his father-in-law, John Willoughby of Payhembury, that he was 'glad to hear of the quiet you enjoy in those parts'.[64] (Willoughby, who had compounded before Exeter Articles and in earlier letters had bemoaned his lot, was not likely to have minimized any disruption or unrest in the county.) The grandees had probably misconstrued the nature of the 1648 rebellion, which was a gentry-inspired revolt against committee rule and heavy taxation, the expression of a Clubman mentality.[65] Taxes were a grievance in Devon but compounding and sequestration had not been especially incisive during 1647 and 1648. Devon had demanded strong government in 1646–47 and had got it. The MPs who had come down to settle the militia and stimulate the sluggish sequestrators worked in a context of sporadic armed revolt elsewhere against a variety of government which could only be described as strong.

For those fortunate enough to compound on Exeter Articles the burden of committee rule was not a punitive one. Others were not as lucky. Even from North Devon, distant from either Plymouth or Exeter, the seats of committee rule and quarter sessions government respectively, a list of eighty names could be produced in response to a Goldsmiths' Hall request for proof of committee action. Only five of these were knights, however; others were yeomen and ex-soldiers and sixteen were marked as 'poor'.[66] The list reflected the good intentions of its compiler, Nicholas Rowe, a solicitor for sequestrations. Rowe was born in Lamerton near Tavistock, may have served the Earl of Bedford when younger, and as a lawyer, was secretary to the Council of War at Plymouth in 1645.[67] His urban background had little in common with those of the county JPs, and Sir John Bampfield criticised Rowe's efforts by reminding him that Goldsmiths' Hall was not interested in the estates of those worth less than £200.[68]

Not only were the committeemen in ill-accord with the county's natural leaders but they were also ill-equipped to foist their order on the county as a whole. Devon was an intractable, hilly and far-flung part of England in which a traveller could be much eased by hospitality and friendliness. The gentry denied the sequestrators such co-operation. Robert Spry, Rowe's fellow-solicitor, was acutely aware of his isolation and tried to apprise the London committee of his difficulties 'in two hundred parishes of fifty miles long'.[69] The north of the county was the least-governed; Spry reckoned that the committee had been there for a total of fourteen days in two years. By the end of 1648 he had persuaded them to sit in the north for a fortnight on end but still complained of inadequate assistance and hinted at some obstruction by Rowe. Even at meetings he found it difficult to elicit accounts from agents and when he told the Lord Chief Justice and John Maynard the MP for Totnes, his patron, he was disappointed further: his proposal for a separate North Devon committee 'by reason of the parlyaments multitude of affayres ... was layd aside'. Despite Spry's efforts the committee was still Plymouth-based, and its work suffered *lucri causa*. 'There are soe few of the comittee that they have not sate constantly, but as much as their occasions would permit them they have attended. Most parte of them are marchants and must at tymes attend their owne business.' They now met at Totnes, Torrington 'and other convenyent places' with Rowe's help: 'without him the comittee cannot sitt, hee having constantly attended them is best able to informe them in all particular concernments'.[70] Spry and Rowe, officially colleagues, seemed in practice to embody an age-old antipathy between North and South Devon.

Goldsmiths' Hall encouraged the sequestrators and the MPs came to Devon to organize the new militia.[71] At the same time the Derby House committee wrote to the Devon assessment commissioners exhorting them to pay in arrears of the monthly assessments. Moreover the still-active separate committee of Plymouth received a letter from Lenthall requesting that the town be inalienably secured for Parliament by the slighting of all potential bastions of resistance.[72] It was all induced by the second civil war and nervousness at Westminster; a long overdue direction of local quasi-military government from the centre. The assessment commissioners, nominated in January, had not yet met together in May and five out of the eighty-six nominees met at Exeter to draft a letter to their fellows plaintively assuring them that 'wee cannot act till there be a general meeting of the greatest part of the commissioners'.[73] They were a motley five, headed by the trimmer Robert Duke of Otterton; an active moderate justice, Peter Bevis, the radical upstart clothier, William Putt, John Marshall, a committed Parliamentarian and minor gentleman from Teigngrace, and John Vaughan, son of Charles Vaughan and newly come down from the Inner Temple. Nicholas Rowe was there to provide legal advice and clerical assistance; he was becoming the chief executive of the Devon parliamentary machine.

They proposed a meeting at Exeter on 19 May, an unhappy choice of venue since the city was still badly disturbed by the presence of Waller's troops. As late as 24 June Waller was proposing to Lenthall that troops be used to assist the Exeter constables in collecting taxes to provide arrears of pay.[74] The hard-nosed committee of Plymouth could distance itself sufficiently from the problems of Ralph Weldon to support the raising of more soldiers. The Plymouth merchants responded to parliamentary exhortations to wariness of the royalists with a strongly-worded letter to their wavering colleagues meeting at Exeter assuring them that there would be 'speedily a considerable number of horse raised here in Plymouth, for the service'.[75] They proposed that the assessment commissioners should invite the well-affected to suppress those who threatened the public safety. Such advice, which glossed over geographical obstacles, the torpor of the assessment committee itself and the difficulties of deciding who was well-affected in a county where commitment was the exception not the rule, revealed how isolated the Plymouth merchants were, and how little they knew of the realities of county government. Theirs was an inclusive concept of government, more suited to urban conditions than to the scattered communities of Devon as a whole.

When the MPs came to settle the militia they brought with them to Devon a world of political nuances unknown in the nearly committeeless county, even though their commitment at Westminster was in their own minds to the county itself and not to any particular parliamentary party. On 11 July, Sir John Northcote, Sir John Bampfield (active in the militia plans since May),[76] Sir John Young and John Waddon attended the midsummer quarter sessions. They attracted thirteen other magistrates eager to display their diligence and doubtless anxious to know the plans for the militia. They were a mixed group of radicals, trimmers and religious presbyterians. No remarkable orders were made at the sessions but instructions to prevent malting, the doubling of rates for the relief of maimed soldiers and fines imposed for failing to attend church and for playing illegal games indicate a concern to minimise social dislocation in the parishes.[77] On the 15th Bampfield and Northcote wrote to Lenthall of their difficulties at their Exeter headquarters in the recently-sequestered Dean's House. The wording of the militia ordinance was not clear, they were short of equipment, and they insisted that (in July 1648 as in 1646) Devon was in 'distraction ... occasioned by the diversity of rates unequally laid upon us beyond any other part of the kingdom'. The remedy would be the passing of 'the grand ordinance of the militia' which would provide three thousand foot and three hundred horse but would be maintained by rates determined by the county itself.[78]

Parliament debated such a measure throughout that summer. There it was viewed as an issue between the county committees who wished to maintain supernumerary forces and the county gentry moderates whose militia ordinance would have given full control back to county gentlemen. Bampfield and Northcote were on the national steering committee and when they wrote to the Speaker in July the names of intended commissioners were being discussed.[79] In Devon the ordinance was not viewed (as it was in Somerset) as a way to draw the teeth of a committee but as a means of rectifying an unfair burden of taxation imposed from above. Locally-raised taxes locally spent were the aim of county leaders. They were not even anti-military; because of royalist invasion scares they requested that Waller's soldiers, who had so enraged the Exeter presbyterians, should stay in the area. The militia commissioners may have shared Waller's suspicions of the Exeter merchant princes.[80] The mayor and aldermen were indignant at the request; that it was granted so readily goaded them into a show of examining debts which the county gentry had incurred to the city when troops were first raised in 1642 and 1643.[81]

By this time arrears of taxes to be collected had been reduced to a three-month backlog but the problems of manpower and materiel remained. The eleven commissioners requested augmentation by twelve assessment commissioners. On 7 August two regiments were ordered to remain in the west and the Devon militia commission was expanded. Three of those who had attended sessions the previous month were added.[82] Meanwhile, commissions to the colonels of the militia foot regiments were issued. One went to Christopher Savery of Shilston who had had to be prodded by the sheriff into coming to sessions. He was instructed to call together his forces, bring in all arms (with the help of constables), arm the well-affected and organise a meeting of them, and collect taxes. The effect was to create a county body which crossed the divisions between sequestrators, assessment commissioners and militia committeemen; commissioners 'and all other honest gentlemen' were to meet as equals.[83] This had been the idea of the Plymouth committee, and Bampfield and the others were happy to adopt it, even though the possibility of bestowing arms on those not named by Parliament, except in a clearly subordinate capacity, was not a practicable one.

In Dorset, Somerset, Kent and several Welsh counties the overlapping personnel and functions of the various committees had welded them into single county standing committees.[84] In Devon this was achieved in a few months during 1648 when partly through pressure from the Derby House and Goldsmiths' Hall central committees and partly through the will of the Devon members of the House of Commons, the first enthusiastic attempts were made to create an effective organ of central government. It was not intended as an act of centralization though that may have been its consequence; the object was to achieve a measure of county autonomy. The week after Sir Francis Drake had requested that Waller's troops should stay, Bampfield and Sir John Young MPs, Arthur Upton, the Brixham radical, and Philip Francis and Justinian Peard wrote to the other commissioners of militia *and* assessments. They had divided fifty-four of them into three committees (each to meet fortnightly) partly because of the 'mayne disservice which the want of a constant meeting brings to the publique and having lately receaved comands from Parliament to be more careful in that particular' but also, significantly, 'soe the burthen may not lye on all at once and that none of us may be troubled but once in three weeks'.[85] Government reform and centralization were a means to achieve a quiet, county-administered life.

There are indications that Bampfield and his colleagues did not achieve a great deal. The House of Commons continued to discuss the *cause célèbre* of the Plymouth garrison finances and in November ordered the Army Committee and the parliamentary committee of the West to examine the case anew in the hope of bringing in more money from the hundreds. On 25 November, the Devon JPs were ordered to bring in assessments there, a clear indication that the Derby House committee was less than pleased with their efforts.[86] And it would appear that the committee for compounding at Goldsmiths' Hall was no more impressed; after March 1648 only one new delinquency case was opened during the rest of that year. In any case, time was running out for the MPs. Despite the flirtation of some of them with the army in 1647, by 1648 when they were active in promoting militia ordinances they had aligned themselves with a policy which in parliamentary terms indicated hostility to the army.

In December 1648 the results of over six months' work appeared in the announcement of committees for the national militia in England and Wales. The second civil war had rendered the Welsh committees inoperative because of their members' involvement in the revolt. Only those whose loyalty had been proven remained in the smaller December commissions. The composition of the Devon committee was determined by the participation of the MPs in the drafting of the ordinance and by requests from the original local commissioners. Underdown describes the militia ordinance as a last-ditch effort by the Presbyterians to abolish county committees and how to the Rump it was a 'malignant' act which all could vote to repeal without qualms.[87] The Devon list suggests that the Presbyterian MPs (defined as such by their treatment during Pride's Purge of four days later) did not have their way in the composition of the committee. It was naturally based on the June ordinance which applied specifically to Devon but the balance in the new committee had shifted from MPs to magistrates. Seven MPs were omitted from the list and every one was secluded by Colonel Pride; one, Charles Vaughan, was imprisoned. The abstaining and conformist members were left, with three Devon Presbyterians and, as if to redress the balance, two Dorset Presbyterians, Thomas Earle and Richard Rose. The Devon MPs included more Presbyterians than men of other groups, but the fact that no others were removed from the list of the June ordinance suggests a struggle in committee for control of the militia.

Only three non-MPs were omitted from the new ordinance, among them Christopher Savery. This may have been aimed at separating civil and military power since he had been recently granted the colonelcy of the militia. The county names which appear on the commission comprise members of the 1647 and 1648 assessment commissions and the most prominent magistrates. Their names had been settled in August on the day that Waller's two regiments were ordered by the House of Commons to remain in Exeter; another Presbyterian defeat.[88] Nevertheless the ordinance and its supporters were viewed not unreasonably by the army as hostile to itself for its net effect would have been to return military power to gentry hands.

The letter from Exeter supporting Waller did little to help the Devon MPs. On 6 December, Samuel Clarke, Ellis Crimes, John Doddridge, John Elford, Sir Edmund Fowell and his lawyer namesake Edmund Fowell, John Harris of Hayne, Sir Nicholas Martin, John Maynard, Robert Shapcote, Simon Snow and John Waddon were secluded by Thomas Pride, and Charles Vaughan and Thomas Gewen were imprisoned. Not for the first time did the remaining, horrified, Devon men withdraw. Sir John Bampfield, Sir Francis Drake, Christopher Martin, William Morrice, Sir John Northcote, Hugh Potter, Sir John Young and Walter Young disappeared from London until at least 6 April 1649, by which time opinion in the Rump had hardened against them. Only Thomas Boone and Edmund Prideaux were left as conformists, with the absentee Laurence Whitaker. Skippon supported the Purge though he had no real Devon connections.[89]

For the Devon MPs Pride's Purge was the culmination of an extended period of hedging, of refusal to set local interests in a wider national context and a willingness to allow the complaints of the county against taxation to acquire a prominence which could not be accommodated in current political debate. The preservation or creation of a quiet life at home had been the singleminded goal of Devonians. They listened to the mutterings of the population when it suited them, but the small part played by the 'official voice' of the people, the jury system and the other organs of the county infrastructure show how limited was the interest of JPs in harnessing popular support. Typical of their opportunism was their readiness to espouse 'centralist' politics in order to further the most 'localist' of aims, that of being troubled 'but once in three weeks'. They had drifted into the Presbyterian camp almost by default. From 1646 to 1648 Devon had had numerically strong representation at Westminster which had failed to make a proportionate impact on the House of Commons or to establish institutions linking Westminster with the county. After the nemesis of Pride's Purge the problem facing the decimated Devonians would be how to restore the capacity to influence policy, based on personal contact, which had prevailed before December 1648.

NOTES

1. J. S. Morrill: 'Mutiny and Discontent in English Provincial Armies 1645–1647', *Past and Present*, LVI (1972), pp. 49–74.
2. D(evon) Q(uarter) S(essions) O(rder) B(ook) 1640–51; J. S. Cockburn (ed.): *Western Circuit Assize Orders*, Camden Soc., 4th series XVII (1976), pp. 240–41.
3. J. S. Morrill: *The Revolt of the Provinces* (1976), pp. 84–87.
4. DQSOB. Midsummer 1646. The volume is unpaginated.
5. J. S. Morrill: 'The Army Revolt of 1647' in A. Duke and C. Tamse (eds): *Britain and the Netherlands*, VI (1978), pp. 54–78.
6. DQSOB Michaelmas 1646, Epiphany 1647. P.R.O. PROB. 11/316/50 for Richard Harris's will.
7. F & R I, pp. 936–38.
8. DQSOB Michaelmas 1646, Epiphany 1647. Paulett destroyed Ash House, in Musbury, the house of the Drake Family: *C.C.C.*, pp. 865–66.
9. E.g. DQSOB Easter 1647 for Edmund Davy as the examiner of the case of North Bovey against Major Ford and his levy there for the maintenance of his troop.
10. DQSOB and Cockburn: *Assize Orders*, pp. 240–41, 256, 275–76.
11. DRO QS Box 55/bundle Epiphany 1648; DQSOB Epiphany 1648.
12. Morrill: *Cheshire 1630–1660* (1974), pp. 238–39.
13. QS Box 55/bundle Midsummer 1647/Petitions.
14. *LJ*, IX, pp. 171–72; Morrill: *Revolt of the Provinces*, p. 126.
15. For full details see S. K. Roberts: 'Participation and Performance in Devon Local Administration 1649–1670', University of Exeter PhD thesis 1980 pp. 19–20 and notes.
16. *CCC*, pp. 1021–22; W. C. Trevelyan, C. E. Trevelyan (eds.): *Trevelyan Papers* III, (Camden Soc., 1872), p. 262.
17. *Trevelyan Papers* III, p. 257; D. Underdown: *Somerset in the Civil War and Interregnum* (1973), p. 139; Historical Manuscripts Commission, *13th Report Appendix II: Portland*, I (1891), p. 414.
18. Morrill: 'The Army Revolt of 1647', pp. 57–58.
19. F & R I, pp. 936–40, 953–54.
20. This may have been the result of the Devon Committee's efforts to disband Barnstaple garrison: Bodl. Lib., Tanner MS 57 f 805; *The Kingdom's Weekly Intelligencer* 5–11 May, 1647; *Perfect Weekly Account* 5-12 May. One is reminded of the return of the shattered Rhé expedition of 1627.
21. *DNB; L.J.*, VII, pp. 374, 661, VIII, p. 43; *T.D.A.*, XVII, p. 237; Alan Everitt: *The Community of Kent and the Great Rebellion* (1966), p. 184.
22. For women as agitators, Brian Manning, *The English People and the English Revolution* (1978) *passim*. H. Cary: *Memorials of the Great Civil War* (1842, 2 vols.), I, pp. 324–27; *C.J.*, V, pp. 229, 231, 262, 266; Morrill: 'Discontent ... in Provincial Armies', *Past and Present*, LVI, pp. 59–60.
23. Cary: *Memorials*, I, pp. 327–29.
24. *Moderne (sic) Intelligencer* 26 August–2 September (30 August); Cary: *Memorials*, I, pp. 344–46.
25. *CJ*, V, pp. 286–87, 343, 362, 441.
26. *Ibid.*, pp. 467, 632, 656; *Moderate Intelligencer* 17–24 February, 1648 (18 February); *Kingdom's Weekly Account* 16–23 February.
27. John Rushworth: *Historical Collections of Private Passages of State etc.* (1659–1701, 8 vols.), VII, pp. 742–43.
28. Based on Underdown: *Pride's Purge*; V. Pearl: 'London's Counter Revolution' in G. E. Aylmer (ed.): *The Interregnum* (1972), pp. 29–56; Thomas Edwards: *Gangraena* (1646).
29. Morrill: *Revolt of the Provinces*, p. 98.
30. *Gangraena*, Part 2, pp. 28–29, 84.
31. D. Underdown: 'Party Management in the Recruiter Elections 1645–1648', EHR, LXXXVII (1968), pp. 235–64.
32. Underdown: *Pride's Purge*, pp. 81–83; Cary: *Memorials*, pp. 339–40.
33. *Parliaments of England: Members of Parliament*, I (1878); Underdown: *Pride's Purge*, pp. 366–90; *T.D.A.*, LXXII, p. 260.

34. Underdown: 'Recruiter Elections', pp. 245, 249–53; Robert Bell (ed.): *Memorials of the Civil War* (1849, 2 vols.), I, pp. 268, 273–74, 277–78, 289–90.
35. Underdown: *Somerset*, p. 130; idem; 'Recruiter Elections', pp. 260–63; Morrill: *Cheshire*, pp. 173–79.
36. For a fuller account of the Devon recruiter elections and the sources, Roberts: 'Participation and Performance' pp. 24–27.
37. *The Copy of a Letter to his Excellency Sir Thomas Fairfax* (1647); DQSOB Michaelmas 1647.
38. *L.J.*, IX, p. 385; H.M.C. *Egmont*, I, p. 440 (for a variant list of Sir Philip Percevall's); Underdown; *Pride's Purge*, p. 83.
39. HMC *Egmont*, I, pp. 443–44; Bell: *Memorials*, I, pp. 367–68. (For John Rolle: Keeler: *The Long Parliament*, and Edward Edwards: *Exmouth and its Neighbourhood* (1868), pp. 101–06); Underdown: *Pride's Purge*, p. 84.
40. George Yule: *The Independents* (1958), p. 113, describes him as an Independent because he conformed to Pride's Purge. He was hardly active in 1647 to 1648, however.
41. *CJ*, V, pp. 329–30, 344; *Mercurius Pragmaticus* 5–12 October 1647 Classification of John Corbet's committee is based on lists in Underdown: *Pride's Purge*, Appendix A.
42. QS Box 55/Bundle Midsummer 1647, Petition with papers attached.
43. The petition was an attack on two ordinances, of 23 June 1647 and 16 February 1648 F & R: I, pp. 958, 1072, *L.J.*, X, pp. 48–62. The June ordinance produced an independent protest to Lenthall from the M.P. for Plymouth, Sir John Young, and his son, Walter, who petitioned on behalf of Colyton for exemption from assessments since the town had been ravaged by fire, collapse of trade, widespread disorder, plague and exactions from the nearby garrisons of Lyme Regis and Axminster: Tanner MS 58 f 524.
44. Epiphany sessions first met on 11 January 1647, and although this would seem to preclude the possibility of a gathering of signatories as a result of the February ordinance, it should be noted that sessions were adjourned often for over a month, without a note being made in the order book.
45. Population figures from A. J. Howard (ed.): *The Devon Protestation Returns 1641*.
46. For local support for entrepreneur and royalist, Thomas Bushell: *A Declaration of the severall passages '... concerning surrender of the garrison of Lundy* (1647); *The Case of Thomas Bushell* (1649) and other 'Tracts on the Mines' at BL C 27 f 1; W. C. Abbott: *Writings and Speeches of Oliver Cromwell* (1937–47, 4 vols.), IV, p. 321; William Rees: *Industry Before the Industrial Revolution* (1968, 2 vols.), I, pp. 400, 470–71; J. W. Gough: *The Superlative Prodigall* (1932), p. 83, for Bideford and Barnstaple merchant support of his Combe Martin scheme. As well as governor of the mines royal (see Rees *op. cit.*) Bushell had been a silk monopolist before the civil war: C/66/14/2824.
47. Rushworth: *Historical Collections*, VII, p. 1027.
48. *Ibid.*, VII, p. 1067; *CJ*, V, p. 543.
49. There had been trouble at Exeter in February as Waller's account makes clear: Tanner MS 57 ff 127–29; DRO City Act Book IX (1647–58), p. 16.
50. *LJ*, X, pp. 269, 270, 272; HMC *Report on the Records of the City of Exeter* (1916), p. 212; City Act Book, IX, pp. 27, 28; *Gangraena* Pt. 3, pp. 41–45.
51. *CJ*, V, pp. 550–51.
52. *Mercurius Pragmaticus* 9–16 May 1648. The debates may be followed in *CJ*, V, pp. 550 *et seq.*; Underdown: *Pride's Purge*, pp. 100–01.
53. *CJ*, V, pp. 569, 585; *LJ*, X, pp. 310, 311.
54. G. Oliver: *Ecclesiastical Antiquities in Devon* (1840–42, 3 vols.), II, p. 86; R. Pearse Chope (ed.): *Early Tours in Devon and Cornwall*, p. 107.
55. *Trevelyan Papers* III, p. 268; *LJ*, X, pp. 372, 274.
56. R. L. Taverner: 'The Corporation and Community of Okehampton 1623–1885', p. 51; Bell: *Memorials*, I, pp. 367–68; Underdown: *Pride's Purge*, pp. 70, 210. Potter had been an official in the household of the Earl of Northumberland.
57. DRO Commissions of the Peace 6/3/47, 26/7/47; DQSOB marginalia for attendances at sessions.
58. The Plymouth committee accounts were published by R. N. Worth in *TDA*, XVII, pp. 215–39, and were padded out by E. A. Andriette: *Devon and Exeter in the Civil War*, p. 129 *et seq.* This ground will not be traversed yet again but an additional source for Plymouth garrison is PRO SP28/127, 128, 153, 197 in their relevant parts.

59. The accounts of Clapp, Revell, and Vaughan are in SP28/128 (Devon), 208 (Devon); L. E. Stephens has Inglett as deputy clerk of the peace from 1646 (*Clerks of the Counties*, p. 79) but DRO DD 55874 makes it clear that he held this appointment in 1641.
60. BL Add 5494 f 99r; *DCNQ* XXII, pp. 10–16; *TDA*, XVII, p. 217, LXXII, p. 259, XCVIII, p. 211.
61. Joshua Sprigg: *Anglia Rediviva: England's Recovery* (1854 ed.), p. 247; Andriette, *op. cit.*, pp. 165, 166, 169.
62. Composition cases in *CCC* passim; see 71–75 below.
63. Bodl. Tanner MS 57 f 805; MS J. Walker c. 4. ff 162, 163, 190, 195, 207, 208, 369, 419.
64. Abbott: *Writings and Speeches of Oliver Cromwell*, I, pp. 606–07; Tanner MS 57 f 173; *LJ*, X, p. 269; *Trevelyan Papers* III, p. 268.
65. A. Everitt: *The Community of Kent and the Great Rebellion*, pp. 240–59; Ivan Roots: *The Great Rebellion* (1966), p. 127; Underdown: *Pride's Purge*, pp. 97–100.
66. *CCC*, pp. 97–98.
67. SP 28/208 (Devon); *TDA*, XVII, p. 228, pp. 39–41, 175 below.
68. *CCC*, pp. vii, 98.
69. *CCC*, p. 97.
70. BL Add 5494 ff 99, 100.
71. *CJ*, V, p. 606.
72. BL Add 44058 ff 32–34.
73. DRO 42080 (Transcript in BL Add 44058 f 32 v). Marshall signed *Three Petitions presented by the grand inquest at the assizes of Exeter* (1642) and for Vaughan: *Students Admitted to the Inner Temple* (1877). The others are described elsewhere.
74. HMC 13th Report Appendix II: *Portland*, I, p. 466.
75. DRO DD 42081.
76. *CJ*, V, pp. 550–51.
77. DQSOB. Young and Waddon were MPs for Plymouth.
78. HMC, *Portland*, I, p. 484.
79. *CJ*, V, pp. 550–51, 558–59, 597, 607, 623, 634–35, 663, 665; Underdown: *Pride's Purge*, p. 127.
80. Underdown: *Somerset*, pp. 121–53, esp. pp. 148–49; *CJ*, V, p. 663; *Kingdom's Weekly Intelligencer* 1–8 August 1648 (7 August).
81. City Act Book, IX, pp. 44–45.
82. Tanner MS 57 f 173; *CJ*, V, p. 663.
83. BL Add 44058 ff 23v–24r, 35, 36v–38r.
84. C. H. Mayo: *The Dorset Standing Committee 1646–50* (1902); Underdown: *Somerset in the Civil War and Interregnum*, pp. 124–29; Everitt: *The Community of Kent and the Great Rebellion*, p. 172 ('The General and Sequestration committees were virtually one institution'); A. H. Dodd: *Studies in Stuart Wales* (2nd ed., 1971), p. 115; Morrill: *Revolt of the Provinces*, pp. 66–67.
85. Add 44058 ff 26v–27.
86. Rushworth: *Historical Collections*, VII, pp. 1338–39; *CJ*, VI, pp. 87, 90.
87. Dodd: *Studies in Stuart Wales*, p. 141; Glanmor Williams (ed.): *Glamorgan County History*, IV (1974), p. 279; Underdown; *Pride's Purge*, pp. 127, 164–65.
88. F & R I, p. 1236; *CJ*, V, p. 663.
89. Based entirely on Underdown: *Pride's Purge*.

Chapter Two:

Local Government under the Rump Parliament 1649-1653

Nineteen Devon justices appeared at the Epiphany Quarter Sessions on 9 January, 1649, under the shadow of events of the previous month. The purge had severely weakened county representation in the House of Commons, and the repeal of the militia ordinance of 2 November had repudiated the attempts at compromise and synthesis of opinion achieved in parliamentary committee.[1] Not until the summer of 1654 were such numbers at quarter sessions recorded again. Among those at Exeter in early January 1649 were Sir Edmund Fowell and Sir Nicholas Martin (both secluded) and Sir John Bampfield and William Morrice who disapproved of the coup and who subsequently failed to resume their seats. Their fellows broadly represented the post-war Bench. Presbyterian baronets and county gentry mixed with half a dozen lawyers and minor gentlemen. While it lasted there may have been little to suggest that this meeting had any particular significance but in retrospect it must have appeared as something of a watershed. Of the nineteen, only two came again before the middle of 1650 and one of those died within the year. Seven never returned and the others drifted back during the last days of the Rump. Only John Tyrling, a minor gentleman from Awliscombe in East Devon, was confident or insensitive enough to appear at every meeting from January 1649 to Michaelmas 1650 and intermittently thereafter until April 1653.

No more than seven justices appeared at any sessions through the rest of 1649, showing that Pride's Purge and the execution of the king had alienated many who had led the opposition to Charles I back in the earlier 1640s. Those who were named on the commissions of the peace and for assessments seemed cautious and reluctant to be seen acting publicly. In the early days of the Commonwealth more than at any other time during the Interregnum it was true that the appearance of power diverged sharply from the reality. The government relied on men like Sir Hardress Waller, Major-General Disbrowe and Major John Blackmore during 1649 and 1650 not only because of military threats to public safety but also because the response which could be expected from the justices of the peace was uncertain. Insecurity undermined central government and its local servants and pervaded the relationship between them. An analysis of the early republican commissions of the peace nevertheless reveals who was valued by the executive.

The two commissions of June 1649 and January–February 1650 are identical and indicate how slowly the government was forced to move in a

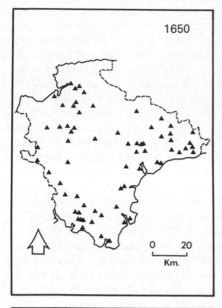

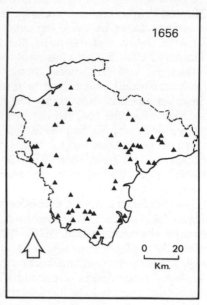

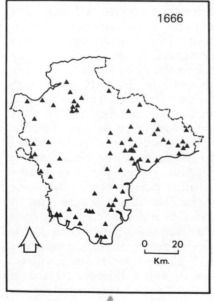

MAPS THREE-FIVE

TOPOGRAPHICAL DISTRIBUTION

OF

JUSTICES OF THE PEACE

IN DEVON

county where there was no local magnate to direct affairs.[2] Headed by
Edmund Prideaux, *custos rotulorum* since 1646, the lists include the names
of three secluded by Pride but omit ten other MPs. Two survivors were
barristers-at-law and the third, Sir Nicholas Martin of Oxton, was not
considered a safe nomination until early in 1650. Also secluded both from
Parliament and from local power was Sir John Northcote, whose
presbyterian faith and failure to resume his seat after the purge and the
execution marked him as hostile to the new regime. The five other
omissions from the 1647 list can be attributed to Pride's Purge except that
of crypto-royalist Sir Samuel Rolle, who died before it occurred. Three
were lawyers and one was the younger son of Sir John Northcote. All were
men prominent from 1646 to 1648. None was purged directly after the
execution of the king, an event which had no effect on the model of the
county power structure.[3]

1649 was thus a year of consolidation, of affirming commitments made
during the winter of 1648. There was little scope for bold executive strokes
through the commissions of the peace. Public action, the humiliation
offered a justice whose name was removed from the commission, was
inappropriate in circumstances in which a diffident government,
conscious of its weakness, needed all the support available to it. It was a
year which foreshadowed political life in the early eighteenth century,
when 'the regulations of the commissions of the peace ... were to some
extent a notional exercise, without much relevance to the real exercise of
local power in the countryside'.[4] But even if the commissions stood as an
invitation to those who remained untainted by parliamentary or royalist
contagion, less formal channels were developed by the Council of State
to monitor the extent of support in the counties. From the core of reliable
partisans came information on the diligence or inactivity of those in
commission; the 'gentlemen who wrote from Exeter' were thanked, and
their information passed on to the House, and lists of attending
magistrates were required from the clerks of assize. At the same time the
application of the Engagement to most local office-holders, conceived as a
means of widening the basis of power, produced a narrowing effect as
dismissals occurred in some cases in its wake. The Engagement
undermined the foundations of personal patronage which could have
supported a rebuilding of the commissions. John Moyle wrote to Francis
Buller in Cornwall in December 1649 that if he wished to resume his place
on the Bench, forfeited by his imprisonment during the purge, Moyle
could have him 'againe to be putt into the commission but you know you
must then subscribe to the engagement'; no other course was possible.[5]
The controversies over both the philosophy of the Engagement and its
enforcement led naturally to more open discussion of allegiances.

The first commission of the peace for Devon to take account of local
commitments was dated 23 July 1650, when the Engagement was a fading
issue.[6] Eighteen months after the Commonwealth was proclaimed
nominations to the Bench began to respond again to political reality, but
even so there was no purge nor was there a flood of new men to drown the
uncommitted. Sir John Bampfield, Henry Walrond and Walter Young

were dead, and only Peter Specott of Thornbury was dismissed, not under a cloud heavy enough to prevent his retention as an assessment commissioner. He embodied the type of moderate 'Puritanism' or presbyterianism prevalent among the Devon gentry.[7] Eighteen new men came in to replace these four and to augment the fifty-odd others. Two were secluded MPs whose experience on the Bench was eagerly sought. Others, like William Putt, were adherents of Parliament during the civil war, elevated after serving as assessment commissioners, or were closely related to men who had already proved themselves reliable. Robert Dillon, son of Sir William Dillon, was educated at Exeter College, Oxford and the Middle Temple in a progression natural for the sons of county gentry. All the rest were minor gentlemen of obscure genealogy and undistinguished marriage connections. John Doble was an outsider, a Somerset barrister who had practised in Devon since at least the mid-1640s, whose legal skills would have made him attractive to those seeking new administrative talent.

These were the fruits of an emphasis on governmental experience as a qualification for inclusion, but seventeenth-century government never approached Weberian standards of bureaucracy. The presence of Henry Walter and Francis Glanville reflected awareness that a Bench composed entirely of administrators and lawyers would lack social *éclat*. Philip Dennis of Ilfracombe, Richard Cole of Meeth, Robert Cockeram of Cullompton and Richard Viccary of Dunkerswell, however, were the most minor of gentlemen, included *faute de mieux*. Soldiers Philip Skippon (MP for Barnstaple), John Disbrowe and Thomas Saunders made up the complement of JPs. Saunders was from Payhembury, a one-time clothier who was governor of Exeter. His two brothers were presbyterian clergymen.[8]

These, the only substantial changes in the commission of the peace during the life of the Rump, achieved an even physical distribution of magistrates throughout Devon. There was no shift in the pattern of distribution from one geographical area to another. The social composition of the Bench in 1650 compared with its precursor of 1647 can be assessed in Table One. The need to stiffen Devonian resolve can be measured by the inclusion of outsiders from Cornwall and Somerset,[9] but the changes broadly effected a shift within the county gentry class, as in Kent and Lancashire. Minor gentlemen were still outnumbered by their 'county' social betters by almost two to one.

The commission of the peace was an open gesture of goodwill offering places to those who would serve, but the county had to be governed. There was no John Pyne or Anthony Weldon in Devon, but there had to be effective channels between London and the county government.[10] Edmund Prideaux remained as Attorney-General and on the Council of State, but his tenure as *custos* was weak. In a dispute over the clerkship of the peace the two contenders resolved their differences when Charles Vaughan conceded the place to Nicholas Rowe, not by intervention from Prideaux, who seemed to abandon local power for central high office.[11] The gap was filled by soldiers working at the behest of the Council of State

Table One: *The Social Composition of the Devon Bench and Assessment Commissions 1647–1666*

1647 Bench	Number	Percentage	1647 Assessments	Number	Percentage
Baronets	5	7.3	Baronets	4	1.3
Knights	7	10.3	Knights	6	7.7
Esquires	34	50.0	Esquires	29	37.2
Gentlemen	7	10.3	Gentlemen	11	14.1
Merchants	2	2.9	Merchants	9	11.5
Lawyers	10	14.7	Lawyers	12	15.4
Out-County	3	4.4	Out-County	7	9.0
	—			—	
	68			78	

1650 Bench	Number	Percentage	1650 Assessments	Number	Percentage
Baronets	4	5.5	Baronets	2	2.6
Knights	2	2.7	Knights	2	2.6
Esquires	31	42.5	Esquires	23	29.9
Gentlemen	18	24.6	Gentlemen	28	36.4
Merchants	2	2.7	Merchants	11	14.3
Lawyers	8	10.9	Lawyers	6	7.8
Out-County	8	10.9	Out-County	5	6.5
	—			—	
	73			77	

1657 Bench	Number	Percentage	1657 Assessments	Number	Percentage
Baronets	2	3.7	Baronets	4	2.9
Knights	—	—	Knights	2	1.5
Esquires	24	45.3	Esquires	41	30.1
Gentlemen	10	18.9	Gentlemen	45	33.1
Merchants	5	9.4	Merchants	15	11.0
Lawyers	10	18.9	Lawyers	27	19.8
Out-County	2	3.8	Out-County	2	1.5
	—			—	
	53			136	

1661 Bench	Number	Percentage	1661 Assessments	Number	Percentage
Peers	2	2.8	Peers	—	—
Baronets	14	19.7	Baronets	15	14.1
Knights	9	12.7	Knights	16	15.1
Esquires	34	47.8	Esquires	43	40.6
Gentlemen	5	7.0	Gentlemen	14	13.2
Merchants	1	1.4	Merchants	5	4.7
Lawyers	7	9.8	Lawyers	12	11.3
Out-County	—	—	Out-County	1	0.9
	—			—	
	71			106	

1666 Bench	Number	Percentage	1666 Assessments	Number	Percentage
Peers	1	1.3	Peers	—	—
Baronets	14	18.6	Baronets	18	18.0
Knights	11	14.6	Knights	10	10.0
Esquires	34	45.3	Esquires	45	45.0
Gentlemen	6	8.0	Gentlemen	11	11.0
Merchants	1	1.3	Merchants	2	2.0
Lawyers	7	9.3	Lawyers	9	9.0
Out-County	—	—	Out-County	5	5.0
Bishop	1	—		—	
	—			100	
	75				

(Numbers exclude the nominal appointments of high government office-holders) and Parliament itself. Disbrowe assumed military control late in 1649 and quelled the discontent at Plymouth garrison, supported the assize judges in their charges to the local body politic, and sat on the Devon bench after delivering a charge to the jury.[12]

The repeal of the militia ordinance had left a vacuum; local grumblings and threats of insurrection demanded that it be filled. The kind of abstract power politics, based on compromise and consensus, prevalent in 1648, was no longer practicable in Parliament in 1649. Parliamentary faction had been temporarily checked and local conditions called for swifter action. At Plymouth the gaols overflowed with French pirates and a Leveller-Royalist rising was planned there for the summer. There were rumours of an invasion of North Devon by Irish rebels.[13] John Moyle wrote of a plan to seize Exeter and 'the proclayming of Charles the Second through all these shieres and the suppressing and cutting the throats of all as would withstand it'. He had to admit lamely: 'whether it bee true or not I knowe not'. Royalist action was not as effective as its propaganda. Sir Hardress Waller was said to have defeated a thousand rebels near Plymouth.[14] In some ways the Presbyterian clergy were more formidable opponents. In Exeter Ferdinando Nicholls persuaded many JPs to stay at home, and the Engagement made matters worse. Church doors were locked to prevent subscription and the form of the oath was altered to suit Presbyterian consciences. By the middle of 1650 the clergy were being scrutinized more closely by the committee of plundered ministers than they had been during the 1640s. To meet these difficulties a dependable militia was a crying need.[15]

The first instructions to the militia appeared in April 1649 and enjoined monthly meetings. Papists were to be disarmed, conspiracies exposed and arms caches seized. The Council of State proposed to use troops to collect taxes and in February 1650 soldiers moved corn supplies from Devon to London. The county militia was augmented, from three troops of horse and three of dragoons to six of horse, but there were no plans to introduce fully military government. Only the magistrates among the militia commissioners were to examine suspects.[16] The militia commissioners had been joined by Major John Blackmore, who had served in Cromwell's regiment. Blackmore persuaded the justices to prosecute 'seditious' preachers. (No letters were sent by the Council to the JPs themselves, confirming their remoteness.) He also advised the demolition of Dartmouth Castle and the strengthening of the Navy between the Scillies and Cornwall.[17] The militia commissioners nominated officers and the Council of State sent down the first military commissions in March 1650.[18] The officers were headed by county gentlemen William Fry, Robert Rolle, Servington Savery, William Bastard, John Arscot and Arthur Fortescue. Savery and Bastard were still in their twenties. Thomas Saunders and the agents of the sequestration committee from 1646 to 1649, James Clark and James Pierce, provided professional military stiffening. A couple were of families which regularly provided constables and grand jurors and there were two Honiton merchants.[19] The twenty others included three JPs and four who were elevated to the Bench in 1650. For a minority military service provided an entrée to more exalted local offices.[20]

Table Two: *The Avenues of Recruitment to County Office 1649 to April 1653*

Body	New Men
Commissions of the Peace	8
Military Militia Commissions	13
Assessment Commissions	34

The decision to allow local nominations was probably sound policy as well as a gesture of goodwill. Local dignities were not immune to encroachment, however. The *county* militia commissioners appointed the militia committee for Exeter.[21] There were also repeated warnings that inactive commissioners would be dismissed. The militia committee was much more the agency of an intrusive regime than was the somnolent commission of the peace. No commission could be compiled without deferring to the claims of social rank, however, and there were complaints that Richard Foxworthy was unworthy to be a major of dragoons. Centralism prevailed in this case and Foxworthy stayed on assessment committees down to 1660.[22] Another militia ordinance of July 1650 underlined the failure of the magistrates as a whole to re-establish themselves as the dependable 'workhorses' of central government; militia commissioners could now examine the recalcitrant on their own.[23]

The assessment commissions of December 1649, November 1650 and December 1652 provided the best opportunity for the Rump to widen its local support.[24] The commissions bestowed considerable power but could never pose a threat to civil or military stability, if misused. They were not, like the old county committees, a closely-knit group. Assessment commissions expanded inconspicuously and without comment from seventy-five members in 1649 to eighty in 1650, ninety-five in 1652 and one hundred and forty in 1657. Here was where most new men cut their teeth in government during the Interregnum. Thirty-four entered the service in this way although only eight ever became JPs. Minor county gentlemen accounted for half the parvenus. Sympathy with the parliamentary cause before 1649[25] and a good deal of family string-pulling accounted for the presence of most of them. Three more lawyers appeared; one, Hugh Camworthy, had been the Devon escheator in 1625.[26] Another seven merchants joined during 1650; three from Dartmouth, two from Barnstaple and one each from Brixham and Plymouth. Four bordered on yeoman status and a couple of soldiers and a wealthy Cornishman completed the lists.[27] The proportion of esquires and gentlemen in the 1650 commission of the peace was the same as that in the assessment commission—sixty-five per cent. There were fewer knights and baronets in the assessment commission but more merchants—eleven per cent more—than on the Bench. Social status was an important consideration when compiling the commission of the peace, and clearly the merchants were thought to have little to offer.

Attendances at sessions confirm the apathy among JPs. In the first four years of the Interregnum numbers barely rose above single figures. Sixteen per cent attended in 1649, nineteen per cent in 1652. These fell below, but not egregiously below, the pre-civil war attendance rate in three counties of about a quarter or below that of twenty per cent in Cheshire. The Devon proportion is comparable to that of the East Riding to Yorkshire in the seventeenth century.[28] The commission of the peace always had its dead wood. The JPs holding sessions together in the early days of the Rump were Thomas Drake of Winscombe, William Fry and Arthur Upton, county gentlemen whose fathers had been JPs before the civil war, and minor gentlemen like John Tyrling of Awliscombe.

The activities of magistrates were not confined to sessions, however, and attendance there should not be assumed to be an entirely fair measure of magistratic diligence. J. S. Morrill expands 'active' to include those who signed one or more document among the sessions files.[29] This possibly errs towards not too narrow a definition but one too wide, since quarter sessions records contain documents which justices signed in bulk and in haste when administrative initiative and responsibility lay elsewhere. It is therefore better still, in order to draw fair comparisons, to take signatures on one class of document among the files. Recognizances are the most plentiful. Most criminal law enforcement by JPs depended on the taking of recognizances and examinations to be despatched to sessions. A recognizance is a measure of one completed administrative action, and although the variety of work falling to the lot of the magistrates defies rigid classification, the information provided in the recognizance (the name of the JP, the parish where the offence occurred and sometimes the details of the offence itself) offers a means of comparing quarter sessions action with extra-sessional justice.

John Tyrling and John Beare came to eight and five sessions respectively during 1649 and 1650 and were equally busy in the parishes. Tyrling signed forty-one recognizances, Beare, fifty-two, and together they accounted for over twenty per cent of the total number for those years. Other prominent attenders did not consolidate their attendances by action in the parishes.[30] Thomas Drake, who came to four sessions, and Arthur Upton, who came to six, signed two and eight recognizances each. William Fry came six times and signed ten (2.2 per cent of the whole number returned). By contrast, Christopher Wood, gent., and John Drake of Ash, esquire, attended only once each but signed fifty-two (11.5 per cent of the whole) and fourteen (3.1 per cent). On the whole, those who returned the highest number of recognizances (ten or more) were not prominent attenders at all. Nearly a third of those thus judged as active in the parishes did not once go to quarter sessions during these two years. Also, the county gentry returned more recognizances than the minor gentlemen, merchants and lawyers. The efforts of stalwarts of lower rank like John Tyrling, Christopher Wood and John Beare were the exception rather than the rule.

Fifty-five per cent of the work performed outside sessions was still in the hands of the county gentry. The changes in the commission of the peace exaggerated changes in the balance of county power: the county gentry, secluded from authority at Westminster, maintained a dogged grip on county administration. Those associated with the secluded MPs, who had failed to appear at quarter sessions meetings, were among the most active in the parishes. The working proportion of the whole commission was about one quarter, which J. H. Gleason considers typical as an attendance rate at sessions. Thirty-nine JPs out of seventy returned one recognizance or more to the court, and this in a year of pernicious local insecurity in which participation in government might have been

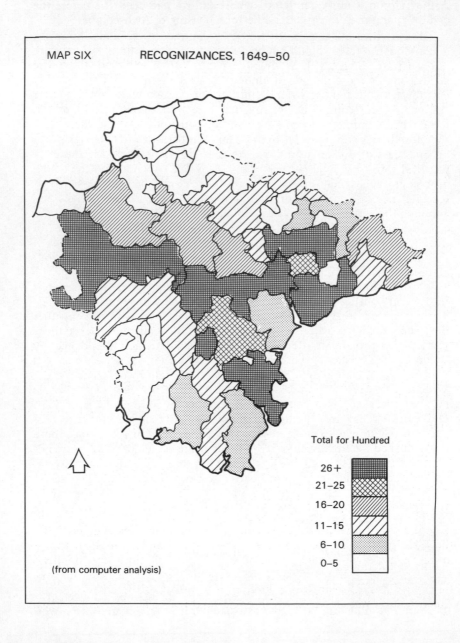

MAP SIX   RECOGNIZANCES, 1649–50

Total for Hundred

26+
21–25
16–20
11–15
6–10
0–5

(from computer analysis)

considered foolhardy. Nor was this action undertaken by individuals in isolation. Twenty per cent of the surviving recognizances were filed by magistrates working together, in accordance with many Tudor and early Stuart statutes.[31]

Yet if the magistrates acting alone or in pairs in the parishes may be set against the quarter sessions system of justice the geography of recognizance-taking demands explanation. More recognizances were filed near Exeter, the permanent seat of quarter sessions, than elsewhere (Map 6). There were large towns in south-west Devon—Plymouth and Tavistock—and in the north—Barnstaple and Bideford—but few recognizances were filed in those areas. It seems highly unlikely that fewer criminal offences were perpetrated there or that justiciary activity accurately measures the extent of crime. Indeed, the recognizance-taking of Major-General Disbrowe and his commissioners was to be concentrated in the Tavistock district, as well as around Exeter. Nor did the pattern of recognizance-taking correspond to the even distribution of magistrates throughout the county. There was no obvious relationship between regular attenders at quarter sessions, who preserved the public, 'political' role of quarter sessions and those who busied themselves at home in administration of an almost private nature. Yet the mandatory despatching of recognizances to sessions at Exeter exercised a pull over the pattern of justice outside sessions: either suspects apprehended near Exeter were more likely to be bound over than others, or much interrogation was conducted without resort to the recognizance. Justice outside and inside sessions now seems to have been less separate. Viewed in one light, recognizance-taking and the holding of 'privy sessions' were extensions of quarter sessions authority and not its antithesis. Even on occasions such as Easter and Michaelmas 1649 and Epiphany 1650 when no more than five JPs sat on the Bench, recognizances were being filed in the parishes by those who had publicly renounced their faith in the drift of events in Parliament, as well as by proselytes and the less scrupulous. Even when the half-empty Bench seemed to mirror political bankruptcy and to typify a regime based on only the most grudging assent in the nation, the law was upheld and order maintained in a topographical pattern moulded by a local institution whose apparent lack of public support was so conspicuous.

The resilience of justices in the parishes despite the unsettled climate did nothing to foster self-confidence among the diminished governing group of Devonshire. Many backed into the shadows and those who remained had to contend with the uncertainties of public opinion. The local leaders under the Commonwealth, more than those of any other Interregnum regime, were liable to feel every rebuff, every questioning of its authority, to the quick. 'Resistance to government was endemic'[32] in the early modern period, and most abuse was simple, unselfconscious invective aimed at anyone in authority. The small fines on offenders suggest that magistrates took a broad view of this. The bailiff who was threatened at Dittisham with a knife in his buttocks suffered very direct violence but it was an attack which posed no threat to local government as a whole.[33] Disaffection within the ranks of the county administration was more alarming. John Huish, bailiff of West Budleigh, remarked cryptically to a grand juror that 'he should see an alteration shortly and that he should not be worth a groat shortly'.[34] Not a particularly seditious sentiment, perhaps, but the justices took their servant to mean political change, and he was dismissed. Even in 1653, when composition and sequestration by delinquents had been largely completed, the magistrates did not hesitate to dismiss Roger Hore of Kilmington from his constableship at Axminster when they discovered that he had 'beene sequestered for his delinquencye'.[35]

Individual justices frequently found themselves the targets of popular ire. Not surprisingly, parvenus were more likely to attract this kind of denigration. Christopher Wood, Nicholas Rowe (the clerk of the peace), Robert Cockeram and Rowland Whiddon, all upstarts and all notable partisans of the Long Parliament during the civil war, were on different occasions the butts of vulgar abuse. A Clayhanger man opined that Cockeram 'had no more wit to be a justice than his breech'; a Beare man thought that William Fry 'was no more justice than his arse' and a fellow-parishioner of Thomas Drake's spread an unlikely rumour that Drake had 'a commission from the King'. These cases were written up in the order books and thus isolated from the run of criminal business, to emphasise the significance with which the Bench endowed them.[36]

Even more serious were overtly political statements. These were fairly uncommon but nevertheless occurred more frequently under the Commonwealth than at any other time until 1670 at least. The man who was briefly gaoled for 'saying he did not care a fart for the justices' was merely shaking his fist at the world through frustration or bravado. George Bond of Mary Tavy was much more threatening when in April 1653 he was accused of saying 'that they had put to death a king that was a god upon earth and that there was not a gentleman left in the land but a sorte of base rogues which weare collers and tinckers that did have sway in the land'. The views of Edward Hyde and the author of *Eikon Basilike* seem to have found an exponent in a small West Devon parish. Five people were found to testify that a Dunsford man had described Parliament as 'a company of knaves ... [that] have sate these three years and cannot graunt a catechize', while in Crediton Oliver Cromwell was considered by one person at least to be 'a rogue and a blood-sucking rogue'. In Tavistock, an industrial town and a centre of unrest and of hostility to Interregnum governments, someone hoped 'to have a kinge again and that ... he should have the carryinge the roundheaded rogues to gaol'. Such egregious behaviour attracted exceptional penalties. The Dunsford man was found guilty, fined a hundred pounds and pilloried. His Tavistock fellow-sufferer was fined ten pounds and stocked for an hour.

Penalties varied widely and depended on the degree of outrage felt by the Bench. The use of the pillory, an unusual punishment at quarter sessions, betrayed the fears of the JPs and their determination to make examples of the disaffected among the lower orders. This was a more direct local deterrent than the imposition of swingeing fines such as that of £500 upon a local critic of Cromwell in 1654. Under the Commonwealth, threats to political stability and social order were considered more dangerous than under the Protectorate bent with a degree of success on 'healing and settling'.[37] There were cases, lastly, where 'political' disaffection was heavily tinged with personal antagonism, petty jealousy and rivalry so prevalent in cases which came before local courts. A drunken Awliscombe cards-player, aggrieved by the turn his game had taken, declared amid uproar that Parliament 'should kiss his arse ... and [he] did hope to see them hanged and [his partner] likewise'. Mrs Ann Davey, the wife of the minister at Offwell, complained of an abusive neighbour who had already been gaoled at the behest of William Fry. She declared, in an attempt to prolong the sentence, that he had averred that 'the Presbeterians and Cavaleers bee devills and that they must be put into one bagg and then throwen into hell'.[38]

Popular contempt for justiciary dignity doubtless mirrors a widespread unpopularity. J. S. Morrill has noted the same symptoms and makes the same diagnosis for Cheshire in the 1650s. But it is no less significant that such cases were singled out by the Bench in its procedures and occasionally in its administered punishments. Offenders were mentioned in the Order Book, unlike those whose disrespect was directed merely towards constables, bailiffs and other lesser officials, and pillorying was a singular penalty. The existence of widespread disaffection to the court of quarter sessions reflected insecurity in the collective consciousness of the governing class as much as it mirrored the objective reality of popular scorn.[39]

A similar test of magisterial self-confidence is the frequency of referrals by the magistrates of cases to others acting outside the direct supervision of the court. Commissions were issued in order to settle disputes between individuals, disputes between parishes or among the inhabitants of single parishes over the apportionment of taxation, particularly local taxation for the relief of maimed soldiers and for the maintenance of gaols and hospitals. Disputes frequently sprang from the settlement and apprenticeship laws, too. There were as many as twenty-two referrals at the Epiphany sessions of 1649 and an annual average of eighteen from 1650 to 1653. The exceptional number early in 1649 arose merely from the large number of attending magistrates. Many of the referred problems suggest that administrative decisions were *ad hoc* and that referrals could cut through work which had been accummulating since 1646. The petty constables of Musbury owed the Axminster hundred constables a half-year's rate; a Sidbury man requested a maimed soldier's pension. Baptist Tooker was at odds with Mr and Mrs Brooking, John Taylor of Cullompton with his father and brother. Robert Hamlyn and Richard Smearden quarrelled over repairs to the church at Widecombe-in-the-Moor—these were among the miscellaneous matters referred to specific JPs or to 'the two nearest justices'.[40]

Almost the only common feature of referrals was that they all involved the problems of the parish; weightier matters of county policy or administrative procedure were not referred. Another restriction was that the initiative allowed referees was bounded by the procedural rules of the court; reports of decisions were to be submitted for the approval of the Bench. With the execution of the King the pattern changed abruptly. The number of cases referred fell away sharply. A decline in the volume of court business would accord with the drop in attendances by JPs but it is not clear why the number of referred cases should also be reduced. Matters were referred in order to lighten the administrative burden faced by the court, and as pressure on the magistrates increased more cases should have been referred. Not only did more JPs stay at home after January 1649, however; the confidence of those who remained was badly shaken. Morrill connects the abuses offered the JPs and the volume of referred cases in a simple correlation of popular consent and administrative performance.[41] The unpopularity of the government provoked abuse and caused JPs to reserve court business for the consideration of sessions only. In Devon, at least, the circumstances are rather more complex. Referrals up to and including Epiphany 1649 reflected accumulated business to be completed. At the next sessions the magistrates lacked confidence to despatch more than five cases to colleagues outside sessions and two of these were matters appearing for a second time for consideration.

The establishment of the Commonwealth thus produced two conflicting symptoms of administrative malaise. There was a lack of confidence about justices in the parishes who had not come to court and whose loyalties were thus suspect; it was safer to reserve cases solely to the consideration of the court. There were also fewer attenders and more and more business, and referral seemed the best relief. From the summer of 1649 a partial resolution of the difficulty was found in referrals to those who were indeed loyal to the government but who were not necessarily JPs. One such was William Squire of South Molton, the father of a local barrister. He had been demonstrably well-affected since 1642 but was little more than a yeoman. With a JP he was asked to arbitrate between two Challacombe people.[42] Zachary Cudmore of Loxbeare was a personal friend of Major Thomas Saunders and settled a similar personal dispute.[43] By January 1650 this policy had been extended to embrace those dismissed from the commission of the peace but who could, if an eye were kept on them, be trusted in minor administrative matters. Sir John Davy of Sandford and Sir John Northcote were asked to consider a petition. Northcote had been dismissed as a magistrate because he failed to dissent from the vote of 5 December, 1648, to continue addresses to the King. Robert Shapcote had been dismissed in 1649 and was never included again despite his seat in the first Protectorate Parliament and his later prominence in Cromwell's government. He, with John Were, a much more typical Rump JP, arbitrated in a Brampford Speke tax dispute.[44] In the same sessions William Squire found himself nominated again, this time to settle the accounts of the Pilton collectors of money for the relief of plague victims.

Many referred problems involved taxation. For a hard-pressed Bench of justices the assessment commissioners represented a useful channel of relief. The tithings of Battisworthy and Nettlesworthy in Witheridge had been in dispute since at least the end of Michaelmas 1648 when William Morrice, Sir John Davy and Henry Walrond had examined the matter. By Easter 1651 the question remained unresolved and the tithings continued to petition the court. The patience of the justices gave way and they testily ordered that the disputants should 'attend the commissioners of this county and that they trouble this court no more about it'. The busy William Squire was an assessment commissioner, albeit during 1649 and 1650 only. The vexatious Widecombe church repairs were delegated to the supervision of John Southmead of Moretonhampstead in July 1649 although the government only rewarded him with a place in the assessment commission in November 1650.[45] Occasionally the justices would abdicate responsibility entirely if they felt that the parishes were well able to look after themselves. When at Easter 1650 a decayed bridge between Chudleigh and Trusham was presented to the Bench, the usual procedure of inquiry into the responsibility for previous repairs was abandoned, 'by a reason a view and inquiry thereof cannot without much difficulty be procured in regard of the scarcity of justices of the peace'.[46] The three nearest parishes were told to split the cost between them. These were hardly circumstances in which a centralised local court could flourish and any decline in frequency of petty sessions meetings could not be attributed to a development in the power and strength of quarter sessions.

Much can be inferred about the composition and aims of a bureaucracy from its treatment of complaints against it. The central Indemnity Committee, established in 1647 to satisfy pressing complaints from the Army, dealt with military matters only; quarter sessions, which in Devon had provided Parliament with its most effective local cadre back in 1647 and 1648, itself judged complaints against it. Most of the Devonshire cases among the papers of the Indemnity Committee concern either the actions of private soldiers during the war, or lawsuits arising from sequestration. John Fortescue of Fallopit, George Bagg of Saltram, Piers Edgcombe and Arthur Bassett of Umberleigh were delinquents who retaliated against the sequestrators, to be checked by the committee, which 'almost invariably' upheld the actions of parliamentary soldiers and officials.[47] Petitions by former mayors and magistrates of the principal towns were common, especially during 1647 and 1648, and they reflected partly the concentration of commitment to the parliamentary cause among the western urban oligarchies and partly the limits of urban magisterial power. Unlike the JPs, who could shelter behind the clear authority of the commission of the peace, the urban leaders found themselves open to attack by men whose property had been distrained for the service of the State.[48]

Lesser men were even more likely to be prosecuted, especially when they were imprudent enough to tread on the toes or the dignities of their social superiors, adept at exploiting opportunities for litigation. Cases involving royalist delinquents were almost all like this; minor functionaries and soldiers appealed to the committee against the suits of royalist gentlemen. A few of these officials were constables seeking indemnity not for actions committed *ultra vires* but for procedures which could be justified by parliamentary ordinance. John Turner, Constable of Broadwoodkelly, tried to distrain the goods of Grenville Southcote, who owed three months' assessment arrears. To do so he entered the house where Grenville stayed. Its owner, John Drake, then sued Turner for trespass. Turner's action was easily justified by the terms of the assessment ordinance, but he had to appeal to the committee for confirmation. John Tooker, customs and excise sub-commissioner at Barnstaple, was accused of unlawfully seizing goods being loaded into a ship there. They belonged to the merchant and former garrison commander, Richard Harris, to prove that the partisans of Parliament in North Devon were not without internal friction.[49] In these two cases the disputes arose from the collection of central government taxes. Here the jurisdictions of quarter sessions and Indemnity Committee overlapped. In May 1647 an excise riot was quelled swiftly by the magistrates at a time when quarter sessions itself exercised authority as an indemnity committee.[50]

By the middle of 1653 the period of total *rapport* between the Bench and central government had cooled, so that the prevailing local attitude was one of caution and an attempt to balance local and central interests:

> Whereas there have been grievous complaints brought to this court by many persons against Middleton and Rice and others in the vigorous prosecution of the acts and ordinances of Parliament for the leavying of the duty of excise to the great injury of many good people, this court doth desire Sir John Davy, baronett, John Beare, William Putt, John Coplestone and Robert Cockeram Esquires or any two of them to examine the said complaints and to use their best endeavours as well to gett in the dues to the State as to reforme the abuses in the collection thereof for the case of the good people of this county.[51]

The court had much more control over its own subordinate officials, and although parish constables were appointed by courts leet or by local patronage the justices were able to remove them if guilty of incompetence or fraud. Alleged abuses of constables in rating and tax collection were probably the most numerous that the Bench had to investigate, especially during the 1650s when the burden of taxation was keenly felt in the localities. Such cases were subsumed in a general acknowledgement of Easter 1649 that 'there have bene many heavy rates and taxes imposed on this county for only reason of the late warres', and that the misdemeanours of constables in misappropriating funds or refusing to present accounts were to be punished by the JPs in their areas.[52] Such general orders frequently convey the impression that the Bench was doing more than it needed in acknowledging administrative failures; almost exaggerating its own deficiencies or those of its subordinates. Public relations could never be entirely ignored by the justices, and on occasions when unrest prevailed in the county, the essentially public nature of quarter sessions government offered a means of satisfying grievances acceptable to both governors and governed.

Public pronouncements were expected, but the public nature of the transacted business and the clarity of the rules within which it was conducted diminished with each successively lower level of responsibility. At the bottom, in the parishes and tithings, the variety in local traditions of appointment and the strength of parochial self-regulation (with a minimal degree of day-to-day supervision) could not be balked by would-be reformers. No amount of breast-beating in sessions could remove the obstacles to a more centralized local administration. As an anonymous Ashburton official wrote to the justices, local customs, acceptable in former times, were at the root of parochial discontent in a period of high taxes:

> The highways cannott be amended without paveinge and therefore it hath beene a custom to make a rate. The rate was made by the constables, the rate is verye unequall never published and men of no estate charged as much as they of very greate estate. Some hath been collected and some wayes that are for the benefitt of the waywardens are mended and others omitted.[53]

Grumbles about taxes could be expressed as attacks on the 'corruption' of officials, but in many other grievances no common pattern is discernible, unless it were a readiness to complain against more minor officials. The villagers of Monkton near Honiton alleged that hues and cries were repeatedly pursued through their village, involving parishioners in a distasteful service; others that parish officers were not relieving the poor, that a man had been wrongly imprisoned, that bailiffs distrained goods unlawfully, that constables took excessive fees. Such perennial local problems fluctuated between complaints that there was too much, and that there was too little government. Depressingly, 'too much' often began when officials and procedures outside the parish were involved.[54]

Nothing was more alien to the gentry-dominated parishes than the pursuit of royalist delinquents. The confidence and activities of sequestrators were maintained and developed under the Rump. After compounding an Exeter Articles in 1646, sequestration business had slackened during 1647 and 1648 but revived in 1649 when thirty-nine new cases were opened. This despite the inadequacy of an administrative machine whose operators were urban merchants more concerned with their own trades than with compositions. Apprehending delinquents and controlling the agents of the committee were never easy, but the rivalry between the solicitor for the north, Robert Spry, and his colleague for the rest of the county, Nicholas Rowe, made matters worse.[55] Many of the officials involved in this work had served the parliamentary cause since early in the civil war, and depended for their appointments on the ruling group which had been superseded in Pride's Purge. Spry owed his post to John Maynard. Charles Vaughan, MP for Honiton before being imprisoned during the Purge, was treasurer of the sequestration committee before being succeeded by Nicholas Rowe who was both sequestrations treasurer and clerk of the peace. Vaughan had been treasurer for Parliament in Devon in 1642. More junior officials whose careers had begun as long ago as 1643 were Giles Inglett (deputy treasurer and deputy clerk of the peace), Samuel Slade and Richard Clapp (commissaries and commissioners for sequestrations). Stephen Revell, another deputy treasurer, was clerk to the committee for sequestrations in 1644, and the solicitor for sequestrations in Cornwall. He owed his position to a family connection with the Rouses. There is no evidence that these men were any more or any less ready to act in 1649 than they had been earlier; reluctance to act was a noticeable feature of the more prominent committeemen, to whom Rowe suggested adding more diligent minor gentry and merchants from areas other than Presbyterian Plymouth.[56]

At the beginning of 1650 the structure of penal taxation was reorganised. The quasi-autonomous local sequestration committees were replaced with county commissioners directly responsible to the central committee for compounding, and the displaced officers had to hand over papers and give all assistance to their local successors. In counties where the committee had been all-powerful this change was a blow to local bosses and a lessening of bureaucratic impositions.[57] In Devon there was no battle between Titans like John Ashe or John Pyne. Because the new county commissioners were to be appointed by the MPs of the individual counties, patronage in Devon was channelled by a very small group, committed to the government but without the local prestige of the secluded Charles Vaughan, John Bampfield and John Maynard, all of whom had formerly supervised compounding. Patronage was now wielded at a distance by men like Thomas Boone and Sir Gregory Norton, the latter drafted to augment the few Devon MPs, even though his parliamentary seat was Midhurst in Sussex and his only Devon connection was an estate in Stokenham.[58] In May 1650 two of the local commissioners complained to Boone that commissions signed by him were delivered by an agent who was not a Devonian. They even questioned their own authority because it had been rumoured that the new compounding procedures had been rejected in Parliament. Sir Gregory Norton also appointed an outsider or at least someone *non persona grata* to commissioners John Searle and Richard Clapp; they wrote to the central committee professing ignorance of Captain Wotton, whom Norton had appointed as their colleague, even though Wotton's military accounts were scrutinized by Clapp himself in 1644.[59]

A local committee of minor gentlemen, subsumed in the assessment and militia commissions, was replaced by a smaller group of minor gentry and soldiers. Captain Wotton, Richard Clapp and Major James Peirce were soldiers. John Searle of Buckerell and Joseph Hunkin of Lifton were armigerous but of parochial influence only. Hunkin and John Marshall of Teigngrace were the only ones who had enjoyed any civilian authority before 1650; the others were new men. Local ties had been weakened as far as possible in the sequestration sub-commission but could not be repudiated altogether. Any sort of local administration depended on goodwill and local custom. The sub-commissioners found that the far-flung nature of the county made all communications difficult and likely to undermine administrative effectiveness. The posting of the new commissions and the calling to account of the erstwhile sequestrators were best done during the quarterly sessions weeks, when reliable information could be had of their whereabouts even if such men were not to be found in Exeter.[60] Local officials also tended to control dependable subordinates. The two retiring solicitors, Nicholas Rowe and Robert Spry, both submitted lists of men 'of integrity and good affection' to Parliament, quite independently, and both lists were dominated by parochial gentry and North Devon merchants. Their suggestions were not adopted, however, and when John Dury, apologist and administrator, wrote to the seven 'great compounders' he recommended some Devon soldiers for promotion. The government tried to minimise county influence in view of the undervaluation of estates and the other ways in which the county community tried to reduce the effect of sequestration and compounding.[61]

Localism of this negative, conservative sort, prevailed in administrative practice as well as in views on appointments and the control of officials. The sub-commissioners found difficulty in persuading the parliamentary committee that local practices in land leasing and manorial court administration could differ from those common in counties nearer London. The minutiae of procedure naturally loomed large in the priorities of the sub-commissioners; the parliamentary committee seemed indifferent to their requests for guidance just as Cromwell and John Thurloe seemed to ignore the beseechings of the major-generals. In both cases, 'indifference' is likely to be a symptom of early modern administrative inadequacy, of failure, even in a centralised government, to maintain adequate communication between the centre and the localities. Compounders and major-generals both floundered in a system, which proceeded not from any established rules but which consisted in a series of accretions, of *ad hoc* decisions accumulating to form its own frame of reference. Searle and Clapp became concerned that the courts of manors under sequestration were likely to be suspended if not supervised, and appointed their clerk, Henry Fitzwilliam, as steward. Their initiative was not commended by the compounders, who wrote back to suggest that clerk and steward be different individuals, and implied that local resistance to peculation was not absolute.[62] The sub-commissioners discovered that the land market was contracting in Devon. Their superiors suggested that the low prices fetched by delinquents' estates sprang from official connivance, and they compared the low level of Devon rents unfavourably with those in counties nearer London. The suspicious yeomanry declined to make good offers and insisted that charges for tax assessments be deducted from the price of land and that prices be set by survey. The commissioners had to allow seven-year leases; they had begun by confining them to a year only.[63] The 1650s saw the development of a recognizable 'county' interest which during the previous decade had been blurred and shot through with ambiguities, and a principal agent of this process of clarification was the sequestration commission.

For every problem without there seemed to be two within. One of the consequences of a close relationship between a central body and a local sub-committee was that the latter was liable to appeal to the higher authority to arbitrate in its minor internal squabbles. These arose from appointments made without reference to those already in office, especially when the newcomers were not Devon men. Captain Wotton was ignored by Searle and Clapp even though he had been an army captain at Plymouth; Richard Carter was 'a stranger', objectionable because he enjoyed something of a special relationship with the compounders and proved himself less susceptible to parochial pressure. Nicholas Tripp's qualification for a post was, in John Searle's view, his 'godliness' but he was made treasurer, a post of extraordinary difficulty and unpopularity. In 1652 Searle and Clapp admitted sourly that 'Mr Tripp being uselessly added lessens the salary'.[64] The last resort against an unsympathetic compounding committee was to offer one's resignation, which both Peirce and Hunkin did in the summer of 1650. Like Ralph Weldon, garrison commander of Plymouth, however, they had to remain in office to complain incessantly.[65]

The compounding committee reforms in 1650 probably stood for revolution to the gentry more than any other activity of government. The sub-commissioners admitted that rumours abounded of an aggressive drive against the once ill-affected and the struggle between the old committeemen and their successors enhanced their revolutionary associations. In fact, the gentry stood to gain by the change because the structure was certainly made less formidable, less effective. Unlike quarter sessions and even assessment commissions (commissioners setting rates on their own hundreds and parishes were at least a minor palliative to local sensibilities) the compounding committee in Devon was a peripatetic small group at home nowhere and seen as hostile by most. Searle and Clapp confessed that pressure of work prevented them from holding enough meetings; the typical quarter sessions response to such pressure would have been to hold more.

Another difference between county-based government and the compounding commissions was that informing, which had faded away with the pressure to enforce the so-called 'penal statutes' (fairly intense during the 1630s) enjoyed something of a revival during the period 1651 to 1652 when acts of sale of delinquents' estates were accompanied by a drive against those avoiding composition in an attempt to provide the government with desperately-needed cash.[66] Prominent in the informing trade was James Clark who personally exposed nearly thirty delinquents who had undervalued their estates. Clarke owed his position to John Searle, whose commitment to godliness both as a qualification for public office and as a principle of local administration, concealed a ruthless and somewhat treacherous nature. Searle's fellow-parishioner and sometime well-wisher, John Willoughby, was one of those who suffered at his hands in the drive against under-valuers.[67] The information laid before the compounding committee resulted in some forty-eight new cases in 1651 and sixty-seven in 1652, but thereafter penal taxation dwindled to a trickle, except during the imposition of the decimation tax in 1655 to 1656.[68]

NOTES

1. Attendance figures at quarter sessions from DQSOB marginalia; militia ordinance F & R I, pp. 1233–1251 (repeal 1251–52).
2. DRO commission of 30/6/49; PRO C 193/13/3.
3. The survivors: Sir Nicholas Martin, John Elford, Edmund Fowell; those dismissed: Sir Edmund Fowell, John Harris of Hayne, Ellis Crimes, Robert Shapcote, John Doddridge, John Waddon, John Maynard, Charles Vaughan, Samuel Browne, Sir Walter Earle. For the basic biographical details of JPs, assessment commissioners and militia officers: J. L. Vivian: *The Visitations of the County of Devon* (1895), idem: *The Visitations of Cornwall* (1887); F. T. Colby (ed.): *The Visitation of the County of Devon* (1872); M. F. Keeler: *The Long Parliament*; A. H. A. Hamilton: *The Note-Book of Sir John Northcote* (1877); PRO PROB 11 (wills). For their education: J. Foster (ed.): *Alumnii Oxonienses* (1891–92, 4 vols.); J. and J. A. Venn: *Alumnii Cantabrigienses* Pt. I (1922–27, 4 vols.); *Students Admitted to the Inner Temple 1547–1660* (1877); H. A. C. Sturgess (ed.): *Register of Admissions to the Honourable Society of the Middle Temple*, I (1949); *The Records of the Honourable Society of Lincoln's Inn, Vol. I Admissions 1420–1799* (1896); J. Foster (ed.): *Register of Admissions to Gray's Inn 1521–1889*, I (1889). Also Howard (ed.): *Devon Protestation Returns;* DNB; GEC: *Complete Baronetage* (1900–09, 6 vols.); M. M. Rowe, A. M. Jackson: *Exeter Freeman 1266–1967* (Devon and Cornwall Record Society Extra Series: I, 1973); John Prince: *The Worthies of Devon;* William Pole: *Collections;* articles in *TDA, DCNQ.* For their wealth: PRO E 179; DRO Q/RTR 1/1–36 (Hearth Tax Returns). In terms of public outrage the purge provoked more hostility from some than did the execution: Lucy Hutchinson: *Memoirs of Colonel Hutchinson* (Dent ed., 1908), pp. 263–67; B. Worden: *The Rump Parliament* (1974), pp. 49–50. Underdown: *Pride's Purge*, pp. 186–87 is a more orthodox evaluation.
4. L. K. J. Glassey: 'The Commission of the Peace 1670–1720' (Cambridge PhD, 1973), p. 397.
5. *CSPD 1649–50*, pp. 262, 408; R. N. Worth (ed.): *The Buller Papers* (1895), pp. 111–12. For the terms of the Engagement: PRO SP 18/3/9; Underdown: *Pride's Purge*, p. 310; idem.: 'The Settlement in the Counties' in Aylmer (ed.): *The Interregnum*, p. 169; Worden: *Rump Parliament*, p. 227.
6. DRO Commission of the peace.
7. A. G. Matthews: *Calamy Revised*, p. 123; I. W. Gowers: 'Puritanism in the County of Devon between 1570 and 1641' (Exeter University MA, 1970), p. 217.
8. BL Loan 29 (Thomas Larkham's Diary) *passim; DCNQ* XXV, pp. 106–07, XXI, p. 284; PROB 11/289/185 (Glanville), 379/13 (Walters); DNB (Disbrowe and Skippon); *TDA*, LXXII, p. 260; *CSPD 1649 50*, p. 439; *TDA*, XLVIII, p. 334; *Exeter Freemen; Calamy Revised* (Lawrence and Richard Saunders); E. S. Chalk: *Kentisbeare*, pp. 86–87; *CSPD 1651*, p. 353, *1651–52*, p. 74.
9. E.g., John Carew of Antony; Francis Rous; Henry Henley of Winsham and Sir Henry Rosewell of Limington. For the last two: Colby: *Visitation of the County of Somerset* (1876), p. 48; Chalk: *Kentisbeare*, p. 18; Pole: *Collections*, p. 185; Underdown: *Somerset*, pp. 47, 125, 130–33, 140, 158; *TDA*, XX, pp. 113–22.
10. The State Papers suggest that the presence of a local 'boss' was decisive in securing an early revision of the commission of the peace; for example, Somerset in March 1650.
11. DQSOB Epiphany 1649; *TDA*, LXVI, pp. 260–61; Stephens: *Clerks of the Counties*, pp. 77–79.
12. Bulstrode Whitelocke: *Memorials of English Affairs* (1732), pp. 439, 447–48, 465; *CSPD 1649–50*, pp. 422, 439; DQSOB for Disbrowe's attendances.
13. Bodl. Tanner MS 56 f 72; SP 25/94/198; *CSPD 1649–50*, pp. 76, 79, 162, 314, 354–55, 450; Whitelocke: *Memorials*, pp. 403, 451, 459.
14. R. N. Worth (ed.): *The Buller Paper* (1895), pp. 109–11; *The Declaration of ... Lord Hopton* (1650); *Prince Charles His Message to the Levellers in the West* (1649).
15. Whitelocke: *Memorials*, pp. 390, 395, 444; *CSPD 1649–50*, pp. 307, 408; SP

25/95/71–72; Worden: *Rump Parliament*, pp. 231–32; I. M. Green: 'The Persecution of "Scandalous" and "Malignant" Clergy during the English Civil War', *English Historical Review*, XCIV, (1979), pp. 522–23; *The West Answering to the North* (1657), pp. 67–68; Underdown: *Pride's Purge*, p. 303.

16. SP 25/63/338, 618–19; *CSPD 1649–50*, pp. 418–19, 510.
17. *CSPD 1650*, pp. 19, 74–75, 106, 130, 137, 159; C. H. Firth, G. Davies: *The Regimental History of Cromwell's Army* (1940), p. 202; W. C. Abbott: *Writings and Speeches*, I, pp. 606–07.
18. SP 25/119/16, 17 or *CSPD 1650*, pp. 504, 507–08.
19. William Sumpter of Cullompton, Henry Marwood of Axminster, Gabriel Barnes and Samuel Searle. For the last two, *TDA*, LXIX, p. 406, LXVI, p. 261; PROB 11/363/71, 373/62.
20. Six men who first appeared as militia officers in 1650 later became JPs.
21. *CSPD 1650*, p. 332. The names of the civilian commissioners for Devon are not known but they must have comprised the active MPs, JPs and assessment commissioners. PRO SP 28 gives these names for some counties but not for Devon.
22. *CSPD 1650*, pp. 289, 374. (The calendar entry on p. 374 has 'commission of the peace' instead of militia commission: SP 25/11/10–13.)
23. F & R II, pp. 397–402.
24. *Ibid.*, II, pp. 295–96, 463–64, 660–61.
25. For William Squire and Robert Dillon, for example, see: *Three Petitions Presented by the Grand Inquest at the Assizes of Exeter* (1642).
26. *DCNQ*, XVI, p. 207.
27. Yeoman/parish gentry: Stephen Sowton of Mary Tavy (constable there 1642, grand juror at sessions 1658–59), William Drewe of Okehampton (successively constable, bailiff, principal burgess and mayor there), Robert Cruse and Richard Foxworthy. *Protestation Returns*, QS bundles; PROB 11/359/37 (Sowton); West Country Studies Library Exeter: Burnet Morris MS index. Soldiers: Saunders and Henry Hatsell. For James Erisey of Erisey: Vivian: *Visitations of Cornwall*, p. 155; *TDA*, XLVIII, p. 334; B.L. Add. 18, 448 (Pedigrees of Devon and Cornwall), f 35 v.
28. DQSOB marginalia; J. H. Gleason: *The Justices of the Peace in England 1558 to 1640* (1969), pp. 104–05; Morrill: *Cheshire 1630–60*, p. 9; G. C. F. Forster: *The East Riding Justices of the Peace in the Seventeenth Century* (1973), pp. 20, 21, 32.
29. Morrill: *Cheshire*, p. 257.
30. Local practice, as evidenced in recognizances and private papers runs contrary to the view of J. H. Langbein that magistrates came to sessions to support evidence offered in writing, to see cases through. Langbein: 'The Origins of Public Prosecution at Common Law', *American Journal of Legal History*, XVII (1973), pp. 313–35. The evidence from the 452 recognizances, 1649 and 1650, was analysed by computer. I am grateful to Mrs G. M. Skinner of the Department of Economics, University of Exeter, for her help with and interest in this topic.
31. Michael Dalton: *The Countrey Justice* (1619), pp. 18–20 *et seq.*
32. Underdown: 'Settlement in the Counties' in Aylmer (ed.): *The Interregnum*, p. 181.
33. DQSOB Epiphany 1652.
34. *Ibid.* Michaelmas 1650.
35. *Ibid.* Epiphany 1653. Hore had only been in office for a few months but was re-appointed in 1666 and served for two years.
36. *Ibid.* Midsummer 1649, Midsummer 1651, Easter 1652, Midsummer 1652; QS Box 59: recognizances on suspicion of felony, Midsummer 1653.
37. DQSOB: Gaol Calendar Epiphany 1650; QS Box 59: examinations and bills of indictment Easter 1652, bills of indictment Midsummer 1652; DQSOB: Gaol Calendars Easter 1652, Midsummer 1654; Underdown: 'Settlement', pp. 170–74.
38. DQSOB: Midsummer 1649; QS Box 57: Petitions Epiphany 1650; Box 59: Bills of indictment Easter 1652.
39. Morrill: *Cheshire 1630–60*, p. 227; for crime as the result of conflict between sectional interests: T. C. Curtis: 'Some Aspects of Crime in Seventeenth Century England with special reference to Cheshire and Middlesex' (Manchester PhD, 1972), *passim*.
40. All in DQSOB Epiphany 1649.

41. Morrill *op. cit.*, pp. 227, 234–35.
42. DQSOB Midsummer 1649; *Three Petitions* ... (1642); J. Cock: *Records of the Antient Borough of South Molton* (1893), p. 173.
43. DQSOB Midsummer 1649; Chalk: *Kentisbeare*, pp. 86–87; PROB 11/269/432.
44. DQSOB Epiphany 1650; *TDA*, LXVII, p. 324; G. E. Aylmer: 'Checklist of Central Officeholders' (deposited at University of London, Institute of Historical Research) for Shapcote.
45. DQSOB Epiphany 1649, Midsummer 1649, Easter 1651.
46. *Ibid.* Easter 1650.
47. PRO SP 24/1/75, 77, 84, 114, 143; 24/2/2, 57, 85; Morrill: 'The Army Revolt of 1647' in *Britain and the Netherlands*, VI, pp. 61–63. M. J. Hawkins briefly discusses indemnity legislation in his introduction to *Unpublished State Papers of the English Civil War* (microfilm), Part I (1975), p. 12.
48. SP 24/1/77, 135, 172; 24/2/13, 30, 81, 91, 93, 139, 160, 162; *Some of Mr Philip Francis's Misdemeanours Discovered; The Misdemeanours of a traitor; A Most True and Unanswerable Answer of Charles Vaughan.*
49. SP 24/1/68, 164; 24/2/110; F & R I, pp. 981–82; SP 24/1/137; 24/2/36.
50. DQSOB Easter 1647.
51. *Ibid.* Midsummer 1653.
52. QS Box 57: examinations Epiphany 1648–49, petitions Michaelmas 1649; DQSOB Easter 1649. Cf. similar cases in DQSOB Michaelmas 1651, Easter 1653; QS Box 58: Petitions Michaelmas 1651.
53. QS Box 58: Petitions Michaelmas 1651. S. and B. Webb: *English Local Government, II, The Manor and the Borough* (1908), pp. 12, 28, 29, 116–17 for a pessimistic view of local variations in appointments and the decline of democracy.
54. QS Box 56: Petitions Epiphany 1649; Box 57: Petitions Michaelmas 1649, Epiphany 1650; Box 58: Petitions Michaelmas 1651; Box 59: Bills of indictment Easter 1652.
55. B.L. Add. 5494 ff 99, 100; *CCC*, pp. 97–98, 152.
56. *CCC*, pp. 152, 219; SP 28/128 Part I (Devon): Charles Vaughan's accounts 1643; Richard Clapp's accounts 1649 (f 26 v for Revell); SP 28/208 contains 1661 list of sequestration officials; Coate: *Cornwall in the Great Civil War*, p. 221.
57. F & R II, pp. 329–35; Aylmer: *State's Servants*, pp. 12–13; Underdown: 'Settlement', pp. 169–70. The committee withered away in Kent and Somerset: Everitt: *Community of Kent*, pp. 276–77; Underdown: *Pride's Purge*, pp. 301–02; in Wales the changes affected structure but not personnel: Dodd: *Studies in Stuart Wales*, Chapter 4, *passim*.
58. G.E.C. *Complete Baronetage*, I, p. 257; O. Ogle, W. H. Bliss, W. D. Macray, F. T. Routledge (eds.): *Calendar of the Clarendon State Papers* (1869–1970, 5 vols.), V, p. 41.
59. *CCC*, pp. 198–99, 321–22; SP 28/128 (Devon) Part I: Clapp's accounts.
60. *CCC*, pp. 293, 321–22, 470–71.
61. *Ibid.* pp. 152, 180, 463. The most recent evaluation of the compounding papers suggests that local collusion to reduce assessment was rife. C. B. Phillips: 'The Royalist Composition Papers and the Landed Income of the Gentry', *Northern History*, XIII (1977), pp. 161–74.
62. *CCC*, pp. 321–22, 352, 359, 384–85, 397. Fitzwilliam, a lawyer, continued as steward and clerk: *CCC*, pp. 422, 474, 734. The government was not attempting to 'separate powers', merely to reduce local corruption.
63. *Ibid.* pp. 219, 397, 401, 407, 418, 445.
64. *CCC*, pp. 321–22, 352, 373, 381, 422, 441, 476, 527, 536–37. By 1652 the reduction in business led to Carter's dismissal and a campaign by Clapp and Searle against Tripp: *Ibid.* pp. 590, 593, 605, 608–09, 612. Carter served in Cornwall in 1648: *Buller Papers*, p. 107.
65. *CCC*, p. 210, 219, 228, 272.
66. *Ibid.* pp. 321–22, 367, 470–71; Devon, pp. 487, 501, 518, 543; for the 1630s and earlier: M. W. Beresford: 'The Common Informer, the Penal Statutes and Economic Regulation', *Economic History Review*, 2nd series, X (1957–58), pp. 221–37; M. J. Hawkins: 'The Government, its Role and its Aims' in C. Russell (ed.): *The Origins of the English Civil War* (1973), pp. 45, 49–50. The texts of the Acts of Sale are in F & R II, pp. 520–45, 591–98, 623–52. Twenty-one Devon delinquents were named in these.

67. For Searle's ambivalent attitude to Willoughby S.R.O. DD/WO Box 53: letters, Searle to Westcomb 17/9/53, 3/4/52; another bundle Searle to Willoughby 7/2/42; Box 57: bundle 'Westcomb Willoughby Composition 1642', letter Westcomb to Willoughby 29/11/51 (Clark as Searle's 'great companion ... in London'), same to same 16/12/52: ('Mr Searle of Buckerell who I believe is your greatest adversary.') Searle was himself pursued by a royalist place-seeker in 1660: PRO SP 29/22/19.

68. During February and March 1652 the 'great compounders' had to listen to the grievances of thirty-five Devonians claiming unjust persecution by informers: *CCC*, pp. 2955, 2959, 2966–67, 2971, 2986. The episode of the major-generals in Devon has been considered by S. K. Roberts: 'Alehouses, Brewing and Government: Legislation, Policy and Enforcement', (Exeter MA, 1976), pp. 69–73.

Chapter Three

County Politics and Government 1653-1659

The membership of the commission of the peace changed very little in Devon between 1650 and the fall of the Rump, but there is evidence that in the last few months of its life the Long Parliament was attempting, in a small way, a programme of reconciliation in the country as a whole which Cromwell was later to declare one of his principal aims. The last *liber pacis* to survive for the Rump is to be found in the Cambridge University Library and was compiled between 25 March and the expulsion on 20 April 1653.[1] It contains the names of six more justices. Two, Robert Bennet and Anthony Rous, were Cornishmen active in their own county from before 1649.[2] John Coplestone and John Fowell would probably have appeared as JPs in the 1630s, although Fowell's entry into politics had been delayed by the seclusion of his father, Sir Edmund Fowell, at Pride's Purge, and the imputing of the sin to the second generation.[3] John Davy was the son of a presbyterian baronet who, like Fowell, had kept aloof from county government since 1649, although unlike him, had been named on commissions of the peace almost continuously since then. The last appointment was the most surprising. John Tuckfield of Crediton was not a former royalist, but had done nothing positive to ingratiate himself with the Rump, apart from a brief period as an assessment commissioner in the late 1640s. He had played no part in government from 1649 until his nomination and his later career followed the pattern of that of a moderate Anglican county gentleman.[4]

The new list widened the power base of the government in the county, and may support the notion that the Rump was not, after all, bent on perpetuating its own oligarchic power. Under the Nominated Assembly this development was reversed. The number of Devon JPs dropped to the level it had been during the uncertain years of 1649 and early 1650. Thirty-three justices were dismissed and twenty-two new ones were sworn in.[5] As one might have expected, a record of loyalty to the Rump was now no recommendation, particularly if one had been an MP or a prominent presbyterian. Men like Sir John Pole, who had not acted as a magistrate since 1649 but whose support had been eagerly sought by the Rump, now forfeited their chances of reconciliation. The changes of 1653 cut through anomalies in the Rump's listing. The dismissal of Sir Henry Rosewell, also, was pragmatic; Rosewell was from Somerset and had contributed absolutely nothing in his six-year nomination to the Devon Bench. Thomas Boone was not allowed to remain because he had been a prominent Rump MP. A sizeable proportion of the casualties were men of comparatively humble 'peasant gentry' origins whose colours had been

47

firmly nailed to the Commonwealth's mast;[6] Clarendon's view of the Barebones representatives as 'inferior persons of no quality or name' should not obscure the fact that an unexalted social background was at no time in the 1650s a prerequisite for political survival.[7]

For the first time since the execution of the King, the Devon commission of the peace was drastically 'purged' in an upheaval typical of the country as a whole.[8] The result may have been a lurch to the left but the changes were cautious; more cautious than those of the later Rump. No fewer than three-quarters of the newcomers had had previous experience in county government. Nine had been militia officers under the Rump,[9] and a baker's dozen had been committeemen at one time or another.[10] Viewed in this light, the commissions of the Nominated Assembly were a consolidation of the support won after 1649, a development of tendencies under the Rump. Three new men had prominent family connections. Edmund, son of Edmund Prideaux the Attorney-General, and Thomas Bampfield, brother of the late Sir John, were obvious candidates if they would consent to serve, and John Bury was the son of an experienced committeeman of the same name.[11] John Blundell was a friend of Thomas Bampfield's.[12] Three others did not immediately satisfy the criteria of former service, family recommendation or personal connection. Lionel Beecher was a Barnstaple merchant who was to nag the Protectorate government to reimburse him for sums he laid out in the service of Parliament as long ago as 1642;[13] Christopher Clobury was a poetaster and a relation of George Monck, and Gideon Sherman was a minor, undistinguished but armigerous Ottery St Mary gentleman.[14] None could really be described as 'impenetrably obscure'.[15]

The Devon purge was an ejection of Rumpers wedded or glued to the disgraced regime, and a shuffling up the government ladder of the more flexible. Religious enthusiasm or partisanship played little part in this, and 'godliness' in Devon remained the moderate presbyterian/Independent middle ground held by Richard Baxter. The military tightened its hold in the elevation of militia commissioners and officers, and in the assumption by John Disbrowe of the clerkship of the peace, instead of Edmund Prideaux. Out went Nicholas Rowe, clerk since 1649, as part of this change, to be replaced by Edward Raddon, religious Independent, secretary to Disbrowe, friend of the misanthropic Rev. Thomas Larkham of Tavistock, and post office official.[16] Raddon soon demonstrated a dour sabbatarianism by creating a fuss about a letter delivered on a Sunday.[17]

Against the sneers of critics who from Clarendon onwards have sought to ridicule the proceedings and participants in the Nominated Assembly, it must be argued that at least its members tackled genuine legislative issues including law reform and the role of tithes instead of becoming bogged down, as the Rump had, in the minutiae of executive details. It is in accordance with the tone of Barebones policy as a whole that there were no more local committees appointed, and adherence to the government has to be measured solely on the evidence of the commissions of the peace.

When the Barebones moderates resigned their authority to Cromwell it might have seemed that yet another purge of local governors was imminent. But Oliver's talk of 'healing and settling' was proved sincere by the moderation of local changes. The Protector was installed on 16 December 1653, and the first commission of the peace for Devon after this to survive is dated 4 March 1654.[18] Former Rumpers were invited to serve; among those spurned by the previous Council of State but now reappointed were Sir Francis Drake, Sir Henry Rosewell, Sir John Young, Hugh Fortescue, Robert Duke, Thomas Boone, Henry Pollexfen, Arthur Perryman and Christopher Wood. Some rejected the call, and attitudes both in government and in the localities hardened after the abortive first Protectorate Parliament, in which the shadow of the dismissed Rump proved hardier than the spirit of healing. Only seven out of fifteen former Commonwealthsmen restored to local power in the first few months of the Protectorate remained in office for the rest of Oliver's reign.[19] Among them was Thomas Boone, who became the Protector's ambassador to the Baltic, and who had been among those *rarae aves*, the Devon MPs who had survived Pride's Purge.[20] The others were county gentlemen whose social status, presbyterian godliness and easy-going politics made them useful to a regime whose leader took a personal interest in moral 'reformation'. Over half—fourteen out of twenty-two—of those brought in to serve the Nominated Assembly were no longer considered fit for the magisterial Bench, but most departed quietly. Their rejection was cushioned by continued membership of assessment commissions and their own past reluctance, in many cases, to come to sessions during the apogee of their public careers. But the quietism was of an ominous sort and was personified by Thomas Reynell, the most regular attender at quarter sessions, 'ready to act in the country as a justice of the peace, though he could not as a parliament-man'.[21]

The episode of the major-generals has been well-worked by historians[22] and although the scheme originated in the South West, as a response to Penruddock's rising, its course was not spectacular, Major-general John Disbrowe, while conscientious, was not of the same feral zeal as his colleague in Cheshire, Charles Worsley, who worked himself into an early grave on behalf of the godly and the government.[23] The most interesting feature of the one-and-a-half years' regime, the way in which the attempt to control representative institutions grew out of a concern for public order, will be treated separately. Here the course of events will be outlined with the aim of showing how far-reaching were the interests of one major-general but at the same time how little was his behaviour that of an *apparatchik*.

Although the major-generals' commissions were in themselves innovatory the ethos of the experiment cannot be said to have been sprung upon an unsuspecting public. The point has been made elsewhere that the moral dimension to the major-generals' brief already had a respectable pedigree;[24] what is equally clear is that the practical aspects of their work had emerged before August 1655. In March of that year JPs were urged to be vigilant against 'loose persons' and 'malignants' and were encouraged to beak up dangerous assemblies.[25] Richard Creed, secretary to the generals of the fleet, was surprised at the welcome Disbrowe received at Exeter that

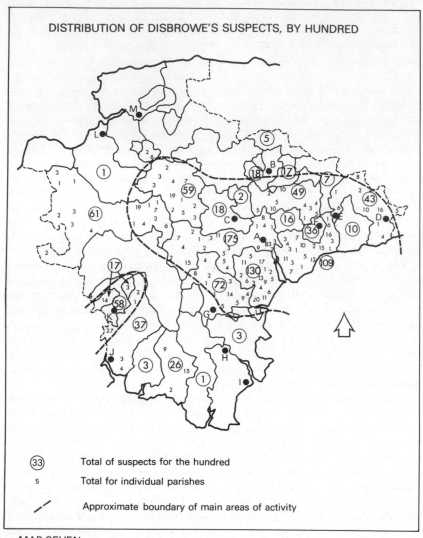

DISTRIBUTION OF DISBROWE'S SUSPECTS, BY HUNDRED

㉝   Total of suspects for the hundred

5   Total for individual parishes

⟋   Approximate boundary of main areas of activity

MAP SEVEN

Key: A. Exeter; B. Tiverton; C. Crediton; D. Axminster; E. Honiton; F. Ottery St. Mary; G. Ashburton; H. Totnes; I. Dartmouth; J. Plymouth; K. Tavistock; L. Bideford; M. Barnstaple.

month; his colleague, Henry Hatsell, settled in at Plymouth to use his local knowledge in an attempt to break the collusion between the magistrates and the drink interest in the town, thereby exacerbating a conflict between the Plymouth council and the excise office.

Three phases may be discerned in the first four months of the major-generals' tour of duty, from October 1655 to January 1656: first, a preoccupation with settling the militia, secondly a concern to deal appropriately with the enemies of the State and its friends ('decimated' royalists and candidates for the shrievalty) and lastly, from late November 1655, the beginnings of protracted grumbling about pay for the county troops.

From May 1655 the militia came under scrutiny, with a directive from the President of the Council of State, Henry Lawrence, to Major James Pierce to take the accounts of former militia officers. By June the sum required to maintain the county militia establishment had been settled upon. The new militia comprised three troops each of a hundred soldiers under the command of Sir John Coplestone, Captain Thomas Saunders and Captain Henry Hatsell. Some five per cent of the total of over £3,000 considered to be the annual cost of this establishment was earmarked for administrative expenses, including salaries for a doorkeeper and two messengers. After the difficulties encountered by the militia in every county in raising adequate local financial provision the establishment was reduced to three troops each of eighty soldiers, and the clerk's salary was halved and one messenger dismissed. Five hundred pounds was saved, with administrative costs not surprisingly bearing most of the burden.[26]

The salient features of administration by Disbrowe in Devon were a cautious cooperation with quarter sessions government, a lack of confidence in his own authority and a zealous, imposing drive by his commissioners in military affairs. Relations between the Bench and the major-general were respectful and fruitful, a direct result of Disbrowe's caution. Beyond nominating a few new justices, and those, Philip Francis and Anthony Rous, valuable for their experience not their zeal, he preferred quiet progress to the grand gesture.[27] The modest achievement (and the even more low-key progress) of jury reform was typical.

Much could be made of the persistent clamours by 'the men on horseback' for whole-hearted support from Whitehall.[28] Calls for copies of 'the instructions' were frequent and arose from the need to prove indemnity for their actions. It may have been a further indication of Disbrowe's insecurity that indemnity was so highly prized; in the 1646–49 period, as the papers of the Indemnity Committee show only too clearly, soldiers were not generally loth to chance their arms in conflict with individual civilians or even with corporate bodies. Possibly it was simply that the lesson of these years had been well-learnt, but in either case Disbrowe was among the loudest in his calls for instructions, issued separately by Thurloe for each town or district.[29]

Apart from the reorganisation of the militia, other aspects of the drive towards State security prevailed in Disbrowe's 'canton'. Henry Hatsell left off badgering the Plymouth town fathers to embark on a pressing campaign for the navy early in 1656. Despite the use made by Hatsell of both hundredal and petty constables—and in this the military could easily have been seen as grossly intrusive—the results were disappointing, largely because of the limitless opportunities for escape available to intended victims.[30] Even Hatsell, not normally given to diffidence, wrote to the Admiralty commissioners enclosing warrants so 'that you may see I have not stretched the power given me'.[31]

It was the commissioners here, as elsewhere, who had 'borne the heat of the day'[32] in the past, who had been rewarded with 'cantonisation' and who now found themselves again engaged in warm work. After several years of semi-guerilla warfare they now emerged with real power and exercised it not only against political elites—there was nothing new in that—but against the broad mass of the population. Hatsell followed the pressing trail, Thomas Saunders was in the van of the local response to the demands of the major-generals' registry.

The brief history of the registry may be followed in the calendars of domestic state papers and in a recent short account.[33] The experiment attempted to endow an ancient practice with bureaucratic and statistical respectability. Tudor statutes had encouraged the observation of 'strangers' in parishes,[34] an observation which doubtless came naturally in rural areas. On this occasion county-wide coverage was sought and achieved by the sub-commissioners, as the map on page 50 shows, and an efficient social analysis was sought by the registrar in London, Thomas Dunn.[35] Dunn congratulated Hatsell on his zeal in June 1656 but asked for more:

> You have observed a very good method, but in regard the addicions of distinction of most of the persons therein contayned are not inserted (if you review but the Generalls instructions) you will find requisite.[36]

By July Hatsell's deficiency had been remedied and the appropriate social designation—yeoman, husbandman and so on—appeared against each name forwarded to the registry. In Devonshire thoroughness was the ultimate bureaucratic virtue; in London a more sophisticated criterion was emerging: that of consistent social cataloguing, a comprehensive and statistical twist to the methods of the heralds' visitations.[37]

It is, however, the thoroughness of the registration which ultimately impresses. A list of over five thousand names was compiled from the western counties, of all social ranks.[38] Licences were issued to those on the move—in itself only a tightening-up of periodic demands that all gentlemen should leave London, not uncommon under the early Stuarts, but on a scale hitherto unknown. How typical it was of mid-seventeenth century administration that men from remote Devon parishes could successfully be issued with 28-day passes to visit London, that certificates could be recorded to this effect in London letter-books and that there could be howls of frustration from the major-generals because registrar Dunn, unassisted by his employers in his search for office accommodation, was slow to swing the registration scheme into life.[39]

From June 1655 the movements of royalists were to be observed more closely and parish ministers were to play a leading role, as community leaders, in this monitoring.[40] The major-generals brought with them a brief to play a more positive role in the parishes, however. They were petitioned by those who sought augmentations to parish livings and frequently became the arbiters in disputes over parochial finance. In March 1656 Disbrowe was ordered, perhaps on Cromwell's own authority, to provide 'such one of the best publique meeting places as is best in repair' for the Baptist congregations in Exeter.[41] The commissioners began to scrutinize the public accounts of various parishes near their homes. Their signatures on highway surveyors' and churchwardens' accounts represent not so much a centralist intrusion as their integration into the pattern of increasing involvement by magistrates in parish affairs.[42]

In addition, of course, there was the necessarily divisive process of 'decimation'—making the royalists pay for internal state weaknesses. But even here there was room for compromise; when John Coplestone wrote to Sir Edward Seymour he stressed that he would 'be as civil ... as possibly I may ... I know you to be a person of worth and honour ...'.[43] Despite decimation, registration and the terrors of pressing, the abiding impression left by Disbrowe in Devon is of his behaviour before the 1656 election, when he consulted with as many 'honest people in every county' as possible, and his method of rooting out the disaffected—'with as little noyse as I could'.[44]

Cromwell's preference for 'conservative settlement' had by 1657 prevailed over the divisiveness of the major-generals and of decimation. A. H. Dodd judged the 1657 Welsh committees to be 'the most representative ... since the war'. There is, however, another side to the development of government support under the Protectorate, and it may be discerned in the composition of those same committees.

Dodd and Underdown regard the 1657 assessment commissions as a fair indication of the intentions of the Protector; they 'tell the same story' as the commissions of the peace.[45] This is to gloss over their origins. The commissions of the peace were compiled in the privacy of the Council Chamber where the ideals of Protectoral government were most likely to be enshrined in orders and directives. The assessment commissions of 1657 were, by contrast, put together over a period of three months in 1657 in a Parliament which had not been notably successful, even though by the standards of the 1650s it had accomplished a good deal by way of statute. James Nayler's case and the fall of the major-generals were divisive, but less so than the offer to Cromwell of the crown. Oliver's agonizing (or temporising) continued as the House agreed on the sum to be raised by assessment for the war with Spain, decided that the money should be paid to the Exchequer as in settled times before 1642, and ordered that the names of county commissioners should be decided by their MPs.[46] On the day that Cromwell refused the crown, the whole House met in committee, doubtless in an atmosphere fraught with emotion, to consider the assessment ordinance.[47] A list of commissioners, authorised on the Protector's second installation on 26 June, was substantially the same as that agreed on the ninth of that month. The assessment commissions reflect, then, not the views of the Protector and his Council, but rather those of a suspicious Parliament.[48]

The origins of the commissions are evident in their size and in their composition. With each group of MPs bringing in a list of nominees, and within the county groups factions attempting to scramble over their rivals, it was natural that the lists should be larger rather than smaller than those of the Rump. As the 1650s progressed, so faction grew with each successive constitutional failure, and faction swells committees prodigiously. The last Commonwealth committee had numbered ninety-five; that of 1657 included one hundred and forty[49] and was the largest county committee until 1672. Its members were an ill-assorted collection of relics from the past, pointers to Cromwell's ideal future, and a leavening of complete unknowns. No fewer than thirty-eight had never been in county office before. There were ten county gentlemen,[50] many of them youths untainted by royalism, although John Willoughby and Mathew Halse had been scrutinized by the compounding commission. A group of trusted Rump military men appeared, to mirror the influence of Henry Hatsell, Navy Commissioner at Plymouth, and John Coplestone, a hero of Penruddock's rising. These included Samuel Searle, the Honiton foot captain and postmaster, Gabriel Barnes and Francis Rolle.

John Maynard and Thomas Bampfield seem to have exerted a particularly decisive influence on this commission. Maynard was MP for Plymouth and had overcome a temporary disgrace when his support for the merchant, George Coney, in a tax case had landed him in the Tower in 1655.[51] He was temporarily excluded from Parliament in 1656. By 1657, however, he had become a popular member of the House and a leading spokesman of a group drawing closer to the Protector's confidence, the lawyers. Speaker Widdrington noted the symbolism of Oliver's donning a black gown in his second installation ceremony.[52] No fewer than nine assessment commissioners for Devon were lawyers, three of them outsiders from Somerset. Most had been to an inn of court, but Thomas Westlake, William Williams and Gilbert Eveleigh were only local attorneys. In Richard Cromwell's Parliament it was noted that 'the lawyers … have shewed themselves fierce cavaliers of the new stampe and Sir (sic) John Maynard sways all and is the only oracle'; during the second Protectorate Parliament (particularly in its second session) he was beginning to build a party based on local loyalties and professional interests.[53] Several others were appointed probably by association with Maynard. He had been MP for Totnes through the Long Parliament to Pride's Purge, and his namesake Christopher Maynard was a merchant who had been mayor there in 1648.[54] Thomas Brooking was mayor in 1649 and Richard Brooking (his brother?) was at the Middle Temple in 1641. Ellis Bartlett was at the Middle Temple (Maynard's inn) in 1635.[55] Some of the most obscure appointments in the decade were made to this commission. Thomas Allen may have been an army captain who was to be suspected of disaffection by the government in 1665; Samuel Codnor was probably a physician who was related to a dynasty of Haytor hundred bailiffs, and Richard Lee was a Clyst St Mary minor gentleman who was a friend of the deputy clerk of the peace and Tiverton town clerk, Henry Fitzwilliam.[56] Bampfield brought with him the town clerk of Exeter, Thomas Westlake, and possibly the other local lawyers.

1657 did not simply mark a drift back to the 'natural order' in local government. Efforts were made to attract representative gentry leaders, but the net was cast wider to include men of as humble social status as any appointed in the 1650s. The expansion and composition of the 1657 committees were a direct result of circumstances at Westminster. They were the first summary of local support outside the commissions of the peace since 1652. (The committee for scandalous ministers of August 1654 was a mere cabal.[57]) Since 1652 Devon representation in Parliament had changed from a demoralised clique whose influence in the county was limited, either by lack of personal interest or by inadequate social contact with the gentry, to a numerically healthy group of twenty-odd MPs, all committed to furthering local interests, but otherwise divided between Cromwellian officeholders and their 'Presbyterian' critics, some of whom flirted with 'thorough-paced' republicanism.[58] Under the Rump there had been something of a simple relationship between central government and the localities on the question of committees. Widespread reluctance among the uncommitted gentry to participate, with the forced exclusion of the sequestered royalists and only a tiny body of Devon MPs, produced unanimity at Westminster and a unanimity by default in the county on the names of appointees. The government had to take whoever it could get. In the later 1650s, by an irony not immediately apparent to contemporaries, political conditions had relaxed sufficiently to tempt more participants—not only county gentry—into service, but the legacies of nearly two decades of bitter, often bewilderingly complex political feuds, physical conflict and uneasy alliances had made the construction of local committees a task not easily accomplishable. Not only did the interests of the government—sound administration and local political stability—have to be protected and the aspirations of local men eager to offer their services satisfied, but the shades of Westminster opinion—a third variable in itself and not merely a mirror image of the local community—had to be reconciled as well. It was this last task which took the most time and which resulted, by a narrow margin, in a victory for the pragmatic Maynard group which was to be so influential from 1659 to 1660.

While opinion in the government and in Parliament swung between what was arguably a conservative policy of bringing up reliable soldiers, experienced in the ways of the county since the early 1650s, to the forefront of local government, and the radical departure of tempting back the old gentry families, attendances at quarter sessions remained stable and displayed the ease with which the remnants of the county gentry kept control of the court, and the reluctance of the new men to attend. On average sixteen attended each sessions from the beginning of 1654 to the end of 1658. No more than seventeen attended any sessions under the Commonwealth. The military group of John Coplestone, Henry Hatsell and John Blackmore, who, under Disbrowe, formed the presence of the major-generals in Devon, persisted in attending long after 'cantonization' had received 'a foil' in the second Protectorate Parliament. Coplestone, who commanded the reformed county militia in 1655, retained the office of sheriff for three years from 1654 to 1657 and used his power to further government policy on ejecting scandalous ministers.[59] More eminent men combined the duties of justice of the peace as best they could with service in Parliament. Thomas Bampfield was new in 1656 to Parliament and had only two years' experience as recorder of Exeter and three as a county justice behind him. He had become a barrister in 1649, and returned to Devon to head a family whose most eminent scion, his brother, Sir John Bampfield, had untimely died.[60] In the county his dour religious scruples were offended by the easier-going lives of some of his peers. In April 1654 Bampfield wrote, rather sententiously, to young John Willoughby, the son of a delinquent royalist:

> That justice must be equally administered unto all without respect to the quality of a person or to the relation of a friende I know I need not acquaynt you; the matter is out of question and it is as cleare that the sinn is at least as great in great men as in others.

Willoughby had offended against the 1650 act against swearing, and paid a ten-shilling fine to the churchwardens of Broadclyst.[61] In Parliament Bampfield proved himself the spiritual heir of Exeter's Ignatius Jourdain, another implacable Puritan; he proposed legislation against those living at 'high rates', and led the hawks who sought James Nayler's death for blasphemy: 'If you lay this aside and do nothing in it I shall say it is no more Nayler's sin but set it upon your doors'.[62] Critic of the Instrument of Government, critic of barely competent Speaker Widdrington, critic of the excise—his views were those of the Country member, suspicious of executive power, though hardly positive in his own suggestions.[63] His presbyterianism shone through his proposal that all the Exeter churches be joined under the patronage of the city[64]—which would have dealt a mortal blow to the Independent congregations—and through his support for the 1646 *Directory of Worship* and for legislation against Quakers and like evils of religious toleration.[65]

Not all Bampfield's fellow MPs were as consistent. He remained outside the circle of government office-holders, but some, like Thomas Gorges and Robert Shapcote, were tempted inside. Gorges had returned from the deputy governorship of Maine in 1643, and may have been a friend of Attorney-General Prideaux. His brother commanded Exmouth fort in 1647, but both were dismissed from the Somerset commission of the peace in 1653 for their criticisms of the local manager, Colonel John Pyne. Gorges became recorder of Taunton and MP for that town in the first Protectorate Parliament but his second marriage strengthened his Devon connections; he married into the family of Mallock of Cockington and came to live at Heavitree.[66] During the second Protectorate Parliament he was appointed to commissions dealing with fraudulent debentures and new buildings in London,[67] and as a government placeman he had to endure the attacks of such as Bampfield. On the Nayler question, however, he was as for 'the higher punishment' (death) as any, when many government supporters spoke out against breaching the provisions of the Instrument for toleration.[68] If Bampfield represented the view of the 'Country' presbyterian critics, and if the middle ground of ambivalence was held by men like Gorges and another lawyer, Edmund Fowell,[69] then Robert Shapcote consistently took the government view. He had overcome suspicions among MPs in the Long Parliament and among the Devon electorate in 1654 that his loyalties lay too far in the direction of the royalists. With Thomas Gorges he was among the five Devon commissioners for the security of the Protector, named in November 1656; he was a commissioner for fraudulent debentures and new buildings. He was Solicitor-General in Ireland and Attorney-General there from 1658.[70] In Parliament he was a moderate on Nayler, and in the second session after the acceptance of the Humble Petition and Advice, he argued that Cromwell deserved full honour as Protector when, to men like Bampfield, he should have remained 'Chief Magistrate'.[71]

Apparent stability in quarter sessions contrasted with a diversity of opinion and interests among Devon's representatives in the second Protectorate Parliament. The sources have doubtless compounded this impression; the fluke survival of Burton's Diary has given us an unusually vivid insight into parliamentary debates, and nothing similar has survived to be a measure of opinion in the county. Yet there were quite tangible differences in the pattern of participation in the central legislature and in the local executive. Dissenters from the prevailing view at quarter sessions registered disapproval by staying away. Parliament, as its history in the 1650s shows only too clearly, attracted dissenters in superabundance, and they had to be forcibly excluded by the executive. At Westminster things were said which could not be said at home.[72] Nayler's case is an example. It raised the issues of the future of religious toleration, the narrowness of support for the Instrument, genuine differences of conscience among factions already numerous enough, and threatened the survival of the Parliament and settlement in the country. Yet in Devon attitudes to Nayler and Quakers were uncontending. The persecution of Quakers began in the north of England from the autumn of 1652.[73] By May 1655 they had appeared in Devon and were prosecuted with particular vigour in the towns.[74] The justices suspected that men like Thomas Salthouse of Dringlebeck in Lancashire and Miles Halhead of Kendal, Westmorland, had come to stir up trouble which would not have been fostered without their particular influence. Thus, at the end of the Midsummer 1656 sessions meeting the seventeen JPs present agreed on a declaration against Quakerism and vagrancy. They affirmed a belief that the laws then in force—including Clause 37 of the Instrument, which established religious toleration by law—were sound but that the alarming increase in wandering persons and Quakers were the result of 'the remissness of some inferior officers'. There was a need for watches and wards and the participation of those of 'estate and ability of body'.[75] The seventeen included five who in the space of a few months became MPs in the Parliament which viciously punished Nayler after protracted debate of the most intemperate kind, and most spoke against him.[76] The moderation of public pronouncements and the blaming of inadequate administration for the ills of the county were features of local government which recur with tedious regularity in the sessions order books and they contrast sharply with the actions of magistrates in Parliament and in the county.

In December 1656 Westlake and Bampfield brought petitions 'of many thousands' in Exeter against Quakers to the House of Commons,[77] introducing populist arguments against toleration. Quaker polemical works, contemporary and later, agreed that persecution was as intense in Devon as anywhere. During the Nayler furore the Devon and Exeter Association of churches began to meet, its establishment endorsed by most JPs. Those singled out for attacks by Quaker writers included John Blackmore, John Champneys, Thomas Saunders, Edmund Fowell, William Putt, Thomas Drake, John Arscot, John Beare, William Morrice and Thomas Gewen.[78] Blackmore and Saunders were firm Cromwellians, Morrice and Gewen had resented the seclusion of the presbyterians in 1648, but in local politics they could agree that Quakers should be prosecuted as deviants. Men like Bampfield knew the attitude of the Council of State towards Quakers even before the parliamentary committee on Nayler's case reported to the House, it should be noted; on 2 October, 1656, Disbrowe was ordered to release the Quakers gaoled at Exeter and to ensure they returned whence they had come.[79] In this light, the behaviour of the Devon MPs at Westminster may be viewed as sheer provocation of a government for which they had scant sympathy. If Joseph Besse may be believed, it was during 1657 that Quaker prosecutions reached their height; during that year George Fox held a meeting at the Seven Stars Inn at St Thomas, Exeter.[80] In November the Council received a remonstrance alleging that Quakers had been ill-treated at Exeter gaol. In keeping with Cromwell's own criticisms of Parliament which had reserved to itself judicial power beyond the spirit and the letter of the Instrument, Lord President Lawrence wrote to the Devon JPs in November 1657. He enclosed the Quakers' paper and explained that

> To the intent the Councell may have a right understanding of the truth of the fact in some other of the cases which assigne noe other reason for proceeding against the persons but their goeing to some meeting place for worship on the Lord's Day and the not yeilding that due respect unto persons in authority that becomes them to doe, the Councell have thought fitt to transmitt to you these papers with theire desire that you will enforme yourselves of the severall cases from those who were principallie concerned in the comittments and proceedings there in specified. And to certifie to this Boord the true grounds thereof with your first opportunity.[81]

At the same time a circular letter was despatched to all the counties enjoining them to act against Quakers with moderation; JPs were advised rather 'to exercise too much lenity then too much severity'.[82] There is no evidence that the order had any effect; Besse's *Abstract* continues its woeful chronicle of impositions and outrages against the Friends. In 1658, all Quaker books in Devon seized by the court of quarter sessions were ordered to be burnt.[83]

The political climate in the county after the major-generals was one of suspicion of a government which had continued a divisive policy towards royalists[84] but which seemed to offer inordinate protection to religious radicals, who, like vagrants, threatened property and the social order.[85] It was not simply that 'those who wished ill to Quakers were those who resented Army rule';[86] central/local suspicions and genuine scruples of conscience ensured that local army officers like Saunders, Hatsell and Blackmore were as severe against Quakers and, in Parliament, against James Nayler as any disgruntled republican or presbyterian. The shock waves of the Nayler affair spread further than Westminster, to jeopardise still further the chances of settlement damaged by swordsmen and decimators. In Devon a tight rein was kept on expressions of dissent from the prevailing 'presbyterian' ideology; Quaker justice Henry Pollexfen was even briefly gaoled at Totnes in 1656 but before this he had kept in the shadows of the governing circle. Criticisms of the government, and hence of soldiers like Coplestone, Saunders, Blackmore and Hatsell and of civilian officials like Prideaux, Shapcote, Raddon and Gorges were avoided by attributing the unacceptable face of religious toleration to the alleged inadequacies of constables, who became the scapegoats for less assailable public men.[87]

Professor Everitt has written of the *rapprochement* of royalists and moderates in Kent in the late 1650s which was prompted by the perception that a government more stable than that of Oliver (or Richard) Cromwell was needed. They united to form, as it were, an opposition waiting in the wings for the collapse of the Protectorate.[88] There is no evidence that anything so schematic developed in Devon. After the catharsis of county resentment, expressed in the second Protectorate Parliament, magistrates settled to a degree of stability and unanimity unknown since the 1630s. Repression continued against Quakers and against the holidays of 'revels'. Orders enforcing the game laws (a useful indication that landowners felt firmly in control) were issued.[89] Cromwell's invitation to county gentlemen to resume their places on the Bench at last evoked a response, from Nicholas Duck, Richard Coffin and Sir John Northcote. John Willoughby, fined in 1654 by the dour Thomas Bampfield for swearing in public, was approached in the summer of 1659 by sheriff John Blackmore because his presence would 'putt a lustre upon the representative body of the county'. Sir William Courtenay was another who had stayed neutral but who now dismayed royalist schemers by consenting to serve on the assize grand jury.[90]

This should not obscure the omens detected by many in Richard Cromwell's Parliament. It was a parliament in which political groupings were as fluid as ever, and in which interest groups had everything to gain by striving to extend their influence. As the royalist correspondent, Brodrick, wrote to Sir Edward Hyde:

> The best and wisest of each faction entertayne fortune by the day and know not what tomorrow will produce so evenly are they balanced by neutrall country gentlemen and young lawyers who, wavering in themselves, are not yet fixt to either party; when the house is fullest and debate hottest no vote being carryed by more than 6, 7 or at most 10 voyces; in which condition god only knows how long it will continue.[91]

The Parliament was elected on the old franchise,[92] which favoured the boroughs at the expense of the counties, and political commitments divided the Devon representatives still further. Cryptoroyalists like Coplestone Bampfield and presbyterian grandees like Sir John Northcote, who had stayed aloof from the politics of the 1650s, mingled with gentry careerists like John Coplestone, presbyterian lawyers like Thomas Bampfield and John Maynard (serving for the Isle of Wight after election for Bere Alston as well) and soldiers like Hatsell, Samuel Searle, John Pley and Thomas Gibbons.[93] Thomas Bampfield, after his scathing criticisms of Speaker Widdrington in 1657, found himself taking the chair. Even though he had spoken against all constitutional developments since Pride's Purge, one correspondent regarded him as a 'well-wisher to the Commonwealth's men or Independents, they are one and the same'.[94] Maynard was the pre-eminent lawyer. After his appointment as Sergeant-at-Law in May 1658, he responded by leading, not only the government legal interest but also the lawyers as a whole. His influence over the 'new Cavaliers' like Coplestone Bampfield, gave grounds for optimism to exiled royalists.[95] Yet despite the eminence of these two and one or two others like Attorney-General Prideaux and Edmund Fowell (both Cromwellians) this was emphatically the Parliament of Sir Arthur Haselrige, Thomas Scot and Sir Henry Vane. Their negative pettifogging had about it an air of unreality,[96] as in the country at large events began to overtake the house of Cromwell.

Since 1650, leading Devon royalists Sir Hugh Pollard, the Seymours, Sir John Grenville and Sir Chichester Wray, had been in contact with all plotters from Lord Hopton through John Penruddock to Sir George Booth in 1659.[97] In October 1658 Pollard was 'at liberty' after his involvement with Penruddock.[98] The collapse of Richard Cromwell's government on 22 April, 1659, reversed the policy of cautious accommodation with the royalists. The army committee of safety placed the county militias on alert, and Coplestone, Hatsell and Francis Rolle, who had served in both civilian and military office since 1650, were the natural leaders in Devon.[99] The final militia committee, whose names were published on 26 July,[100] were a mixture of presbyterians like Thomas Reynell, William Morrice, William Fry—no government of the 1650s could have done without them—and the upstart soldiers who had provided a reserve of civilian manpower in the 1650s. There were a few nominations made more in hope than anything; among them the Plymouth mayor and town clerk, Samuel Northcote and Edmund Pollexfen.[101] Successive Interregnum governments had run through practically the whole gamut of non-royalist political opinion, so when the restored Rump issued its militia list and on 8 July a commission of the peace,[102] 'angling for support' had been resumed. Purges were no longer practicable, nor was there an obvious group to be elevated to the commission. James Pierce became a JP; he had been a customs officer and a collector of funds for the propagation of the gospel in New England under the Old Rump.[103]

In August 1659 the military preparations of the Rump were justified by the attempted presbyterian/royalist coup of Booth's rising and by a wave of panic which spread across the country. A midnight alarm at Tiverton was laid at the door of sectaries and Quakers, whose influence was said to have developed apace at the Exeter garrison since 1655 (although some attributed the scare to royalist *agents provocateurs*).[104] John Coplestone was despatched to Cheshire to help extinguish the incipient fires of rebellion, while Henry Hatsell, drawn away from naval security to command a troop in the South Hams, and Francis Rolle, who seized arms at Torrington and detained suspects there, provided a stout defence in the county against royalist insurrection.[105] Lord Mordaunt contacted the royalist leaders Wray, Sir John Grenville and Lady Ellen Drake, and cautious approaches were made to Sir John Northcote and Cornish leader Boscawen, but to no effect; the Devon royalists remained passive.[106] It was the ear of faith which heard that 'Exeter and Poole hath declared for his Majesty and that Cornewal is rysen'.[107] Another correspondent reported to the exiles on 8 August that 'there have been dark reports raysed of Plymouth',[108] and Sampson Larke, a soldier from Combe Raleigh, Axminster,[109] who had been despatched to Plymouth to secure it found there a less than warm reception. He was faced by a local government strike; the warrant declaring the Booth rebels traitors

came from the high sheriff of this county, by the constable of the hundred to a petty constable who according to the usuall manner applyed himself therewith to the mayor craving his countenance and assistance in the publication thereof, who utterly refused to take any cognizance of it.

The ministers of the town, including the redoubtable presbyterian, George Hughes, similarly refused, and Larke and the constable were left to read it in the market place 'not without being scoffed at by divers merchants and others and raged against by the gentility in generall'. The sullen presbyterian elite of the town, who had withdrawn from committee government in Devon after Pride's Purge, had looked to Booth for succour after a decade of rule which had been almost as unsympathetic as that of Charles I. Larke managed to contain these resentments by increasing the military force with 'such well-affected persons as may be judged compitent to defend themselves'.[110] After Lambert's decisive victory at Winnington Bridge on 19 August, the Rump could breath again, but reprisals had to be taken against those who did not 'own Parliament' in the recent disturbances. John Blackmore, in a letter to Speaker Lenthall, appreciated that Lambert's timely intervention had quelled 'a flame in the west which otherwise I feare, all your friends would not have bin able to have prevented'.[111]

General George Monck's army in Scotland was beginning to assume an ominous significance in national politics, as in the event of a more successful royalist or presbyterian rising his was the force which could prove decisive in its defeat or its victory. Monck had been close enough to Richard Cromwell to offer him advice earlier in the year, but of greater moment was his connection with leading presbyterians. Monck was of an 'ancient and noble family' perhaps, but it was neither ancient nor noble enough to earn for its elder scions a place in the pre-civil war commission of the peace or in the local subsidy assessment commissions.[112] Monck's educational background was hardly typical of the Devon gentry of the early Stuart period; he went to King's College, Cambridge, when Exeter College, Oxford, was *de rigueur*, and his career as a professional soldier befitted more the younger son or the declining gentleman than the prosperous, well-connected esquire. Hagiographers like John Prince sought to embellish Monck's claim to be a 'worthy of Devon' by bestowing on him an impeccable genealogy but it cannot disguise the fact that Monck was not of the first order of gentry.[113] But he did have Devonshire contacts which were of particular significance in the circumstances of 1659 to 1660. Among his relations were Sir John Grenville, the leading Devon royalist, and William Morrice, who by this time had become one of the most experienced Devon MPs and justices of the peace.[114] Morrice was a presbyterian (not a royalist *pace* Mary Coate[115]) and represented the views of most of the Devon gentry still in power. Monck was not a naturally trusting man but he consistently relied on family friends in his political dealings,[116] and in 1659 to 1660 several of these had achieved positions of great power in the State. Morrice was the Rump's Secretary of State, and John Maynard, though powerful, seemed to be uncommitted. Some thought he led 'the Cavaliers of the new stampe'; others, as late as April 1660, thought him 'suspected by the honest [royalist] party'.[117] At any rate he was a Devonian and a name to conjure with. Monck's key position in 1659 was only partly the fruits of military strength; had he not enjoyed the confidence of a group of presbyterians swept back to power late in 1659, a confidence founded on the accidents of his place of birth and upbringing, the Restoration might have assumed a quite different complexion, even if it is admitted that some sort of Restoration seemed inevitable.

NOTES

1. Cambridge University Library MS Dd 8/1. It is dated 1653 and internal evidence identifies it as a Rump *liber*.
2. Underdown: *Pride's Purge*, pp. 261, 299, 308–09, 316, 322, 329–31, 345, 351, 360; Vivian: *Visitations of Cornwall*, p. 413.
3. *TDA*, LXXII, p. 261, XCVIII, p. 212; PROB 11/355/136; Keeler: *The Long Parliament* for Sir Edmund.
4. *DCNQ*, XXII, p. 48; DRO Z 1/44/45 for Tuckfield's will.
5. PRO C 193/13/4; DRO commission of the peace dated 26/9/53.
6. Such as Robert Hatch, Philip Crocker, Richard Coles, Maurice Rolle, John Doble, Robert Cockeram, Richard Viccary. All had become magistrates for the first time in 1650, and some resumed their places under the Protectorate.
7. Edward Hyde, Earl of Clarendon: *The History of the Rebellion* (Macray ed., 1888, 6 vols.), V, p. 282. The Devon Barebones MPs were undistinguished but included Francis Rouse and George Monck. Christopher Martin survived the fall of the Rump, and only John Carew and Richard Sweet were radicals: Tai Liu: *Discord in Zion* (1973), pp. 167–69.
8. Underdown: *Pride's Purge*, pp. 340–41.
9. John Arscot, John Whichalse, James Erisey, William Venner, John Hunkin, Servington Savery, John Rowe, John Blackmore, John Cruse.

10. Whichalse, Erisey, Venner, Hunkin, Savery, Rowe, Cruse, Shilston Calmady, Henry Hatsell, John Marshall, John Drake, John Searle, Richard Sweet.
11. *DNB* (Bampfield and Prideaux); Vivian: *Devon*, p.621; *TDA*, LXI, p. 212, LXVII, p. 324; (Bampfield became recorder of Exeter and Speaker in Richard Cromwell's Parliament: *Burton's Diary*, IV, pp. 149–50, 430–33; *CJ*, VII, pp. 613–14, 640); *Christ's Reward of a Christian's Watch and Ward* (1655) for the funeral sermon for John Bury senior.
12. PROB 11/386/18.
13. *CSPD 1655–56*, pp. 157, 247, 302–03, 458, 462, 470, 491, 494, *1656–57*, pp. 246, 279, *1654*, pp. 134, 338, 550, *1655*, p. 369.
14. Vivian: *Devon*, pp. 201, 680; J. M. French: 'Thorn Drury's Notes on George Wither', *Huntingdon Library Quarterly*, XXIII (1959–60), pp. 386–87.
15. Underdown: *Pride's Purge*, p. 340.
16. SP 29/449/90; DRO QS Box 60, bundle Michaelmas 1654: letter to Benjamin Braburne; BL Loan 29 (Larkham's Diary) ff. 42 v, 44 v; Aylmer: 'Checklist of Central Officeholders'; L. E. Stephens: *Clerks of the Counties*, pp. 77–79. For more on Raddon see my note in *BIHR* (1980), pp. 258–65.
17. *CSPD 1653–4*, p. 84.
18. DRO: Commissions of the peace.
19. Robert Duke, Thomas Boone, Henry Worth, Christopher Wood, Henry Walter, Francis Glanville, John Rolle of Bicton.
20. PRO PROB 11/363/71; Bodleian Lib. Clarendon MS 61/172; *TDA*, VII, p. 364, XLIII, p. 353; Lady Eliott-Drake: *The Family and Heirs of Sir Francis Drake* (1911, 2 vols.), pp. 30–31.
21. Underdown: 'Settlement in the Counties' p. 173; A. R. Bayley: *The Great Civil War in Dorset 1642–1660* (1910) p. 365.
22. E. W. Rannie: 'Cromwell's Major-Generals', *EHR* X (1895) pp. 471–506; Ivan Roots: 'Swordsmen and Decimators' in R. H. Parry (ed.): *The English Civil War and After, 1642–1658* (1970) pp. 78–92; G. E. Aylmer: *The State's Servants* (1973) pp. 48–9, 312–14; discussions by D. Massarella, S. K. Roberts in Ivan Roots (ed.): *'Into Another Mould': Aspects of the Interregnum* (Exeter 1981).
23. Aylmer *op. cit.*, Morrill: *Cheshire, DNB*.
24. Aylmer *op. cit.* pp. 312–13, Roberts in *'Into Another Mould'* p. 37; K. V. Thomas: 'The Puritans and Adultery: the Act of 1650 Reconsidered' in Pennington and Thomas (eds.): *Puritans and Revolutionaries* (Oxford 1978) p. 258 *et seq.*
25. SP 25/76a/38–39; *CSPD 1655* pp. 135–6, 145, 499.
26. *CSPD 1655* p. 192; SP 25/77/861–880 (Devon ff. 867, 890); *CSPD 1655–56* p. 262.
27. *Thurloe State Papers* iv pp. 337, 413, 439, 520.
28. Roots: 'Swordsmen and Decimators'.
29. *Thurloe State Papers* iv pp. 300, 413, 472, 520.
30. *CSPD 1655–56* pp. 154, 157–8, 439; BL Add. 38848 f.44 (Hatsell to Navy Commissioners).
31. SP 18/124/9–10.
32. *Thurloe State Papers* iv pp. 171, 225, 451. Cf. Major-general Goffe: 'I doe see the stress of this business must lie upon the midle sort of men'.
33. Roberts in *'Into Another Mould'* pp. 36–38; A. R. Bax: 'Suspected Persons in Surrey during the Commonwealth', *Surrey Archaeological Collections* xv (1899) pp. 164–89.
34. Alehouse legislation of the Tudor and early Stuart period (5, 6 Edward VI c.25; 1 Jac. 1 c.9; 4 Jac. 1 c.4, 5; 7 Jac. 1 c.10; 21 Jac. 1 c.7; 1 Car. 1 c.4; 3 Car. 1 c.4) taken *in toto* sought to distinguish *bona fide* travellers from drinking residents; the Proclamation Concerning Alehouses of 19 January 1619 stipulated that lodgers were to report to constables on arrival at inns: P. L. Hughes, J. F. Larkin: *Stuart Royal Proclamations* (Oxford 1973) pp. 409–13. Under the Commonwealth the role of the alehouse as listening-post—despite abolitionist rhetoric—was developed: *CSPD 1649–50* p. 392, *1653–54* p. 328.
35. *CSPD 1655–56* p. 227 for discussions over Dunn's clerical establishment.
36. BL Add. 19516 f. 64r.
37. *Ibid.* f. 80r.

38. For a later direct link between heraldry and political arithmetic, Philip Styles: 'The Herald's Visitation of Warwickshire 1682–83' in *Studies in Seventeenth Century West Midlands History* (Kineton 1978) pp. 108–149.

39. BL Add. 34011–17 are the registration books; *CSPD 1655–56* p. 75 for Dunn's brief.

40. *Thurloe State Papers* iv pp. 190, 216–17, 287, 316; *CSPD 1655–56* pp. 129, 277; Proclamation of 6 July 1655: text in SP 25/76a/73–75 (*CSPD 1655* pp. 232–33).

41. *CSPD 1655–56* p. 224.

42. E.g. Bere Ferrers (DRO PO 20, PS 1, PW 43–47, 56).

43. *HMC 15th Report Appendix VII* p. 91.

44. *Thurloe State Papers* iv p. 396, v pp. 302–03.

45. Underdown: *Pride's Purge*, p. 343, 'Settlement', pp. 174–77; Dodd; *Studies in Stuart Wales*, p. 161.

46. *CJ*, VII, pp. 487–88, 500; *Burton's Diary*, I, pp. 171–74.

47. *CJ*, VII, p. 533.

48. No goodwill was engendered by the exclusion of many republicans and other hostile spirits at the beginning of this Parliament, among them John Young, John Doddridge, William Morrice and John Hale—presbyterians all: *A Narrative of the Late Parliament* (1657) in *Harleian Miscellany* (1808–11, 12 vols.), VI, pp. 456–81; Whitelocke: *Memorials*, pp. 651–53; *CJ*, VII, p. 425; C. H. Firth: *The Last Years of the Protectorate* (1910, 2 vols.), I, pp. 12–15; Abbott: *Writings and Speeches*, IV, pp. 281–86.

49. F & R II, pp. 1065–66, 1245.

50. William Courtenay, Edmund and William Walrond, John Willoughby, William Martin, John Chichester, Henry Northleigh, William Kelly, Richard Duke. *CCC*, pp. 1027, 2966.

51. S. R. Gardiner: *History of the Commonwealth and Protectorate* (1903, 4 vols.), III, pp. 300–01.

52. *Narrative of the Late Parliament*, p. 477. Abbott: *Writings and Speeches*, IV, pp. 561–62, for the ceremony itself.

53. Bodleian Lib., Clarendon MS 60/279–80; cf. ff 224, 228. Maynard's developing influence was recognized by Oliver when he appointed him Sergeant-at-Law in May 1658: *Burton's Diary*, II, pp. 458–62; E. Foss *The Judges of England* (1848–64, 9 vols.), VII, pp. 325–34; *DNB*.

54. *TDA*, XXV, pp. 229, 230, 232; XXXII, p. 114.

55. *Ibid.* XXXII, p. 128; *Register of Admissions* ...

56. SP 29/449/90; *DCNQ*, XLII, p. 265; PROB 11/233/36, 398/5; Vivian: *Devon*, pp. 527, 671; *TDA*, LXXII, p. 263.

57. F & R II, pp. 968–90 (esp. pp. 970, 979).

58. *Burton's Diary*, II, p. 393.

59. Cromwell on 27 February 1657: Abbott: *Writings and Speeches*, IV, p. 417. For Coplestone: *CSPD 1655*, p. 241, *1655–56*, p. 262; SP 25/77/867, 890; Bodleian Lib.: Rawlinson MS A 27 f 381 (militia 1655); MS J. Walker C 4 f 181; *A Narrative of the Late Parliament*, p. 467; J. F. Chanter: *The Life and Times of Martin Blake B.D.* (1910), pp. 140–49.

60. *TDA*, LXI, p. 212, LXVII, p. 324; Vivian: *Devon*, p. 40.

61. SRO DD/WO Box 57 file marked 'Bampfield': T.B. to J.W. 18/4/1654; F & R II, pp. 393–96. Willoughby remained 'friend' enough to merit a place in the 1657 assessment commission. (Sir Richard Grenville's son, Richard, was fined fifty shillings for swearing five oaths, in 1653: DQSOB Michaelmas 1653.)

62. *Burton's Diary*, I, pp. 24, 29–30, 32–33, 40, 118, 164–65, 167, 263, II, p. 229. For Jourdain p. 206 below.

63. *Ibid.* I, pp. 237–38, 273–74, 292–93, II, pp. 27, 149, 159–60.

64. Partly as a defence against such proposals, the Tavistock and Exeter Independent churches met to discuss a measure of association; Bampfield's proposed scheme would have extended the Devon Assembly: *TDA*, IX, pp. 279–88; Bodleian Lib. Rawlinson MS D 1352 ff. 148–53; W. A. Shaw: *A History of the English Church ... 1640–60* (1900, 2 vols.), I, p. 281, II, pp. 446–47.

65. *Burton's Diary*, I, pp. 168, 224, II, pp. 68, 113, 204–05.

66. BL Add. 11314 f 12; M. F. Stieg (ed.): *The Diary of John Harington, MP, 1646–53*

(1977), p. 34; Raymond Gorges: *The Story of a Family Through Eleven Centuries, being a history of the Family of Gorges* (1944), Chapter 16, *passim*; Underdown: *Somerset*, pp. 168–69, 172–73.

67. Aylmer: 'Checklist of Central Officeholders': *A Narrative of the Late Parliament*, p. 469.
68. *Burton's Diary*, II, pp. 159–60, I, pp. 73–74, 85–86; Roots: *The Great Rebellion*, pp. 205–08. Henry Hatsell and Robert Shapcote, Devon officeholders, doubted whether Nayler could legally be executed: *Burton's Diary*, I, pp. 125–26, 146–47.
69. Fowell sought Nayler's execution, was critical of the Spanish War but supported claims that the 'Other House' should be styled 'House of Lords': *ibid.* I, pp. 168, 176, 191, 209; II, pp. 34, 61, 159–60, 163, 165, 167, 448–50.
70. F & R II, pp. 1038–42; Aylmer 'Checklist'; B. L. Lansdowne MS 822 f. 290.
71. *Burton's Diary*, I, pp. 125–26, II, pp. 159–60, 274–75, 298, 377, 402.
72. For the view that Parliament simply responded to electoral pressure: Conrad Russell: 'Parliamentary History in Perspective 1604–29', *History*, LXI (1976), pp. 25–27; D. M. Hirst: 'Court, Country and Politics before 1629' in Kevin Sharpe (ed.): *Faction and Parliament* (1978), p. 131.
73. Whitelocke: *Memorials*, pp. 544, 568.
74. Joseph Besse: *An Abstract of the Sufferings of the People Call'd Quakers* (1733, 2 vols.), I, pp. 55–62, 63, 64–67, 71, 72; DRO QS Box 60, mixed bundle 1655: examination of Thomas Salthouse *et al.*, bundle Epiphany 1656: examinations of Caleb and John Pearce *et al.*
75. DQSOB Midsummer 1656; A. H. A. Hamilton: *Quarter Sessions from Queen Elizabeth to Queen Anne* (1878), pp. 164–65; Besse: *An Abstract*, p. 70. Cf. *CJ*, VII, p. 439.
76. Bampfield, Hales, Hatsell, Fowell and Reynell: *Burton's Diary*, I, pp. 78, 91, 150–51, 168.
77. *Ibid.* I, p. 168, *CJ*, VII, p. 470.
78. *The West Answering to the North*, pp. 63–64, 77–78, 84–85, 88–89, 93, 107, 164–66; Besse: *An Abstract*, pp. 65–72; PRO SP 18/157A/87.
79. *CSPD 1656–57*, p. 122; SP 25/77/422.
80. Besse: *An Abstract, passim*; N. Penney (ed.): *The Journal of George Fox* (1911, 2 vols.), I, p. 270; Barry Reay: 'The Quakers, 1659 and the Restoration of the Monarchy', *History*, LXIII (1978), pp. 193–213, is perhaps inclined to take Quaker literature too much at face value: Henry Pollexfen, *pace* Fox, was a JP from 1649 and not from forty years earlier: Reay, *op. cit.*, p. 201; *Fox's Journal*, I, p. 237; DRO Commissions of the peace. Mark Grime, the 'Quaker' governor of Cardiff, was a client of Sir Arthur Haselrige's—not a man celebrated for sympathy with religious radicals: Reay, p. 201, *CSPD 1659–60*, p. 293.
81. BL Add. 38856 ff. 71, 73–74 (Copies in BL Add. 44058 ff 55–58).
82. SP 25/78/259–60, 840–41; SP 18/157A/87, 88; *CSPD 1657–58*, p. 156.
83. DQSOB Midsummer 1658. Oddly enough, Charles II's government enjoined clemency: DRO DD 60351.
84. Cf. Reynell and Bampfield in December 1656: 'If the Cavaliers be never so wicked, let us be just to them and keep our faith'. *Burton's Diary*, I, pp. 236, 241.
85. Fowell: 'They deny all ministry and magistracy'. *Ibid.* I, p. 168.
86. Christopher Hill: *The World Turned Upside Down* (Penguin ed., 1975), p. 235.
87. The notion of defusing controversial issues by blaming those not in direct contact with the government in their administrative duties accords well with a concept of political sensitivity outlined by Edmund Fowell and Speaker Widdrington in May 1657; Cavaliers should be allowed to hold offices of trust but not of profit; if they were excluded from the former, 'You will have neither sheriffs nor constables'. *Burton's Diary*, II, p. 34.
88. Everitt: *Community of Kent and the Great Rebellion*, pp. 298–301.
89. DQSOB Easter 1658, Midsummer 1658, Midsummer 1659.
90. DQSOB marginalia; SRO DD/WO Box 53, B. to W. 8/7/1659; Bodleian Lib. Clarendon MS 57/173–74.
91. Clarendon MS 60/224.
92. Cf. *England's Confusion* (1659) in *Somers Tracts* (1809–15, 13 vols.), VI, pp. 513–30.
93. *Official Returns of Members of Parliament* (1878, 2 vols.).

94. *Burton's Diary*, II, pp. 88–89 (I, p. 224, II, p. 68 for his presbyterianism), Clarendon MS 60/226.
95. Clarendon MS 60/224, 228, 279–80; BL Add. 5138 (transcript of Guybon Goddard's Diary) ff. 62 v, 83 v, 92 v, 118. The original unpaginated diary is in WRO Ailesbury (Savernake) MSS, but it is available, *almost* entirely and accurately transcribed in *Burton's Diary* (J. T. Rutt ed.).
96. Recorded in *Burton's Diary*, III and IV.
97. D. Underdown: *Royalist Conspiracy in England 1649–60* (1960), pp. 27–35, 150, 153.
98. Clarendon MS 59/125–27, 57/173–74.
99. *CSPD 1658–59*, p. 360, *1659–60*, pp. 8, 15–16, 24, 65, 79, 100, 119; SP 25/98/26; SP 18/204/2. Exeter had been re-fortified against possible royalist invasion in 1658: Clarendon MS 57/44.
100. F & R II, pp. 1320–42, esp. pp. 1322–23.
101. *TDA*, XCII, p. 293; *Students Admitted to the Inner Temple* for Pollexfen.
102. DRO commission of the peace.
103. PRO E 122/232/21; *CSPD 1659–60*, p. 252; E 190/952/3; *CTB*, I (1660–67), p. 634; DRO 1429 A/PWI, Chagford churchwardens' accounts 1480–96, loosely inserted parish accounts 1653 (F & R II, pp. 197–200).
104. *Mercurius Politicus* (21–28 July 1659), pp. 617–18; *Publick Intelligencer* (25 July–1 August, 1659), p. 617; *TSP*, III, pp. 259–60; B. R. Vandevelde: 'Quakers and Fifth Monarchy Men: Problems of Public Order' (Exeter MA, 1978), pp. 35, 52; Underdown: *Royalist Conspiracy*, p. 256.
105. Clarendon MS 63/113–14; PRO SP 18/204/2; SP 25/98/155–56; *CSPD 1659–60*, pp. 65, 100.
106. Clarendon MS 65/59–60, 77; 61/204; Underdown: *Conspiracy*, pp. 260, 264–65.
107. Clarendon MS 64/7–8.
108. *Ibid.* 63/88.
109. For Larke's career: *CSPD 1654*, p. 585, *1655*, pp. 253, 446, 542, *1656–57*, p. 445, 448, 558.
110. Bodleian Lib. Tanner MS 51/125; C. H. Firth (ed.): *The Clarke Papers* (1891–1901, 4 vols.), IV, pp. 290–91; *CJ*, VII, p. 769. For Booth's rising in general: M. Coate (ed.): *The Letter Book of John, Viscount Mordaunt 1658–60* (1945); J. R. Jones: 'Booth's Rising of 1659', *Bulletin of the John Rylands Library*, XXXIX (1957), pp. 416–43; Underdown: *Royalist Conspiracy*.
111. *CSPD 1659–60*, pp. 219–20; Tanner MS 51/103, (reprinted in *Clarke Papers*, IV, p. 295). By contrast *A Faithful Remembrance and Advice to the General Council* (May 1659) offered some Devon support for the 'Good Old Cause'.
112. Maurice Ashley: *General Monck* (1977), pp. 3, 149. (1630s commissions of the peace: PRO C 193/13/2, SP 16/405; subsidy commissions in *Statutes of the Realm*.)
113. Venn: *Alumni*; Ashley: *General Monck*, p. 71 for a more realistic assessment of his background than that offered in Prince: *Worthies of Devon*. Monck's membership of Gray's Inn and Lincoln's Inn was bestowed after 1660. Cf. Joan Thirsk: 'Younger Sons in the Seventeenth Century', *History*, LIV (1969), pp. 358–77.
114. For the Monck/Grenville axis: Clarendon MS 59/125; *DNB* 'Grenville'; *TSP*, I, pp. 2–3 for the friendship between Morrice and Grenville's father, Bevil.
115. Bell: *Memorials*, II, pp. 140–44; *West Answering to North*, p. 107; Coate: *Cornwall*, p. 300.
116. Another family favoured by Monck was that of Clobury. John C. was a soldier, Christopher a 'Country' poetaster: Ashley: *General Monck*, p. 171, note 14 above.
117. Clarendon MS 60/279–80, 72/59–60.

Chapter Four:

The Juries of Devonshire

The English jury system offered opportunities to the gentry and middling sort for something approaching mass participation but has been largely neglected by historians since the surveys of Sidney and Beatrice Webb early in this century. The Webbs concluded that juries, with the rest of local government after 1660, ossified as gentry control became absolute. Editors of quarter sessions records have mentioned the jury system in passing but editors of archival source material have naturally been concerned to outline the structure of government rather than to trace developments in that structure.[1] More specific studies differ in their appraisal of what William Lambarde called 'the eyes of the Law'. J. S. Cockburn concludes that assize juries were conservative, parochial and preoccupied with the 'predominantly uncontroversial' details of county business; by contrast J. S. Morrill regards the Cheshire grand jury at both assizes and quarter sessions as increasingly independent and assertive.[2] Much has been made of the rhetoric of jury-summoning. 'Charges' to juries by visiting dignitaries have been seen as indices of changing views on the constitution and as guides to 'real' attitudes behind parliamentary rhetoric. They were certainly used as a means of advertising the legitimacy of the government of the Commonwealth in 1649.[3] In more settled times charges invariably blended a curious mixture of flattery, cajolement and bullying. The views of law reformers on juries have also been explored in detail.[4]

The juries of Devon can be judged by the plentiful lists and less abundant presentments among the quarter sessions bundles[5] and by miscellaneous evidence elsewhere.

The Quarter Sessions Grand Jury

Three kinds of jury met at Exeter Castle for each sessions meeting.[6] They were the grand jury, the trial or petty jury and the hundred jury. The grand jury was the most socially exalted and fulfilled both a judicial and an administrative purpose. It considered whether bills of indictment brought against those charged with felony or misdemeanour deserved answer. If they did not they were each endorsed *billa vera* or 'true bill'; if they did not, *ignoramus* was written on the back of the indictment and the suspect was free to leave the court. After consultation with the magistrates and the clerk of the peace jurors could decide to 'traverse' a case; that is, to accept a plea from the accused or his counsel, or suggest themselves, that a case be postponed until the next sessions meeting or reserved to the consideration of the assize jury. The trial jurors brought in guilty or not guilty verdicts and considered large numbers of cases in succession. The hundred jury was supposed to present grievances to the court from the thirty-three hundreds of Devon, but as few such presentments have survived and because those that have were made by individual jurors to the court, it may be assumed that the hundred jury had atrophied into a reserve of available freeholders from which the petty jury could be augmented by the procedure known as *tales de circumstantibus*. While the trials of those whose indictments had been judged *billae verae* were proceeding, the grand jury presented the grievances of those in the parishes (to whom the grand jurymen were supposedly closer than the exalted members of the commission of the peace) to the Bench. The jury system at each sessions, therefore, involved upwards of forty men for a space of two or three days in a well-defined hierarchy of function.[7]

The grand jury was summoned by a writ of *venire facias* issued in the sessions before the one in which the jury was to serve. The jury at the Easter sessions was thus summoned by a writ issued during the Epiphany meeting. According to Lambarde, the writ could not be issued by the *custos rotulorum* alone;[8] in Devon in the mid-seventeenth century the custos was an absentee, and so it was normal for two justices of the quorum to issue it. The writ was addressed to the sheriff, who was to

> cause foure and twenty free and lawfull men (every of which maie have forty shillings by the yeare of freehold at the least) to come before the keepers of the peace publique and justices of peace of this ... county assigned for the hearinge and determyninge of divers felonies, trespasses and other misdemeanours in your county committed and done, at the gaol garden neere the castle of Exon ... and alsoe at the same tyme ... some twenty foure as well knights as others honest and lawfull men of the bodye of your county, as well within liberties as without, whereof every one maie have forty shillings by the yeare at least in rent, land or freehold, to inquire upon those things which then and there shalbe enjoyned them.[9]

It is clear that there was a legal distinction between juries of issue or trial and those of inquiry, even though in practice the grand jury combined both these functions.[10] At the beginning of the sessions the writ was returned to the court by the sheriff, together with lists of freeholders from the hundreds, compiled by the bailiffs as a cumulative compilation of potential jurors.[11]

The writs of *venire facias* authorised the summoning of twenty-four grand jurors, of whom, according to Dalton, at least twelve had to be sworn. In Kent an odd number was always sworn so that a verdict could always be reached by a majority. In Cheshire the number sworn rose from an average of between thirteen and seventeen from 1625 to 1642 to twenty-one or over from 1646 to 1659.[12] No change in the size of the jury is discernible in Devon; the average size from 1649 to 1670 was just over seventeen.

A major task of the grand jury was to deliver presentments to the court. Here the capacity of the jury for independent action should have been at its greatest, and it is clear from William Lambarde's charges that the

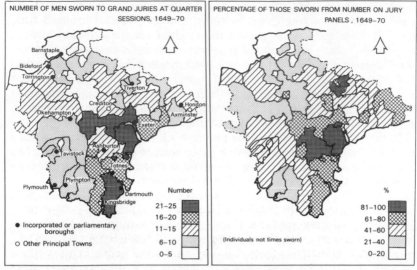

MAP EIGHT   MAP NINE

quality of presentments traditionally exercised the concern of justices of the peace. The characteristics of Devon jury presentments are a mingling of a lofty tone of moral censure, an enumerating of lapses in communal responsibilities and a tendency towards spiteful attacks on specific individuals, including other jurors. An interest in roads and bridges was natural in those who had to foot most of the bill for their repair and even supervise their upkeep. Such presentments were usually of specific neglects. At Easter 1667 roads at Halberton, Tiverton, Poltimore and between Pinhoe and Huxham parishes were presented; at Michaelmas 1664 Wonford bridge at Heavitree was said to be in disrepair. Such presentments were likely to be repeated subsequently, a pattern also discernible in the orders of magistrates.[13] The Easter 1667 road presentment was first made, in its essential details, at Michaelmas 1661. Presentments also reflected moral concern, as in the 'grievance of unlycensed alehouses' or merely the jurors' anxiety to be seen to be diligent. At Epiphany sessions 1649 it was ordered that 'upon petition of the grand jury in respect of this week's service, no amerciament be extracted against them for not appearing at the precedent sessions'. There could be a virtual cash reward for dutiful conduct.[14]

A remarkable feature of the grand jury at the Restoration was its interest in the re-establishment of the Church of England. Inhabitants of a dozen parishes were presented for absenteeism from church and although the lists recurred in subsequent presentments at least 35 individuals were thus singled out.[15] Such condemnations occurred throughout the 1660s, but began in earnest between the passing of the Act of Uniformity in May 1662 and its 'deadline' for ministers who intended to conform, 24 August.[16] As early as 1 November 1661, the jury presented 'all ministers that doe neglect or refuse to read the booke of common prayer, and those that doe not administer the Holy Sacraments'.[17] Does this support Dr R. S. Bosher's view of an Anglican—indeed 'Laudian'—revival inspired from below? He detected a 'spontaneous and gradual' recovery from as early as May 1660 in some places but the true picture must be drawn from events in each diocese and although chapter meetings began at Exeter in August 1660 it was not until October that a registrar began work. Ordinations recommenced in January 1661.[18] In the local context, then, jury interest in Anglican recovery was not as remarkably early as it might seem if compared with the chronology of parliamentary debate.

The jury also requested that the prayer book be read again and pointed out two examples of incumbents who were failing to do so. The Midsummer 1662 grand jury presentment included a list of 31 habitual absentees from church and the information that Simon Parsons, vicar of Sidbury, and James Haddridge, vicar of Halberton, had failed to read the prayer book and to administer the sacraments at divine service. The timing of this presentment suggests that the jury was contributing to the preparations for the date when clerical ejections would begin in the parishes. The Act of Uniformity was passed in May 1662 and incumbents were given from the 19th of that month until St Bartholomew's Day to conform to three conditions. They had to read from the revised Book of Common Prayer, to declare before the ordinary of the diocese that it was unlawful to take up arms against the King, and to repudiate the Solemn League and Covenant.[19] By 8 July, therefore, when the Devon presentment was made, the preparatory period was well-advanced. These complaints by the jury, an inverted form of the tendency of the Cheshire jury to suggest positive improvements in the structure of parochial authority,[20] were apparently unique, but one common fact linked the parishes of Halberton and Sidbury. They were both in the gift of the Dean and Chapter of Exeter Cathedral before the Civil War and their Interregnum incumbents were thus intruded, not by private patronage of right, but by the exercise of an alien authority, by national or local committee. Haddridge and Parsons were thus fair game for a grand jury which had consistently shown itself respectful of the rights of its local social superiors.

Jostling with appeals for ecclesiastical revival and secular reform were less lofty concerns. Minor infringements of respectable behaviour and actions detrimental to public welfare were frequently presented. The tithingmen of Farringdon, Aylesbeare and Poltimore failed to keep rook-nets, Hugh Smeardon of Ilsington diverted a water course, John Penny of Halwell laid 'dung and soyle in the king's highway leading from Dartmouth and Totnes'. Thomas Venning of Abbotskerswell was presented for 'keeping of geese in our potwater and other annoyances to the sum of the parishoners'.[21] A nuisance was defined as an offence 'to his majesty's liege people'—to the public—but the difference between public interest and private advantage was here as everywhere likely to be blurred. Jurors presented other jurors and officials and there was no 'professional' unity or defence against outsiders. Hugh Smeardon of Ilsington was sworn to five juries between 1665 and 1670 but he was presented for diverting water. An erstwhile mayor of Bradninch, Robert Jerman, was presented by his fellow-townsman, John Venman, as 'a common drunkard and an incourager and procurer of others as committ the same sinne'.[22]

An assessment of the contribution of the grand jury to trials at law is not easy to make. True bills were not guilty verdicts and although random sampling indicates that bills were quite likely to be rejected by the jury, the clerks of the court were entitled to frame them anew or to remove the case to assizes. Trial juries, on the other hand, could be relied upon to convict in half the cases before them and the quarter sessions order books and the informal papers of the court reveal no difficulties perceived by magistrates in achieving successful prosecutions. Once in court, a defendant was lucky to escape conviction.[23]

The overall impression, from its parochial concerns, frequent *'omnia bene'* statements and invariable endorsement of other presentments is that the Devon grand jury was by no means the healthily independent and vigorous body which Morrill has discovered in Cheshire. Specific presentments reflect the origins of jurors who made them. The Abbotskerswell potwater case was raised by William Stoneman of Abbotskerswell. The alcoholic mayor of Bradninch was presented by a Bradninch juror. The same feature can be discerned in Cheshire but in Devon it led to a reluctance by jurors to conceive of a 'county' interest as anything more than the sum of the problems of parishes. The 'county community' was not a concept prominent or implicit in their deliberations. There is, however, the question of where the initiative in jury selection lay. Were jurors sworn because sheriffs or justices felt that certain areas needed attention, or was it merely that of those present on a given day in court only those with something to say were sworn? The parochial flavour of presentments suggests the latter. It is difficult otherwise to account for the incongruous juxtaposition of items in presentments; concern at 'ministers that doe neglect or refuse to read the booke of common prayer' is hardly the same sort of concern as that informing the attack on Thomas Venning's methods of poultry farming. There was no purge of jurors in 1660 and yet the jury suddenly assumed an interest in religious affairs which it had hitherto lacked. There was, on the other hand, an extensive scrutiny by central government of the commission of the peace[24] and the Devon Bench was enthusiastic in its support of Bishops Gauden and Ward. The hint of magisterial domination cannot be ignored.

The Cheshire grand jury like that of Devon was used by its members to pursue private quarrels. It is worth summarising other points of similarity and difference. In Cheshire there was a more formal institutional structure to support presentments endorsed as true bills. In cases of church absence there is no evidence that the justices ever issued orders except in response to a presentment, and county rates had to be endorsed by the grand jury before finding acceptance by the magistrates. The Webbs noticed that in some areas bridge repairs were not put in hand until the grand jury had presented the delapidation.[25] The Devon grand jury was not completely independent. There is reason to believe that some presentments were drafted by the staff of the clerk of the peace, although the jury was not always willing to accept this usurpation. The appearance of presentments deploring the laxity of game laws did not really accord with the social status of the jurors, and during the 1660s the signatures of JPs had to be appended to lists of freeholders. The Cheshire quarter sessions and assizes distinguished between private petitions and presentments by juries. The Cheshire grand jury did not concern itself with the repair of bridges, the operation of the poor law or the illegal erection of cottages or keeping of 'inmates' or lodgers. By contrast, these problems were preoccupations in Devon. The Cheshire jury was a county inspectorate and frequently presented county officials. So far was this from the case in Devon that its grand jury commonly reported that it had no presentments to add to those of the constables. Only once did the jury present officials and then it was a general statement against 'constables who have not paid in proportions of rates',[26] a problem which exercised the justices of the peace to a remarkable extent during the 1660s.

The sessions grand jury was undistinguished. For its members the most burning issues were likely to be ones touching them personally or which bore upon the humdrum reality of their daily lives. Far from seizing opportunities for self-expression they seemed to prefer to endorse the lead offered by the justices. On the other hand the magistrates indulged in a stream of orders and declarations but seemed unable to move the jury from a regular pattern of performance. This puzzling discrepancy between official attitudes and the documentary record upon which the jury has been judged can be partly explained by examining the pattern of recruitment to the jury and the social and economic structure of the county itself.

Jury service was a recurrent fact of life for a section of Devon society. Apart from the average grand jury of seventeen members there was a wider group whose names appeared on the sheriffs' panels but whose faces were never seen in the jury chamber at Exeter Castle. On the jury panels for 1649 to 1670 (an artificial period, obviously) are the names of 672 men. Of these, 391 were actually sworn to grand juries. Even after allowances for missing panels, misspellings and administrative lapses of various kinds there can be no doubt that a large body of men were involved on the fringes of the jury system. Many were called but few were chosen. Of the 391 sworn, the largest group (149) served once only, 69 served twice and the remainder can be divided into ever smaller groups of those who served more frequently. Most men sat on no more than three juries each.[27]

There was no obvious common characteristic among the leaders. Anthony Coplestone and John Land came from the most junior of cadet branches of armigerous families. Others were substantial yeomen or minor gentlemen. The relatives of Richard Moore of Cullompton had 'gent.' carved on his tomb when he died in 1674. Moses Tirrell held property in Exeter as well as in his own parish of Pinhoe.[28] At least three sessions grand jurors became commissioners for assessments and a few more were merchants. Many were hundredal constables.[29] The property qualification for service was still the 40-shilling one, meaningless since the beginning of the century at least. The act of 1665 provided that henceforth they were to have a minimum yearly income of £20, or in Wales, a land of poor if litigious squires, £8. Jurors remained the 'middling sort', below the level from which magistrates were sworn but above that of the most minor copyholders.[30]

The topography of Devon is dominated by the division between highland and lowland zones running from north to south along a line marked by the Exe valley. This most obvious geographical feature, marking East Devon off from the central and West Devon moorland plateau, conceals other less obtrusive but equally important differences. East Devon itself was a sheep-rearing district characterised by large manors and during the sixteenth century by a high degree of aristocratic landownership. By the mid-seventeenth century it had become less dominated by the aristocracy but remained the home of some of the most eminent gentry families: the Drakes, the Poles, the Youngs, for example.[31]

The South Hams district, the Dartmouth/Kingsbridge hinterland, was relatively densely populated and its land was the most fertile in the county. In the sixteenth century it was the most wealthy region, while its sheep supplied the wool for the cloth trade of Ashburton and Totnes. Arable farming was practised here, too, as it was in the Exe Vale below Exeter and the Barnstaple region in the north of the county.[32]

The rest of north and west Devon was thinly populated and poor, except for the Tavistock district which still lived off the fruits of the expansion of the tin industry, in a depressed condition by the 1640s.[33] The soil was infertile and the region included Dartmoor and Exmoor. Leland's opinion of the moor, 'All by forest, barren and moorish ground where is store and breeding of young cattle but little or no corn or habitation', was confirmed in even starker terms by the businesslike surveyors of confiscated crown lands in the sixteen-forties: 'A mountainous and cold ground, much beclouded with thick fogs and mists'.[34] A contemporary view that commoners on Dartmoor were 'substantial men' does find some support, however, in the movement of the land market in the west of the county in general. Late settlement meant a large freeholding class; in the mid-sixteenth century the supply of land exceeded the demand for it and led to an invasion by carpet-baggers.[35]

It might be expected that the grand jury would have been recruited from those districts in which land had long been held by a numerically healthy freeholding class, but such a simple model is not helpful. Dartmoor was under-represented: Lydford, a huge parish covering much of the moor, sent not one juror to Exeter, and neither did Widecombe-in-the-Moor. In areas where prosperity rested on industry, the impulse to participation in government clearly focussed on towns rather than on the nebulous county administration. It would not have been clear to a small cloth producer from the Tiverton region, recovering in the 1650s from earlier economic disruption, that a place on the grand jury would have bestowed benefits as valuable as those brought nearer to the grasp by service in the parish. Tiverton, the capital of the new draperies cloth trade, sent only six men to the grand jury. The Teign valley, by contrast, which had enjoyed a tin boom in the previous century and which remained as a quasi-urban economy of small boroughs and large villages, was well-represented.[36]

The sworn jurors came from a wide spread of parishes but the regions returning most jurors to Exeter were those of the south-east (the South Hams) and the area around Exeter. The South Hams included the boroughs of Dartmouth and Totnes, populous but economically depressed in the shift in the cloth trade from old broadcloths to new draperies.[37] The economy of Exeter itself attracted a large population to its surrounding villages. The evidence of the Compton Census, the Protestation returns of 1641 and the Hearth Tax returns of the 1660s and 1670s, together with the geographical distribution of royalist sympathisers examined during the 1655–56 visitation of Major-general Disbrowe and his commissioners indicates, on balance, a spread of population which accords broadly with jury recruitment.[38] The population of Devon was heaviest in the south and east, with another concentration around Plymouth and Tavistock; the north and west were (the towns excepted) more lightly peopled.

It is instructive to identify those parishes which sent more jurors than average to Exeter Castle. Forty-four Devon parishes sent at least four jurors on at least one occasion each between 1649 and 1670, and one might expect these parishes to be the homes of the magistrates of Devonshire. In fact only six were the homes of justices, although it is interesting that these six were dominated by leading families: East Allington by the Fowells, Broadclyst by the Bampfields, Kenton by the Courtenays, Tavistock by the Wreys, Sandford by the Davys, and the crowded parish of Ugborough which found room for the Saverys, the Fowells and the Strodes. Nevertheless, jury recruitment, a wider participation in the life of the community and the pattern of social organisation are not unrelated. The grand jurors were more likely to come from hundreds where farming was mixed arable and pasture, the area of the most stable agrarian wealth and where communities were frequently nucleated rather than 'open'.

Professor David Underdown has found the field/forest or pasture antithesis relevant in explaining the taking of sides during the civil war. This typology of rural communities was outlined by Dr Thirsk,[39] and Underdown has shown how the royalist clubmen of Dorset, Somerset and Wiltshire were more likely to come from the nucleated villages of downland districts of sheep and corn farming, while parliamentarian neutralists were more strongly associated with the scattered communities of wood and pasture areas.[40] This generalisation applies more to the 'middling sort' than to the common people. Underdown concludes that the evidence 'does little to support the hypothesis that settlement patterns by themselves had much to do with' the allegiances of the ordinary soldier. Here the pattern of industrial activity and the survival of forms of popular culture are important and Underdown suggests that literacy and the effectiveness of propaganda would be other significant variables.[41]

The recruitment of the grand jury was not a crude manipulation of the yeomanry and wealthier tenantry by the resident gentry magistrates of the parishes, but the field/pasture model may still be relevant, for the areas of highest recruitment were those where corn and stock-raising mixed farming predominated and where villages were nucleated rather than scattered. These were communities in which manorial discipline was more easily maintained, and there is a clear association between healthy representation on the sessions jury at Exeter and an active manorial elective system at home. Manors like Alphington (three grand jurors, ten petty jurors), Kenton (two grand jurors, five petty jurors), Morchard Bishop (five grand jurors, one petty juror) and Newton St Cyres (one grand juror, five petty jurors) maintained a vital tradition of manorial jury presentments and meetings. With the exception of towns like Hartland (five grand jurors) which elected a vigorous 'select vestry' or 'Twenty-Four Governors', the north of the county was under-represented on the jury and it cannot be pure coincidence that the survival of manorial records from the north and west of the county is comparatively poor.[42] The grand jurors' appearances at Exeter were likely to confirm their status as men with a say in the running of their parishes.

Settlement patterns in rural Devonshire would therefore appear to be relevant to a study of jury summoning but the evidence is not one-sided. The South Hams and East Devon were singled out by Bishop Ward in 1663 as 'especially ... disorderly and troublesome' because of a Puritan tradition there.[43] There were Baptist and Independent congregations at Exeter, Colyton, Tiverton, Chulmleigh, Dartmouth, Plymouth, Kingsbridge, Kilmington, Uppottery, and Honiton from the 1640s onwards, many with the tacit support after 1660 of county gentry whose own religious persuasions could more accurately be defined as presbyterian.[44] The bishop noted how the East Devon nonconformists profited from the proximity of the Devon border, 'which being the border of three dioceses as wel as of three counties gives great oppportunities to the sectaries to play their tricks and escape.'[45] It was true that in a wider sense East Devon belied the orthodox notion that a 'county community' counted for more than physical geography, economic reality and administrative accidents: the thriving pasturing economy of the region looked away east to the cattle trade with Dorset and London.[46] In the 1660s Puritan Dartmouth in the South Hams turned awkward on the government, anxious to manipulate a by-election.[47]

We are faced, therefore, with the apparent paradox of a rather slothful and somnolent jury system springing, Venus-like, from the same sea which brought forth a Puritan activism of quite formidable proportions: the same conditions producing an almost contradictory pattern of participation. One line of explanation, perhaps so far given insufficient weight, is the secular pattern of participation itself. Only six of the parishes where quarter sessions jury service was a regular obligation were dominated by magisterial families, but most of the parishes were geographically well located for travel to Exeter. Some—Alphington, Aylesbeare, Chudleigh, Newton St Cyres, Rockbeare and Sowton—were all either near Exeter or were situated on main roads to it. Others, like Bishopsteignton, Halberton, Milton Abbot and Swimbridge were on other principal highways. A few remain unaccounted for; Withycombe Raleigh near Exmouth sent two grand jurors and seven petty jurors but was situated at the end of a 'blind' road—a cul-de sac. Black Torrington was a scattered and large parish in West Devon from which eight grand jurors travelled to Exeter.[48] But in most instances the spread of population reinforced the harsh imperatives of travel in hilly terrain to determine the ways in which juries were recruited. Distance from Exeter, difficulty of travel and scattered settlements ensured that for the north of Devon the bailiffs' lists of freeholders had deteriorated into stylized repetitions. Administrative effectiveness diminished as distance from Exeter increased.

The increasing self-confidence of the higher gentry on the Bench of magistrates and the survival, and in some cases the re-shaping, of the parish elites after 1660 would seem to contain within them the makings of conflict. Yet the behaviour of the grand jury suggests that participation in county government could act as a 'buffer zone' between two powerful and cohesive social groups. The gaps in our knowledge might suggest that for too long the county has been the focus of attention at the expense of the parish. Similarly perhaps we have been too preoccupied in explaining social unrest and not sufficiently exercised by the phenomenon of rural quietism. Devon was largely enclosed as early as 1600 and despite depression in the textile industry and in mining, the disruption of war, the visitation of plague and some appalling harvests in the late 1640s, was not noted for crowd disturbances or a degree of middling-sort radicalism which could not be accommodated in the prevailing political and social structure.

The Hundred Juries

The existence of a cohesive hundredal jury system by the mid-seventeenth century seems doubtful. From the practice in other counties and from the bailiffs' description of the men in their returns of freeholders as 'hundreders' it may be judged that the hundred still played a prominent part in jury administration but in the summoning of the jury rather than in its operation at court. The hundreders named on the lists were of petty juror status—mostly middling yeomen. The lists of returned hundreders and those of sworn trial jurors can be compared; a survey of twenty-seven chosen at random reveals that an average of 5.2 men were recruited each sessions to the trial jury from the hundredal lists.

In some counties there was a jury for each hundred. In Essex there were nineteen. In Kent the sixty-three hundreds justified 'virtually autonomous' sessions at Maidstone and Canterbury and in the 1580s William Lambarde had noted 'no small hindrance to the service' when only one man served there for each hundred.[49] As Morrill has suggested, hundred juries were more likely to be summoned in counties where the hundreds were numerous, but the very size of large counties reduced their effectiveness. There were thirty-three hundreds in Devon as well as an 'artificial' hundred comprising the manors of the Duchy of Lancaster. About twenty hundreders' presentments have survived from the 1660s.

None was made by more than one individual and they were greatly outnumbered (in an approximate ratio of two to one) by constables' presentments. The hundreders had to be sworn in court; a presentment of Colyton bridge was endorsed: 'The grand jury will not take it without oath in court'.[50] Hundred presentments ran the range of those offered by the grand jury, except that none called for moral reform or related to national politics. The juror was one of a number of presenting officials: surveyors of highways, petty constables, hundred constables, county treasurers of rates for hospitals, gaols and maimed soldiers, and even JPs all offered presentments to the court. In the ideal court-room described by Dalton and Lambarde all would have been referred to the grand jury to 'join in one good and serviceable mind, voice and presentment',[51] but in Devon there were many independent presentments; the structure of county government was more flexible. It was, in fact, something of a free-for-all, and it further weakened the power, cohesiveness and independence of the grand jury.

The Trial Jury

The structure and performance of trial or petty juries is clear: twelve men invariably formed a trial jury and their sole task was to bring guilty or not guilty verdicts on alleged criminals. The names of the petty jurors cannot be found on the sheriffs' lists of grand jurors summoned and sworn and on average only five of the twelve were chosen from the lists of freeholders and hundreders. To account for the presence of the others it may be helpful to note any common characteristics among those sworn. The evidence for trial jurors is from fifty-nine panels surviving out of the minimum possible sworn of eighty-eight.[52] The grand jury was empanelled once for the sessions, but two or three trial juries could be sworn if the criminal side of court business was unduly heavy.

Lambarde thought it 'no small privilege ... which the subject of this land enjoyeth ... that he is not to be judged but by his peers and men of his own condition neither by such that be of remote dwelling but even by those of the same shire and neighbourhood where the matter doth arise ...'.[53] All jurors were Devonians, it is true, but it is unlikely that a defendant from north Devon felt among sympathisers from the same 'neighbourhood' when he stood trial. We know where the members of sixty juries lived. Three hundred and ninety of seven hundred and twenty attendances were by men from Wonford, Exminster and East Budleigh hundreds, all adjacent to Exeter. Of the hundreds producing more than a dozen attendances each, only one, Lifton in west Devon, lay outside a sixteen mile radius from Exeter. This takes no account of jurors sitting on more than one occasion, and the figures for Wonford, Exminster and East Budleigh are swollen by those who came many times. Thomas Eliot of Upton Pyne in Wonford sat on fifty-two juries, Thomas Harris of Kenton in Exminster on forty-eight, John Turner of Alphington (Wonford) on forty-six and his fellow-parishioner, John Pawling, on forty-two. They may have sat on juries before 1649 and after 1670. Yet a good three-quarters of the jurors came only once or twice,[54] so that the prominence of the 'suburban' hundreds cannot be gainsaid. Within these hundreds the numbers of sworn petty jurors bore no relation to the population of the parishes. Doddiscombsleigh, nestling in the Haldon hills to the west of Exeter, had an adult male population of one hundred and two in 1642[55] and sent one man as a trial juror; neighbouring Dunchideock, even more remote and with an adult male population (according to the same source) of only fifty, sent seven. Alphington had one hundred and ninety-six adult males and sent eight. The Dunchideock jurors travelled down to Exeter more frequently during the 1660s than during the Interregnum. Taking the period 1649 to 1659 as a whole, four Dunchideock men sat on the jury sixteen times. For the decade 1660 to 1670 four men (one served on either side of the 1660 watershed) sat thirty-seven times. This pattern is writ large in the jury system. Between 1649 and 1659, one hundred and eleven different men sat on twenty-one juries, but between 1660 and 1670, seventy-six men were sworn to thirty-eight. Attendances were more likely to be multiple in the Restoration decade. The trial jury developed into a body led by an exclusive cadre within easy reach of the court officials and not subject to the vagaries of the hundredal bailiffs who summoned other jurors. This was the substantive contribution of the Restoration justices and their servants, the clerks of the court, to jury control.

The social position and wealth of the trial jurors lay below those of the grand jurymen. The petty jurors were not 'gentlemen' even by courtesy; the lists of their names were plain. Their comparative obscurity compounds the problem of source material. Only two trial jurors were royalist delinquents, and doubt attends even these identifications.[56] The 1662 and 1674 hearth tax returns have again been sampled. From a sample of fifty-two jurors an average of 3.1 hearths per individual is revealed; the average for the grand jurors was over five. Statistical sources soon peter out, but insight into the class of trial jurors may be derived from a brief study of the one or two who by the accidents of history are not entirely obscure. They are not necessarily typical nor is this an exercise in 'collective biography'. They appear here *faute de mieux*.

Peter Bartoe of Awliscombe was summoned once to the grand jury (in Epiphany 1665) but was spared probably because he was insufficiently wealthy to serve without challenge, and once to the trial jury (in Easter 1652). He was never constable of the hundred. Bartoe was an abrasive man, never far from the centre of parochial controversy. A neighbour, Peter Holway, gentleman, swore in the Consistory Court of the Bishop of Exeter that Bartoe was worth £60 per annum, and that he owned two tenements, one of which he let. In 1662 Bartoe was involved in a dispute over property rights in seats in Awliscombe church,[57] and the following year in the Epiphany quarter sessions it was made amply clear that events had escalated into a quarrel between Bartoe and the other prominent parishioners of Awliscombe. Peter Bartoe was overseer of the poor that year (he could aspire to parish, if not hundredal office) and contended that 'remiss officers' had abdicated their responsibility for 'order and good government'. He skilfully played on what he hoped would be magisterial horror at 'drunkennesse, fornication, unlicensed alehouses, masterlesse persons, nourishers of schysme, deceivers of the pore, unjust raters'—all rife in the parish, according to him. His indignation appeared to spring from the failure of his predecessors in office to clear their accounts and hand over rate-books: their only legacy to him 'was to grace him with a bastard' whom he had had to maintain. Bartoe's protestations apparently went unheeded by the Bench. Indeed, it seems that the rot which in Bartoe's view pervaded Awliscombe had crept within his own walls; in October 1667 John Willoughby of Payhembury examined Bartoe's son, John, for stealing a saddle.[58]

Bartoe was not the only juror whose family occasionally strayed into crime or moral turpitude. Hugh Bidwell of Newton St Cyres (petty juror four times between 1650 and 1652) found himself giving evidence in 1663 against his own brother, who lived in nearby Brampford Speke and who was accused of adultery. From the cross scrawled at the bottom of the deposition it may be judged that Hugh Bidwell was illiterate.[59] Bidwell was probably not the only petty juror to be so. Some petty jurors came from families once much more eminent. Thomas Suxbitch of Marsh Barton, Clyst St George, sworn four times between 1656 and 1666, came of a family prominent in the Middle Ages but by the fifteenth century already settling into oblivion. To Tristram Risdon, writing in the 1630s, they were a family 'never of any great eminency, yet worthy memory'. By Polwhele, a century later, they were judged more harshly as 'living almost in total obscurity within themselves, no better than a race of unpolished peasants'.[60]

In parish affairs, petty jurors were likely to be in the second rank of participants in office and discussion, behind the local gentry and the most prominent yeomen. Just as the appellation 'gent.' enhanced the prestige of grand jurors, so the conventions of jury service at the lower level reinforced wider social distinctions. Devon trial jurors, unlike their Cheshire counterparts, served on petty juries only. Of the one hundred and fifty-eight trial jurors whose names are known, only seventeen ever served on the grand jury and only ten on more than one occasion. Of these ten, only four served more often on the grand jury than on the petty jury and cases where service on both grand and petty juries was approximately equally balanced were invariably those where the total of services was low. Thus Peter Bartoe and William Westlake served once on each jury and Richard Smeardon of Ilsington served once on the grand jury and twice on the petty jury, as did William Seymour of Aylesbeare. Petty jury service offered no-one a means of social advancement. Most petty jurors were undoubtedly yeomen farmers or minor tradesmen. James Paddon of Ide, who served twice in 1665 and 1666 when in his late fifties, lived in a three-hearthed dwelling in the village where he had lived all his life and where he carried on the trade of a clothier. His neighbour, Charles Scutt, who served in 1670, kept an alehouse and was married to a woman of nonconformist sympathies.[61] Their 'middling sort' economic independence went unexploited in the structure of county government.

Trial juries were kept busy throughout sessions, returning verdicts on indicted prisoners. By far the greatest number of offences tried at sessions—nearly seventy per cent—were thefts. The other most frequent misdemeanours were forcible entry, assault and vagrancy. A small but significant group of offenders were those who in the 1640s denounced Parliament or drank healths to King Charles and in the 1660s (though one assumes they were different individuals) spoke against the Prayer Book or refused the Oath of Allegiance. The number of cases per sessions could be swollen by offences committed by a group of people; among the twenty-nine tried at Easter 1658 were fifteen charged with riot. The highest number at a single sessions between 1649 and 1670 was thirty-eight at Midsummer 1662 but eleven of these were traversed to a subsequent meeting. The lowest figures are more tentative since lists of offenders may be missing but totals of five and six were recorded at the sessions of Michaelmas 1649, Epiphany 1650, Easter 1651, Epiphany 1654, Michaelmas 1654, Epiphany 1663 and Midsummer 1669. The average was just over thirteen, and no differences can be discerned between the decades before and after 1660.[62]

Changes in the composition of the trial jury had little effect on the pattern of verdicts. It might be thought that juries under the control of the Bench would be more likely to bring in a high proportion of guilty verdicts than those where a substantial number of those sworn were new to the task before them. During the period 1649 to 1656 it was usual for up to five of the twelve trial jurors to be men who served once only; that is, those whose names are not found on jury lists surviving from 1646 to 1649 or on subsequent lists after their one service. Men serving once only might be thought less likely to be from a 'typical' social background or summoned in an evasion of the hundred bailiffs. There were two ways to control the trial jury; one was to maintain a large number of newcomers. In the summer of 1656 all twelve were new to the service. The other was more subtle and probably more generally acceptable. Between 1662 and 1670 the number of jurors serving once only never rose above two on any one occasion, and on sixteen of these juries there were no new men at all. Multiple attendances instead testified eloquently to a manipulation of the jury system which played on the tendencies within the summoning procedure towards stylisation and repetition. Bringing in new men to fill half the jury places was probably a consequence of stifling completely the initiative of bailiffs. In any case, the degree of initiative left to a trial jury was strictly limited, not only in the sense that it had to choose one of only two alternative verdicts. That, in itself, was latitude enough, since a verdict made an enormous difference to a defendant. But a case at trial jury was in the last stage of a procedure to pass through which implied, with each successive step, a greater degree of guilt. A defendant was originally bound by recognizance out of sessions, would have been examined, would have been the subject of a bill of indictment and a *billa vera* decision by the grand jury. In the court itself there was no studied attempt to maintain impartiality. Even in central courts, jurors interrupted testimonies and judges blatantly directed witnesses and juries.

Attempts in the House of Commons in 1667 to prevent Chief Justice Keling from fining jurors on the western circuit who brought in verdicts against his directions were celebrated because of the boldness of the commons' action not because Keling's practices were outrageous.[63] Most of the initiative in local courts lay with the presiding body, both in common law courts of quarter sessions and assizes and in ecclesiastical and Admiralty Courts where civil law procedure left no room for a jury system at all. Not surprisingly, then, the percentage of guilty verdicts at sessions bears no relation to the number of newcomers to the jury. In Midsummer 1656 when every one of the jurors was a stranger eighty-one percent of the verdicts were 'guilty', but in Michaelmas 1659 when there were no strangers, the percentage was even higher, at eighty-six percent. No correlation can be made between jury structure and the pattern of justice, although the percentage of guilty verdicts was higher during the 1650s than it was during the next decade.[64]

The Problem of Control

Control over representative institutions was of no small importance to a government concerned at once to establish a wider basis of support (implied in Cromwell's commitment to see the first Protectorate Parliament succeed), to obtain financial solvency and to meet squarely the problem of how to shift the very mores of the nation in a particular direction. The electoral body, like the jury system, lent itself, superficially at least, to outside influence and direction, and with a cadre of government supporters in the countryside the first of these aims, bringing a compliant Parliament to Westminster, may reasonably have been expected to succeed. It did not, however. The contingent from the county and the boroughs of Devon was, it is true, as sympathetic a body as any seventeenth century government could hope to obtain but the MPs were not wrung from their towns without opposition. The Tiverton election of 1654 was fought amid propaganda and subterfuge which followed the successful candidate, the lawyer, Robert Shapcote, even to London.

The government candidate at Tiverton, Major John Blackmore,[65] was opposed by Shapcote, whose commitment to Parliament even before 1648 had been doubted and who was one of the many secluded at Pride's Purge. Blackmore's supporters at Tiverton were led by Henry Fitzwilliam, the deputy clerk of the peace, on the grounds that Shapcote's allies were crypto-royalists with no record of fidelity to the governments since 1649. Blackmore's voters, by contrast, had 'most of us served the commonwealth in person, and all of us given testimony of our hearty affections to the same in all the late changes'. Shapcote himself was allegedly a gamer and an alehouse-haunter, whose cock-matches and bowls games drew 'many loose gentlemen together'. Depositions against Shapcote by Lewis Stucley and John Chishall, Independent ministers of Exeter and Tiverton respectively, made it clear that Presbyterian-

Independent rivalries complicated the contest.[66] Shapcote, the more obviously local candidate, who had represented Tiverton from 1646 to 1648, again secured his election, but while he was at Westminster a speech of violently anti-Protectorate sentiments was fraudulently attributed to him when published.[67] Representing the hundred-odd republicans who withdrew from the Parliament on 12 September 1654, the pamphlet accused Cromwell of ruling arbitrarily: 'If we must needs have a king againe, why not he whose undubitable right it is?'. (Although these views would not have found assent among the cautious Devonians the idea that serving the government was only to be tolerated as a means of serving the 'country' was voiced privately by a prominent trimmer, Thomas Reynell.[68]) It was Robert Shapcote himself who drew the attention of the House to the 'treasonable, false, scandalous and seditious' pamphlet, and his good affection to the government was demonstrated by his appointment as Solicitor-General in Ireland.[69] Nevertheless, one of Shapcote's supporters, Aquila Skinner, was dismissed by Disbrowe from the Tiverton corporation in March 1656 with four others who were considered 'scandalous in their lives or enemies to the Commonwealth'.[70] But by then the first Protectorate Parliament had irremediably soured; control over the electorate, the freeholders, the 'middling sort', had proved more consequential than many had realised—Cromwell's dissolution speech is a measure of his disappointment.

Control over juries was thus a natural preoccupation for those attempting to sway representative institutions into line with government policy and in 1655 at least, to obtain specific results from the specially-commissioned trial of the Penruddock rebels.[71] John Disbrowe's association with the south-west began in June 1649 when he re-organised the militia there. He was at quarter sessions in Devon in 1650 and was thus a natural choice as agent to a vengeful but nervous government anxious to nip the cankerous bloom of Penruddock's rising firmly in the bud. In the event, however, the rising was ended by the Wiltshire county troop led by Colonel Unton Crooke, who pursued the rebels as far as South Molton in North Devon, where the chase ended with little bloodshed at two in the morning of Thursday, 13 March 1655.[72] There was some discussion between John Thurloe and his local correspondents on the likely composition of the jury responsible for trying the one hundred and thirty-eight rebels confined at Exeter Castle. Disbrowe promised to work with Sheriff Coplestone to obtain a suitable jury and was optimistic (an unusual frame of mind for him) that as the rebels were not themselves Devonians they would not evoke particular sympathy in the surrounding area. On 11 April, Commissioner Hatsell at Plymouth wrote to Colonel John Clerke, with heavy irony, that the rebels could expect 'a good deliverance by a Devonshire jury'.[73] In any case, the government chose to minimise the chances of hostile collusion by trying the case by commission of oyer and terminer, making good use of the Tudor statute empowering the trial of treason cases in the counties by specially-picked commissioners sitting with a jury.[74] The advantages of oyer and terminer were partly that its *ad hoc* composition reduced delay between apprehension of malefactors and their trial (although in this case the trials coincided with the spring assizes) and partly that its members, local magistrates, were more likely to swear in a jury sympathetic to their ends than were the assize judges, who were supposed to be above local influences. Hatsell realised that although some prisoners were merely 'old grooms and serving-men', 'the longer they lie the more pity will be got towards them' and promised to send up jurors to Exeter from Plymouth. Sheriff John Coplestone assured Disbrowe that he would do his 'utmost to get fit jurymen'. At the same time directions to the justices on security matters were issued and the militia commissions were despatched, in a mood which became formalised in the August commissions and October instructions to the major-generals.[75]

Oyer and terminer dispensed with the need for a grand jury; the indictment for treason was assumed *billa vera* and could proceed to trial by petty jury. As with normal assize procedure the trials were held separately in the several counties of the west; the ringleaders remained at Exeter. Their trial was conducted on 18 April, a month after their arrest, and Penruddock did as much as he could to disrupt the arrangements of the government by challenging twenty-two jurors—without cause, in Henry Hatsell's view. His rather disingenuous claim was belied by the desperate Penruddock who alleged, doubtless with justification, that 'the jurors were so pact that had I known them the issue would have been the same as it was ... one of the jury being asked by a gent. why he found me guilty, answered he was resolved to hang me before he did see me'.[76] The government could not afford to relax its grip on affairs and although the outcome may have seemed inevitable to Penruddock his own last letter to his wife implies that there was sympathy for him, somewhere at least: 'If I should forget this City of Exeter for their civilities to my own self in particular and indeed to all of us I should leave a reproach behind me'. Perhaps, however, this is death-cell magnanimity in an age when, as Ivan Roots reminds us, men 'knew how to die'; in the same letter Penruddock thanked John Coplestone who had done as much as anyone to bring him to the scaffold.[77]

The commissions to the major-generals were thus a temporary abandonment of the aim of widening support in favour of achieving solvency and righteousness not by electoral consent but by personal persuasion or even coercion. Yet democratic forms could not be wished away (not the Protector's wish, in any case) and the problem of control remained as a thread running through the 1650s. It is the corollary of the problem of consent. Control over elections would be tackled vigorously in the campaigns for the second Protectorate Parliament. Control over juries was an aspect of the major-generals' brief, appearing first in the Penruddock trials. The difference between these two aims was that control over elections was always liable to encroach upon the limited politics of the urban oligarchies, not always conducted with an eye to issues wider than the specifically municipal, whereas the views of the government on the administration of the jury system accorded with those of those who wielded real power in the shires, the JPs, whose powers had steadily increased at the expense of the sheriffs (except during the 1630s) since at least 1600. Review of the freeholders' books was normally undertaken by sheriffs and justices jointly and the Commonwealth Bench was enthusiastic in its scrutiny. Between Epiphany 1650 and Michaelmas 1652 the magistrates discharged ten men from future jury service, in all cases but one because of old age; the jurors were over sixty years old. Roger Fowler of East Budleigh was discharged because he was 'both a physitian and a chirugeon'. The decision to discharge was taken by the justices alone; the sheriff was 'to take notice' of the exemptions. The magistrates displayed a keen interest in the quality of jurors but by the time that Cromwell was installed as Protector they had realised that weeding out the unsuitable in court could not shore up the weakness in the jury system itself. An interest in jury reform had been evident in the deliberations of radical lawyers in the Rump and in the Nominated Assembly; in the latter it was proposed that in order to prevent multiple attendances county registers of freeholders should be compiled.

At the Epiphany quarter sessions 1655 the Devon Bench made plain its intention to alter the procedure by which juries were summoned:

> It is ordered and this court doth desire that the sheriff ... for the future doe from henceforth forbeare to summon or retorne any person to appeare at the assizes and sessions for the service of his highness ... except it be for once in the yeare and that no bayliffe of any hundred ... doe from henceforth make retorne of any person to attend the service aforesaid untill he hath showed the same unto the next justice of peace and by him approved and his hand thereunto.[78]

They were attempting justiciary control over the composition of all juries, grand and petty, at assizes and quarter sessions. The following sessions proceeded without any notable change in the names of the jurors or any reference in the order books to the working of the jury, yet an unofficial meeting was held by fourteen justices, only six of whom attended sessions officially that month, when the sole subject under scrutiny was the jury.[79] Seven of those present, however, had recently come down from Westminster as members of the recently-dissolved Parliament, and all were committed to the Protectorate.[80] The meeting may have been prompted by a determination to eliminate as much dissidence in the county as possible, to achieve control so that the next parliament should not be addled for the same reasons as the last. Determination was certainly the key-note of the remarkably specific resolutions. At the next assizes the jurors for civil trials should be drawn from lists of at least one hundred and thirty-six names (four from each hundred) to be returned to court by the magistrates.[81] Grand jurors were to be selected from the ten summoned from each of the three grand divisions of the county and for the sessions grand juries, eight were to come from each such division. Jury service was to become the duty of a reduced body of freeholders chosen and closely supervised by the JPs rather than by the sheriff. That the resolutions were propounded with national events in mind is strongly suggested by the concluding desideratum: the magistrates should 'be verry wary in retourning anie to serve in juries who have ayded the late kinge etc., and continue their affections unto that interest'.[82] This was not the 'healing and settling' which Cromwell had expounded as the 'great end' of the first Protectorate Parliament but was more akin to the 'cantonization' and 'decimation' which were to follow.

During the summer of 1655 Disbrowe was preoccupied with the settling of the new militia in the west and the principal matter arising in his correspondence with Thurloe was the perennial one of arrears of pay for the soldiery. Jury administration proceeded as it had done, with no perceptible alteration in the pattern of summoning. The matter was not dropped, however, and it was of sufficient importance to the Protector for him to write personally to Disbrowe on 29 January 1656, entirely on the question of jury control.[83] The letter was to be forwarded to Sheriff John Coplestone. That it was written, as the Protector confessed, as a response to his having been 'much pressed' to instigate jury reform and that it appeared at the end of a year of concern among the government's friends in Devon at inadequate control suggest that Oliver was responding to pressure from within the county. His opening sentence made it clear where he thought the problem lay: 'the law and justice hath been much lyable to bee perverted by the waye that is generally held by deputy sheriffs in the choice of juries.' This criticism was levelled at those charged with the permanent administration of the system; their professionalism was placing them beyond the control of JPs. Cromwell endorsed the proposals of the latter:

If ... the justices of the peace, especially such of them as are best spiritted for the worke, name some of the freeholders of clearest integritte and prudence of honest and blameless conversation which for their number maie be proportioned to the businesse of the countye to which they related to serve uppon juries for the yeare next ensuing both between party and party and in cases cryminall and offer the names so agreed uppon to the sheriffe and undersheriffe of the countye; I doubt not butt that they would bee found willing to receive kindly such an assistance.[84]

These were the previous year's specific proposals in general terms. Cromwell alleged that such a system was working elsewhcrc and that as things stood the names of the jurors who would serve were known before trials, since names were delivered by the undersheriff to the clerk of assize. The results were bribery, 'the ensnaring of the weaker and the tempting the avaryce of the more subtill wholie in wayte for their owne advantage'. The Protector ended by requiring Disbrowe to root out bribery in the counties under his control.

Justice Christopher Savery, among whose family papers Cromwell's letter came to rest, had been at the Exeter meeting in the previous year. There is more evidence that he was particularly interested in the jury system and that he diligently observed the directions which the Protector had given. Among the Savery papers were lists of 'the names of such persons as were presented by the gentlemen and the chieffe inhabitants of the severall parishes within the hundreds of Coleridge and Stanborough' (in the South Hams: the Dartmouth-Kingsbridge coast and its hinterland).[85] These lists, compiled by Christopher Savery, John Beare, William Bastard and John Hale on a specific day in May exactly a fortnight before the opening of the Devon assizes, named two hundred and eighty-five men from thirty-four parishes. Although the lists were intended only as a reserve from which jurors could be drawn, the names of only thirty-three can be found among the surviving jury lists—that is, an average of roughly one for each parish. The lists were compiled in descending order of status (esquires, then gentlemen and yeomen) and although there are no assize jury panels extant, it is possible to compare the ranking in the lists with status designations given for quarter sessions juries where all members were *ex officio* 'gentlemen'. Of those who served on the jury at Exeter from the South Hams seventeen were gentlemen and twenty-one were yeomen. No esquires were sworn, even though there were seventeen on Savery's list. If these figures are divided into groups of those who served from 1649 to 1660 and those who did so from 1661 to 1670 (and the names of those who served across the 1660 division are included twice) it is seen that the balance of jury composition shifted in favour of more yeomen and less gentry participation after 1660. There were nine yeomen and eleven gentlemen in the earlier decade, twelve yeomen and six gentlemen in the later one. Statistically negligible though these numbers are, the trend supports complaints circulating since at least the 1620s that the quality of jurors was declining in Devon.[86]

No other hundredal listings have come to light. Yet the compiling of lists, so typical of seventeenth-century reform drives,[87] was no guarantee that changes in the jury system would actually occur. Disbrowe, in Plymouth on 4 February 1656, at the end of a trying tour of the south-west, wrote pessimistically to Thurloe:

> I have ... received command relateing to the sheriffs, justices and juries, and shall do my utmost in it; though when I have don all I fear it will be to little purpose. I shall respit my reasons untill I come in person, however nothing shall be wanting in me to obtain a reformation therein.[88]

Disbrowe's 'reasons', beyond his natural tendency to pessimism, remain obscure, but the success of the venture may be judged on the evidence in the quarter sessions file. Until Midsummer 1656 there is nothing to suggest that the jury system had been moved from its wonted course. But in that summer, at a time when the vigorous campaign by the major-generals to secure reliable returns to the second Protectorate Parliament was under way, the trial jury displayed some unusual features. The twelve men had apparently never served before and were not to do so again in the period up to 1670. Moreover they came not from the hundreds nearest Exeter but from a wider area.[89] The usual freeholders' lists, compiled by undersheriff and bailiffs and returned with the *venire facias* were replaced by a shorter list of seventeen from whom the twelve were sworn. They tried twenty-one cases (the highest number since 1649) of which seventeen were convictions. For the grand jury more continuity was retained but seventeen out of the twenty-five were new men. Ten of the seventeen sworn were new.[90] The wide geographical origins of jurors and influences outside the court made it impossible to control jury composition completely.

Jury control was a realistic aim when central government, the shrievalty and the Bench of magistrates were agreed on common ends. The sessions of Michaelmas 1656 showed, however, how short-lived the attempt had been. To a grand jury list of twenty-six names the sheriff or the deputy added: 'These above named were returned the last sessions by the justices but noe others except three by the justices being returned the sheriffe alsoe returned these following soe as the service may not be neglected',[91] and inserted twenty-one more names. The sheriff, who relied heavily on professional, permanent (if half-time) subordinates, had doubtless drawn on this assistance to produce these. Cromwell had feared the consequences of too much initiative among subordinate local officials, a fear conveyed by magistrates who detected a threat to their own power. 1656 was a year of common agreement on the aims of government, agreement which assured the jury reformers of some success.

The Restoration brought with it no moderation in the JPs' pretensions to complete administrative control; in the unique period of Cavalier euphoria immediately after 1660 they were as committed to the policies of central government as those in power in the mid-1650s had been. Not the undersheriffs but the bailiffs bore the brunt of their vigour on that occasion. In Michaelmas 1661 the following order was agreed:

> Forasmuch as complaint is made unto this court that the bayliffes of the severall hundreds in this county doe somon very many persons to appeare and serve as freeholders at the generall sessions but for their owne private gaine in taking rewards make retourne of very few ... it is therefore ordered that all bayliffes ... doe procure the next justice of peaces hand to their retournes and somon such persons onely as the said justices shall thinke fitt and allowe under his hand to serve as aforesaid.[92]

This was a modified version of what had been tried in 1656; not the comprehensive listing of jurors but only their approval was now the self-assigned task of the JPs. For the next few sessions the freeholders' lists were endorsed with their signatures as an indication of their approval, but they could not keep up this procedure. Moreover, the annotations were vigorously struck out by the court officials in what was presumably an expression of disapproval of the encroachment on their tasks. Attacks on bailiffs were an unchanging feature of seventeenth century quarter sessions. These obscure officials, appointed by private patronage not through the collective consent of the court, offered a standing affront to the power of the JPs and were fined at each sessions for neglect or absence. Since there was never an occasion when a jury could not be sworn, one may wonder what prompted their concern; one is drawn to conclude that control itself was the issue at stake rather than administrative efficiency as such.

In September 1664 the justices again assayed the elusive summit of total control:

> The justices of the peace in this county in their severall subdivisions are desired ... to make inquirie of all freeholders within their severall subdivisions and to bringe in a list att the next sessions of all who are fitt to serve in the grand jury and the petty jury at the sessions to the end that the many complaints made against the bayliffes of hundreds and otherwise for insufficient and improper retournes may be prevented and avoyded.[93]

Again listing seemed to offer the reality of control but not even the Act 'for the returning of able and sufficient jurors', which passed the Lords on 2 March, 1665, achieved much success. The preamble spoke of 'the reformation of abuses in sheriffs and other ministers who for reward doe oftentimes spare the ablest and sufficientest and returne the poor and simpler freeholders less able to descerne the causes in question and to beare the charges of appearance and attendance thereon'. The statute replaced the hopelessly unrealistic forty-shilling freehold qualification with one of an annual income of £20, and made inadequate wealth of jurors a 'good cause of challenge'. Penalties were imposed on negligent sheriffs and corrupt bailiffs and at the next Easter quarter sessions the JPs were empowered to review the freeholders' lists. The only evidence that the act was observed in Devon is the higher than average number of new men sworn to the quarter sessions grand jury during 1665 and 1666. There were no purges and no general orders arising from the statute, however, and from 1667 the pattern of recruitment resumed its wonted course. The act produced the merest hiccup in the procedure of jury summoning.[94] This was perhaps because the intentions of the statute and the aspirations of Devon JPs were not in harmony. Despite its directions for registration the act regarded the justices as the temporary agents of reform, an inspectorate whose task was to be completed within the space of one sessions, whereas since the mid-1650s the magistrates had been trying to oust the shrievalty from its control over juries. The architects of the statute had no plans to weaken the powers of the sheriff who, after all, was a more closely accountable officer of the Crown than ever the justices were.

Other Juries

For the Devon assize grand jury nothing substantial can be added to the thorough survey of all the assize circuits made by J.S. Cockburn.[95] His account of juries as 'conservative' and 'preoccupied with the familiar and predominantly uncontroversial details of county administration'[96] accords with our knowledge of quarter session juries. But what emerges from a number of sources is that sheriffs were eager to enhance the prestige of the jury by empanelling as many of the county jury as possible by personal persuasion rather than by the peremptory demands of the bailiffs. There had been criticisms that the quality of jurors had perceptibly declined. Robert Oland was the father of a constable and grand juror. In 1625 he wrote to the Duke of Buckingham, an unlikely man to appear in the guise of local government reformer:

> At our assizes [in times] passed our grand jury have been esquires and gentlemen of quality and the best farmers and yeomen to serve at sessions and none but freeholders in both; but now the case is altered. If there be three or four gents., at the assizes the rest are yeomen. Gentlemen count themselves too high for that service and farmers [being] the best yeomen of £100 a year, think it too base to attend at sessions, for they say a clerk of the peace will record their appearance for five shillings yearly.'[97]

In 1634 John Bampfield of Poltimore, sheriff for that year, wrote to Christopher Savery a letter characterised by cajolement, flattery and lofty exhortation so typical of jury charges. The next assize grand inquest should be 'culled out of the most antient and active gentrie' whose appearance would be an 'honour and ornament' to the county, a 'terrour to vice' and a 'favour ... to vertue'. Savery's absence from assizes, if unavoidable, should be justified in 'a speedie answeare and gentle interpretation'.[98] A similar tone was adopted by John Blackmore, sheriff 1659, when he wrote to the once-sequestered alleged delinquent, John Willoughby. After some pleasantries Blackmore comes to the point:

> But not to make the porch larger than the house my request in short is that you would not only honour mee with your good company the next assizes but by your presence putt a lustre upon the representative body of the county.[99]

There seems little doubt, however, that despite these sorts of personal blandishments the numbers of jurors required for the service and the onerous duties of the sheriff in sessions week made this personal approach impracticable as a routine. More typical were the letters of undersheriff Thomas Northmore to sheriff Richard Coffin in 1685; he assured him that he would 'take care for the grand jury', having received instructions from the judges to impanel the 'better sort'.[100]

We know the names of few Devon assize jurors. All that has survived is a list in a civil minute book for the western circuit from 1656. Its information can confidently only be applied to the *nisi prius* side of assize business.[101] It is a list of 129 names, many of them to be found on lists for quarter sessions grand and petty juries, many otherwise unknown. It seems likely that here was material for the assize petty jury to hear civil cases. Some names have opposite them 'attended all week'. None were from the social *milieu* of the JPs. The list appears in the minute book when Cromwell's directive was being enforced; the 129 names may be part of the comprehensive listing scheme.

The sheriff could influence the deliberations of grand jurors by appealing to baser appetites. John Morrill has described the convivial entertainment enjoyed by the Cheshire grand jury,[102] and this provision was always the responsibility of the sheriff. J.S. Cockburn has shown how, in some areas, the generosity of sheriffs caused concern to seventeenth century governments but fails to square this with the evidence to suggest that the office of sheriff was dreaded by likely incumbents because of the expense it entailed.[103] After the Restoration, Cockburn shows, many espoused the spirit of economy, though in view of this marked reluctance to assume the office, it seems unlikely that the legislation of 14 Car. II c. 21 went against the disposition of the sheriffs. John Willoughby was sheriff in 1664. His accounts include the expense of six pounds for entertaining the grand jury at each assizes, with an additional expense of eleven pounds at each meeting for 'fiddlers that played at the ordinary'.[104] In Buckinghamshire in 1680 articles had been drawn up by JPs to recommend that no more than three shillings for meat and drink per person should be spent. The maximum number in the grand jury was twenty-three so that by their reckoning assize entertainment should not have exceeded three pounds ten shillings. Willoughby's outlay greatly exceeded this frugal allocation.[105] The Devon assize grand jury was not the illustrious body it may once have been but those who served did not go unrewarded.

Finally, it may be useful to examine briefly some juries in a nearby county and in corporate towns within Devon. In Wiltshire, Barnstaple and Dartmouth the institutions of government and their participants had not been physically estranged. The Wiltshire quarter sessions were held in sequence at Salisbury, Devizes, Warminster and Marlborough. In a county where local government was not centralised, presentments flourished. Hundred presentments were made by jurors from only the hundreds nearest the seat of sessions but these juries comprised fourteen to sixteen juries each, in contrast to vestigial performance in Devon. Presentments in mid-seventeenth century Wiltshire dealt with much the same issues that vexed Devon jurymen; minor infringements of regulations and neglect of public duties were prominent.

There was a varying degree of collusion between constables and jurors. Although by the end of the 1660s the Devon grand jury was largely subordinate to the hundred constables, in Wiltshire juries frequently adopted an independent stance and presented matters not mentioned by constables. Sometimes they were prepared merely to endorse constabulary presentments. What is certain is that the jury, despite independence in presenting, was much under the control of the magistrates. Presentments, particularly those of the hundreds, were made in response to a series of 'articles', probably based on the Book of Orders of 1631, just as hundredal constables in Devon had submitted returns to the Privy Council before the civil war. The Wiltshire articles persisted through the civil war and Interregnum into the 1660s.[106] Control of the jury, and of the presenting function, were both made easier by a peripatetic sessions which made contact between the sessions court and the parishes reliable and regular.

It was not only in county government and the higher courts that the jury system flourished. It was the basis of manorial courts from the local leet to the hundredal court,[107] but nowhere was the presenting function more vigorously sustained than in the mercantile towns.

During the seventeenth century Barnstaple had been eclipsed as an economic centre by the new draperies and the development of the East Devon cloth trade. Even its role as a landing place for Irish wool imports was undermined by the physical difficulties imposed on the mercantile community by the silting up of the River Taw. It proved impossible to dredge, and the port of Bideford grew at Barnstaple's expense.[108] In its politics, Barnstaple was suspicious both of county government and of the central authority. Its own economic welfare came before wider issues. In 1647 the military governor of the town was a local man who supported municipal interests against the county committee. During the 1650s the principal agent of the government in the town was the merchant, Lionel Beecher, who by 1657 was sorely repenting his commitment to the Protectorate and the decline, as a consequence, of his business.[109] Religion divided the town from the county. The minister, Martin Blake, supported by townsmen like Richard Harris, was hounded by county committeemen and the local military establishment throughout the 1650s. As a moderate Anglican Blake was to be removed from his living although it was much to the discomfiture of John Coplestone and the Plymouth Presbyterian merchants Timothy Alsop and Philip Francis that the Puritan lecturer at Barnstaple, Jonathan Hanmer, as a personal friend of Blake's. Coplestone was appointed recorder of the town in February 1656 and his campaign against Blake culminated in his arrest and despatch to the Scilly Isles. Blake had retained influential supporters, however, including Edmund Prideaux and Sir Hardress Waller.[110]

Barnstaple could not be relied upon, therefore, by Interregnum governments, but the restored monarchy was no more popular there. From the first moves to re-establish the local militia the town opposed what it took to be the attempt, by the Duke of Albemarle, to overturn local customs by Privy Council *diktat*. By February 1662 the government faced a strike by Barnstaple ratepayers who resented the introduction of military rates without reference to the aldermanic body.[111] As in the 1650s local privileges and interests were defended fiercely against encroachment or intrusion. Did the jury structure of the town contribute to this spirit of truculent independence?

At Barnstaple the court leet and the local sessions or aldermanic court had been amalgamated into one court dealing principally with minor civil cases, and criminal matters involving property rights, including trespass. Jury lists have survived from the 1670s, and show that presentments were regular and lengthy. At a meeting of the 'general sessions of the peace and court leet held before the mayor, deputy recorder, aldermen and steward' on 12 October 1674, no fewer than forty-five separate presentments were offered by the grand jury.[112] An alehousekeeper, 'althou bound yet very unfitt', six unlicensed alehousekeepers, an idle beadle and a man whose swine 'run the street' were reported but most cases were of broken pavements, noisome dunghills and weaknesses in the masonry and equipment of the quay. Dilapidated 'penthouses' (outhouses) were a matter of great concern to the Barnstaple jurors and their prominence indicates the operation of elementary planning laws or the internal regulation of economic interests. Merchants and tradesmen who developed their property were carefully scrutinized. The quay was naturally an area of interest and was keenly watched. In August 1674 three 'penthouses', two access roads and a pavement there were presented. The quay itself near 'The Crane' inn needed attention.[113] From the late 1670s presentments for absenteeism from church began to appear, possibly to reflect concern at the popish plot and the Exclusion crisis, but otherwise presentments were of internal regulative matters only. Those presented for their neglect or deliberate infringements of local standards were punished by an established scale of fines. In the county penalties were determined by the discretion of the magistrates. A broken pavement attracted a fine of three shillings, a 'broken penthouse' five shillings and all other offences six shillings and eightpence, except allowing a house to be in dangerous disrepair which carried a penalty of ten shillings.[114] Compare these with three shillings and fourpence for illegal drinking, five shillings for drunkenness and twenty shillings for running an unlawful alehouse—penalties determined in early Stuart statutes—and it becomes apparent that the Barnstaple court took regulative presentments seriously. Their effect was to reinforce the introspective tendencies in Barnstaple's government: to focus popular participation on issues crucial to the economic life of the town, which in the mid-seventeenth century must have caused concern in most propertied residents.[115]

At first glance, Dartmouth had much in common with Barnstaple. Both were seaports, both were parliamentary boroughs with a freeman franchise,[116] and both had flourishing local courts. Apparent similarities concealed many differences. In Dartmouth, quarter sessions and the court leet remained separate, even if their civil and criminal functions overlapped. Dartmouth was a primary port for the new draperies exports and had adapted to economic necessity. Dartmouth, unlike Barnstaple, had seen much military action during the civil war, and was dominated in the 1650s by men like Thomas Boone, one of the few Devon survivors of Pride's Purge. Although Major John Blackmore advised the demolition of Dartmouth Castle in May 1650, his fears sprang from the possibility of a sea invasion by Irish rebels or exiled royalists not from any imagined designs by the local populace.[117] Barnstaple and Dartmouth were 'Puritan' in their government but Dartmouth was not introspective. Merchants and mayors there like John Budley and William Barnes became county assessment commissioners and Barnes presided at the customs office.[118] The town was open to benign intervention and goodwill was offered by outside authorities. When Christopher Savery and Edmund Fowell arbitrated in a tithes dispute there they made it clear that they had acceded to 'all your demandes which wee seldome or never do to any'.[119] John Disbrowe settled amicably a dispute there over the living of Townstall in 1656, between the Independent minister, John Flavell, and the Presbyterian, Allen Geare; he intervened after the normal procedure of popular election had failed.[120]

After 1660 goodwill soured. Dartmouth considered itself betrayed by the Privy Council which was alleged to have favoured Merchant

Adventurers' trade monopolies.[121] In the 1667 by-election at Dartmouth the candidate of the Earl of Arlington and of the local patron, Sir Thomas Clifford, Joseph Williamson, was defeated by a late entry into the competition by Sir Walter Young of Colyton, backed by Sir William Morrice. A third candidate, Sir John Colleton of Exeter, an excise farmer, was supported by the Duke of Albemarle and several local magistrates. B·it the corporation was 'fickle' and Colleton's involvement with the Canary Company proved decisive in his defeat.[122] Dartmouth politics were thus conducted with an eye to wider issues than those of the North Devon towns but was political consciousness confined to the merchants who dominated government there?

Jury presentments at sessions and leet contain many items of exactly the same content as those made in Barnstaple. Neglected roads, pigs in the streets, dunghills in public places, walls in imminent danger of collapse: these are plentiful. But a striking difference was the readiness of jurors to attack prominent individuals and the Chamber itself for their shortcomings not only with regard to local matters of concern to tradesmen and propertyholders but also in their enforcement of statutes and proclamations. In July 1660 the Presbyterian minister, James Burdwood, who enjoyed the support of Thomas Boone, was presented 'for riding on Whitsunday last'. (He was asked for his reasons and then excused by the court.) Four cases of 'opening windows' and working contrary to a Proclamation were also presented. The churchwardens were criticized for not erecting the king's arms in the church, the receiver was censured for not repairing the north conduit and the Chamber was accused of granting 'foreign' shopkeepers the same privileges as freemen.[123] No-one was exempt from criticism, however eminent; Thomas Boone, Captain John Pley and Mr William Spurway were censured for minor neglects of pavements and property.[124] But this was October 1660 and the temerity of the court leet in pursuing these affairs may have owed not a little to Restoration politics; all three had been notable Common-wealthsmen. The presentments may simply reflect the royalist euphoria so prevalent in 1660. To the fore of the 1660 presentment, too, is concern for the observance of the Sabbath, church attendance and the maintenance of the church fabric. Even as late as July 1662 the neglects of the town scavengers were presented with 'the towne for not haveing the commandments in the church of St Saviours'.[125] Unfortunately the series of Dartmouth presentments is brief and fragmentary and perhaps the years 1660 to 1662 were not typical ones in the consciousness of the jury, but if the series is compared with that for the county in the same period, the Dartmouth jury seems much more abrasive. In both Barnstaple and Dartmouth the jurors were minor freeholders whose names mean nothing to the student of government in the county but they were prepared to speak independently, in Barnstaple against those who failed in their obligations to the community and in Dartmouth against those who transgressed against government edict and the prevailing religious code. In both cases the jury harmonised with the impression offered by the townsmen to the world outside and in neither instance was the jury in any way moribund. In both cases the tyranny of geography held no sway. The withering of the jury system doubtless began before the 1640s and continued into the eighteenth century. Devonians spoke of the deteriorating quality of jurors in the 1620s and the parochial flavour of presentments at quarter sessions was a chronic condition of the jury, not a sudden attack of 'depoliticization'. The key to the history of the jury in the early modern period lies probably in the sixteenth century. Marian legislation established pre-trial examination by JPs and whether this was a borrowing from continental practice or a development from medieval English precedent it ratified the expanding power of magistrates. The statutes led also to that 'specialization of function' which distinguished felony from misdemeanour by reserving the former to the attention of assizes; but JPs now possessed formidable powers of examining and initiating prosecutions, which developed through the seventeenth century to help destroy the reputations of the 'Squire Westerns' in the eighteenth.[126] As magisterial initiative increased, that of juries atrophied. Even Marian juries were no longer self-informing, and were dependent on other bodies for their information. The recent work on jury charges has tended to take at face value the oratory of men like William Lambarde; unless corresponding charges and presentments can be compared there is no reason to assume that the description of the 'eyes of magistracy' was realistic. The sub-structure of local government was a source of strength in periods of political instability, but changes in these institutions occurred so slowly as to make a twenty-year period for study too limited to notice real shifts in practice and participation. It has yet to be proved that the Devon quarter sessions grand jury was ever other than a pooling of parochial problems.

NOTES

1. S. and B. Webb: *English Local Government from the Restoration to the Municipal Corporation Act: The Parish and the County* (1906), p. 458; H.C. Johnson (ed.): *Wiltshire County Records: Minutes of Proceedings in Sessions 1563, 1574 to 1592* (1949); D.H. Allen (ed.): *Essex Quarter Sessions Order Book 1652-1661* (1974).
2. Conyers Read: *William Lambarde and Local Government* (1962), p. 69; J.S. Cockburn: *A History of English Assizes, 1558-1714* (1972), p. 113; J.S. Morrill: *The Cheshire Grand Jury* (1976), pp. 33-39, 45.
3. R. Cust, P.G. Lake: 'Sir Richard Grosvenor and the Rhetoric of Magistracy', *Bulletin of the Institute of Historical Research* liv no. 130 (May 1981), pp. 44-49; Conrad Russell: *Parliaments and English Politics 1621-29* (Oxford, 1979) p. 431; *Sergeant Thorpe ... his charge to the grand-jury at York Assizes* (1649).
4. Donald Veall: *The Popular Movement For Law Reform 1640-1660* (Oxford 1970); G.B. Nourse: 'Law Reform under the Commonwealth and Protectorate', *Law Quarterly Review* lxxv (1959) pp. 512-29; Russell, *op. cit.* pp. 90-91, and sources there cited.
5. DRO QS Boxes 57-75, bundles 1649-70.
6. As in Essex, Kent and Wiltshire but not Cheshire: Joel Samaha: *Law and Order in Historical Perspective: The Case of Elizabethan Essex* (1974), p. 48; Allen (ed.): *Quarter*

Sessions Order Book, introduction; William Lambarde: *Eirenarcha* (1582), p. 306; Johnson (ed.): *Wiltshire County Records*, p. xxii; Morrill: *Cheshire Grand Jury*, pp. 41-43.

7. The description of procedure at quarter sessions has been kept to a minimum; many accounts are available from other counties and may be applied *mutatis mutandis* to Devon. See the sources in notes 1 and 4, also Michael Dalton: *The Office and Authority of Sheriffs* (1628), pp. 197-203, R.H. Silcock: County Government in Worcestershire 1603-1660' (London PhD, 1974), pp. 179-89.

8. Lambarde *op. cit.*, pp. 291-92.

9. Random example from QS bundles. The writs were in Latin until November 1650, and again after 1660.

10. Dalton *op. cit.*, 197-200.

11. That these are not in themselves exhaustive lists of freeholders is plain from the limited number of names they contain, that they are not grand or petty jury lists is evident from a comparison with other lists of jurors actually sworn and that they are not hundred jury lists is suggested by internal divisions into 'hundreders' and 'grand jurymen' sections.

12. Lambarde *op. cit.*, p. 308; Dalton *op. cit.*, p. 200; *The Complete Justice* (1638), pp. 119-20; Morrill: *Cheshire Grand Jury*, p. 11.

13. QS Box 70, Epiphany 1665 (misplaced presentment of 1 October 1661); Box 72 loose presentments of 4 October 1664, 16 April 1667. William Lambarde: *Eirenarcha: or of the Office of the Justice of the Peace* (1582), pp. 383-84; Conyers Read: *William Lambarde and Local Government* (New York 1962) pp. 72-73.

14. QS Box 68 loose presentment 12 January 1663; Box 67 bundle Easter 1662; Box 72 loose presentment 16 April 1667; Box 73 loose presentment 14 July 1668; Box 64 bundle Easter 1660; Devon QS Order Book (hereafter DQSOB) Epiphany 1649.

15. Absenteeism from church was no longer an offence from 1650: C.H. Firth, R.S. Rait (eds.): *Acts and Ordinances of the Interregnum* (3 vols. 1911) II. pp. 423-25.

16. QS Box 68 loose presentment 12 January 1663; Epiphany 1664; Box 70 bundle Epiphany 1665 (misplaced from Michaelmas 1661); Easter 1665 (misplaced from Midsummer 1662); Box 71 loose presentment Midsummer 1666; Box 72 loose presentments; Box 73, loose.

17. QS Box 70 bundle Epiphany 1665 (misplaced presentment from Michaelmas 1661).

18. R.S. Bosher: *The Making of the Restoration Settlement* (London, 1951), pp. 163-164; I.M. Green: *The Re-establishment of the Church of England 1660–1663* (Oxford, 1978), pp. 42-43; E.A.O. Whiteman: 'The Re-establishment of the Church of England 1660-1663', *Transactions of the Royal Historical Society*, 5th series, v (1955), pp. 113-115.

19. QS Box 70 bundle Easter 1665 (misplaced presentment of Midsummer 1662); I.M. Green *op. cit.*, pp. 143-47, Chapter 7 *passim*; A.G. Matthews: *Calamy Revised* (Oxford 1934) pp. 20, 241.

20. Morrill: *Cheshire Grand Jury* pp. 33-39.

21. QS Box 68 loose presentment of Epiphany 1663; Box 67 bundle Easter 1662; misplaced presentment of April 1659; Box 70 loose presentments; bundle Epiphany 1665, misplaced from Michaelmas 1661.

22. QS Box 67 bundle Easter 1662 (misplaced presentment 12 April 1659); Box 68 loose presentment 12 January 1663. For the public/private ambivalence pervading government see G.E. Aylmer: *The King's Servants* (London 1961) pp. 338-9.

23. Endorsements on the bills of indictments, lists of indictees in QS sessions bundles. The grand jury frequently rejected up to two-thirds of the indictments; the trial jury found 66.75 per cent of defendants guilty during the 1650s and 57.7 per cent guilty during the 1660s.

For the difficulties of assessing the evidence for judicial procedure, J.S. Cockburn: 'Early Modern Assize Records as Historical Evidence', *Journal of the Society of Archivists* V, (1975), pp. 215-31; *idem, A History of English Assizes 1558-1714* (Cambridge, 1972) p. 114; J.H. Baker: 'Criminal Courts and Procedure at Common Law 1550-1800' in J.S. Cockburn (ed.): *Crime in England 1550-1800* (London, 1977) p. 19.

Multiple attendance was more common among the trial jury. 76.58 per cent served once or twice, 12.6 per cent served ten times or more, and the most frequent attenders lived in the Exeter area, suggesting a closer degree of control by the court.

24. Edward Hyde, Earl of Clarendon: *The Life of Edward Hyde, Earl of Clarendon, being a Continuation of the History of the Great Rebellion from the Restoration to his banishment in 1667* (Oxford, 1759) pp. 42-43; PRO C 220/9/4 (1660-62), British Library (hereafter BL) Egerton 2557 and Add. 36781 f. 42 (1661) are commissions of the peace, the earliest evidence for Devon changes in the 1660s. The last two are not included in the list given by T.G. Barnes and A.H. Smith in *Bulletin of the Institute of Historical Research* XXXII (1959) pp. 221-42. In 1649, fifteen out of seventy justices were removed from the Devon Bench; in 1660, twenty-three out of fifty-four disappeared (in the first case 21 per cent, in the second 42 per cent.)

25. *English Local Government: The Parish and the County*, p. 449.

26. QS Box 72 bundle Easter 1667, misplaced presentment 19/4/64.

27. At the extremes, 3 men served 10 times, 2 men served on 11, 12 and 13 juries each, one man served fifteen times and another eighteen times.

28. J.L. Vivian: *The Visitations of the County of Devon* (Exeter 1895); A. Mozley: 'The Land Family of Woodbear Court, Plymtree', *Transactions of the Devonshire Association*, xxiii (1891), pp. 217, 213; personal observation of Richard Moore's tomb; DRO QS Box 63, bundle Epiphany 1660 (Deposition by Moses Tirrell); Public Record Office (hereafter PRO) E 179/245/12.

29. Firth and Rait *op. cit.* for committee lists; DRO QS bundles passim.

30. *Statutes of the Realm* v pp. 553-54. The hearth tax returns reveal the names of 49 grand jurors who occupied properties with an average of 5.2 hearths each. In Cambridgeshire this would have placed them firmly among the yeomanry. DRO Q/RTR (Hearth tax returns) 1/1-36, PRO E 179/245/17, 375/13, 102/530; M. Spufford: *Contrasting Communities: English Villages in the Sixteenth and Seventeenth Centuries* (Cambridge 1974) pp. 38-41.

31. W.G. Hoskins: *Devon* (1954) pp. 13-21.

32. Joan Thirsk (ed.): *The Agrarian History of England and Wales iv, 1500-1640* (Cambridge 1967) p. 4; Hoskins *op.cit.* pp. 115-16; John Kew: 'Regional Variations in the Devon Land Market, 1536-1558' in M.A. Havinden, C.A. King (eds.): *The South-West and the Land* (Exeter 1969) pp. 32-36.

33. Kew *op.cit.* pp. 30-32; R. Pearse Chope (ed.): *Early Tours in Devon and Cornwall* (London 1918, reprinted 1967) pp. 98-99.

34. Thirsk (ed.): *Agrarian History of England and Wales iv* p. 76; P(ublic) R(ecord) O(ffice) E 317/36/18.

35. Thirsk *op.cit.* p. 76; Kew *op.cit.* pp. 31-32.

36. Analysis of QS jury lists; Kew *op.cit.* pp. 36-38.

37. Hoskins: *Devon* pp. 62, 66, 115, 127; idem, 'The Rise and Decline of the Serge Industry in the South-West of England' (University of London MSc thesis 1929) pp. 1-8; J. de L. Mann: *The Cloth Industry in the West of England from 1640 to 1880* (Oxford 1971) p. 27.

38. Robin Stanes: 'The Compton Census for the Diocese of Exeter, 1676, Parts 1 and 2', *Devon Historian* ix (1974) pp. 14-27, x (1975) pp. 4-16; A.J. Howard (ed.): *The Devon Protestation Returns, 1641* (2 vols., privately printed, 1973); hearth tax returns in PRO E 179, DRO QS. An article with C.R. Roberts is in preparation on these sources for the population of seventeenth-century Devon. For the major-general's suspects, see pages 50–52 above.

39. Thirsk: *Agrarian History iv* Chapter 1.

40. David Underdown: 'The Chalk and the Cheese: Contrasts Among the English Clubmen', *Past and Present* lxxxv (1979) pp. 25-48 *passim*.

41. David Underdown: 'The Problem of Popular Allegiance in the English Civil War' *Trans. Roy. Hist. Soc.* 5th ser. xxxi (1981) pp. 81, 92 and *passim*.

42. DRO jury lists; DRO 1508M for the manors of Alphington, Kenton; Z1/54 for Morchard Bishop; 63/2 for Newton St Cyres; 1201A for Hartland. See also I.L. Gregory (ed.): *Hartland Church Accounts 1597-1706* (1950).

43. J. Simmons: 'Some Letters from Bishop Ward of Exeter 1663-1667', *DCNQ* xxi (1940-41) p. 226.

44. K.M. Beck: 'Recusancy and Nonconformity in Devon and Somerset 1660-1714' (Univ.

of Bristol MA thesis 1961) pp. 80-81, 94, 101; S.K. Roberts: 'A Poet, A Plotter and A Postman: A Disputed Polemic of 1668' *Bulletin of the Inst. of Hist. Res.* liii (1980) pp. 264-65; E.A.O. Whiteman: 'The Episcopate of Dr. Seth Ward, Bishop of Exeter (1662-67) and Salisbury (1667-1668/9) with special reference to the ecclesiastical problems of his time' (Univ. of Oxford DPhil thesis 1951), map appended.

45. Simmons: 'Some Letters from Bishop Ward' p. 226.

46. Robin Stanes: 'Devon Agriculture in the mid-eighteenth century: the evidence of the Milles Enquiries' in Havinden and King (eds.): *The South West and the Land* pp. 47-48. For a comment on the county community debate so far, J.E.C. Hill: 'Parliament and People in Seventeenth-century England' *Past and Present* xcii (1981) pp. 100-24.

47. See below, pages 145-146.

48. Statistics from jury lists and (ed. W.L.D. Ravenhill), Benjamin Donn: *A Map of the County of Devon, 1765* (Devon and Cornwall Record Society, new series ix, Torquay 1965).

49. Samaha: *Law and Order in Historical Perspective*, p. 48; Peter Clark: *English Provincial Society from the Reformation to the Revolution; Religion, Politics and Society in Kent 1500-1640* (1977), p. 114; Lambarde: *Eirenarcha*, p. 306, idem: *Perambulation of Kent* (1826 ed.), pp. 27-49. The grouping of the hundreds of Kent into six lathes effectively supplanted them as units of county government.

50. QS Box 73 loose presentment 15/7/68.

51. Read, *op. cit.*, p. 99.

52. Found attached to lists of indictments in sessions bundles.

53. Read, *op. cit.*, p. 99.

54. 76.53 per cent served once or twice, 12.6 per cent served ten times or more.

55. *Protestation Returns.*

56. William Cleake of Newton Abbott was under suspicion only temporarily and so his estate was never investigated; there were two George Churchills at Rockbeare, one worth £1,000 by the estimates of the committee for compounding, but hearth tax returns show one with three hearths, the other with only one. *CCAM*, pp. 1104, 1353; *CCC*, p. 1121; PRO E 179/375/13.

57. DRO Bishop's Consistory Court MS 868 (unpaginated): cases 23/9/62, 27/4/63. Bartoe was fined £187 as a royalist delinquent in July 1646: *CCC*, p. 1385, and had been nominated for the constableship of Hemyock hundred in 1633. At that time he was in trouble for abusing Edmund Prideaux esq., later Attorney-General: DQSOB Michaelmas 1633.

58. QS Box 68 bundle Easter 1667, Petition of 13/1/63; Box 72 bundle Michaelmas 1667: examinations; DQSOB Epiphany 1654. Bartoe's apprentice was discharged in 1669 because his master had abused him: *ibid.* Midsummer 1669.

59. QS Box 68 bundle Midsummer 1663: examinations.

60. Hoskins: *Devonshire Studies*, pp. 105-09.

61. DRO Q/RTR Hearth Tax 1/17; Bishop's Consistory Court MS 872 (unpaginated) case of 8/10/69; DRO Q/RLV (Victuallers' Recognizances): Wonford Hundred 1646; QS Box 68 loose presentment inc. of Elizabeth Scutt, of 12/1/63.

62. 13.8 1649-59, 13.4 1660-70.

63. Cockburn: *History of English Assizes*, p.114, 'Assize Records as Historical Evidence', *passim*, J.H Langbein: 'The Criminal Trial before the Lawyers', *University of Chicago Law Review*, XLV (1978), pp. 263-316; D.T. Witcombe: *Charles II and the Cavalier House of Commons 1665-1674* (1966), p. 74; Kenyon: *Stuart Constitution*, pp. 420, 426-30. Bushel's case in King's Bench 1670 confirmed the judgement against Keling. In the North American colonies juries conversed about cases in open court: G.L. Haskins: *Law and Authority in Early Massachusetts* (1960), p. 213.

64. 66.75 per cent 1649-59, 57.7 per cent 1660-70.

65. The son of an Exeter glover. Born in 1616 he went to Exeter College, Oxford, in 1634 (BA 1640, MA 1649 while a major in Cromwell's regiment). He was in Scotland with Overton's regiment in 1652 but returned to Exeter to live at Mount Radford. He was hostile to Quakers, was knighted by Cromwell and was sheriff in 1659: Foster: *Alumni Oxonienses*; Rowe and Jackson: *Exeter Freemen*; Firth and Davies: *Regimental History of*

Cromwell's Army, pp. 202, 209, 550, 606, Abbott: *Writings and Speeches*, I, pp. 606-07; SRO WO Box 53, Blackmore to John Willoughby 8/7/1659; *West Answering to North*, pp. 77-78.

66. PRO SP 18/74/1-2, *CSPD* 1654, p. 279. Fitzwilliam's distinctive hand, recognizable in quarter sessions order books for the 1650s, penned the petition to the Committee for Elections. *Calamy Revised* pp. 115, 469, for Chishall and Stucley.

67. *Colonel Shapcott (Knight of Devonshire) his Speech in Parliament the 30 of October 1654* (1654), *passim*.

68. A.R. Bayley: *The Great Civil War in Dorset* (1910), p. 365; Underdown: 'Settlement in the Counties'. p. 173.

69. *CJ*, VII, p. 383; BL Lansdowne MS 822 f 290.

70. Dunsford: *Historical Memoirs of Tiverton*, p. 191. Skinner was discharged by quarter sessions from jury service in 1654, perhaps because of his politics.

71. E.W. Rannie: 'Cromwell's Major Generals', *English Historical Review*, X (1895), pp. 471-506; A.H. Woolrych: *Penruddock's Rising* (1955).

72. Abbott: *Writings and Speeches of Oliver Cromwell*, III, pp. 646-62; Woolrych, *op. cit.*, pp. 19-20.

73. *TSP*, III, pp. 281, 305-06, 306-08; *CSPD 1655*, p. 84.

74. Names of commissioners may be found in PRO C 181/6/98; *CSPD 1655*, p. 90; G.R. Elton: *The Tudor Constitution* (1960), pp. 80-82.

75. Abbott: *Writings and Speeches*, III, pp. 836-51; *CSPD 1655*, pp. 77-78, 92-93, 99, 120, 123.

76. *CSPD 1655*, p. 131; WRO Penruddock MSS 332/265/58, pp. 2, 6.

77. Penruddock MSS 332/265/58, pp. 10, 14; Roots: *The Great Rebellion*, p. 37; Woolrych, *op. cit.*, p. 26 for doubts about the provenance of Penruddocks's 'last letter'.

78. DQSOB Epiphany 1655. For discharges 1650-52 *ibid*. Epiphany 1650, Epiphany 1651, Easter 1651, Michaelmas 1651, Epiphany 1652, Michaelmas 1652. Also *Somers Tracts*, VI, pp. 218-19; F.A. Inderwick: *The Interregnum* (1891), p. 205.

79. 'Resolutions at Devon Quarter Sessions 3rd April 1655', BL Add. 44058 ff 42 v – 44 r.

80. *Parliament of England ... Official Returns* (1878), I. The MPs were William Morrice, Arthur Upton, Thomas Boone, William Bastard, John Hale, William Fry, Henry Hatsell. The others: John Coplestone, William Putt, Christopher Savery, Thomas Saunders, Robert Duke, John Blundell, Henry Walter.

81. The concern to control the jury is indicated by the desire to reduce the number of attending jurors. A projected 120 was increased to 136 to accord with statute law governing writs of *venire facias*, 'the law being very strict in this particular'. Add. 44058 f 43 r.

82. *Ibid*. ff 43 v – 44 r.

83. A transcript is in BL Add. 44058 ff 40 r – 42 r, and a reprint in Abbott; *Writings and Speeches*, IV, pp. 87-88. There is some doubt as to the origins of this letter, but is seems likely that although it was composed in response to the Devon situation it was subsequently sent to other counties. See S.K. Roberts PhD thesis pp. 153-154.

84. Add. 44058 ff 40 r – 42 r; TSP, IV, pp. 511, 523, 534. Cromwell believed that grand juries had been 'superficiall' in their prosecution of the reformation of manners: Morrill 'The Government of Cheshire during the Civil Wars and Interregnum' (Oxford DPhil, 1971), p. 311. For Cromwell's general interest in law reform: Abbott: *Writings and Speeches*, IV, p 274.

85. Add. 44058 ff 44 v – 52 v.

86. Add. 44058 f 18 r. SRO DD/WO Box 53 bundle 3: letter, J. Blackmore to J. Willoughby 8/7/1659.

87. E.g., the response to the Book of Orders. The need to list free holders appeared in Somerset in 1648: Cockburn: *History of English Assizes*, pp. 119, 331-32.

88. *TSP* IV, p. 501.

89. QS Box 61 Midsummer 1656 jury list and indictments.

90. The grand jury newcomers, unlike those on the trial jury, continued to appear on lists during the later Interregnum and into the next decade.

91. QS Box 61 Michaelmas 1656 grand jury panel.

92. DQSOB Michaelmas 1661.

93. *Ibid.*, Michaelmas 1664.
94. *Statutes of the Realm*, V: 16, 17 Charles II c. 3 (pp. 553-54). John Broadmead of Willand was discharged from future service in 1666 because he was only worth £3 p.a.: QS Box 71 bundle Michaelmas 1666, certificate.
95. *History of English Assizes*.
96. *Ibid.*, p. 113. This description fits that of the Worcestershire grand jury: R.H. Silcock: 'County Government in Worcestershire', p. 66.
97. *CSPD Addenda 1625-1649*, pp. 85-86.
98. Add. 44058 f 18 r.
99. SRO DD/WO Box 55 bundle 3, Blackmore to Willoughby 8/7/59.
100. DRO Pine-Coffin letters (letter book D), letters of Northmore to Richard Coffin 10/8/85, 17/8/85, 26/8/85. In 1681 Bishop Lamplugh of Exeter wrote to Archbishop Sancroft of the exceptional grand jury comprising 36 baronets: *DCNQ*, XXII, p. 144.
101. PRO ASSI 22/1.
102. Morrill: *Cheshire Grand Jury*, pp. 19, 49, note 35.
103. Cockburn: *History of English Assizes*, pp. 105-06; L.M. Hill: 'County Government in Caroline England' in Russell (ed.): *The Origins of the English Civil War* (1973), p. 72; T.G. Barnes: *Somerset 1625-1640: A County's Government during the Personal Rule* (1961), p. 131.
104. SRO DD/WO Box 53 (loose). At the Lincoln assizes, Lent 1632, the under sheriff laid on a dinner for 23 grand jurors at 2s. 6d. per head, although other 'gentlemen in the Great Chamber' dined five times at that rate: Nottinghamshire R.O. DD F vii/69-72.
105. Cockburn: *History of English Assizes*, pp. 67. 305. Willoughby's total of £268.2s. 9d. for incidental expenses while sheriff should be augmented by at least £48, the amount which Sir Francis Drake paid out in 1647 while passing his accounts at the Exchequer in 1645. £48 covered the fees to the clerk of the pipe, the foreign apposer, and a baron of the Exchequer: DRO CR 20, 133.
106. WRO QS Great Rolls sampled: Hilary 1648, Trinity 1648, all sessions 1653, Hilary 1656, all sessions 1661, Hilary 1668. For the returns in the 1630s, PRO SP 16.
107. Ralph Josselin complained that the constables chosen by the Earl's Colne jury were 'unfit to order the alehouses': Alan Macfarlane (ed.): *The Diary of Ralph Josselin 1616-1683* (1976), p. 31.
108. Hoskins: *Devon*, pp. 327-30.
109. PRO SP 18/153/48. For Beecher's career in government: *CSPD 1654*, pp. 134, 338, 550, *1655*, p. 369; *1655-56*, pp. 157, 247, 302-03, 458. 462, 470, 491, 494; *1656-57*, pp. 246, 279.
110. Bodl. MS J. Walker c. 4 ff 176-90, 350, 356, 369; J.F. Chanter: *Life and Times of Martin Blake, passim*, but esp. Chapter 4; *Calamy Revised*, p. 247 and pp. 343-44 for Nathaniel Mather, Blake's successor.
111. North Devon Athenaeum, Barnstaple Borough MSS 576-90.
112. *Ibid.* no. 1856.
113. *Ibid.* no. 1858.
114. On dorse of *Ibid.* no. 1856.
115. Other presentments examined: *Ibid.* 1857, 1859, 1860, 1861, 1862, 1865.
116. D.M. Hirst: *The Representative of the People? Voters and Voting in England under the Early Stuarts* (1975), Appendix 3; Weinbaum: *British Borough Charters 1307-1660* (1943), pp. 22-24.
117. *CSPD 1650*, p. 137.
118. F & R II, pp. 660-61; *CSPD 1652-53*, p. 584; PRO E 122/222/66; Aylmer: 'Checklist of Central Officeholders 1649-60' (Unpublished list deposited at University of London, Institute of Historical Research, 1976).
119. DRO Dartmouth Corporation MSS DD 62722.
120. *Ibid.*, DD 62817 B; Edmund Calamy: *The Nonconformists' Memorial* (Palmer ed. 1802-03), p. 14.
121. DD 62924-26, 63528. DD 67716 is the charter for Newfoundland trade, reissued in 1660.
122. SP 29/183/35-37, 44, SP 29/188. For Colleton: Robert Steele (ed.): *Bibliography of Royal Proclamations* (1910), I, pp. 401, 409; *CTB*, I, p. 639.

123. DD 63018. For Burdwood see *Calamy Revised*, pp. 57-58.
124. DD 63020.
125. DD 63114. Other presentments are DD 63017, 63019, 63112, 63113. Note a Puritan drive against moral offences in eve-of-Restoration Plymouth, where constables presented illegal drinkers and church absentees: West Devon RO Plymouth City MSS W 359/79. This campaign was almost certainly government-inspired: *Clarke Papers*, IV, p. 295.
126. J.H. Langbein: *Prosecuting Crime in the Renaissance* (1974), Chapters 4, 5, passim, esp. pp. 118-21; Elton: *Tudor Constitution*, p. 456; Kenyon: *Stuart Constitution*, p. 494; J.H. Baker: 'Criminal Courts and Procedure at Common Law' in Cockburn (ed.): *Crime in England*, p. 20.

Chapter Five
Bailiffs and Constables 1649-1670

The Hundred

The hundred emerged before the Norman Conquest as a unit of local government and remained the basis of county administration below quarter sessions, and of national taxation, until 1834.[1] The thirty-three hundreds of Devon, with the artificial unit of the Duchy of Lancaster, were each represented at sessions by a bailiff and at least two constables. The effectiveness of the jury system rested on the bailiffs. The constables executed writs and warrants of the court of quarter sessions, supervised the collection of national and local taxes and after 1660 provided administrative links between the local units of the county militia. Their authority was bounded by the hundreds which they served, and the significance of these hundreds as administrative units and as items of property should first be made clear.

The significance of the hundred in government has obscured the fact that hundreds, like manors, could be bought and sold. Moreover, as in manors, the privileges of lords and the rights of tenants were exercised in courts held regularly within the hundred. When the parliamentary surveyors visited Devon they noted the places where, at regular intervals of six months, hundred courts were held. They did not, however, note the names of the lords of the hundreds, leaving the impression that the hundreds were under direct crown control. It is important to bear in mind the surveyors' intentions in coming to Devon. Parliament's purpose in selling the hundreds was to realise a readily obtained fixed sum of money in exchange for what had become an uncertain revenue derived from an increasingly otiose manorial sub-structure: the many tithings of each hundred. (There were fifty tithings in Wonford hundred, nineteen in Exminster.[2]) Yet the hundreds were regarded by the Trustees for the sale of Crown lands as anomalous possessions of the Crown, to be considered not as manors but as revenues only and therefore the Devon hundreds were offered for sale under the Act of Sale of Fee Farm Rents of 11 March 1650. The hundreds of neighbouring Somerset were sold under the Act for Sale of Crown Lands.[3] Revenues rather than rights were sold in Devon, and in the absence of evidence for the sales of the Devon hundreds it may have been the case that the lords remained unaffected by the legislation.[4] In Easter 1650 the lord of Stanborough hundred, Sir Thomas Hele, was fined £30 for not appointing a bailiff and this was on 23 April, over a month after the act which had supposedly placed Stanborough hundred on the market.[5] Apart from commentators like Sir William Pole, who wrote before the civil war, and Daniel Lysons who studied manorial descendents

101

in the early nineteenth century (from which perspective Interregum changes in ownership would have appeared as temporary aberrations) the sources for sales of hundreds are scrappy, miscellaneous and rather obscure. Little information has been derived from the 1650s. Royalist delinquents found that the profits of their hundred courts were alienated from them during their sequestrations but this was a temporary diversion of income rather than confiscation.[6] The only example of a hundred being acquired by an official outside the county gentry group is that of Ermington, bought from Stephen Revell by Sir Peter Fortescue in 1685. Revell was a Cornishman who became clerk to the Devon and Cornwall sequestration bodies before the changes of 1650.[7]

In 1822 Lysons offered his readers a list of incumbent lords of the hundreds.[8] He made no attempt to trace hundredal descents but from asides by him and by Pole and from other miscellaneous material an incomplete list of hundred owners in the mid-seventeenth century has been compiled (Table 3). The ownership of the hundreds did not mirror the power structure of local administration. At least eleven hundreds were in aristocratic and non-Devonian hands. The distribution of the estates of Sir Edward Courtenay introduced a powerful Cornish element into Devon hundred ownership, and the Pophams and Pauletts were magnate interlopers from Somerset. Families like the Russells and the Earls of Donegal branch of the Chichesters were no longer forces to be reckoned with in local politics. Some lords of hundreds fell below the ranks of the JPs. John Slowly of Fremington played no part in local government and Thomas Lethbridge of Winkleigh served on the quarter sessions grand jury five times between 1650 and 1670.[9] In hundreds divided among branches of family it is not possible to discover the most powerful interest because where patronage rights were still attached to the hundreds they were not necessarily held by the interest holding most of the profits.

The rights of hundred lords were severely circumscribed by local government procedure and central intervention. In the Middle Ages private ownership had been more significant than it was in the seventeenth century; in the time of Richard I only Plympton and Lifton hundreds had 'return of writs' and were exempt from the sheriff's authority.[10] Writs of *venire facias* to the sheriff in the 1650s and 1660s enjoined them to enter liberties, but the private franchise was no longer a potent force. Only Francis Popham, knight, (and after his death, his son, Alexander) had to account at the Exchequer for the issues of the office of lord of the hundred of Coleridge. The sheriff's issues amounted to £30 annually, Popham's to a mere twenty pence, and Popham was able to include his nominal accounts with those offered to the Exchequer by the undersheriff or an attorney representing the sheriff.[11] Coleridge and Tavistock hundreds were the only ones not to be surveyed for the trustees of fee farm rents and although the Tavistock profits of office were not separately presented at the Exchequer it may be assumed that it was considered with Coleridge to be a 'liberty' so far as hundredal profits were concerned.

Hundred courts were still being held in the mid-seventeenth century. They were similar to courts leet in form with twelve jurors or homagers being appointed, manorial dues being paid and registered, and presentments of decayed bridges and minor nuisances being offered for the consideration of the court. Small fines were imposed for minor transgressions. At Ottery St Mary, where the hundred court and the leet were co-extensive, lists of assize-breaking alesellers were presented. Court meetings were in practice held more frequently than the minimal twice a year for the paying of feudal dues which the parliamentary surveyors noted. At Ottery there were monthly meetings; the Exminster hundred court met as often and was peripatetic.[12] In the town of Ottery St Mary it was doubtless the hundred court/court leet which appointed constables but in hundreds comprising many manors and parishes there was no appointing power since the hundred constable was under the control of the justices. Hundred courts were presided over by seneschals or stewards whose offices were likely to be hereditary and certainly in the gift of the lords. When Charles I's commissioners on fees wrote to the Devon magistrates in the 1620s for information on the hundred courts they were told that there was 'much difference in their severall fees' between the individual courts. The JPs thought that 'much might be abated for the generall' which is now turned to private mens uses to the vexacion of poore men';[13] hundred courts were considered as vexatious as church and stannary jurisdictions. Not surprisingly, most stewards offered a different opinion. Fees in many of the courts had not been altered in thirty years and where they had been increased it was 'agreed upon by divers freeholders ... of the hundred'. Thomas Osmond, deputy steward of Halberton hundred, offered a description of his court which seems typical: 'Neither counsellors nor attorneys at lawe do use to come to these courts but only countrey persons that do follow plaintes for small debtes or trespasses and no other'.[14] The hundred courts were not powerful but their survival was irksome to magistrates. Where did hundreds or hundred courts touch on the performance of local government?

High or hundredal constables were under the control of JPs in and out of sessions. No appointment of hundredal bailiffs were registered in the sessions order books, however. The assertions both of contemporary pundits and of modern historians have been that they were shrieval appointees.[15] When the parliamentary surveyors visited Devon they stated flatly that stewards and bailiffs were appointed on a temporary basis by the sheriff.[16] We have already noticed that their descriptions of the hundred tend to be over-simple and there is no reason to believe that their view of the appointment procedure for bailiffs was not entirely accurate. Occasionally the court had to reprimand the lords of the hundreds for not appointing bailiffs or had to request that a bailiff be replaced. At the sessions of Easter 1650, Sir Thomas Hele of Halberton, a civil lawyer and royalist delinquent, was fined £30 for not appointing a bailiff in Stanborough hundred.[17] In Michaelmas 1661 it was ordered that 'Mr Lethbridge, lord of the hundred of Winkley, doe authorise a fitt man to be bayliffe there in the room and steed of Michael Brooke now bayliffe there.'[18] In January 1670, James Clifford, a distant kinsman of Sir Thomas Clifford and an assessment or subsidy commissioner from 1661,

Table 3: The Hundreds of Devon and their Ownership in the Seventeenth Century

	Location of Court[1]	Lord of Hundred (Family)	Source
Axminster	Axe Bridge	Petre, but by 1670 Sir Joseph Sheldon	J. Youings: *Calendar of Monastic Lands*, p. 118; D.R.O. 517M/MH1.
Bampton	Bampton	? Earls of Bath	Lysons, p. 28, Pole, pp. 209-10.
Braunton	Barnstaple	Waller or Courtenay	Lysons, p. 64.
E. Budleigh	Clyst Honiton	Duke of Otterton	Pole, p. 152.
W. Budleigh	Washfield[2]	Mohun of Okehampton	*C.C.C.*, p. 1504, Lysons, p. 372, B.L. Add. 11314 f 50.
Clyston	Clyst Honiton	Sir William Morrice	*Charity Commissioners Reports* (Devon), II, pt. 5, p. 29.
Coleridge	?	Sir Francis Popham	P.R.O. E 368/685-88.
Colyton	? Kilmington[2]	Petre/Pole/Drake	Lysons, p. 130, Pole, pp. 135-36.
Crediton	Crediton	John Maynard, John Tredenham	QS Box 57, mixed bundle.
Ermington	Ermington	Stephen Revell (Fortescue by 1685)	PROB 11/382/45
Exminster	Exminster[2]	? Courtenay	Pole, p. 252, Lysons, p. 235, D.R.O. 1508 M.
Fremington	Torrington	John Slowly to 1666, then Hawkins	*C.C.C.* p. 2841, Lysons, p. 241.
Halberton	Sampford Peverell	Paulett	Bodl. Tanner MS 287/103.
Hartland	Yarnscombe	1/12 Arundel, rest Carew, Zouch, Fitzwarren	Abstracts of inquisitions post mortem, Exeter City library.
Hayridge	Feniton[2]	Mohun	As for West Budleigh.
Haytor	Berry Pomeroy	? Putt	Lysons

Hemyock	Awliscombe	? Mohun	Bodl. Tanner MS 287/93.
Lifton	Okehampton	Harris of Hayne	Lysons, p. 267, Pole, pp. 202, 348.
S. Molton	S. Molton	Squire	Pole, p. 349
Ottery	Ottery	Young of Colyton	Lysons, p. 377.
Plympton	Plympton[2]	Courtenay of Trethuse, Cornwall	C.C.C., p. 2658.
Roborough	Bickleigh	Slanning	West Devon R.O., Roborough MS 291.
Shebbear	Taddiport	?	
Sherwill	Sherwill	Chichester of Hall, Raleigh	B.L. Harley Charters 85 H 59.
Stanborough	Brent	Sir Thomas Hele	DQSOB Easter 1650.
Tavistock	Tavistock	Russell	B.L. Add. Charters 11, 168; Youings, p. 4.
N. Tawton	N. Tawton	?	
Teignbridge	Newton Bushell	James Clifford	DQSOB Epiphany 1670.
Tiverton	Tiverton[2]	?	
Black Torrington	Exbourne	George Marks, Robert Tothill	P.R.O. E 372.
Winkleigh	Winkleigh	Thomas Lethbridge	DQSOB Michaelmas 1661.
Witheridge	Ashmill (Bishop's Nympton)	Chichester of Donegal	Lysons, p. 564.
Wonford	Alphington	Mohun	As for West Budleigh.

1 From P.R.O. E 317/10/1-5.
2 Hundreds divided among co-heirs of Edward Courtenay — in 1557: Mohun, Trelawney, Arundel, Vivian, Buller: C.R.O. Fortescue MSS DD F 83.

was amerced twenty shillings 'for not haveing a bayliffe within or for' Teignbridge hundred.[19] It was not that the court could exercise no control over bailiffs. The order to Lethbridge was not unique; most bailiffs who proved wayward or dilatory were were dismissed without reference to the appointing lord.[20] Fines and amerciaments were regularly laid upon defaulting bailiffs and on occasion they were prosecuted in open sessions for demanding money from summoned jurors in return for exempting them from service. But the power of the court lay in regulation and dismissal not in appointments. The hundred was a dwindling source of Crown revenue and a very minor unit of local jurisdiction but as an avenue of private patronage it retained some significance in county affairs. The channels of patronage meandered; there could be interests other than those of the lord of the hundred to consider in appointing a bailiff and these interests could include those in exhalted echelons of the county gentry. In November 1674, Sir Henry Carew of Bickleigh wrote to Baron Mohun of Okehampton to remind him that he

> did about a yeare since request a favour from you which was on the behalfe of one John Maunder, my neighbour, to succeed in the office of bayliffe of the hundred of Hayridge in the roome of one Barons deceased the which you were pleased to condiscend unto and thereupon he was by Mr Fitzwilliams then steward admitted to the said office who hath for ought I can understand hitherto behaved himselfe very civilly since which tyme Mr Fitzwillams hath either by your order or otherwise resigned the place to one Mr John Hawkings of Crediton, a person well knowne to me and as I am informed ...a fit and exquisite person . . . Yett nevertheless I make bold once more to recomend the said Maunder to your Lordshipps favour for his former imployment ... he behaving himselfe honestly and not acting anything prejudiciall to your Lordshipps seignory and comporting himself in the execucion of his office civilly which is the desire of yours to love and serve you ... [21]

Carew's concern for Maunder's interests (Maunder was probably his tenant) demonstrates something of the pyramid of local patronage which persisted even when justiciary control was aggressively extended to the composition of freeholders' lists. Carew was a JP, Mohun was not, but it is evident that the prevailing power lay with the outsider and it was a power to be courted.

What control was left to the sheriff? Apart from the task of summoning jurors by writs issued to the bailiffs by deputies, very little, it would appear. In a county the size of Devon it is implausible that control over bailiffs — thirty-four of them — would be exercised personally by the sheriff, in any case. Patronage on that scale could not be deployed by one person. When constables were appointed by the authority of quarter sessions, the selection procedure was invariably left to 'the two nearest justices' with sessions only as arbiter. Dalton describes the avenues of responsibilty not local practice. Devon was not unique in harbouring persistent private control. From 1655 the sessions of Essex ordered that because of malpractices by bailiffs they were all to 'produce to the said court their severall grants and claimes to the said bailiffewicks' and as in

Devon some were discharged and the lords of the hundreds ordered to replace them. As in Devon, too, the sheriffs seem to have exercised little control over these subordinate officials.[22] In a survey of medieval legislation, a 1680 case of a Leicestershire sheriff against the proprietor of a hundred culminated in a judgement for the sheriff on the grounds that grants of bailiwicks since a statute of 1340 were void and that the office of bailiff could not exist independently of the sheriff's authority: 'All escapes by the bailiff are escapes by the sheriff'.[23] It is not clear whether or not this established a general principle of absolute shrieval control.

The Bailiffs

Hundred bailiffs were not the stewards of the hundreds nor were they sheriff's officials responsible for the apprehension of debtors and the distraint of their goods. Stewards of hundreds and manors were usually practised in manorial law and were responsible for the holding of courts and the administration of estates. The appointment of a steward was thus an exercise in careful estate management as well as an opportunity to reward faithful service or to repay a favour. When William Morrice was asked by the son of a recently-deceased steward to award him his father's office Morrice reluctantly acceded but wrote to a friend: 'I looke upon him as one whose youth hath neither authority nor experience competent for such a trust but ordered him keepe this present court and for this one tourne'. The deceased Mr Tamlyn had been allowed to administer the court as he saw fit; Morrice regretted that he could not replace him with Prideaux's nominee because he 'could not suddenly change the steward and put in another as unacquainted as myself'.[24] Service as stewards of the estates of great men offered several clerks an avenue to county eminence. Henry Fitzwilliam is one example; Edward Raddon, whom Fitzwilliam succeeded as clerk of the peace, was another.[25] Particularly in a decade when the clerkship of the peace was a prize open to lawyers other than the younger sons of county gentry, land stewardship could be a successful start to a career in county government. Like the clerks of the justices and the officials of the court of quarter sessions the court stewards were part of a county infrastructure of legal experts who exercised real authority in their domains. When Hugh Camworthy, steward of the court leet of the Borough of Braunton, owned by the Countess of Bath, could not persuade the inhabitants to repair two stone bridges he wrote to the clerk of the peace desiring him 'to take such course ... as is usuall in such aferes'.[26]

Sheriff's bailiffs were the strong-arm men of the sheriff's court, the scourge of debtors and the group of officials against whom most complaints were bitterly made. M. J. Ingram's description of bailiffs as 'more like brigands than officers of the law' and his estimate that a third of them were complained of suggested that he is describing sheriff's bailiffs and not hundred bailiffs.[27] Almost all the evidence for sheriff's bailiffs comes from cases against them but they seem to have been Exeter men who hung around the Castle and the sheriff's ward at Stoke Canon on the outskirts of the city to work more or less casually. Allegations of rough treatment of debtors were frequent. David Hart was appointed governor of St Thomas House of Correction in Michaelmas 1666 but from the first seemed to encounter difficulties in making financial ends meet at the bridewell. By Michaelmas 1668 he had been dismissed but secured a writ from the court of quarter sessions, his employer, that he should retain his liberty. He was coming from Exeter Castle with proof of this indemnity when he was bundled by two men who turned out to be sheriff's bailiffs. His expostulations were useless: 'They would not harken to it but mad a disturbance in they [sic] streate'. By the following January Harte was in the debtors' gaol.[28] In January 1654 two bailiffs, Ralph Porter and John Saunders of Exeter, were found guilty of extortion by a trial jury,[29] a reminder that when evidence comes from those who had fallen into the hands of bailiffs it is prudent to consider the judgments of other contemporaries. Henry Newbury claimed that in 1647 he was 'led ... on foote from Axminster to the sheriff's ward at Stoke Canon ... 22 miles distant' but he was making a case for indemnity to the parliamentary committee.[30] Dissatisfaction with the operation of the laws on debt was not confined to those who suffered under them. A list of prisoners at Stoke Canon sheriff's ward in 1665 shows that some of the forty-one were confined for debts as small as £4.[31] Reform of the laws on debt was a perennial subject in parliaments of the 1650s. The fate of 'poor prisoners' was a matter of personal concern to the Lord Protector and of sufficiently general concern to ensure legislation.[32]

Hundred bailiffs were neither as eminent as court stewards nor as notorious as the heavy-handed sheriff's bailiffs. Apart from the occasional presentment[33] and the delivery of the odd court writ,[34] their sole function was to summon jurors from the parishes to Exeter Castle. Shrieval administration lacked an effective core of supervision over the bailiffs. JPs served longer than subordinate treasurers (who served for one year) and constables (who served for about three years). Shrieval authority was marked by a reverse pattern of service. Sheriffs at the top served for one year only, deputies for longer, and bailiffs for longer still. At the lowest levels private patronage remained powerful enough to add its own distortion to the chain of responsibility. By the mid-seventeenth century the dichotomy in local government between a shrievalty responsible to assize judges and ultimately to the Exchequer and a commission of the peace beholden to the Lord Chancellor, each with its subordinate staffs of undersheriff and bailiffs on one hand and treasurers and constables on the other, had narrowed considerably. Central taxes were collected by the head constables (appointed by the JPs) under the sheriff who was finally accountable for the sums raised. In matters of local taxation the JPs were all-powerful, and jury summoning and the prosecution of debtors were all that were left as sole responsibilities of shrieval officials. Even in jury service there were attempts by the magistrates to control the bailiffs. The patterns of participation by the sheriff and his subordinates were institutional weaknesses. They contributed to the decline of the shrievalty as much as did neglect by central government and assertiveness by the justices.

Sheriffs changed annually; medieval legislation and later commentaries established that no bailiffs should have served longer. The case of 1680 in which the right of the sheriff to enter any bailiwick was upheld traversed this ground before judgment. In Dalton's view the same restriction should have been imposed on under-sheriffs. [35] The thirty-four hundred bailiffs in Devon remained in office for much longer, hardly surprising in a large county with many hundreds, a fixed sessions meeting at Exeter and a substantial concession to private patronage. Hundredal variation was enormous. In Bampton hundred the average length of service was much the same before 1660 as after and for the period 1649 to 1670 was over 1.8 years. [36] This concealed the restriction of the office to only four men, Thomas Quick, Henry Warman, William Dyer and John Tanner. This pattern was common. Men served for a time, stood down and resumed service some years later. The longest continuous period in office was achieved by Thomas Cloutman of Hartland (1601–1680)[37] who summoned jurors in the hundred of Hartland for nearly twenty-five years.

Distance from Exeter exerted no decisive influence on the bailiff's service, and neither did the size of the hundred. Of those nearest Exeter, the average length of service in Wonford was 1.07 years, in Exminster 10.37 years and in East Budleigh eleven years. These were hundreds where trial jurors came to sessions with the most frequency and regularity. Two of the largest hundreds were Black Torrington and Lifton, both in West Devon. The bailiffs served in the former hundred for, on average, 1.68 years and in the latter for 7.33 years. The regional variations are exaggerated by the custom in some hundreds for bailiffs to serve frequently but for short periods. Thomas Brewer of Wonford served seven times between 1649 and 1670 but on three of those occasions served for less than a year. The ownership of the hundreds cannot be said to have determined the patterns of service in them. Local traditions and family dominance were important, however. T. E. Hartley noticed that in Kent 'family specialisation' prevailed in some bailiwicks. [38] In Devon the hundred of Haytor was under the control of the Codnor family; the office of bailiff passed from Nicholas to Joseph and to Edward of that name. [39] In Hemyock the office passed from Mark Peter at his disgrace to Nicholas Burcombe for seven years and then reverted to Moses Peter in 1661. Some bailiffs served for long enough to have observed several dynastic changes in other hundreds. Thomas Cloutman of Hartland served for over twenty years; John Kerswell of Exminster and Thomas Eastcott of Lifton served each for over fifteen. The average length of service by bailiffs in the whole of Devon between 1649 and 1670 was 6.26 years.

The office of bailiff was not subject to 'political' pressures, was not a pawn in struggles for control by partisans of the central authority. Like the jury itself, the bailiwicks were left unpurged in 1660. Eight of the thirty-four posts changed hands that year as in 1654, 1656, 1662 and 1664. Ten bailiffs were replaced in 1650 and twelve in 1651, the highest proportion (over a third in 1651) removed during this period. If the magistrates were responsible for the dismissals the imposition of the Engagement may have been decisive but if this were the case the order books give no hint of it. What seems more likely is that the new appointments were part of an accelerated rate of change among county officeholders in the reconstruction after the 1640s. Parochial initiatives of the later years of that decade were an aspect of this revival. The owners of some hundreds were prosecuted for delinquency — Baron Mohun of Okehampton was among them — to add to instability in the bailiwicks. Purges of bailiffs had occurred elsewhere in earlier troubled times; in Radnorshire all the hundred bailiffs were replaced at the accession of Queen Mary in 1553, but those were years of shrieval power and hundredal vigour.[40]

Historians have judged bailiffs harshly. Parish constables have been pitied as 'poor constables' burdened with an office they could scarcely afford to bear.[41] Bailiffs, however, included 'the shiftless and the desperate', 'more like brigands than officers of the law'. They were 'venal' and grossly corrupt.[42] The failures and excesses of bailiffs were waved under the noses of magistrates at the opening of each session when it would become apparent that writs for jurors directed to certain hundreds had not been executed or that the bailiff was not in court to offer a list of freeholders. The neglects of the bailiffs were almost invariably written up as the first item in the entry for a session and there was an average number of cases in each session of nearly two and a total in twenty years of at least seventy-eight.[43] These regular derelictions of duty did not provoke the same response from the Bench on each occasion; fines imposes varied from as low as 2s.6d. to as high as £10. In general, however, fines were heavier during the Interregnum. In 1655, 1657 and 1660 the bailiffs of East Budleigh, Hartland and the Duchy of Lancaster were fined £10 for not appearing in court or for neglect. In Michaelmas 1651 three defaulters were fined only ten shillings each,[44] perhaps because more severe penalties would have deterred others from serving at all. Twenty or forty shillings were more typical forfeits. Variations do not suggest a routine problem routinely treated but rather an appraisal of each offence by the Bench. The composition of the presiding Bench changed slightly from sessions to sessions, and levels of fines could fluctuate in differing appraisals of offences. From 1664 onwards fines dropped to a norm of ten shillings and in only five cases from then until 1670 were heavier penalties imposed.[45] Below ten shillings there were fines of three shillings (on at least three men) and in Easter 1669, John Wills, bailiff of Wonford, was fined only 2s.6d.[46] Lighter penalties corresponded with dwindling interest in jury control. Spasmodic attempts at accurate listing of freeholders and supervision of bailiffs had been strengthened by heavier fines. Cockburn describes efforts to list freeholders as a 'most persistent illusion' which 'probably foundered on local lethergy'.[47] But the magistrates of the 1660s were in no sense lethargic. Juries were apathetic, and the Webbs probably erred in taking their apathy as a general mood at post-Restoration quarter sessions.[48] Jurors abdicated their responsibilities, their presenting function, spontaneously, and magistrates enjoyed unchallenged power as a consequence. Crude manipulation of the jury system and ancillary officialdom was henceforth no longer necessary.

Fines on bailiffs fluctuated with the degree of importance the justices attached to juries they summoned. But bailiffs were much more frequently punished in quarter sessions than were hundred constables even though the latter outnumbered them by two or three to one, and even though the range of responsibilities shouldered by the constables was much wider and much more demanding. This imbalance in reliability implies inadequate control by magistrates, control exercised through dismissals of egregious offenders and in the case of constables, through the appointments of their successors. If constables could be controlled, why could not bailiffs? The difference between them was that bailiffs were appointed through the exercise of private patronage operating with ends other than those of the 'county' (or more precisely other than those of the court of quarter sessions) in view. As jury control came to matter less to the justices so the private appointing rights in hundreds were likely to remain unchecked. If the 'middling sort' on juries had proved more tender of their own privileges the magistrates might have sought greater control over bailiffs' appointments as a balance.

In 1689 the catatonic hundred jury tradition was finally allowed to expire on the pretext that the enormities, 'extortions and oppressions' of bailiffs could be allowed to continue no longer.[49] This was a parting shot in a war of attritition against bailiffs. But the charge against them must be examined. How venal, in fact, were the bailiffs?

There were no more than half a dozen cases of bailiffs accepting bribes or abusing their power for pecuniary gain or acting with violence in this twenty-year period. In nearly all these cases the magistrates launched extensive enquiries into the alleged abuses but there is no evidence that corruption was prosecuted with any degree of severity.

At Michaelmas 1650 Mark Peter, the bailiff of Hemyock, was gaoled briefly for offering sheriff Robert Rolle 'two or three stitches of corn for his paines' if he excused Robert Bowerman of Hemyock from grand jury service. The sentence was imposed as much for impertinence as for bribery, but it was no deterrent. In the following year, Peter, still in office, was the subject of allegations by a respectable grand juror and his wife, Henry and Katherine Butson of Culmstock.

> Mark Petters came to their house in Culmstock ... the day befor Easter and the said Mr Henry Butson and Katherine his wife being in their court hee the said Mark Petters told them he was com for easter-dueties then shee the said Katherne Butson demanded of him what it was. The said Mark Petters replyed it was a peece of bacon shee told him hee could not come in a worse time, shee being not soe well furnished then the said Mark Petters being denied said hee could have favoured the said Mr Butson and then presently warned him to be a juryman on the Tuesday seventhnight which was the last easter sessions and see how he will answer that ...

Peter seems to have been singularly unsuccessful at bribery. As the court took a lenient view he continued as bailiff until early in 1654 when he was replaced by Nicholas Burcombe.[50]

Dismissal was invariably the result if in the early 1650s bailiffs expressed monarchical sympathies or criticised the government. The point here was that as well as spreading disaffection among the lower classes such criticisms were an unwelcome display of political initiative and independence. So when John Huish, bailiff of West Budleigh and the appointee of royalist delinquent, Warwick Lord Mohun, told William Reynolds in 1651 that 'he should see an alteracon shortly and that he should not be worth a groat shortly' he was instantly dismissed from office.[51]

At Easter, 1664, the magistrates conducted an inquiry into allegations of irregularities in the bailiwick of Coleridge. Coleridge was the only Devon hundred to account separately at the Exchequer and the extent of the enquiry may have been connected with national concern at the quality of jurors, which bore fruit in the act of 1665.[52] Benjamin Beasley was appointed bailiff in 1664 and disgraced himself by not appearing at the first sessions for which he had summoned jurors. At the Easter sessions he was alleged to have summoned many but by taking bribes from those who wished to evade jury service had returned the names of only three to the sheriff. Instead of simply examining who complained of Beasley's conduct the JPs decided to check his activities systematically. The constables of the fourteen Coleridge parishes were ordered by the hundred constable Richard Yoldon to cause those warned by Beasley to attend a special meeting at one in the afternoon of 9 April 'att the house of Mr Edward Hayman in Kingsbridge'. The returns of the constables, as they arrived one by one at the house of the head constable, slowly exposed the extent of Beasley's fraud. No fewer than fifty men were ready to swear that Beasley had summoned them to appear at the sessions of Epiphany 1664. Some made it apparent what had occured. Edward Luscombe had given him two shillings to be excused. A South Pool juror had given an undisclosed amount. Two Cornworthy men were summoned but 'neither appeared' for the same reason. Eight East Portlemouth jurors, warned for service by Beasley, turned out all to be copyholders and thus not entitled to sit on the sessions jury in any case.[53] Beasley was dismissed but like John Huish of East Budleigh, later resumed his duties (after a couple of years, in Beasley's case).

The re-appointments of even those bailiffs found guilty of extensive peculation belie the claims of justices to be ever-watchful for abuses in the hundreds. When in 1661 and 1689 the Bench declared that despite the best efforts of magistrates bailiffs summoned many jurors but returned few, 'for their owne private gaine in taking rewards' its claims were disingenuous . The 1664 case of the Coleridge bailiff demonstrated that in the hundred constables and their parochial subordinates the county had the makings of an administrative inspectorate which could have been employed to examine such charges with a minimal degree of supervision. This machinery was employed infrequently; the indifference implied supports the view that bailiffs were threatened for reasons other than their own incorrigible corruption.

Cases of physical assault by hundred bailiffs were not common and when they occurred, though they were painful to the victims, were no threat to the effectiveness of government or to the hierarchy of county power. Many instances doubtless went unreported. Minor gentlemen and substantial yeoman who served on the grand jury usually employed servants and bailiffs would have been foolhardy to risk attacking their social superiors. Less substantial yeomen, if assaulted, would perhaps have been reluctant to commit themselves to the expense and time which a report to a magistrate may have involved. Charles Vaughan, the former clerk of the peace, was beaten up by a bailiff at his home in Ottery St Mary but this seemingly sinister 'political' attack occurred probably during an arrest for debt. In his will Vaughan bemoaned the declined of his fortune; his estate was 'much decayed' through the 'late unhappy warres'.[54] Bailiffs were in any case themselves open to attack. William Bartlett, a predecessor of Benjamin Beasley in the hundred of Coleridge, was told by Richard Fountain of Dittisham, whom he was summoning, that 'if he did not depart he would thrust a knife in his buttocks'; and in January 1651 John Warren of South Molton reported that he had been assaulted by a recalcitrant juror.[55]

The bailiffs of the hundreds of Devon were an undistinguished lot. Their contribution to the public life of the communities whence they came was confined to their work of summoning juries. No bailiffs served as constables of the hundreds or as treasurers of gaol, hospital or maimed soldiers' funds and rarely are their names to be found on jury lists. The sources for the study of the wealth of social groups are unhelpful. Bailiffs were evidently too poor to attract the attentions of compounding commissioners or pre-civil war escheators and feodaries. The destruction of the Exeter wills has precluded a study of what might have been the most fruitful line of enquiry. As one might have predicted, no bailiffs had their wills proved in London. Even the Protestation Returns of 1641 are not particularly illuminating. The names of many bailiffs occur in the lists for parishes within the hundreds they served to suggest that local knowledge, intimacy with little-visited farmsteads in remote coombs or windswept moorland was the main qualification for their work. Bailiffs must have been more like scouts than administrators. In Kent they remain, despite T. E. Hartley's investigations, 'a biographical unknown quantity'.[56]

For Devon it must be concluded that where something can be ascertained of the bailiffs as a group it confirms that they were men of no more than husbandmen status in most cases. Of the bailiffs whose place of residence can with reasonable confidence be asserted, only seven appear in the hearth tax returns and they were taxed with one or two hearths each only. Indeed, the difficulties of locating even a place of residence for most bailiffs suggest either that bailiffs tended to be among the more socially mobile (in the physical sense) or that the sources for such an enquiry (particularly the tax returns) were not as inclusive of the entire male population as has been supposed by some modern historians.[57] The duplication of surnames and the absence of corroborative evidence, familiar pitfalls to the student of petty officialdom, here seem gaping chasms. Whether the Codnors of Haytor hundred who held that bailiwick for a quarter of a century or more were of the same family as Samuel

Codnor of Ipplepen, physician and Protectoral assessment commissioner, cannot be resolved. Was John Furlong of Black Torrington — bailiff there at odd times during the 1650s and 1660s — the grand juror of Whitchurch in Roborough? It seems unlikely that the bailiffs would have enjoyed such comparatively eminent connections; the right note is more likely to be struck if John Algar, the bailiff of Roborough throughout the 1660s, is identified with a petty juror on one occasion only, in 1660.

Occasionally a bailiff would stumble from the shadows into the glare of temporary notoriety, usually as the result of a neglect or a discovered fraud. The bailiff of Wonford, William Cliffe, anticipated the Restoration by almost two years when he was overhead to say in a shop in Chagford that 'Charles Stuart was King of England, Scotland and Ireland and ... that he would proclayme Charles Stuart King of England ...'. His accusers allowed in mitigation that they thought Cliffe 'was very much distempered with liquour'. Cliffe was not in office at the time and his punishment is unrecorded.[58] But apart from these cases, 'benign obscurity', to misquote Archbishop Parker, would seem to be the most appropriate epitaph to the 119 Devon hundred bailiffs between 1649 and 1670.

The Head Constables

There were up to seventy-five constables serving the hundreds at any one time, and they bore the main thrust of county administration. There were normally two constables in each hundred but in larger or more populous areas like East Budleigh, Wonford, Black Torrington and Hayridge three officers were usually sworn. Control by justices over the appointments and relief or dismissals of high constables was absolute. Retiring constables nominated two or three suitable successors to the Bench; the court then authorised 'the nearest justices' to select one or any other person. This accorded with the practice described by the anonymous author of *The Compleat Constable*; the influence of manorial lords or juries ended with the appointment of parish constables and they could be overruled by the Bench if they made choices unacceptable to the magistrates.[59] No longer was a constable a 'representative' of his township, 'exercising in his own person its communal rights and subject to its communal responsibilities'. More accurately constables of parishes and hundreds were the servants of the ruling elites of those administrative units.

Constables were fined for not attending sessions even though a 1629 assize order had relieved them from this obligation. In 1661 the justices were able to order that henceforth all presentments by constables were to be made at sessions and not at assizes.[60] Length of service was not predetermined but officers who had served for two or three years usually petitioned for their release. Variations among the hundreds were again considerable. In the 'hundred' of the Duchy of Lancaster in the 1660s the average length of service was only just above one year; in the hundred of Exminster at the same time it was six-and-a-half years. No spatial pattern can be discerned in the variations; there were only three constables from 1649 to 1670 in the remote North Devon hundred of Hartland but in equally distant Sherwill, facing South Wales across the Bristol Channel, there were ten constables and from 1660 to 1670 there was an average period of service as low as 2.82 years. Exminster hundred extended to the boundaries of the City of Exeter and the average length of service there was nearly ten years.[61]

Continuity in constabulary service suggests stability and effectiveness in government performance but long service could arise from neglect as well as from paternalistic supervision, from indolence in the office-holder as well from a sense of dedicated professionalism. Each hundred would have to be judged on whether tasks charged to the constables were effectively and swiftly performed, and the information is not available. This was a pre-bureaucratic age.[62] Length of service does not appear to have been considered as important to local government service. The tasks imposed upon constables increased during the 1660s and they were more closely supervised by quarter sessions, but these charges wrought no decisive alteration in the pattern of their service. In most hundreds there was a slight decline in the average length of service during the 1660s but only from 3.79 years in the Interregnum to 3.29 years from 1661 to 1670 — a difference of half a year. The average length of service for all hundreds between 1649 and 1670 was 4.09 years.

Devon head constables survived in office through political change. Evidence for 1648 to 1649 is lacking but the Restoration was accompanied by no purges of the constables of the Interregnum. There were of course changes in 1660 as there were in the years immediately preceding and following but they were the leisurely ones of an established routine not a hasty bundling out of the politically dangerous.[63] The pattern of appointments remained largely undisturbed. Daniel Condy was the only constable to be removed for his opposition to the Restoration and his case includes several peculiar features, not least that he was pushed out from below not as a result of any initiative by the JPs. Condy was a Tavistock clothier who married the daughter of the Independent minister of the town, Thomas Larkham, whose antinomian views and somewhat shady record in New England whence he had returned in 1642 made him a figure of some notoriety. Condy supported Larkham's religious convictions and lent his father-in-law substantial sums of money.[64] In 1658 Condy went as 'an ambassador' to the Exeter Independent minister, Lewis Stucley, about 'a mutuall communion between the churches'.[65] Throughout the 1650s Condy managed the Tavistock house of correction.[66] This entrée into local government service was followed by his elevation to the office of head constable of Tavistock in Michaelmas 1659.

In January 1660 Edmund Fowell, presbyterian lawyer, a former MP for Tavistock and the son of an erstwhile Plymouth town clerk, conducted an enquiry into the accounts of the house of correction on behalf of quarter sessions, a routine check were it not that Fowell had married the daughter of Thomas Larkham's arch-enemy, Francis Glanville.[67] Condy was not criticised, however, on this occasion; it was the proclamation of Charles II as king several months later which precipitated a crisis in Tavistock which Larkham and Condy did nothing to postpone. Condy, to counter what seemed to him a collapse of public order, to others a natural rejoicing at a welcome change, tried to employ his constabulary authority to organise a quasi-military force.[68] He struggled against the tide of popular emotion. Before Easter 1662 Condy's enemies requested sessions that 'he, a grand phanaticke, may be discharged from the office of head constableshipp',[69] and the magistrates heeded their petition. The instigator of Condy's ejection was George Howard, the illegitimate son of Sir Richard Grenville's widow, who had been something of a rakehell in Tavistock and who might thus have fallen foul of Larkham in the 1650s. Howard successfully solicited the support of William Courtenay, baronet, of Powderham, his cousin, a patron of moderate presbyterian ministers, and it may have been his influence with the Bench which hastened the downfall of Larkham and Condy. The former had in any case incensed so many individuals in Tavistock that personal grievances could be harnessed to popular agitation.[70] Condy was dismissed as constable and Larkham's ministry was terminated on St Bartholomew's Day 1662. Condy retained his governorship of the house of correction. His constableship had been brief, and his readiness to participate in local politics had cost him his position. His reliability could be exploited in the politically insensitive governorship of the Tavistock bridewell.

Condy was unusual in employing his constableship to good political effect. Most county-officeholders from the ranks of the minor gentry and the yeomanry were more likely to shrink from participating in what was never viewed either as an inalienable right or as a hard-won privilege for whose survival vigilance had to be exercised. The 'Clubman' mentality was always likely to be strongest when political upheaval was at its most intense. The introduction of the Engagement from early in 1650 may have hardened the reluctance to participate among the Devon yeomanry and minor gentlemen; in Michaelmas 1649 half a dozen men were bound over to the next sessions for refusing to take the office of constable in several hundreds. It was proving difficult to find men to serve on any terms, let alone those involving an additional political test.[71]

The office of constable was not confined to an élite, nor was it unrelated to other avenues of county service. Bailiffs were a group of socially inferior officers who were in all respects beyond the pale of county participation. Not so the head constables. Nearly thirty-five cent of them also served as grand jurors. Only two petty jurors became head constables in this period, to confirm that the public responsibilities of trial jurors began and ended with the limited task of delivering verdicts on criminal cases. Surprisingly, more seniority would seem to have been accorded grand jurors than head constables. Seventy constables served as grand jurors after retirement and almost half that number (thirty-nine) had been grand jurors before taking offices as constables.[72] The opposite might have been expected, since the duties of constables were increasingly onerous and responsible while grand jurors' presentments reveal an apathy, a willingness to be guided by the Bench which might suggest timidity born of inexperience.

The career pattern of the most numerous participants in county office below the level of JP ran contrary to the realities of local power. Local administration seemed to suffer an imbalance between the aspirations of minor officials and the needs of Leviathan, in taxation, in social policy and in law enforcement. Local gentlemen, after serving these needs with frequent reluctance and scant recognition, became grand jurors, the embodiments of an institution from which power had passed, kept alive by administrative inertia (or momentum) and by the persistence of a measure of magisterial flattery of jurors, in 'charges' and in entertainment. This imbalance produced no 'political' unrest among its sufferers and this crucial difference between minor officials and JPs was maintained by the absolute domination of the magistrates and by the inadequacy of political ideology among their subordinates. 'County' ideology was an emotionally powerful but intellectually puny concept but there is little to suggest that even the good of the county was an object of endeavour and discussion among the minor gentry and yeomanry of Devon. A group of officials among whom abstention from office is the sum of their political action was only dimly aware of the encroachments of magistrates, for whom in the 1640s and 1650s 'the country' had been such an attractive rallying-point.[73]

Yet there was a sizeable minority of twenty-one constables who served as grand jurors while they held constabulary office, an indication of how the imbalance between the aspirations of individuals and the needs of government was being corrected. It would not be a great step from the recognition that a serving constable was well qualified to be a grand juror to the awareness that what made him so was his greater knowledge of matters requiring presentment and his capacity to engage in dialogue with the magistrates on the minutiae of local government performance. His role in that performance must now be considered.

A series of constables' presentments from the 1660s has survived among the quarter sessions records and they confirm the vigour of constabulary initiatives in that decade.[74] After total collapse in the 1640s and a slow reconstruction in the 1650s the hundred constables were almost as vigorous in their presenting after the Restoration as the justices had been during the 1630s. In most cases it is not clear to whom the presentments were made. Some were initially presented at petty sessions and thence forwarded to the general sessions,[75] though it was significant that in Ottery St Mary in the Sixties and Seventies the constables sent presentments to petty sessions and not to Exeter. In their view petty sessions existed in their own right, not as an adjunct to quarter sessions. The constables of Tavistock and West Budleigh acknowledged petty sessions.[76] Tavistock hundred centred on the town, so allegiances to petty sessions may have been stronger in areas where hundreds were co-extensive with large settlements and where courts leet survived to be active.

Presentments offered by parish constables, churchwardens or surveyors of highways were sometimes simply endorsed by head constables, with a frequency which suggests that many more parochial presentments were despatched to sessions than have survived.[77] The grand jury, in turn, often underwrote constables' presentments and, in theory at least, considered every presentment and endorsed it *billa vera*.[78] (In fact, presentments by officials were considered *prima facie* as true bills.) Thus the presentments system did not depend on officials having their ears to the ground, being 'better acquainted with the common grievance of the countrie then justices'[79] so much as on effective control. The roots of presentments were more systematic if less challenging to the establishment than J. S. Morrill allows; their flourishing was one of the fruits of hierarchy rather than an independent threat to it. Most decisions, most actions in local government were conceived at the apex of a pyramid of responsibilities, among the JPs. The presentments system began at the base of the pyramid with most information coming from the parishes through petty constables and head constables to the grand jury and the Bench. Most presentments were of parochial matters, of deteriorations in services, in lapses in fulfilling moral and legal obligations by individuals, rather than criticisms of the Bench and of the government. Constables' presentments for the 1660s have been summarised as Table 4.

The subject exercising constables most were the arrears of subordinate officials in the parishes. There were twice as many complaints about these than about the next most vexatious issue, that of decays in roads and bridges. Associated with pressure from the Bench on the hundreds (and thence on the parishes) to clear past accounts and to bring in outstanding local taxes in the 1660s were petitions by constables for the payment of their expenses, and the regular production of fairly detailed accounts. By far the greatest number of complaints against parish officers were aimed at recovering arrears for the annual taxes for the maintenance of county gaols and hospitals and for the relief of maimed soldiers, but considerable effort was expended in securing the payment of *ad hoc* levies imposed for the repair of bridges. Localism was not defined by local boundaries; head constables found it difficult to collect money for the repair of bridges outside their hundreds. Parish constables were occasionally reprimanded for not making presentments or for not making them to the head constables; even *omnia bene* had to be reported in writing.[80]

The thirty-seven presentments for absence for absence from church recall the interest taken by the grand jury in this topic. The adjacent hundreds of West Budleigh and Crediton together accounted for about forty per cent of the recusancy and church absence cases, which began to appear in presentments from around 1662. Nonconformity flourished in this cloth-producing area but constables seemed reluctant to present what frequently accompanied absence from church — attendance at conventicles. During the purges of these two meetings during 1670, the initiative lay entirely with the magistrates. Local officials consistently acted with much hestitation when they enforced new legislation in the 1650s and 1660s; in this sense the new laws of the Rump governing private morality were at one with the Uniformity Act.

The volume of presentments by constables may be compared with the frequency of orders on specific topics by the justices in the order books. The revived jurisdiction of the consistory courts excludes a comparison

Table 4: Constables' Presentments 1660 to 1670

	Constables' arrears, neglects	Church absenteeism	Recusancy	Rates: refusing payment	Roads and bridges	Neglecting roads and bridges	Settlement, vagrancy	Conventicles	Abusing constables	Bastardy	Apprenticeship, poor laws	Disturbing ministers	Alehouses and drinking	Swearing	Poaching
Axminster	6	1			3	3	1						2	1	
Bampton	2	2			2	1	2	1	1				2		1
Black Torrington	5				2	1									
Braunton	6								1				1		
Clyston						1	1			1	1				
Coleridge	3	1			3					1			3	2	
Colyton	3			3	2	2	3			1	5				
Crediton	2	11	2	3	6	3	9		2		6	1	3	1	
E. Budleigh	1		2		4						2				
W. Budleigh	2	6					1		1				2		
Ermington	1				6										
Exminster	3	1			2										1
Fremington	2	1								1			1		
Halberton	7	3			2		2				1		5	1	
Hartland		1													
Hayridge	2			5	1										
Haytor	3	3	5	1		1							2		
Hemyock	2				1	2							1		
Lifton	6			3	1	2			1				1		
North Tawton	7	1									1		2		
Ottery St, Mary	1	3	1		1						2		2		
Plympton	3										1				
Roborough	6	1		1	2				1				2		
Shebbear	6		1												
Sherwill	2		1												
South Moulton	1				1										
Stanborough	2				3										
Teignbridge	4	2			1		1				1		1		
Tiverton	3				3		4								
Witheridge	9				2								1		
Wonford	11				1										
TOTALS	112	37	12	16	48	16	24	1	7	4	20	1	30	5	2

involving cases of absence from church; quarter sessions was not the only, or even the principal, jurisdiction in that matter. Only attacks on conventicles following legislation in 1670 — seventeen cases in the three sessions from Midsummer 1670 to Epiphany 1671 — indicated overt magisterial vigour in defence of the church. (Unofficially, to the gratification of Bishop Sparrow, much help was offered the church courts by a cadre of Anglican partisans.[81]) Even where the process of law was confined to the court of quarter sessions there was a gross imbalance between the number of constables' presentments and the volume of order book entries on specific issues. On roads and bridges, for example, for which forty-eight constables' presentments have survived from the 1660s, the JPs made 131 orders in the same period. Twenty-four presentments on vagrancy and settlement were offered to the court but there were twenty-two court orders in 1662, the year of the Act of Settlement, alone. This was partly because the orders resulted from information not only by constables and juries but by paid informers, nosy neighbours and others with grudges as well as by the magistrates and their seemingly near-omniscient clerks. The discrepancy also highlights the procedures of the court. Not all matters deserved an entry in the order book. Presentments of simple misdemeanours usually resulted in prosecution, and details of offences would be entered directly on bills of indictment. Thus, breaches of the assize of ale and cases of unlicensed or unruly alehouses accounted for thirty constables' presentments — the fourth most numerous category — but very few of these were entered in the order books. Failure to enter each case did not imply an abdication of interest by magistrates in social control, but it suggested that the alehouse laws were clear, uncomplicated and administratively simple. These laws, laid down in the statute of 5 and 6 Edward VI c. 25 with Jacobean accretions, were not substantively amended after the reign of Charles I. Cases brought under them demanded little of the court's time. Moreover, the laws of evidence in early modern England were not demanding[82] so that local consensus against an errant alehousekeeper could combine with high legal costs to prevent a compelling defence against suppression.

A significant difference between the presentments of constables and grand juries was that the former avoided personal attacks on fellow-officials or against other individuals more prominent in government. The grand jury was a co-operative body, a team, in which restrictions of personal initiative were balanced by anonymity for individuals on the principle of safety in numbers. Teams also foster personal rivalries, however. Constables worked singly and lacked both the stimulus to, and protection against, personal vendettas and their consequences. But those outside the charmed circle of local government could expect no immunity from criticism, however exalted their social position. Even the humble constables of Churston Ferrers parish did not flinch from presenting the London parvenu, Sir Peter Lear, in 1668 for not paying 'his proportions to severall rates for the repaireing of severall county bridges'.[83] Papists were excluded from local administration by statute, and several prominent Roman Catholics were presented by constables for recusancy.[84]

In the 1660s and probably in the 1650s although direct evidence is lacking, the fecundity of constables' presentments offered a contrast to the withering of the grand jury. Control over constables had been secured and maintained in quarter sessions and since regular presentments could be produced from each hundred, a continuing and distinctive role for the grand jury was becoming difficult to envisage. But other organs of government should not be judged against the performance of the moribund grand jury. Constables' presentments flowed in frequently but they did not provide the bulk of the administrative caseload by any means. The constables' apologies that they had made other presentments to petty sessions were ominous straws in the wind. By the late 1660s in rural areas like Black Torrington hundred and by the late 1670s in *all* hundreds, the presentments by constables at quarter sessions had become mechanical repetitions of *omnia bene*, a sterile ritual in which all participated with no effect on the executive tasks of government.[85]

The presentments of constables had deteriorated even more rapidly than those of the grand jury, but hardly in the same circumstances. The grand jury had represented the claims of the amateur against those of the professional. It was dependent on a system of selection recognised as grossly fallible even in an age when 'efficiency', in government was only a welcome refinement of 'effectiveness', rarely experienced. The office of constable, by contrast, was much more suited to the role of representative of the parishes because its incumbents were in regular contact with parochial subordinates. The grand juror was likely to bring to quarter sessions the grievances of his parish; the constable had access to a dozen parishes or more, and it was in his interests to cultivate this access. It was not through devotion to the ideals of the county that the constables presented the neglect and arrears of parish officials on over a hundred occasions in the 1660s, but because their own discharges from office, the carrot dangled by quarter sessions before so many gentlemen in its service, depended on the clearing of their accounts and thus of those of subordinate officers.[86] The professionals won a scarcely-perceived struggle in quarter sessions by a kind of natural selection but quarter sessions itself was not an immutable guardian of 'county' interests. The apogee of sessions was achieved during a period of frequently severe tensions between central (Privy Council) and local (court of quarter sessions) government, when the interests of justices were defended in sessions meetings where petitions to Whitehall were drafted and in which local pecularities of procedure became bulwarks against which the tides of centralisation should beat in vain. The 1660s did not see a revival of 1630s-style local and central government relations, however, just as they did not witness the resurrection of prerogative courts, fiscal feudalism, or even Laudianism. Political patronage and the disinterested exercise of local power could never be separated, but it was in the 1630s when pressure from the centre was at its most intense that it was realised that the sway over the parishes by JPs could most safely, effectively and easily be conducted in petty sessions. Freed from central pressures, it was natural that there was a rediscovery in the 1660s of what administrative *blitzkrieg* had almost casually revealed under the proponents of 'Thorough'. As petty sessions developed apace so presentments to quarter sessions became increasingly irrelevant, whether by grand jury or constables, since petty sessions were more sensitive to the apprehension and summary binding over of alleged felons. Seen in this light the dominance by the office of constables over the grand jury was merely a shift of emphasis in an organ of government, but the eclipse of presentments altogether was a sign that that organ itself was passing through a substantial modification.

Presentments were easily choked by pressure from above and by shifts in the balance of administrative power. At no time, however, were presentments the principal burden on constables' time. The main function of a local official at any level was as 'an intermediary between different concepts of the community'[87]—the JP representing the county to central government for example—and the head constables mediated between the hundreds, as the sum of their constituent parishes, and the county, represented in sessions. In no area was this function exercised more regularly or to better effect than in the responsibilities of constables for the collection of local rates. In Norfolk, at least until the 1630s, local taxation was ad hoc, and levied for the repair of specific roads and bridges or for the relief of named distressed persons.[88] As a result, the proportion payable by individual hundreds had to be determined on each occasion and so the Norfolk Bench was plagued by continual disputes between magistrates claiming reductions in the rates for their areas.[89] In mid-seventeenth century Devon, stability in rating had been achieved. Although it is not clear how the sums were decided, an established annual rate in each hundred division had been agreed and was accepted by each constable. The rates were to maintain hospitals and houses of correction and to relieve maimed soldiers by providing pensions. Sums fixed on hundreds were then divided by constables into levies on the parishes in their stewardship, not into equal impositions but into proportions based on the population and thus the capacity to pay of the parishes. The establishment of fixed rates ended dissension among the justices but did nothing to prevent disgruntled petitions by those who resented the assessments made of their financial means by the constables. An annual average of eighteen complaints from individuals in the parishes were received by the magistrates during the Commonwealth. Accusations that the constables set the rate to favour the parishes where they lived[90] mingled with darker grievances; the Chudleigh ratepayers complained of 'the ill suggestions of William Babb, gentleman, constable of the hundred who findeing noe direct meanes to leavye the [local rates] hath and doth still use the power of the sword in a most rigorous course'.[91]

County rates were steady. Robert Coombe of Willand was constable of Halberton hundred in the later 1640s and presented his accounts in 1648.[92] The charges levied in his division for gaols and hospitals were exactly the same—fourteen shillings and seventeen shillings and four pence respectively—when the annual rates were copied into the order books in 1667.[93] Ralph Richards, accounting in 1661 for an eight year period of office in Hayridge hundred, paid the same annual sums over to sessions for hospitals and gaols throughout his term. They, too, were the same in 1667.[94] The reasons for this continuity are fairly obvious. County provision for relief of the sick and for the punishment of offenders was forced into the procrustean mould of the physical capacity of the hospitals and houses of correction. Despite plans to build new houses of correction, there were chronic difficulties attending all attempts to implement these schemes. More poor people or more chronically sick could only mean worse provision—overcrowding, disease and hunger. The debate over the future of bridewells was conducted mainly in terms of the capacity of the Bench to control them. Not all local rates remained constant, however. Fees for mustermasters—the professional NCOs responsible for co-ordinating the efforts of the trained bands—were a charge erratically met during the 1630s and the 1660s and were paid directly to the mustermasters by constables.[95] Gaolers and wardens of hospitals were paid from the central funds administered by the treasurers for gaols and hospitals; head constables contributed the sums they collected from the parishes to these funds. Mustermasters were paid after the Restoration at the pre-civil war rate. George Palmer's last duty, before he retired from the constableship of Hayridge in 1661, was to pay Grenville Weekes thirteen shillings and two pence from the six parishes under his supervision. Direct payment hardly encouraged regular payments. Even though the mustermaster had a powerful interest in seeing the sums collected, the size of the county made personal intervention on each occasion impracticable.

Mustermasters' fees fluctuated through administrative weakness arising from magisterial wavering, but it was another aspect of the county militia which increased the rate charge on the population—the burden of relief for maimed soldiers. By the late 1640s the rates imposed for the relief of former soldiers had dropped, at pre-civil war levels, below the sums levied for gaols and hospitals. Robert Coombe of Willand was responsible for collecting only ten shillings and eight pence from the parishes of Willand and Sampford Peverell for this purpose, as against fourteen shillings for mustermaster's fees and the same amount for gaols. Seventeen shillings and four pence went to the hospitals.[96] By the 1650s these proportions had been reversed, doubtless as a result of numerous petitions to sessions by soldiers and soldiers' widows, supported by serving and former officers. The Hayridge constables paid £4.6s.8d. each year from 1653 to 1660 for maimed soldiers. In 1653 the JPs confirmed that the soldiers' rate had been doubled between 1648 and 1653. The quarter sessions order book names at least eighty people wounded in the service of Parliament or whose husbands had been killed, who were relieved by pensions or by lump sums in 1649 and 1650 alone, and this is likely to be a minimum estimate. In 1660 the problem was even greater. Even though all those who had fought for Parliament were now excluded from county relief, the disbanding of the army impoverished many whose past allegiances in arms could no longer adequately be proved. In January 1661 eighty-three soldiers were awarded a total of £235.3s.4d. per annum, with a bonus of twenty shillings each for their 'present relief'. Throughout the rest of 1661 additional lists of another ninety were complied, but the clamour for county provision led inevitably to reduced individual pensions.[97]

In the early 1650s the partisans of Parliament could each expect fifty shillings a year but pressure on funds which could not be raised quickly had reduced this in 1661 to a mere ten shillings at most for those on supplementary lists. A sub-committee of the leading magistrates established rules for the payment of pensions more stringent than any compiled during the Interregnum. All soldiers were to produce testimonies from field officers that they had been loyal to the late king, and certificates from surgeons to confirm their disabilities. The certificates were to be produced at Easter sessions, when other accounts were to be produced by officials.[98] Although the county was able to reap certain benefits from this pool of dependents, many of whom were willing to work for quarter sessions if they could, the burden of the rates was bound to increase, and by 1667 the charge on the part of Hayridge hundred, formerly in the care of George Palmer, then under the supervision of Zachary Travers, had risen to £6.10s. per annum for maimed soldiers, three times the sum of other rates.[99] To maintain some perspective on what were in their own terms massive rate increases it should be noted that local taxes remained light in comparison with the demands of the State. For example, the entire annual rate burden on Ermington hundred in 1667 was £30.17s., while the monthly contribution of three of the eleven parishes of the hundred towards the assessment had in 1653 amounted to £37.12s.6d.[100] By 1662 and the act of 13 and 14 Charles II c. 10, which established the hearth tax, Ermington hundred was expected to produce £177.17s. every six months on its 2,357 hearths.[101]

The onus of local rate collection fell entirely on the backs of the head constables and although they escaped some of the burden of national tax-collecting, government policy after the Restoration imposed more duties on them. The hearth tax was administered by the provisions of 13 and 14 Charles II c. 10 county by county, with the collection of the dues and the surveys of taxable hearths left to petty and high constables. There was no overt opposition to the hearth tax from the parishes, although one or two like Gilbert Burrington of Crediton refused to let the constables survey his dwelling.[102] At a higher level, it was Sir Courtenay Pole, the MP for Honiton, who first introduced the hearth tax bill to the Commons, supported by Sir William Morrice. Morrice wrote to Edmund Prideaux of Padstow that the Court Party had 'made the chymnyes smoake for it (though they never chance fire) and have approved ourselves good subjects'.[103] Returns of chargeable hearths were to be made by constables to the clerk of the peace who was in turn to engross them in one account to the Exchequer. The allowances to the collecting officials indicate where the burden of administration was expected to fall. Sheriffs were allowed three pence in the pound, petty constables two pence and high constables and clerks of the peace one penny each. On the face of it this was realistic because the surveys, as well as the collection of the tax, were entrusted to petty constables.[104] But as Chandaman and Meekings demonstrate, the 1662 act was undermined by the instability of administration at its lowest levels; parish constables changed annually in many parishes and this made continuity difficult to maintain. 'The humble status of the constables hardly gave them an authority commensurate with the heavy responsibilities placed upon them.'[105] Meekings exaggerates in extending the annual turnover in local offices to include head constables, however; in Devon it was they who maintained continuity, who more than any others were suited for the administrative task involved in hearth tax collection, since they stayed in office for extended periods. A constable in office in 1662 would very likely have been there still when the alleged negligence of local officers was cited as the reason for introducing officials responsible only for the hearth tax.[106] Head constables enjoyed regular contact with the justices and clerks of the peace, grandees who would have seemed remote to parish constables.

The 'devolution' of the 1662 hearth tax thus increased the burden on the county and on its work-horses, the head constables. The restoration of the militia, along the lines of that which prevailed in the 1630s, was an even greater imposition on them. The orthodox government view of the ideal militia as a volunteer force supported by central taxation was swamped by the Country preference for locally-raised, locally-paid trained bands: a substantive concession to localism. There were difficulties in the government and in Parliament over the terms of this concession, of course. There was the undercurrent of opinion against an outright return to the militia of the 1630s; there was the failure by the Court to exercise prerogative control over the musters in 1660 and there was a prolonged feud between the House of Lords and the House of Commons over the respective powers and privileges of lord lieutenants and their deputies. William Morrice noted the resentment of the Lords 'that they shalbe sett to horse and armes by deputy lieutenants' but by May 1662 these issues had been resolved by a series of tactical compromises. The fiscal integrity of the Lords was protected by a system of separate assessment.[107]

There was probably much less dissension in the localities. From the summer of 1660, with the uncontested appointment of Monck as Lord Lieutenant and a dozen others (royalists with a decent leavening of presbyterians) as deputy lieutenants, the way was clear for the disarming of suspected republicans and 'Oliverians'.[108] The lieutenants were to 'be sure at least to keepe up the full number both of horse and foote which the trayned bands of that our county were formerly wont to consist of'.[109] No-one could be sure how the arms stocks and muster assessments in the parishes had fared since the beginning of the civil war, and so a survey was undertaken, parish by parish, into their condition, and the head constables supervised it. The returns to the deputy lieutenants have survived for the hundreds of Coleridge and Stanborough and within these hundreds conditions varied widely.[110] Some parish constables were able to produce comprehensive lists of the taxable population, even though many of those on them had died since 1640. On the other hand, the constables of Malborough parish insisted to the deputy lieutenants that 'there is an impossibility in fulfillinge the extreame of yor honours warrants, viz. a list in 1640, parties being unready and at a vast losse of memory to recount the auncient charges as specifically registered in the muster rolle'. They promised 'as our expresse of loyalty' the complete arms for twenty foot-soldiers instead.[111] There was no widespread reluctance to refurbish the musters, which were akin to festive church-ales for many parishioners; they were 'inclined to treat the occasion as a holiday'.[112]

The militia ordinances of the 1640s and 1650s had exempted from local contributions those who had an annual income of less than £10. Statutes of 1660 and 1662 first increased the minimum taxable income to £15 but then removed such qualifications altogether. Restoration militia legislation widened the social basis of taxation but lowered the scale of payments.[113] The changes burdened the poorer classes and increased the number of individuals taxable. Moreover they added to the administrative tasks of local officials. In Norfolk it seems that the militia of the 1660s functioned outside the range of quarter sessions, and that the deputy lieutenants, clearly intended as an 'inner circle' of Court dependents, continued to administer the musters separately.[114] Yet as Richard Dunn shows, the infrastructure of quarter sessions government and militia administration was a shared one, in which the head constables played the key role. The militia naturally depended on effective communications to co-ordinate its activities. In Devon, as well as company musters four times a year, there was an annual general rendezvous of horses and men, and warrants from the deputy lieutenants were directed to petty constables, to individual contributors, to 'loyal and indigent officers', to 'maimed soldiers' and to the tinners, all of whom were expected to appear at particular meetings.

Other specific tasks had to be accomplished by the deputy lieutenants: ammunition stores had to be checked, and their transfer from one place to another authorised, by warrants of the deputies delivered by head constables. Arthur Prideaux, one of the two constables of Ermington hundred, executed forty-two militia warrants in 1662 and 1663. Prideaux was in charge only of part of the hundred, and was accountable at quarter sessions also for presentments, local rates, the delivery of civilian warrants and the levying of *ad hoc* taxes. In the same period, John Avent of Plympton executed twenty-four militia warrants. The burden did not diminish as the decade progressed; Avent's successor, Thomas Geale, received twenty-one warrants between June 1666 and August 1667. In Black Torrington hundred, far-flung and thinly populated, John Tickell, one of the three head constables, delivered thirty warrants in 1666 and 1667.[115] The statutes of 14 Charles II c. 3 and 15 Charles II c. 5 provided that sums raised by constables for the maintenance of the militia should be paid to deputy lieutenants; this has led R. M. Dunn to exaggerate the independence of the militia from quarter sessions. Administrative expenses incurred by constables were met by the justices, however, and so the accounts for the delivery of warrants were presented at sessions. The workload on head constables was heavy enough to justify the regular employment of footposts.

Footposts were agents of county government who took up the delivery of letters where the government post office—under direct control in the 1650s, afterwards in farm—left it. They were an improvement on the slow and unreliable common post which county government in Somerset had relied upon in the 1630s. In the surveys of the Devon militia in 1660 the names of the footposts were appended to the lists of the taxpayers, and they gradually assumed the physical task of delivering the warrants, under the close direction of the head constables. They were paid directly by the constables and it was for reimbursement of these sums that the constables presented accounts of militia warrants to sessions.[116] Footposts were paid for the miles they travelled and although head constables were apt to refer to their 'footpost', lists of militia assessments give the names of the footposts in each parish, and the number of miles covered suggest how necessary a number of footposts in each hundred was. The returns of miles travelled were inevitably notional but they make the point that assistance for the head constables was necessary. John Avent's footposts covered four hundred and sixteen miles, an average of seventeen miles a month, on militia business. During the Interregnum there was no 'settled pay' for footposts but by the 1660s they were paid, and constables reimbursed, at the rate of a penny per mile. The expenses of constables on footposts became another link binding constables and quarter sessions since repayment could only be made on presentation of accurate accounts.[117]

The sessions bundles of the 1660s are an eloquent testimony to the development of administrative techniques. From the 1660s the haphazard scrawls of officials who, in recalling their transactions has jotted them down as each came into their heads were no longer typical. Each warrant delivered, each administrative action undertaken, was now numbered and frequently underlined to separate it from the next. Double entry accounting and the balance sheet were unknown but just as the condition of the sessions order books have been taken as an indication of bureaucratic standards,[118] so the painstaking accounts of head constables in the Restoration period mark a shift towards 'professionalism' in local government at a level afforded inadequate attention by historians.

The restoration of the county militia fell heavily on constables and tried their patience because it was not the only charge to fall upon them. The county rates increased largely because of military disbandment. The introduction of the hearth tax was fiscal 'devolution' in its terms, although it was not long before the government repented of its surrender to local pressures. As the volume of local government business expanded so the status and prestige of the magistrates were enhanced. Pressure on the resources of the magistrates from below was not complemented by strong direction from the Privy Council above. In Western's view, the militia, which had contributed so much to heavier local responsibilities, 'suffered severely from the long decline in central interference in local administration that set in after the Restoration'.[119] Whether or not this was true as a general principle, petty sessions developed apace and accorded with the social and political aspirations of a magistracy restored to what it considered a natural and rightful inheritance.[120] For the constables, however, the lapse of central direction brought with it no spoils or rewards, only the highly dubious privilege of recognition by justices that their work was more and more important, a recognition couched in terms no more gracious than a torrent of orders and warrants against defaulting officials.

For the head constables the 1660s brought with them no change in kind but only in the volume of business. The constables had to combine to insist on adequate reimbursement. At the Midsummer sessions of 1662 ten head constables, half of whom had served during the Interregnum, had to remind the Bench that they were 'continually put to very great charges and expences by footposts in the dispersing of warrants and other messuages to the severall parishes within our respective limitts and divisions ... and hitherto had nothing allowed or paid us for the same'.[121] In the Michaelmas sessions of the previous year it had been established by the JPs that footposts would be paid from martial rates on the parishes, in an attempt to relieve the county rates for gaols, hospitals and maimed soldiers.[122] The uncertainty of this revenue prompted the constables' complaint and the immediate order by the magistrates that footposts should get a penny a mile from the county stock.[123] Even this was not considered adequate by some constables. Eighteen composed another petition and presented it at the Michaelmas sessions of 1662. This petition received more support than the earlier one, but still under a third of the seventy-odd constables signed it. Seven of the eighteen had drawn up the summer petition; they pointed out that they were 'likely to be frustrate' of the magistrates' good intentions, 'by reason that the stores and treasuries (vizt., the gaols, maymed soldiers and hospitals) out of which your worshipps did allott the same are scarce sufficient for the particular services for which they were appointed'.[124] They requested permission to raise *ad hoc* rates from the parishes upon presentation of accounts to the nearest JPs, but such initiatives could not be encouraged by magistrates whose control of county government was becoming more and more absolute. The petition met with stony silence.[125]

This was as near as the justices came in the 1660s to a revolt among their subordinates and it was but a brief display of discontent which never received widespread overt support among the head constables. Through the rest of the decade the pressure was firmly, continuously and irreversibly exerted by the magistrates on the constables to produce accounts in arrears, a pressure maintained by social differences between county gentry and 'peasant gentry' or yeomanry and by the structure of government itself, in which constables and jurors had adopted a firm stance of subservience. This was demonstrated by the manner in which the work of bailiffs and jurors fell into fixed routines in which the limits of their authority and expected performances were unquestionably defined. Magisterial control over constables was expressed in very different terms: it was expressed in the constables' role as a reliable taskforce which could be called upon to fulfill the more irregular functions of local government.

Bridges (unlike roads) were not maintained in the seventeenth century, but were simply repaired when they became dilapidated or dangerous. In some counties bridge repairs could only be authorised by grand jury presentments[126] but one result of the decay of the Devon grand jury was that bridge repairs were speeded up because they were initiated instead by private petition to sessions. In most cases the magistrates inquired into the history of repairs to decayed bridges in order to discover where responsibility lay. Some bridges were repaired by private landowners, some by hundreds or parishes and some by the county. There were inevitably disingenuous disavowals of responsibility, but some problems were genuine. The history of an Exminster bridge was a puzzle because 'it is uncertaine by whom the sayd bridge ought to be repayred for that (as this court is informed) the same hath not been in decay formerly within the memory of any man'.[127] But wherever responsibility was judged to lie, the burden of rate collection usually fell upon the head constables, who acted as receivers from the parish officials if repairs were charged to the parishes of a single hundred, or as collectors under an independent, purposely-appointed treasurer if more than one hundred was involved.[128] Yet all initiative in bridge repair assessments lay with the justices, who retained the right to view the bridges to estimate the cost of making good the decay, and to appoint able workmen. The sums involved were frequently very large. Richard Osborne, treasurer for Christow and Spera bridges in 1667 was responsible for collecting £170 for one bridge alone—more than the annual levy on the whole county for the maintenance of its prisons.[129] The larger the assessed sum, the longer it took to raise, and so bridge funds arrears orders were almost as frequent as efforts to retrieve county rates. The demands made on the time of the justices called for some delegation of bridge repair procedure but where this occurred the initiative passed not to constables but to a group of men even more devoted to the interests of the magistrates: their clerks.[130]

Other *ad hoc* tax collections administered partly if not exclusively by the constables were the funds for plague relief in the late 1640s[131] and voluntary contributions towards the relief of the poor or those whose homes had been destroyed by fire.[132] Such collections were made for objects of charity outside Devon.

The delivery of warrants was a regular aspect of constabulary duties and probably attracted more hostility towards them than even the collection of taxes. Head constables delivered warrants or orders from the court to the parish constables and reported to the court on the consequences of their delivery. Thus in January 1651 the constable of East Budleigh hundred presented to sessions the returns of the parishes in his charge to an inquiry of the court into the number of maltsters operating in the area and into the number of waywardens.[133] Warrants were despatched in bundles, distributed to the parishes and then returned with the endorsement of either success or failure. The system depended on undisputed authority; defaulting head constables were as liable to the threats and censures of the Bench as were the parish officials to them. Two constables of neighbouring parishes indicated their healthy respect for the office of head constable in their recriminations over a neglected warrant:

> I told you that you should make returne on Monday night, I made returne of the rest of the warrant this morning but how you will spake for not making of your returne I knowe not, unlesse you goe to Exeter tomorrow verie earlie and enquire for the high constable for your own discharge ... [134]

There were warrants other than those of quarter sessions or assizes. The militia warrants of the 1660s proceeded from deputy lieutenants and during the Interregnum warrants were sent by Admiralty commissioners to hundred constables and thence to parish constables in order to organise naval pressing compaigns.[135]

It has already been noted that three-quarters of the sessions grand jurors served as constables and so much of what has been discovered of the social position of jurors can be applied to the head constables as a group. A sample of the hearth tax ratings of fifty-one constables indicates that their average of hearths each was 5.1, almost exactly the same as the grand jurors,[136] and as before the average conceals enormous variations. Robert Cliverdon, who served Hartland hundred for sixteen years, had no fewer than eighteen hearths. Peter Elbow of Buckfastleigh had twelve, Robert Rawleigh of Sheepwash in Shebbear had eight. A sample of forty-seven lay subsidy rolls values produces an average land assessment of £2.3s. Assessments for militia contributions are another source for wealth. From the Protestation Returns of all adult males in 1641 and from the 1640 charges for the militia compiled by the petty constables in 1660 it may be concluded that only a minority among parishioners contributed towards these levies.[137] Among the parishes of Coleridge hundred only seventeen of the thirty-six Loddiswell men were chargeable and in South Brent the proportion was as low as twenty-five out of two hundred and sixty-seven. Nine of the seventy-two Woodleigh men contributed. In these three parishes, therefore, the average percentage of the adult male population contributing to the militia was only 12.33 per cent. Constables were always among these dubiously-privileged men. The most each contributed was a musket and a pike and for most it was either one or the other. One or two had to provide only a corslet (or more usually, its cost). Here the difference in status between magistrates and the very minor gentry and yeomanry becomes most apparent. JPs could not expect to escape contributing less than a horse each and many were assessed at a horse and a man's arms complete. John Kellond, JP, of Painsford in Ashprington, had to pay for a horse and two foot soldiers' arms (he had sixteen hearths). Sir Edmund Fortescue, JP of East Allington, who paid on an eighteen-hearthed property, was considered wealthy enough to pay for a light horse complete with arms and a pike and musket. Below the level of the most wealthy, the cost of the militia was spread fairly evenly among the dozen or so leading parishioners, but the head constables always fell in the latter rather than in the former group.

The destruction of the Devon wills has left a large gap in the sources for a study of the wealth of constables. Nevertheless one or two of the surviving inventories suggest the wide variation in their moveable wealth. Thomas Tucker, of South Molton, constable of that hundred in 1650, possessed at his death only his house and its contents. William Heywood of Bondleigh, on the other hand, was a farmer whose livestock and crops contributed substantially to the posthumous assessment of his wealth. William Searle of Dartington was assessed similarly as a yeoman and head constable. In these three cases the value of their personal estates did not amount to £100 each.[138] The selection of surviving inventories cannot substantiate hypotheses about the wealth of the Devon yeomanry as a whole but it may be of note that the three known grand jurors whose inventories are still available were worth much more than the constables. Thomas Dyer of Shobrooke was assessed at £278.18s., John Viccary of Farway at £222.9s.4d. and Scipio Heywood of Winkleigh at £463.3s.[139] None of them served as grand jurors during the 1660s and it is interesting to speculate whether the Restoration decade saw a rise in the status of selected constables while grand jurors became less prestigious. Such a shift would accord with the relative importance of the two groups in the performance of government although in at least one other county it was the high constables who as a group dwindled in status after 1660.[140] Most of the constables and grand jurors were undoubtedly involved primarily in agriculture as a source of income but as with the jurors there were exceptions. Daniel Condy of Tavistock was a merchant, Giles Moore of Broadclyst (constable during the 1650s despite having been sequestered for royalism) was a brewer who had enjoyed royal patronage under licence in the 1630s.[141]

As well as a common background in social position, constables and grand jurors both held office in their parishes as an invariable administrative apprenticeship. Burnell Rider of Bere Ferrers was churchwarden there in 1645 and continued to serve as a supervisor of parish accounts through the Interregnum while sitting on the sessions grand jury from 1656 to 1658.[142] In the later 1640s, Nicholas Drewe of Chudleigh supervised the repair of the market house after having served as churchwarden and overseer of the poor in the 1630s.[143] During the Interregnum he was a grand juror. Robert Cliverdon, constable of Hartland hundred from 1650 to 1666, had been overseer of the poor in Hartland parish in 1645 and was so again in 1668. He was also one of the twenty-four 'governors' of the parish.[144] William Mallet was churchwarden of Iddesleigh in 1643 and 1651 and overseer in 1655.[145] From 1651 to 1653 he was a head constable and sat on the grand jury in 1660 and 1662. This pattern was universal in Devon and doubtless elsewhere but the tasks falling to the attention of these men were not merely an apprenticeship in drudgery. Parochial service involved participants in the wider political life of the county and in a variety of legal procedures and in some cases demanded skills in representing the interests of the parish to others. Bere Ferrers, a maritime parish in the South Hams, had to be represented at the Court of Admiralty in cases of shipwreck and it was the parish gentry who undertook this.[146] The parish constable supervised 'the plucking down the king's armes from the church'. The churchwarden claimed 1s.2d. in 1650 for his efforts to lessen the burden of the soldiery on the parish: 'Spent at Plymouth in too severall jurnies to free our parish from the county troop and on journey to Tavestock, spent at Tavestock in a quarter of wine to have some of these shouldiers removed out of the parish'.[147] The Chudleigh officers had to co-operate with such soldiers in 1648 in the collection of 'the British rate [for the relief of soldiers in Ireland] for dyett for horse and man'. When

Nicholas Drewe presented his accounts for the repair of the market house he included as an expense six pence paid for 'a book of ordinances of Parliament'.[148] There was nothing in their administrative apprenticeships which inevitably predisposed constables and jurors towards lassitude or political indifference.

NOTES

1. Helen Cam: *The Hundred and the Hundred Rolls* (1930), *passim*. The medieval descents of the thirty-three Devon hundreds in private hands (Cam, *op cit.*, p. 137) may be studied in the series of articles in *TDA* by O. J. Reichel.
2. PRO E 317/10/1.
3. F & R II, pp. 358–62; M. J. Hawkins: introduction to *Unpublished State Papers of the Civil War and Interregnum*, Series 2 (microfilm, 1977), pp. 6–8, 32–33; S. J. Madge: *The Domesday of Crown Lands* (1938), Chapter 4, *passim*, pp. 384–85.
4. A search for the purchasers of the Devon hundreds in PRO E 315/138 (particulars for sales of fee farm rents) has been in vain. E 315/319 (Order Books of the trustees for the sale of fee farm rents); E 315/140 (Accounts of sales of fee farm rents), 141, 142 (Contracts), 173 (Contracts and purchases of crown lands), Index 17353 (Palmer's index to sales of crown lands) and material listed on pp. 104–105 below.
5. DQSOB Easter 1650; E 317/10/4 for the survey of the hundred on 4 April, 1653.
6. E.g., *CCC*, p. 1504 for Mohun.
7. PROB 11/382/45; Mary Coate: *Cornwall and the Great Civil War*, p. 22; PRO SP 28/208 (list of sequestration agents, July 1661).
8. Lysons, p. xxii.
9. According to R. L. Taverner (thesis, p. 81), the 'big man' of Winkleigh was Richard Dunning (author of *Bread for the Poor* and *The Plaine and Easy Method*, both poor law tracts) but Dunning seems to have originated from Walkhampton. He was constable of Roborough hundred 1662 to 1666 and was a grand juror between 1660 and 1670 (QS bundles).
10. Cam, *op. cit.*, p. 138. Not until 1680 was it was legally established that a sheriff could enter any hundred and that the Crown had no right to grant away hundreds. Defence counsel argued that 'where ancient grants are dubious they shall be construed and expounded according to usage'. H. A. Merewether, A. J. Stephens: *The History of the Boroughs and Municipal Corporations* (1835, 3 vols.), III, pp. 1727–31.
11. PRO E 368 (Lord Treasurer's Remembrancer Memoranda Rolls), 635–88; T. E. Hartley: 'Undersheriffs and Bailiffs in Some English Shrievalties c. 1580–1625', *Bulletin of the Institute of Historical Research*, XLVII (1974), pp. 166–67 demonstrates that most sheriffs making statements at the Exchequer employed undersheriffs to appear for them.
12. DRO CR 20, 086–20, 092 (Ottery court rolls 1662 to 1670); University of London Library Fuller MS 34/1 (Ottery St. Mary hundred court rolls 1682); DRO 1508 M/Devon/Manor/Exminster/1 (Exminster hundred court book 1675 to 1678), 517 M/MH 1 (Axminster hundred court roll 1676). For the period before the civil war cf. DRO CR 96 (West Budleigh court roll 1631 to 1632), 162 (Hayridge court roll 1624), 1314–1316 A (Sherwill court rolls 1632 to 1640), 393–94 (Tiverton court rolls 1636), 434 (Wonford court roll 1621). The Axminster rolls are the only ones to include the names of the lords, but Hayridge hundred court was also a court for recovery of minor debts: QS Box 62, bundle Epiphany 1658, examinations of two hundred court bailiffs.
13. Bodl. Tanner MS 287/72. The returns to the commissioners from the Devon stewards are in *ibid*. ff 68–139 and Tanner MS 101/126.
14. Tanner MS 287/102.
15. Michael Dalton: *The Office and Authority of Sheriffs*, Chapter 120, *passim*; S. and B. Webb: *English Local Government: The Parish and the County*, p. 453; T. E. Hartley: 'The Sheriffs of the County of Kent 1580–1625' (London PhD, 1970), p. 144; *idem*: 'Undersheriffs and Bailiffs', p. 169; but see Barnes: *Somerset*, pp. 129–30, note 14.
16. E 317/10/1.

17. DQSOB Easter 1650, *CCC*, p. 1239, *CCAM*, p. 698.
18. DQSOB Michaelmas 1661. Brooke had been bailiff since at least Easter 1653: QS bundles, names on returns of jurors from the hundreds.
19. DQSOB Epiphany 1670; *Statutes of the Realm*, V (for 1660s commissions); Vivian, p. 70.
20. Orders against the lords of Hartland, Hemyock, Stanborough and Hayridge and all defaulters who failed to appoint bailiffs were made in Easter 1648: DQSOB.
21. BL Add 11314 f 50. Henry Fitzwilliam was a Tiverton attorney whose county career began as clerk to the sequestration committee in 1650. He supported Major John Blackmore, the government candidate at the Tiverton election of 1654, and was deputy clerk of the peace, and clerk from 1658 to 1660. He was appointed county treasurer in 1667.
22. D. H. Allen (ed.): *Essex Quarter Sessions Order Book 1652–1661* (Chelmsford 1974), pp. 74, 78, 110. Mr. Allen offers no comment on this in his introduction. It may have been connected with Cromwell's directives on juries. Cf. K. Wrightson: 'The Puritan Reformation of Manners, with special reference to the counties of Lancashire and Essex, 1640–1660' (Cambridge PhD, 1973), p. 200.
23. Merewether and Stephens: *History of the Boroughs*, III, pp. 1727–31.
24. Prideaux Place, Padstow, Volume 'Miscellaneous MSS' enfoliated: letter, Morrice to Edmund Prideaux 27/9/1671. I am grateful to Mr J. F. Prideaux-Brune for permission to examine his family MSS.
25. See p. 74 above. For Raddon *CCC*, pp. 474, 3263. Giles Inglett, another deputy clerk of the peace, was steward to the Mallock family at Cockington: DRO 48/13/2/2/7.
26. QS Box 73 bundle Midsummer 1668: letter, Hugh Camworthy to John Northcote. He was able to add as a postscript that the bridges had just been repaired; perhaps the threat of an estreat had had the required effect.
27. M. J. Ingram: 'Communities and Courts: Law and Disorder in early Seventeenth Century Wiltshire' in Cockburn (ed.): *Crime in England*, pp. 123–25.
28. DQSOB, Michaelmas 1661, Michaelmas 1668, Epiphany 1669; QS Box 73 bundle Michaelmas 1668: letter, David Harte to John Northcote. For allegations against other bailiffs: DRO DD 55805, 56151.
29. QS Box 64, indictments 1654 to 1660. Cf. fines of ten shillings each upon two who assaulted bailiffs in 1651: QS Box 58, bundle Michaelmas 1651, bills of indictment.
30. DRO 123 M/E/16. Cf. the alleged persecutions of bailiff Andrew Thorne in 1652: QS Box 59 bundle Midsummer 1652, petitions.
31. SRO DD/WO Box 19/3a (indentures re John Willoughby's shrievalty).
32. F & R II, pp. 240–41, 321–24, 378–79, 754–64, 911–15, 943–45; Ivan Roots: 'Cromwell's Ordinances' in Aylmer (ed.): *The Interregnum*, p. 148.
33. John Mitchell, bailiff of Colyton, presented three bridges in that hundred in 1649: QS Box 56, bundle Epiphany 1649, presentment.
34. E.g., Sheriff William Putt's writs to Philip Ellis and Paul Southwood, bailiffs of Plympton and Wonford hundreds respectively, to be served on defaulting local ratepayers: QS Box 58 bundle Midsummer 1651 (warrants), also a warrant to the bailiff of Lifton in 1663 to summon twelve recognizance breakers: QS Box 68 bundle Michaelmas 1663, warrants.
35. Dalton: *Office and Authority of Sheriffs*, Chapter 120, *passim*; Hartley: 'Undersheriffs and Bailiffs', pp. 169–70. Bailiffs changed annually in Lincolnshire: S. A. Peyton (ed.): *Minutes of Proceedings in Quarter Sessions held for the parts of Kesteven … 1674–95* (1931), pp. xix–xxi.
36. Names of bailiffs and hundred constables may be found in lists of freeholders bound up with writs of *venire facias*, among sessions bundles. Lengths of service have been calculated from these.
37. Devon and Cornwall Record Society: *Hartland Parish Registers* (1934).
38. Hartley: 'Undersheriffs and Bailiffs', p. 169.
39. The name of Codnor is to be found frequently in the Protestation Returns for Haytor, particularly in the parishes of Kingskerswell, Newton Abbot, St. Marychurch and Torbryan. In Epiphany 1665 three JPs were ordered to examine Joseph and Nicholas Codnor to discover which was entitled to the bailiwick: DQSOB. A Nicholas Codnor was a tenant of Sir John Stawell: PROB 11/334/145.

40. E. J. L. Cole: 'Minor Officials in Radnorshire under the Great Sessions in Wales', *Transactions of the Radnorshire Society*, XLV (1975), pp. 59–60.
41. E.g., Carl Bridenbaugh: *Vexed and Troubled Englishmen 1590–1642* (1968), p. 249.
42. M. J. Ingram: 'Communities and Courts', *op. cit.*, pp. 123–25.
43. On occasion the entry was general, that all defaulting bailiffs were to be fined a certain sum, suggesting the frequency and routine nature of the problem.
44. DQSOB Michaelmas 1651, Midsummer 1655, Midsummer 1657, Midsummer 1660.
45. All in 1669 and 1670: DQSOB Easter 1669, Midsummer 1669, Epiphany and Easter 1670.
46. *Ibid.*, Easter 1666, Epiphany 1667, Easter 1669.
47. J. S. Cockburn: *History of English Assizes*, p. 119.
48. S. and B. Webb: *English Local Government: The Parish and the County*, p. 480. Cf. F. W. Bretherton: 'Country Inns and Alehouses' in R. Lennard: *Englishmen At Rest and Play* ... *1558–1714* (1931), p. 162 for the view (partly correct) of an 'abdication of authority by the central government after the Restoration' over social policy. Cf. Chapter Seven below.
49. S. and B. Webb: *English Local Government: the Parish and the County*, p. 459.
50. DQSOB Michaelmas 1650, Easter 1651; QS Box 58 Midsummer 1651, examinations. Bailiffs' names are on freeholders' lists.
51. *Ibid.*, Michaelmas 1650. Huish was re-appointed in less sensitive times, from 1653 to 1656.
52. Chapter Four, p. 88 above.
53. QS Box 69 bundle Easter 1664: bundles of papers on Coleridge bailiwick 1–16.
54. DQSOB Epiphany 1653; *TDA*, 66, pp. 260–61; Vivian, p. 644, PROB 11/320/67.
55. DQSOB Epiphany 1651, Epiphany 1652.
56. Hartley: 'Undersheriffs and Bailiffs', p. 168.
57. W. G. Hoskins and C. A. F. Meekings have stressed the value of these records. See Hoskins: *Exeter in the Seventeenth Century* (Devon and Cornwall Record Society, 1957); List and Index Society, CLV (1978).
58. QS Box 62 bundle Epiphany 1659, examination of October 11th before John Davy. Cliffe was something of a 'relief' bailiff; he served on six separate occasions between 1649 and 1670 but never for more than the duration of one session.
59. DQSOB, *passim*, for appointments; *The Compleat Constable* (1692), pp. 7–9 *pace* the Webbs in *English Local Government: The Parish and the County*, p. 453.
60. H. B. Simpson: 'The Office of Constable', *English Historical Review*, X (1895), p. 630; PRO ASSI 24/19/1/1; DQSOB Epiphany 1661 and *passim*.
61. Names of constables on returns of hundreders in QS bundles.
62. At hundredal level and below, much business must have been transacted verbally, thus transgressing against one of the six points in Weber's definition of bureaucracy: R. Bendix: *Max Weber: An Intellectual Portrait* (1960), pp. 418–25.
63. It was ordered in Michaelmas 1661 that all constables should swear 'their allegiances to the king's majestie and ... new sweare ... to execute their office': DQSOB.
64. B. L. Loan 29 (Diary of Thomas Larkham) ff 28, 30 r, 33 v, 38 v, 39 v, 56 r, 62 v. I am grateful to Mr James Hopkins for lending me his transcript of this diary. Secondary accounts of Larkham are in *DNB*, H. P. R. Finberg: 'A Chapter of Religious History' in Hoskins and Finberg: *Devonshire Studies*, pp. 385–86; *TDA*, XXIV, pp. 96–146. A bowdlerised version of the diary was published by William Lewis in 1880.
65. Loan 29 f 46 v.
66. DQSOB 1649 to 1660 *passim* for payments of his salary.
67. *Ibid.*, Epiphany 1660. For Fowell: *TDA*, XV, p. 468, XLVIII, pp. 336–37; *Register of Admissions to ... the Middle Temple*; Vivian, p. 369; PRO E 121/2/2 (his purchase of Sutton Pool, Plymouth), PROB 11/329/54. Larkham's opinion of Glanville may be judged by his private exultation at his death: 'while Grylls and Glanville at your feet in dust/ly mouldering, to our God singe praise we must'. Loan 29 f 45 r.
68. Loan 29 f 50 v; QS Box 73 bundle Michaelmas 1668, petition of 4 September, 1668; *TDA*, XXIV, p. 140, PRO SP 25/99/225.
69. QS Box 65, loose petitions by William Courtenay, George Howard and Richard Vivian (undated). For a further attack on Condy in 1668: *Ibid.*, Box 73 bundle Michaelmas

1668, Petitions, DQSOB Midsummer 1668.

70. For Howard: QS Box 58, bundle Michaelmas 1651 indictment for assault and unlawful meeting; Roger Granville: *The King's General in the West* (1908), pp. 25–39, 205–07; (also scattered references *passim* in Amos Miller: *Sir Richard Grenville of the Civil War* (1979). Howard represented Tavistock in the Cavalier Parliament. For Courtenay: *TDA*, XCVIII, p. 212, Vivian, p. 247, K. M. Beck: 'Recusancy and Nonconformity in Devon and Somerset 1660–1714' (Bristol MA, 1961).

71. QS Box 57 bundle Michaelmas 1649, recognizances. PRO SP 18/3/9 for the terms of the engagement. One of Condy's predecessors as head constable at Tavistock, John Leare, was nominated by a retiring constable in Easter 1650, ordered to be sworn at the following sessions and to be bound over to the next assizes if he refused. This is presumably what happened, for there is no record of his service: DQSOB Easter, Midsummer 1650.

72. Thomas Chapple of Witheridge and Henry Eustace of Roborough were both hundreders immediately before commencing as constables in 1649 and 1650. Cf. East Sussex, where quarter sessions grand jurors were all constables: C. B. Herrup: 'The Common Peace: Legal Structure and Legal Substance in East Sussex 1594–1640' (North Western Univ. PhD 1982) pp. 140–143.

73. The sessions grand jury, in contrast to the assize jury (and that only during periods of political upheaval, when it was infiltrated by JPs) was neutral, indeed was apolitical. This is not Morrill's neutralism (an articulate statement of county integrity or inviolability) nor Manning's view of the neutral as a moderate in disguise, but more like H. A. Lloyd's description of the South West Wales ruling class as lacking political awareness. The difference between Devon and West Wales was that in the former political awareness distinguished the gentry (JPs) from their subordinates. Devon jury presentments never reveal any commitment to the 'county' or towards any ethos other than that of the parish. Morrill: *The Revolt of the Provinces*, pp. 36–38, 213 note 89; H. A. Lloyd: *The Gentry of South West Wales 1540–1640*, pp. 211–12. The county ethos has been definitively outlined in Everitt: *Community of Kent*, pp. 45–55.

74. DRO QS/constables presentments 1/1–34/27. Devon archivists have removed these from the sessions bundles but some may still be found in those bundles for summer 1661 (seven presentments), Michaelmas 1661 (one), Easter 1662 (four), summer 1664 (two), Epiphany 1665 (three), Easter 1665 (two), Easter 1667 (eight).

75. Constables Presentments 1/2, 10, 11 (Axminster), 7/14 (Colyton), 11/1 (Exminster), 13/6 (Halberton).

76. *Ibid.*, 20/2, 5, 7, 9 (Ottery St. Mary), 27/1 (Tavistock), 30/7 (West Budleigh).

77. *Ibid.*, 2/1 (Bampton), 3/7 (Black Torrington), 5/2 (Clyston), 6/4, 5 (Coleridge), 8/3, 4–21 (Crediton), 13/4, 5 (Halberton), 30/9 (West Budleigh).

78. QS Box 70 loose presentment, 9 January 1666; Box 71 loose presentment 8 January 1667; Box 72 loose of 9/7/1667, 16/4/1667, 7/1/1668; Box 73 loose of 12/1/1669. Presentments endorsed *billae verae* include 1/9, 10, 2/1, 3/7, 4/2, 5, 6/3, 7/1, 8/12.

79. Morrill: *Cheshire Grand Jury*, pp. 5, 45–47.

80. This is an interesting comment on the development of bureaucracy in the counties and is further evidence of the hierarchy on which presentments rested. QS/Constables' Presentments, 1/14, 30/5, 2/4.

81. DQSOB Midsummer 1670 to Epiphany 1671, *DCNQ* XXII, pp. 45, 46, 48, 72, 73, 74. Kenyon: *Stuart Constitution*, pp. 383–86 for a comparison between the 1664 Conventicle Act (which elicited no response from the Devon JPs) and that of 1670. Perhaps the penalties in the 1664 act on JPs who 'wilfully and wittingly' failed to complete prosecutions persuaded the Bench to steer clear of the statute altogether.

82. J. H. Langbein: 'The Origins of Public Prosecution at Common Law', *American Journal of Legal History*, XVII (1973), pp. 316–17.

83. QS/Constables' Presentments 16/14. Lear came to Devon after a successful career as a Barbados planter. He was made a baronet in 1660, sheriff in 1673, and lived at Exminster. He was not a JP. J. and J. B. Burke: *Extinct and Dormant Baronetcies* (1841); G.E.C.: *Complete Baronetage*, III, p. 72; *CSPD 1673–75*, p. 46. He also defaulted on muster contributions: PRO PC 2/55/522.

84. Constables' Presentments 20/4 (George Eveleigh gent. of Ottery, not to be confused

with the Totnes town clerk), *CCC*, p. 1642. Presentments 16/5 (Kirkham of Paignton), *CCC*, pp. 1396, 1469, Pearse Chope: *Early Tours*, pp. 106, 110.
85. In 1679 no fewer than thirty-three hundreds had 'nothing to present'.
86. Cf. D. H. Pennington: 'The Accounts of the Kingdom 1642–1649' in F. J. Fisher (ed.): *Essays in Social and Economic History Presented to R. H. Tawney* (1959), pp. 182–203, for exactly the same incentives to efficiency.
87. Peter Clark: *English Provincial Society*, p. 125.
88. A. Hassall Smith: *County and Court: Government and Politics in Norfolk 1558–1603* (1974), p. 95.
89. *Ibid.*, p. 96.
90. E.g., in QS Box 56 bundle Epiphany 1648–49; DQSOB Easter 1653.
91. QS Box 57 bundle Michaelmas 1649, Petition.
92. They are in QS Box 56 bundle marked '1648 loose'.
93. DQSOB Midsummer 1667.
94. *Ibid.*; DRO Carew and Martin MSS DD 56035.
95. From 1642 to 1646 the mustermaster was one Captain Cockayne; from 1660 Grenville Weekes, probably the uncle of Richard Weekes of Hatherleigh, a debtor who had fallen foul of William Morrice, and who died in the Fleet Prison, London, in 1670. DQSOB Epiphany 1661, Easter 1661, Vivian, p. 776, PRO C 108/93/letter William Morrice to William Martin, BL Add. 34012 (Alphabetical index of Disbrowe's suspects 1655 to 1656); QS Box 73 bundle Michaelmas 1668, Petition of Richard Weekes.
96. QS Box 56 bundle '1648 loose'.
97. QS 'Maimed Soldiers' File: 146/1–3; DQSOB Easter 1653.
98. Maimed Soldiers File 144/1. 'Chirugeons' were not paid extravagantly. Ellis Veryard received ten shillings for examining all claimants from five hundreds, Thomas Fidoe of Ottery had the same for examining soldiers from Colyton and Axminster: 144/2, 3.
99. It was ordered in 1662 that since 'the number of souldiers which ought to be relieved is growne soe great and consequently the charge, as that the present rates are not able to supply their wants', the total levy was to be £565.8s. per annum; DQSOB Midsummer 1662. So many soldiers clamoured for their pensions during sessions that in 1664 the court ordered that henceforth head constables were to send them their money: *Ibid.*, Michaelmas 1664.
100. DQSOB Midsummer 1667; PRO C 103/17, loose assessment for Plympton and Ermington hundreds 1652 to 1653.
101. PRO E 360/37; Webbs: *English Local Government: Parish and County*, p. 497; List and Index Soc. CLV.
102. DRO Q/RTR 1/9, 29; Crediton 1660 A/262, 265.
103. C. D. Chandaman: *The English Public Revenue 1660–1688* (1975), pp. 76–82; Prideaux Place, Padstow: 'Misc. MSS', letter Morrice to Prideaux 15 March 1662. Chandaman argues that the act cannot be ascribed to any single person.
104. A series of 1662 hearth tax returns for Exminster, Crediton, Tavistock and part of Stanborough hundreds, extracted from the sessions bundles, are in DRO Q/RTR Hearth Tax Returns 1/1–36. A stray for Trusham parish is in QS Box 57, bundle mixed 1614 to 1693.
105. Chandaman, *op. cit.*, p. 82, C. A. F. Meekings: *Surrey Hearth Tax 1664* (Surrey Rec. Soc., XVII, 1940), p. xvi. Lydia Marshall: 'The Levying of the Hearth Tax', *English Historical Review*, LI (1936), pp. 628–46 for limits of local initiative.
106. Along the lines of assessments, subsidies and customs administration. Chandaman *op. cit.*, p. 84.
107. J. R. Western: *The English Militia in the Eighteenth Century* (1965), pp. 7–8, 10, 14–15, 25; Prideaux Place, Padstow, 'Misc. MSS' Morrice to Prideaux, 15 March, 1662.
108. PRO SP 29/8/183–89, 11/157.
109. SP 29/8/188–89.
110. WRO 1332 (Duke of Somerset MSS) Box 55: militia.
111. *Ibid.*, Stanborough hundred returns.
112. A. Browning: *English Historical Documents VIII: 1660–1714* (1953), pp. 781, 796.
113. Western, *op. cit.*, pp. 16–17.
114. R. M. Dunn (ed.): *Norfolk Lieutenancy Journal 1660–1676* (Norfolk Rec. Soc., XLV,

1977), introduction, p. 14, and *passim*; Western, *op. cit.*, pp. 16–17.

115. These accounts may be found in QS Box 69 bundle Epiphany 1664, bundle Midsummer 1664; Box 73 bundle Midsummer 1668, bundle Michaelmas 1668.

116. Barnes: *Somerset*, pp. 87, 274. Some constables' accounts of 1660 to 1661 muddle militia warrants and warrants to or from petty sessions in their accounts; as the military activities in the county increased, however, so it became conventional to separate these responsibilities when accounting because the JPs refused to reimburse footposts for journeys other than those on militia business: DQSOB Michaelmas 1663.

117. DQSOB Michaelmas 1650. Some constables, later in the decade were awarded an annual sum from which to pay their footposts; provisions such as these were necessary because churchwardens could no longer meet bills for footposts: QS Box 68 bundle Midsummer 1663, petition of William Rider; Box 71 bundle Midsummer 1666, petition of Halberton constables.

118. T. G. Barnes: *The Clerk of the Peace in Caroline Somerset* (1961), p. 46.

119. Western, *op. cit.*, p. 27.

120. Chapter Seven below, pp. 183–87.

121. QS Box 67 bundle Midsummer 1662, petition of hundred constables.

122. DQSOB Michaelmas 1661.

123. *Ibid.*, Midsummer 1662.

124. QS Box 67 bundle Michaelmas 1662, petition of hundred constables.

125. There was no vendetta against its composers, who continued in office until their relief was, as usual, overdue.

126. Assizes were important in co-ordinating bridge repairs: PRO ASSI 24/21 *passim*.

127. DQSOB Easter 1650.

128. *Ibid.*, *passim* for the very frequent references to this particular task of government. Treasurers were of the social group from which the head constables themselves were selected.

129. QS Box 73 bundle Epiphany 1667 to 1668; DQSOB Midsummer 1667.

130. Chapter Seven pp. 175–83 below.

131. DQSOB Midsummer 1646 to Michaelmas 1648, although the royalism of constables in 1646 which rendered them 'evill instruments to the State' led to their subservience to other treasurers.

132. DQSOB Epiphany 1657, *CSPD 1657–58*, p. 218, *1658–59*, p. 25.

133. QS Box 58 bundle Epiphany 1651, presentments.

134. *Ibid.*, Box 73 bundle Epiphany 1668, warrant endorsed with a note from William Payne to 'cozen' Browne, n.d.

135. *CSPD 1655–56*, pp. 157–58; SP 18/124/9–10.

136. PRO E 179/245/17; DRO Q/RTR Hearth Tax Returns 1/1–36.

137. WRO 1332 (Duke of Somerset MSS) Box 55 (militia) returns for Coleridge and Stanborough; *Devon Protestation Returns*.

138. Margaret Cash (ed.): *Devon Inventories of the Sixteenth and Seventeenth Centuries* (Devon and Cornwall Rec. Soc., new series XI, 1966), pp. 110, 114, 153.

139. *Ibid.*, pp. 118–19, 137–38, 141–42. Heywood was a suicide whose goods were forfeit to the King's Great Almoner, the Bishop of Winchester. As a contrast, John Salkeild of Uffculme was head constable of Bampton from 1654 to 1656, and a grand juror from 1661 to 1667. When he died in 1688 his property was assessed at £134.0s.4d., of which £100 was the value of leasehold land interests. WRO Uffculme wills.

140. Philip Styles: 'The Social Structure of Kineton hundred in the reign of Charles II' in *Studies in Seventeenth Century West Midlands History* (1978), pp. 165–66.

141. For Moore: SP 16/377/65, 66; *CCC*, pp. 1125. Moore was fined £100 by the compounding commissioners.

142. QS lists and DRO, Bere Ferrers PO 20, PW 56, PS 2, PW 39, 43, 44, 45, 47.

143. DRO Chudleigh PW 1 ff 604–05, PO 1.

144. DRO Hartland PW 2 A.

145. DRO Iddesleigh PO 1.

146. Bere Ferrers PW 41, 42, 47.

147. *Ibid.*, PW 42.

148. Chudleigh PW 1 ff 604–05, 645.

Chapter Six

The Sixteen-Sixties

The Restoration Spoils of Patronage

The collapse of political stability in 1659 is even more remarkable than the events of 1660. In September 1658 Richard Cromwell had been proclaimed Protector in Exeter, and the crowds had shouted 'Amen, Amen' in a ceremony as impressive as any seen in the city within living memory.[1] Ten months later panic was sweeping the county to accompany political changes as bewildering as any in the later 1640s. Anti-sectarian scares were not smoke without fire: in June the Rump had received a petition of 'many well-affected persons' of the western counties who demanded the abolition of tithes (a 'soul-oppression') and the use of meeting-houses 'commonly known as churches'. They condemned the dilatoriness of the law and the persecutions against them launched in the name of the law, and requested that the godly be appointed to civil office. The petition was duly read in Parliament but MPs declined to execute their proposals.[2] Interest groups were drifting apart, and well might Major Blackmore acknowledge the narrowness of Lambert's quelling of the Booth rising, for in the Exeter garrison itself the commanding officer, Major Brocklehurst, was secretly treating with royalist agents.[3] In December 1659 public order in Exeter virtually collapsed and martial law was imposed by Brocklehurst—a 'hasty, rash fellow' in the view of a newspaper correspondent—while civilian republicans, who held Portsmouth, played for his support, not knowing his earlier commitments.[4] In these circumstances of civic unrest, widespread intrigue and civil and religious instability the Devon quarter sessions meeting took place in January 1660. Only six names are to be found in the order book, those of William Putt, Edmund Fowell, Thomas Reynell, John Coplestone, John Searle and James Pierce, a group of military and civilian office-holders and moderately presbyterian careerists. There was certainly, however, another meeting—of committed presbyterians, led by Thomas Bampfield and including some of the secluded MPs of 1648. More vocal than the 'official' JPs, who were men of executive action, not words, the group agreed on a petition to Parliament in the name of the inhabitants of Exeter, 'groaning under high oppressions and a general defect of trade'. Popular and bourgeois grievances had been exploited by those determined to recover the power at Westminster which they had forfeited in 1648; Northcote, Courtenay and Sir Simon Leach were apprehended by Unton Crooke for provoking riots at Exeter. Only the return of the MPs secluded in 1648 could provide for the safety of the city, which was in the hands of apprentices and others who had seized the keys of the gates 'without taking notice of the magistrates and less of the souldiers'. Bampfield presented this petition to the Rump, which had been restored for the second time,[5] and at least one correspondent read the portents correctly.[6] The implications of the call for a free parliament included the restoration of the monarchy, as Monck quickly pointed out in open letters to Robert Rolle[7] and William Morrice, who with Northcote, Thomas Bampfield and his nephew, Coplestone Bampfield, and William Courtenay, led the presbyterian-tending-to-royalist group dominating the press. Monck counselled restraint and argued that interest groups in the country had to be satisfied by any political settlement. On these grounds, monarchy was not comprehensive enough a basis for settlement. The government 'must needs be a republic' and the present Parliament should be left to determine its own future.[8] Monck's letter provoked three replies from Devon, which suggested that something of a pamphlet war had developed, possibly stage-managed, probably with the aim of testing public opinion.

Monck's personal views are hopelessly opaque to modern historians, just as they were to contemporaries,[9] but the arguments of the Devon gentry were clarity itself. 'The force upon the Parliament in 1648 was the great breach at which our confusions have entered like a torrent';[10] from this assertion in the anonymous *Letter to General Monck* sprang the gentry commitment to a free parliament and hence to a restoration of monarchy.[11] Religious presbyterianism had been thoroughly discredited after the Scots invasion of 1651 if not before, and the 1655 Devon Association had been a voluntary, watered-down meeting of moderates. Thus political presbyterianism was allied to a call for the restoration of the Church of England as the guarantor of toleration, with a sneer that the sects were 'not fit to be secured, unlesse ... in the souldier's dialect, to be restrain'd'.[12] The problem of new interest groups created by sales of royalist, crown and church lands, an intractable one to Monck, was brushed aside by less cautious local opinion. The Harringtonian concept of the necessary relationship between power and wealth in land was dismissed with classical and renaissance examples to the contrary, and on the more pragmatic grounds that Interregnum purchasers would be willing to give up some of their lands voluntarily in order to retain the rest.[13] Ironically, it was argued that a restored monarchy would be able to 'abate' the excise and leave land purchasers alone. Only one pamphleteer from the West Country adopted the view that a free parliament could lead to a new republic, on the naive grounds that it had been 'Parliament', as a single, continuous and consistent institution, which had abolished monarchy and sold crown lands. The author, 'J. Trev.' realised that if the secluded members were admitted 'then you will have none less to oppose you but the damme Cavaliers',[14] but without appreciating that most secluded MPs would now be active royalists seeking monarchical stability to enjoy power at Westminster. The 'county community' was never so introverted as to repudiate parliamentary politics. The Devon gentry were set on returning a large quota of 1648 MPs, but observers saw their early forthright declaration to Monck as a way for the latter to evade strictly parliamentary procedure: 'This will be a patterne to all the countys in England, and very many, especially the western counties, have declared their concurrence in the same particulars and many beleeve that Monck will take that to be the sense of the kingdome then what the men at Westminster shall determine'.[15] By late February and early March, Northcote, Sir William Courtenay, Coplestone Bampfield and Robert Rolle had become overt royalists, Morrice had been rewarded for his fidelity to Monck with the office of governor of Plymouth,[16] and on 10 May the citizens of Exeter and Plymouth were celebrating the Restoration with military parades, watched by the county gentry.[17]

On 7 May the Convention ordered that all officers in posts on the day that Charles II was declared rightful king should keep them[18] but his assurance did little to disguise the extent of the revolution among office-holders. The Court was plagued by requests from would-be clients of the king; a clamour which had begun as soon as Charles had set foot on English soil.[19] A host of minor gentlemen and opportunists emerged from utter obscurity to request manorial stewardships in the King's gift, rectories, postmasterships and stannary offices.[20] Sir Courtenay Pole and Coplestone Bampfield led the royalist and conformist 'presbyterian' groups respectively, to disarm potential rebels, dismantle caches of arms (one was found near Exeter Guildhall early in 1662[21]) and supervise the removal of adherents of the old regime from public office.[22] Pressure on officeholding thus came both from below, from those who could not aspire to county office as JPs because of their obscure social standing and who would not seek office as constables because financial gain was a principal motive, and from above, from those whose vision of a reconstructed community included no role for the remnants of the old regime who could now be regarded only as a subversive threat.

The local offices in the royal gift fell into three broad groups: those which had fallen into abeyance during the Interregnum, such as collectorships of ecclesiastical revenues and stewardships of royal property; those formerly in the hands of army officers and others appointed by Interregnum governments, in the post office, the customs and the other bodies of taxation, and offices peculiar to the Restoration circumstances. In this last category would be placed Edmund Fortescue's desire to succeed his late father, Sir Edmund Fortescue, as governor of the now suitably-named Fort Charles.[23] The prevailing Interregnum ideal of centralisation as the only reliable way to ensure that executive power remained in the hands of the godly was now discredited, and patronage demands could again be met by monopolistic grants and sinecures. Monopolists, always the most persistent, optimistic and flexible of suitors, could trim their petitions to fit the pattern of a government seemingly anxious to establish a reputation for crusading morality. In September 1660 a proclamation against 'debauched persons' enjoined the observance of early Stuart alehouse licensing laws, and Thomas Roberts followed it with a request to regulate alesellers to remedy 'base men during the late

times licensing the locusts and vermin of the nation'; language and
—curiously—sentiments worthy of Major-General Charles Worsley
himself.[24] As in the 1630s there were now many counsels advocating the
surrender of executive functions to private hands, in the interests of
government efficiency and entrepreneurial profit, but with the difference
that in the 1660s the aspirations of the government in social policy soon
contracted, despite the early declarations of reform intent. Before the civil
war, it had seemed that monopolies could have succoured 'Thorough'
government but Privy Council directives on local government seemingly
died with Laud.[25] In the early 1660s there was an explosion in patronage
demands, and it seemed natural to develop the potential of sinecures,
which had been 'drastically cut' during the Interregnum. But the outrages
of the 1660s were carefully avoided by leaving local patronage largely in
the hands of local men. Nicholas Oudart, secretary to Charles II's sister,
Mary of Orange, failed to obtain the sinecure of feodary of the Duchy of
Cornwall in succession to the presbyterian, Thomas Gewen, who died in
1661. The office, with that of keeper of the ports of Plymouth and
Cornwall, went instead to William Morrice and his son. (Among other
grants to Morrice were a pension of £260 a month, a London house, a
baronetcy and the profits of several Devon fairs.[26])

Nowhere was this localistic triumph of the county gentry more apparent
than in the outposts of the central government in Devon. The Honiton
MPs in the Cavalier Parliament, the former royalist delinquents Courtenay
Pole and Peter Prideaux, baronets, recommended that the Honiton
postmaster, 'a fellow of factious preaching', be replaced by a Honiton
man, William Lowman, of sufficiently local and recognizable status to
have sat five times on the Interregnum quarter sessions grand jury.[27] At
Exeter, Edward Raddon was replaced as postmaster by a local merchant,
George Browning, who demonstrated that a surrender to local pressures
was not without its problems by quarrelling with his fellow-merchants in
the ruling body over the water supply to his mill.[28] The Plymouth and
district postal service was placed in the hands of John Clarke, a
tavern-keeper and a client of Lord Arundel and Sir Jonathan Trelawney,
the brother-in-law of the younger Edward Seymour. It was Arundel who
took on the ruling body of Plymouth over claims to Sutton Pool, crown
land which was bought for the governors of Plymouth hospital in 1651, in
a case which amounted to a Crown prosecution.[29]

A similar process developed in the customs offices of the county. At
Barnstaple William Morrice was able to intrude Humphrey Prideaux, son
of his brother-in-law, Edmund Prideaux of Padstow, into the collectorship
of customs, in February 1661. He failed in an effort to have the salary
increased from £50 per annum, despite the approval of the King and Lord
Treasurer Southampton, because of the 'banglings' of the customs
commissioners, who prevailed in maintaining a salary related to the fiscal
significance of the port. In the early 1660s, it was administrators, as
distinct from courtiers and even ministers, who seem to have exercised
virtually the only control over the sale of offices.[30] Morrice was also
responsible for ensuring that the Roope family retained control of the

Dartmouth customs. Anthony Roope had been granted the office of customer by letters patent in 1634, and it was a relation, probably a son, John, who took control in 1660.[31] The Roopes were a prominent South Hams family who regularly sent representatives to the sessions grand jury. John was a cousin both of 1661 assessment commissioner, Ambrose, and of Rump commissioner, Nicholas.[32] Morrice's interest in the office was maintained in 1664 after Roope's death, when his son, John, took control.[33] The pattern of customs appointments in the early 1660s thus favoured 'insiders'—townsmen appointed to their town office—and the clients and families of county gentry. Others who were advanced in this way were Scipio Stucley (a relation of Sir Thomas Stucley of Affeton in North Devon, a former royalist delinquent who was knighted in May 1660.) Scipio became comptroller of Exeter in July of that year[34] and Nicholas Opie, a Plymouth merchant who became customer of that port and Fowey. His wife, Susan, sued the parliamentarian Truro merchant, Edward Nosworthy, after Opie's death in 1662.[35] In 1662, William Noy, the grandson of Charles I's attorney-general, was promised the office of searcher at Exeter and Dartmouth in reversion after George Ley, a flagrant breach of the prohibition of reversions in customs posts. The grant was made because of Noy's 'services and sufferings'.[36] In the late Sixties John Trelawney and Richard Arscot were gentlemen appointed to the Excise Appeals Commission and the Exeter customs respectively: Arscot was a client of the Earl of Bath.[37]

There was some continuity between this pattern of appointments and that which had prevailed during the Interregnum. William Barnes had been collector at Dartmouth from 1649 to the mid-1650s. He had filled the civic offices of receiver and mayor of the town in the 1640s, and retired to become mayor again in 1654. He was also an assessment commissioner for the county in 1652.[38] John Tooker and John Makernes, collector and deputy respectively in Interregnum Barnstaple, were local men, although when Makernes was appointed in 1653 he thanked Robert Blackborne, the Customs Commission secretary, for finding him the post but requested a more lucrative one if it could be found:[39] More typical, however, had been the military influence on appointments. Captain Francis Rolle began his career in the customs as searcher at Dartmouth in 1646 before moving to the more senior position of customer at Exeter in the 1650s. He, also, aspired to civilian office, and was named on a supplementary list of assessment commissioners in 1657.[40] Soldiers were to be found in the excise offices, too. George Rattenbury of Plymouth was excise sub-commissioner there and a captain of foot in the Rump militia.[41] James Pierce was a lieutenant-colonel of foot in 1650, an assessment commissioner from 1650 to 1652 and in 1657 and 1660, and was a JP in 1659, as well as holding an excise post in Exeter.[42] Military men were not necessarily strangers to the county. Francis Rolle was from Holsworthy in West Devon, and after the Restoration James Pierce, suspected by the monarchy of continued disaffection, was described as 'of Exeter'.[43] Walter Deeble, comptroller of customs at Ilfracombe in 1647, was an Exeter merchant who could only achieve the freedom of the city by special fiat so that he could become a common councillor in 1651. He had offered his financial resources to the Plymouth committee in 1645 and became mayor of Exeter in 1659.[44]

In both the 1650s and the 1660s appointments to customs and excise were largely from within the county although in both decades recruitment was not always from within customs towns. In the 1650s patronage of these offices was vested in a diffuse group of local soldiers, central administrators like Blackborne, and MPs—a paradox for a regime generally taken to have been centralistic and hence, presumably, monolithic. In the Restoration decade, by contrast, control was surrendered without a struggle to the county gentry, whose younger sons and clients provided a more socially exalted group of officeholders. County gentry patronage pervaded the excise to a considerable extent. In Richard Cromwell's Parliament the Devon excise farmer, Richard Best of London, was one of several farmers to appear personally before the House of Commons in order to justify having achieved arrears of £14,000 in his farm.[45] In 1660 the statutes establishing the excise as a pillar of Restoration finance enjoined direct collection again, while leaving the option of farming open at a later date, not through tenderness for the feelings of the county gentry but because, with a new Book of Rates, direct control was the only practicable method of collection. Farming was soon tried again, from the end of 1662, but with the provisions that appointments were left to quarter sessions, and that in appeals against the excise office the JPs were to have the final determination.[46] The Devon justices returned five names for consideration, among them that of Sir Thomas Stucley of Affeton, whose relative was the Exeter customer, and Thomas Chudleigh of the Ashton, Exminster, family. The successful candidates were Sir James Smith of Exeter and Sir John Chichester of Pilton, both ex-royalists. Chichester was also MP for Barnstaple in the Cavalier Parliament, and Smith sat for Exeter. He was a relation of Monck's and had been suspected of complicity in Booth's rising.[47] In Michaelmas 1665 the farm was renewed, this time with Smith and Sir John Colleton as principals, and the opposition to the excise which increased after this date has been taken as a wry tribute to the developing efficiency of the tax.[48] In the third reorganisation of the 1660s, from midsummer 1668 to 1671, Smith again retained control, as a 'trustee' empowered to dispose of the county farm to subordinates, and he chose Bernard Grenville, the younger brother of the Earl of Bath, yet another recognition of the power of those who happen to have been in positions of critical importance in 1660.[49] (Sir John Grenville had been elevated to the peerage and showered with the wardenships of the Devon and Cornwall stannaries, the lordship of Bideford and that of three Cornish manors.[50])

The Sixties were characterised, in Chandaman's view, by appointments of 'what were optimistically regarded, by the test of loyalty rather than experience, as more suitable men',[51] yet in the previous decade it was the loyalty, the 'godliness' of the minor gentry which had made them suitable for customs and excise posts, rather than any lengthy experience in government. Head constables were arguably the most experienced local administrators, together with justices' clerks, but it seems that none of these took over as customers[52] or as searchers. The appointees of the Restoration were not successful because they were experienced bureaucrats or even because they were loyal enough to have fought for Charles I or had shown a willingness to do so for his son, but because they were fortunate pawns in the prevailing political climate of indiscriminate dividing of spoils.[53] The efficiency of the customs is, in fact, impossible to measure. Receipts at the outposts clearly depended on the volume of trade transacted there rather than on any diligence on the part of the officials. It is true that a drive against negligence and fraud was launched in the early 1660s but this was at a time when 'deadness of trade' gripped the country, and when receipts needed to be maximised. It was the collapse of trade which had been played upon by the fomentors of unrest in Exeter in 1659. When Thomas Clifford, MP for Totnes, presented a gift of gold to Charles II in August 1660 he hinted heavily that Totnes merchants expected government help by implying that the gift would have been greater were it not for the recession.[54] This state of affairs continued through most of the decade. Moreover, detailed analysis of the cost of customs administration in Devon is not possible because the only source available, the Audit Office Declared Accounts, does not offer any estimates of receipts at the individual outports. Not until 1670 are there any complete lists of the customs officers in the ports, and so it is difficult to estimate, for the earlier period, the other possible criterion of customs patronage. The Treasury Books and the State Papers record the appointments, often by letters patent, of the senior officials in the ports but the establishment lists indicate how large were their subordinate staffs. The annual salaries for the Exeter establishment in 1670, twenty-nine men excluding the 'patent officers', amounted to £795; Scipio Stucley, comptroller of the port, enjoyed an annual salary of £10.6s.8d. John Roope, customer of Dartmouth, was paid £83.6s.8d. a year, and his twelve subordinate officials cost the Custom House £250 a year. There were three 'patent officers' in Plymouth in 1670 with annual salaries amounting to £79.10s.; the thirty-two others were paid £695 a year. Barnstaple seems to have been something of an exception; William Morrice's client, and later his own son, were paid £50 a year when each was customer of the port and in 1670 only two officers wre recorded as serving there, at an annual cost of £75. Sixty-six per cent of the cost of running the Barnstaple customs office seems to have been the salary of a political appointee, but in practice the ports of Bideford and Appledore, though separately accounted for in the 1670 establishment book, should be considered with Barnstaple, just as the ten East Devon and River Exe sub-ports of Seaton, Beer, Branscombe, Sidmouth, Budleigh Salterton, Exmouth, Lympstone, Teignmouth, Dawlish and Starcross were included in the Exeter figures. On this basis, if John Morrice was comptroller for the North Devon ports as a whole, as seems likely (there were certainly no other candidates) his proportion of the annual payroll there is reduced to little over twelve per cent.[55]

There was thus considerably more patronage available in the customs offices of the localities than is suggested by the few names in the Treasury

Books. 'Tidesmen', 'waiters', 'searchers', boatmen and warehousemen comprised the majority of customs officials, and it is clear that most of these were local men who were rooted in parishes in which they served. The names of John Hooper, John Hutchinson and Ely Foster, customer and waiters at Appledore, are not to be found in the Northam parish registers, it is true, but the five other officials, Robert Brook, Hopkin Samms, John Griffiths, Bartholomew Rozier and William Mathews, were married and buried in Northam and rented seats in pews in the parish church.[56] At Topsham, the effective centre for the Exeter customs establishment, the names of tidesmen, waiters and searchers are to be found in the parish registers, and Peter Hagedot, the highest paid official (with two clerks he drew £160 a year) had formerly been, *inter alia*, an exciseman in Exeter before the first farm of the 1660s in 1663.[57] The contrast between the intruded patent officers, from areas other than those in which they served, and the majority of the locally-recruited employees, hired because of their residential proximity to the customs houses rather than because of any role in a 'spoils system', is heightened by the attitudes of the central customs establishment itself. On the 1675 and 1679 lists in the Customs House records, the patent officers are not mentioned at all, as if to emphasise their separateness. At the upper levels of the salary scales the customs collectors and their deputies enjoyed financial rewards comparable with those received by keepers and deputy keepers of weapons in the Ordnance Office. In the customs, the officials were paid a fixed salary but one which was determined by the volume of trade at the port. Thus the two surveyors at Exeter were paid £80 a year each; their colleague at Dartmouth only got £35. The Plymouth surveyor was paid £68 a year. At the lower levels, the remuneration compared badly with that pertaining to the Ordnance Office. Ordnance labourers' salaries were, at £21 a year, comparable with those of middle-ranking provincial customs searchers; the warehousemen and boatmen earned only between £8 and £10 a year.[58]

Patronage cannot be judged simply by volume, however. It is true that numerically and remuneratively the career excisemen outweighed those with contacts in high places, but the impact that the few placemen exercised, and the image of the Customs House itself, may be gauged by their role in the Dartmouth parliamentary election of January 1667. John Fowell, the town governor, Owen Lindsay, the postmaster, and Giles Ivy and William Hurt, customer and surveyor of the port, openly acted as the agents of the Earl of Arlington's candidate, Joseph Williamson.[59] Another supporter of his was John Roope, the patent officer, although in diligence he lagged behind his subordinates.[60] Giles Ivy compiled a list of dissenters in Dartmouth, and it was said to be the 'phanaticke partie' which had been decisive in electing the 'country' candidate, Walter Young of Colyton, (backed by William Morrice) whose principal virtues were a presbyterian background and a career untainted by government office. Williamson strove his utmost to manipulate the machinery of patronage, but to no avail. Among the repercussions of this election in which post office and customs were so visibly the agents of a candidate whose court background associated him with an unpopular Dutch war and the Canary Islands patent, were attempts to oust the Plymouth postmaster, Arlington's client, and a violent incident on Dartmouth quay in which a searcher was beaten up. According to customer, William Hurt, the incident had been prompted 'by that very gangue ... that lately contended with his Majesties patent and proclamacion to the Canary Company'.[61]

The quality of patronage counted more than its volume, and there would seem to have been little difference between the actions of the customs officials in 1666 and the 'strivings' of the major-generals in the elections for the second Protectorate Parliament a decade earlier. There was one peculiar feature of the 1667 election, however; the comparative silence of the Exeter and Dartmouth 'patent officers', Roope, Stucley and Noy. All three were of gentry families and all had been appointed in the great share-out of 1660 to 1662. Williamson's reliance on their subordinates suggests that by the mid-Sixties royalist euphoria had cooled to a degree which had affected the gentry's stake in government office. The gentry representatives in the customs were considered more likely to side with the county than with the government in struggles for local power.[62]

The Commissions of the Peace, Taxation and Lieutenancy

The Restoration was a victory for the county gentry. The 'natural rulers' came to their own again, and so the agency for their rule in the localities resumed a significance lost during the Interregnum. The composition of the commission of the peace was in Lord Chancellor Clarendon's hands, but not to the exclusion of other pressing counsels. Monck's influence was supreme within the county and the lieutenancy was given to him bound hand and foot, but in the Convention a real struggle for power developed between the presbyterians and trimmers, such as Monck and Morrice, and the devout cavaliers. Attempts were made to oust George Kekewich from the governorship of St Mawes in June 1660; his son wrote from Westminster that 'none are prefered to places of trust but Caval[liers] ... G. Monk is not so much respected as he was, he finds himself slighted allready by the Parliament which made him to go out in discontent ...'.[63] The Devonians in the Convention found themselves as hard-pressed by cavalier newcomers as they had been by independents in late 1648 or by Cromwellians and republicans in the 1650s. A list of those 'managed' by Lord Wharton suggests that at least ten Devon MPs were presbyterians and that the royalists were Thomas Chafe and Thomas Clifford (Totnes), Samuel Trelawney (Plymouth) and George Howard (Beeralston). G.F.T. Jones has suggested that a further five were royalists because they were on Wharton's list but unmarked as under his influence but their local careers indicate that two were presbyterians who had retired from politics in 1648 (Sir Francis Drake and his brother-in-law, Ellis Crimes), another was an aristocratic political lightweight (William Russell, third son of the fifth earl) and two were ex-Cromwellians (Samuel Searle and the ubiquitous John Maynard). That they were beyond Wharton's influence suggests not royalism but either genuine independence—Maynard, for example, was 'suspected by the honest [i.e., cavalier] party' in April 1660—or simply that Wharton did not know them.[64] The Devon representatives could hardly be said to reflect the prevailing mood of Parliament, and Morrice soon echoed Monck's 'discontent'; he complained that many had 'with so great expence purchased places in parliament with no other designe than to make themselves wholly breaking this acte [of oblivion]'.[65]

The Act of Oblivion became a symbol of the kind of settlement sought by the King, and Charles's 'goodness ... seconded by reasons of state'[66] brought it to fruition in this Parliament and preserved it in the next, despite attacks by a Devonian, Edward Seymour the younger, MP for Gloucester. Seymour was aged twenty-eight, a young blade who was the despair of his father, the third baronet and the MP for Totnes in the Cavalier Parliament.[67] In June 1661 Seymour brought in a proviso to the Act of Indemnity which one local commentator thought would have passed by one hundred and ninety votes until the king sent a message that 'he should looke on such as noe friende to him that did tuch with that Acte'; the following day the proviso was rejected by ninety-nine votes.[68] In 1660 and 1661, therefore, most Devonians would have followed Morrice rather than Clarendon, and Clarendon rather than Seymour, and local pressures circumscribed the Lord Chancellor's efforts to create a commission of the peace wholly suited to his purposes. Clarendon describes how:

> the commissions of the peace were renewed and the names of those persons inserted therein who had been most eminent sufferers for the King and were known to have entire affections for his Majesty and the laws though it was not possible but that some would get and continue in who were of more doubtful inclinations by their not being known to him whose Province it was to depute them.[69]

An instance of how the latter occurred is provided in Morrice's account of Court estimations of the merits of Edmund Prideaux of Padstow. In July 1661 Morrice told him that 'You were by some men's stickling left out of the commission of the peace', but in September 1662 a struggle between the Earl of Bath (a moderate presbyterian and one of the greatest landowners in Devon and Cornwall)[70] and Colonel Arundel of Trerice (cavalier) for the Chancellor's ear produced victory for the former. Then, in Morrice's words, 'the Chancellor upon inspection of the list asked what the Prideaux was and my lord [the Earl of Bath] answered an honest gentleman of good estate his kinsman and to secretary Morrice his brother-in-law, wherupon you past muster'.[71] The changes in the commission of the peace have to be viewed not as the undiluted preferences of Clarendon and moderate royalist opinion, but as the results of compromise between shifting coalitions of political interests.

The revolution among minor county officeholders in 1648 to 1649 was quite considerable but in 1660 the continuity of government as represented by constables and bailiffs was virtually absolute. For the justices of the peace, however, the Restoration was a watershed. Change in the hundreds in 1649 had been necessary because of the virtual collapse of local government during the 1640s; at the end of the following decade the reconstruction was complete, and this administrative strength helped a purge of the commission of the peace—something of a luxury during the Interregnum—to be accomplished with minimal disruption. More importantly, in 1660 the government did not need actively to seek support; Charles II was proclaimed with a degree of popular assent which had contrasted with the reluctance to participate in government which had been typical of the political nation as a whole since the end of the civil war. Lord Chancellor Clarendon had an eye to the welfare of 'eminent sufferers' for the King but in 1660 there were more of these than could be accommodated in the commission of the peace. With demand outstripping supply, therefore, it was natural that a purge should have been undertaken. In 1649 fifteen of the seventy JPs had lost their places; in 1660 it was twenty-three out of fifty-four, or twenty-one and forty-two per cent respectively.[72] Those dismissed in 1660 were, first, the egregious representatives of Cromwellian government, the military men of comparatively low birth who had risen to prominent places in the civil administration: Coplestone, Hatsell, Blackmore, Saunders, James Pierce, Joseph Hunkin. Others had been associated with central government in a civilian capacity: Thomas Boone, John Searle and John Carew the regicide. The last main category was of trimmers who had exercised local power with scant reference to the government but whose prominence in quarter sessions was a constant goading to the secluded royalist gentry. The trimmers included John Beare, John Elford, William Fowell, John Tyrling and Christopher Wood. Yet among these would have appeared William Morrice himself—he came to sessions on seven occasions during the Interregnum and it was through his influence and that of Monck and the Earl of Bath that the presbyterians among the justices were preserved from complete elimination. In 1664 Bishop Ward compiled a list of fourteen presbyterians and 'Oliverians' who had survived from the 1650s;[73] to their number could be added Robert Duke of Otterton,[74] Sir John Northcote, who was prominent in debates in Parliament on religion and who thought of deans and chapters as mere parasites,[75] and probably Sir Francis Drake and John Maynard. Even William Courtenay sheltered an ejected presbyterian minister at Powderham.[76]

In 1660 and 1661 forty-eight new men were appointed to the commission of the peace, or more accurately new men and those who had not been in government for at least ten years. By the end of 1662 the commission had assumed the characteristics it was to keep for the entire decade. The 1660s were not a period of purges nor was any attempt made during periods of tension between Parliament and the executive to 'tune' the Bench. 'Eminent sufferers' were well rewarded. Twenty JPs had been sequestered for delinquency and had paid fines, while another ten had been mulcted by the agency of semi-penal taxation, the committee for advance of money. Between one-third and a half of the Restoration Bench had a vested interest in royalist revenge, therefore.[77] Yet not all former delinquents of the county gentry class were restored to the Bench. The

Aclands provided JPs and sheriffs in the pre-war county, had paid a composition fine of over £1,500 but in their case there were no adults in the senior branch of the family to assume a place on the Bench. The Culmes of Molland were similarly afflicted. On the other hand Francis Bluett of Holcomb Rogus had been killed at Lyme Regis in 1644 and had two sons who would have been of suitable age for appointment to the commission of the peace but neither served in the 1660s.[78] Sir Peter Ball, a civil lawyer from Exminster, a former commissioner of array, paid a fine appropriate to an estate worth £600 a year (about the same as the Devon lands of the well-favoured Seymours) and might have expected a better reward than merely a place on assessment commissions.[79] It was influence, not wealth, which counted for most in finding a place as a justice and when there were more aspirants than places the least connected went to the wall. Just as it is difficult to account for some of the omissions without invoking the mysteries of patronage, so it is hard to see why certain Interregnum JPs flourished in the next decade. Why was John Elford dropped in 1660 never to be nominated again while his brother-in-law, John Wollocombe, survived in commission until his death in 1663? They were of the same age, moved in the same social circles (among the 'presbyterian' county gentry like the Northcotes, Drakes and Fortescues) and were 'trimmers' during the Fifties. Elford had been an MP, however, and perhaps it was this distinctive experience which disqualified him. On the other hand, Thomas Reynell was the epitome of the trimmer JP and MP and he survived to attend all but seven quarter sessions meetings of the 1660s.

In the early 1650s the commissions of the peace had not reflected accurately the distribution of power within the county. Attendances at quarter sessions revealed the reluctance of many JPs to participate in public. There was a nucleus of committed justices upon whom sessions depended and a larger group who attended more or less erratically. The Restoration attendances were more, evenly distributed and on average were somewhat larger (thirteen in the Fifties, sixteen in the Sixties) than they had been. The most frequent attenders were the remnants of the presbyterians (Thomas Reynell, Henry Worth, Sir John Davy and John Hales) and the ex-royalists and newcomers like Henry Northleigh, Samuel Sainthill, Sir Courtenay Pole and Thomas Carew. If attendances are added (an individual who attended all sessions from 1661 to 1670 would have been present on forty occasions) it is found that the Parliamentarian/ Cromwellian group and the ex-Cavalier group were roughly balanced with 214 and 219 total attendances respectively, with the newcomers, county gentry who had come to government fresh in the 1660s, holding a marginal lead of two hundred and twenty-nine attendances.[80] It was doubtless the salutary effect of this influx of young JPs which ensured that the divisions of the past decades were not as deep in the 1660s. Among the newcomers were a few who, had they become justices in the 1650s would have been described as obscure upstarts. John Hore of Chagford was a lawyer of the Middle Temple whose children married into the minor gentry families of Read (the rector of Drewsteignton), Buck and Cudmore, the last being a family on the best of terms with the Puritans,

Saunders of Payhembury. John Hore himself was a 'good friend' of Hugh Trevilian of Hartland, a JP from 1647 to 1652.[81] Edward Lovett was sworn in as a JP in 1668, probably through the good offices of his 'loving friend' Arthur Bassett, an ex-royalist, although he was not armigerous. Lovett ensured that posterity judged him so, however, by having 'esquire' carved on the tombstone in Tawstock church which he erected before his death.[82] Both he and John Hore were appointed with no previous experience in government but another undistinguished newcomer, George Reynell, had served on assessment commissions before his elevation to the magistracy in 1665. Reynell came from a branch of his family junior to that of the indefatigable Thomas Reynell and in the records of Exeter College, Oxford, he was described as the son of George Reynell, 'gent.'. He married a Somaster, of another ancient but somewhat shadowy South Hams family. His elevation coincided with the removal of Thomas Bampfield and John Davy, presbyterians both, so perhaps it owed something to his Anglican zeal.[83]

The commission of the peace was always an avenue of social mobility rather than a static reflection of the county elite. Nevertheless, Lovett, Hore and Reynell, with three or four others, were the exceptions to the rule. Most Restoration JPs were of unquestionably county gentry status, of esquire level and above. Sixty of the JPs in commission in 1666, or seventy-eight per cent, were baronets, knights and esquires, and the Earls of Bath (Grenville) and Donegal (Chichester) with Monck, who had been elevated to the peerage, restored aristocratic appointments in sharp contrast to the Interregnum pattern.[84] Gentlemen and lawyers numbered six and seven respectively and there was only one merchant, the Gittisham clothier, Thomas Putt, who had first served in 1647.

The county gentry were restored to the full panoply of local power, but the fiscal requirements of central government ensured that the compilation of assessment (and now, subsidy) commissions continued as in the 1650s. Dodd regarded the Interregnum commissions as the development of 'the power of the committee' in the forties, but in their limited scope they were more strictly a reversion to established methods of subsidy administration which were naturally maintained in the new government.[85] Continued, too, was the trend towards large assessment commissions; the 1657 pattern of upwards of a hundred members was developed in a steady growth. In 1665 there were ninety-five members on the committee for the Royal Aid Act of 16 and 17 Charles II c. 4 and in 1679, two hundred and six commissioners for the Supply Act of 31 Charles II c.1.[86] The explosion in the size of the committees brought with it no increased centralisation or central direction in local fiscal affairs; the commissions were unwieldy and power was diffused in the interests of patronage and supposed administrative effectiveness.

Sixty-two tax commissioners in Devon in the 1660s were not JPs.[87] Six had been commissioners but not justices in the previous decade, and each had first served on the 1657 commission, to support the view that that year marked something of a turning point. Seven were political appointments designed largely to satisfy patronage demands. Five were of non-

Devonians. John Ashburnham was a Sussex courtier whose only connection with Devon was a grant of some Crown leases; George Carteret was governor of Jersey and the son-in-law of Sir Nicholas Slanning of Maristow, and Sir Thomas Higgons was a diplomat and a relation of the Earl of Bath.[88] He lived in Southampton. Sir John Mallett and Sir John Speccott were respectively from Somerset and Cornwall.[89] Another two were Devon men who clung to the coat-tails of the mighty. Sir Chichester Wray was well-connected with the Earls of Bath and Donegal; although Tawstock was his ancestral home his will was written from Trebigh in Cornwall. Christopher Monck, Albemarle's son, was a callow youth scarcely out of his teens.[90]

Eighteen commissioners were former royalist delinquents of varying social standing. Sir Peter Ball, Sir Nicholas Slanning and Sir James Smith were of families which had done much for the royalist cause but which were hardly adequately rewarded. Pre-war patterns of participation were constraints on social mobility. The largest group of thirty-one assessment commissioners came from much the same background as their Interregnum predecessors, that of the lower levels of the county gentry and their common characteristic was that they were new to government in 1660s. Some came of families which had provided pre-war commissioners—the Bluetts, the Berrys, the Fownes, the Staffords—but many were merchants, lawyers or minor gentlemen who for reasons so particular, local and individual, had been rewarded with a certain parochial prominence.[91] The expansion of the assessments committee had made it suitable for packing as an 'overflow', both for those who might have expected something better, and for those whose obscurity would have offended men in more exalted stations. The difference between the two decades may be read in the way in which outsiders were treated. In the 1650s they were added to the commission of the peace to strengthen it; in the 1660s they were made assessment commissioners because there were no vacancies anywhere else.

By sharp contrast, the lieutenancy, preserved as a vehicle for the chauvinism of the gentry elite, despite the misgivings of the government and its stated preference for something more effective,[92] maintained social distinctions in the guise of military hierarchy. The enthusiasm of the Devon gentry for quasi-military celebrations in 1660, and their addresses to the restored monarch from militia meetings have been linked by one historian with their fears for the preservation of the established social order. Hence the rounding-up of 'fanatics' by legally-constituted gangs like that of Coplestone Bampfield was one with the popularity of the Clarendon Code among former Cavaliers.[93] In addition, the remarkably swift reconstruction of the militia—the deputy lieutenants were appointed in July 1660, surveys of arms were made in the autumn, and the tinners' regiment was mustered in January 1661[94]—was the sympton of a psychological need to reconstruct a hierarchy which was felt to have been knocked awry by the administration of the 1650s. Thus, the officers and men of sheriff Coplestone Bampfield's regiment, under Lord Lieutenant Monck, presented a loyal address in favour of monarchy and episcopacy in

May 1661; their signatures amount to a roll-call of the gentry in descending order of social as well as of military rank.[95] JPs and tax commissioners served as senior and junior officers while the most minor gentry, constables and grand jurors like William Babb, George Glanville, Thomas Suxbitch, James Paddon and George Weymouth were included as ensigns and sergeants. In the euphoria of the Restoration, the militia was taken up as the symbol of county solidarity; in the fifties it had suffered as the embodiment of centralist intrusion and sectarian divisiveness.[96] Similarly, the basis of military taxation, pre-civil war assessments for arms, could but reaffirm an old order. In 1660 this old order had to be the guiding principle for reconstruction, in the haste which precluded leisurely administration and direction:

> We thought fitt hereby to direct you soe to guide yourselfe therein by the example of former times as may be most for the advantage of our service and least chargeable to our good subjects, so as you be sure at least to keepe up the full number both of horse and foote which the trayned bands of that our county were formerly wont to consist of.[97]

At the lower levels of the gentry and yeomanry the inclusiveness of the restored militia may have been genuine enough, since political commitment at those levels had been tentative and opportunist; at the upper levels the inclusiveness was illusory. The government was forced to scrutinize suggested deputy lieutenants because from 1660 to 1661 the security of the regime in the counties rested literally on their efforts. From the first list compiled in July 1660 were removed the names of Thomas Reynell, ardent presbyterian, William Courtenay, never a royalist, and for less obvious reasons, the ex-Cavalier, Sir James Smith.[98] Left in were nine knights and baronets and three esquires, including the additions in another hand, of two prominent royalists, Sir Hugh Pollard and Sir Thomas Stucley. A deliberate effort had been made to balance the deputy lieutenancy between royalists and presbyterians who had served during the Interregnum. By late 1661 the complexion of the commission revealed a stronger hold by the ex-Cavaliers, for although no presbyterians had been removed, the deputy lieutenants had been augmented by another ten royalists, including Francis Drake, Piers Edgcombe, Thomas Southcott and Sir Thomas Hele (all former delinquents).[99] Social weight may have been lessened slightly by the addition of another four esquires, but their undoubted reliability amply compensated.

Charles II had returned at the behest of the presbyterians not of the Cavaliers, but one of the most striking developments of the Restoration settlement was the way in which a presbyterian majority in 1660 had been turned into a Cavalier and Anglican ascendancy by 1661. In the localities this ascendancy was mitigated; in Devon it was tempered by the prominence of two or three presbyterians who retained powerful links at Court and in the country—Albemarle, Morrice and the Earl of Bath. It was they who advised Clarendon on the composition of the commission of the peace and ensured that a sufficient number of presbyterian JPs remained to irritate Bishop Seth Ward. But apart from the Bishop's almost paranoic private outbursts the JPs of Devon worked together in amity. Although Clarendon's euphoria that "'every man dwelt again under the shadow of his own vine" without complaint of injustice or oppression' was exaggerated in wistful hindsight, there is certainly little evidence of faction-fighting and much of constructive county government.[100] Most presbyterians and royalists were committed to the Restoration settlement. The commission of the peace and the lieutenancy were under closer control than the assessment commissions, however, whose large numbers and narrowly parochial concerns—to achieve 'fair' individual assessments—stimulated faction and political dissent. John Arscot of Tetcott, a presbyterian, wrote to his brother-in-law, William Martin of Netherexe, for a copy of instructions agreed upon at a meeting of the commissioners in Exeter, for levying the 'Free and Voluntary Present' (13 Charles II c. 4). He was a commissioner, and he was particularly embarrassed by his ignorance because he had 'cause to fear that nowe a cru of the commissors of our sub-north[ern division] devise warr at the generall meetinge'.[101] His fears were not, however, sufficiently pressing to move him to attend the meeting; he was kept at home by the visit of his cousin's wife. William Morrice tried to get him to go, which in itself suggests something of presbyterian/Cavalier friction.

In 1663 John Fowell wrote to Joseph Williamson, secretary to the Duke of York, that the assessment commissioners in Devon were reducing the fiscal contribution of the county:

> The persons of 1 or 2,000 per annum pay noe more to the subsidys than those with us that have nott £300 per annum and that the commissioners have justifyed this proportion by a letter to Mr. Secretary Morrice by reason of the great poverty and losses which the county induced in the warr; a dam'd rebellious county and if the commissioners there shall thus passe without rebuke you will find that this county will nott in their two next subsidy be halfe as much as now.[102]

Inside the county, assessments produced friction between Cavalier and presbyterian groups; in Whitehall, Devon's fiscal apportionments were a source of annoyance to a government heavily dependant on parliamentary taxation.[103] But these were minor irritations on the body politic, arising from the endemic resentment of taxation rather than from circumstances peculiar to the 1660s. For the most part, the Restoration offers a picture of political 'ins' and 'outs' with the grey area between most closely approached by amorphous assessment commissions.

The Ousted Officials

What of those who were ejected from the commission of the peace in 1660? It was a vengeful Restoration, and the disarming of Cromwellian and republican partisans was undertaken vigorously and gleefully. On the eve of Charles II's coronation, Shilston Calmady of Bridestowe, a county gentleman who had been nominated as a JP in 1653 and 1654, but who seems never to have acted, wrote to his brother-in-law: 'I suppose your friende Hatsell, that threatned to make you stinke smells ugly himself now, but such knaves commonly have better fortune than honest men',[104] suggesting the contempt commonly felt by the armigerous towards upstarts even when on the same political side. Henry Hatsell, navy commissioner, customs official and Cromwellian MP, may have thought that there was a place for him in the restored monarchical government, or at any rate judged the popular mood to be one of localistic aggression. In a *volte-face* he demanded a £4,000 debt which he claimed the Admiralty commissioners owed the people of Plymouth. He retired to Saltram, the house in Plympton which he had bought from the delinquent Sir James Bagg, an unfortunate who had suffered as much from 'Thorough' as from the predations of parliamentary rule, and although he was still a freeman of Plymouth in 1666 (he was first admitted in 1641) he was not on the governing body when the commissioners for regulating corporations visited in August 1662. When some cattle of his were rustled in 1667 the examining magistrate maintained a studied indifference to his past achievements; he was still *one* Hatsell of Saltram, *gent*. Throughout the 1660s he was watched by government agents as one likely to provoke insurrection but there is no evidence that he was ever interested in more than a life as a quiet gentleman farmer with an interest in the Plymouth business world.[105]

It was the combination of prominent military office with merchant or minor gentry status which seemed to attract the attention of these agents; Francis Rolle, William Venner, Thomas Allen, James Pierce and John Beare were all described in reports as if they still held military rank. Thomas Boone (with the late Edmund Prideaux) and Christopher Martin were the only Devon republican MPs so were inevitably associated with revolution. John Searle of Buckerell, who in the early 1650s had seemed needlessly to be antagonising the royalist delinquents, now found himself under the scrutiny of a type of bounty-hunter who blended Cavalier zeal with the enterprise of the projectors.[106]

For Colonel Spurway and Edward Raddon, former clerk of the peace, the 1660s were a time of active opposition to the government which culminated in Raddon's writing an 'underground' attack in verse on the 'Papist' monarch and then fleeing abroad with Spurway to die in exile and outlawry.[107] Robert Shapcote, Cromwell's Solicitor-General in Ireland, stayed in his adopted country to sit in the Irish House of Commons. In 1663 he was implicated in a rebellion against the Lord Lieutenant, the Duke of Ormond, which arose from dissatisfaction with the Restoration settlements of the church and land questions. In 1665 he was expelled from the House of Commons but was subsequently pardoned. The evidence against him was never more than weak.[108] The Sixties were an edgy, nervous decade, with the government continuously on its guard against plots and plotters. It need not have been concerned about most former Devon officials who were happy to remain in anonymity. The JPs of the county did not seem concerned about their behaviour; they were observed by outsiders instead. Against only one individual did the magisterial Bench direct the full venom of which it was capable. Sampson

Larke was a Combe Raleigh man who had been based at Plymouth since the mid-Fifties as an officer under Disbrowe and as a customs agent. He was the hero of the restored Rump in having the proclamation against Booth proclaimed despite the hostility of the deeply presbyterian Plymothians. He was a friend of Thomas Saunders, who died in 1660, and who had been governor of Exeter and Plymouth under the Commonwealth and Protectorate. In Michaelmas 1661 Larke was imprisoned at Exeter common gaol for refusing the Oath of Allegiance. There he remained 'during the King's pleasure', and not until the summer of 1663 was it made clear that he had been convicted of praemunire, the offence of which those who refused the Supremacy and Allegiance oaths were guilty. Larke spent the rest of the decade in prison and after his release fought at Sedgemoor against the monarchy at whose hands he had suffered so much. He was executed in the bloody aftermath as a 'fanatic Anabaptist' traitor.[109] Two others, Cornishmen but with close Devon connections, had been executed as regicides in October 1660; they were Gregory Clement and John Carew.[110]

Spurway, Raddon and Larke were notable exceptions to the pattern of conformity by local Interregnum officials after 1660. None of them bore county office as constables or quarter sessions jurors, for quite apart from their former commitments they were above that social standing. They hovered uneasily by the ranks of assessment commissioners and probably assize jurors. The later career of John Coplestone is downright improbable and defies both the rule of passive conformity and the exceptional cases of active opposition to the restored monarchy. Coplestone was a lawyer who combined the recordship of Barnstaple with the shrievalty of Devon from 1655 and whose diligence in assisting Unton Croke to suppress Penruddock's rising won him a Cromwellian knighthood. In the later 1650s he served as a captain of horse in the regiment of the republican colonel, Matthew Alured, and was retained in the Devon commission of the peace, although he retired from the local militia which he had led during the rule of the major-generals. Critics described him as 'a great Cavalier formerly' and it would appear that he can be identified safely as one of the Coplestones of Upton Pyne who, it is true, were delinquents. In 1650 he was under a cloud for quarrelling with his neighbour, Mrs Marcella Walters, mother of the Rump JP, Henry Walters. Both were bound over to keep the peace. He commemorated his association with the major-generals by christening his son Desborough, and well might it have seemed to contemporaries that he sought the best of two worlds.[111] After the Restoration he reverted to royalism and by the mid-1660s he had found favour with the King's illegitimate son, the Duke of Richmond, for whom he recounted news at Court. At a later date he appears as a client of Danby's. He never again appeared in Devon commissions of the peace or of taxation but once out of Devon he managed to find a niche on the fringes of the Restoration Court.[112] It seemed that to make any contribution to political life the egregious Cromwellian officials had first to escape the unanimity of the Devon gentry that they should be seen and not heard.

The JPs of 1652 and 1662

How did the Restoration bench of magistrates compare with its predecessor of ten years earlier? In these pages some broad comparisons between the magistracy of 1652 and 1662 will be drawn, with a view to highlighting changes over the decade.

Perhaps the most obvious difference was the exalted status of Restoration magistrates compared with their counterparts of a decade earlier. In 1650 about half the JPs had been of esquire status and above; by 1662 that proportion had risen to eighty-three per cent. The return of knights and baronets, who had formed the spearhead of the great class of sequestered royalists, accounted for much of this, but the largest single category remained that of the esquires. The gentry retained their grip on the local community. Social factors and the demands of government, rather than a healthy rent-roll, account for the inclusion of some JPs and the exclusion of others who seemed worthy of the dignity. The number of gentry in Devon has been calculated by Hoskins[113] and is discussed above, but it includes self-described gentlemen who would not normally aspire to the Bench.[114] The Devon Protestation Returns offer a source for estimating the numbers of gentry in a fairly neutral and realistic way.

Excluding the Exeter parishes, lists for 446 out of 502 parishes have survived. Thirty-nine 'esquire' families have been found in these lists whose members were not represented in the commissions of the peace. Twenty-nine were armigerous and could be found in the Herald's Visitation of 1620. Death and genealogical withering account for the omissions of the Culmes, the Arscots of Bideford, the Gilberts (so eminent in the previous century) and the younger sons of prominent families whose brothers became JPs, such as Reed Fortescue of Cornwood, Peter Speccott junior of Thornbury and Edward Calmady of Bridestowe.

Devon was not a county where recusancy was a highly significant disqualifying factor, but the gentry families of Rowe, Kirkham, the Arlington branch of the Chichesters, the Careys of Cockington and the Coffins of Parkham probably would have been represented in the commission of the peace were it not for their religion. John Rowe of Staverton was sheriff in 1688 and died in office. Edward Carey of Cockington was a knight and thus well-qualified for office. When Cosmo III of Tuscany visited Devon in 1669 Sir William Kirkham rode out to visit him, and he was described as 'the only Catholic gentleman within the county'.[115] Kirkham participated in county affairs to this extent at least. The evidence of the recusant rolls[116] suggests that there were not ten Catholic families of esquire status which could have provided JPs. More—thirteen out of thirty-three on the 1655 roll—were gentlemen, but this proves not that recusancy was concentrated in the 'peasant gentry' but that Catholicism was *evenly* spread in county society; there were *more* minor gentlemen than those of superior status.[117]

More men failed to attain office because they consistently made marriage alliances with obscure families, suggesting that their 'esquire' designations were freakish. Among them were the Newcourts of

Georgeham (married into the Hexts, the Incledons, and the Harris family of Marwood) and the Molfords of Bishop's Nympton (married into the Chollocombes and the Welshes). The view that the length of a family sojourn in a county significantly contributed to the political behaviour of that family is one which may find confirmation in analysis of such families but the question of how this natural selection operated raises insuperable difficulties. In fact, although traditions of county office-holding ran in families, they were not likely to influence the selection of magistrates beyond one or two generations. Nevertheless esquires who lived in Devon but whose descents were not recorded in the 1620 visitation and by antiquarians like Pole and Westcote could scarcely expect a place in a body which represented the hierarchy of the county; some were Cornishmen and Somersetians, the kinds of men who were included in the 1650s only as makeweights.

Although the 1662 magistracy included some who were picking up the threads of local government participation after an enforced absence of twenty years, more significant were the forty-five complete newcomers to county office. In this sense, the Restoration was more revolutionary than the changes of the early 1650s, which had been characterised by expulsions rather than new admissions. The decisive period then had not been the consequences of the execution of the King but the period of the expulsion of the royalist armies from Devon in 1646 and 1647. Of the 1647 bench only thirteen had been active before the civil war or had been named in royalist commissions of the peace; fifty-seven others were drafted in from committees, the army or from the parishes where many would doubtless have been content to remain. Inexperience was no obstacle to diligence, however: indeed some of the most notable zealots were among the novices of the Restoration. Thomas Beare became an Anglican zealot who won Seth Ward's approval; John Davy of Ruxford in Sandford, of a junior branch of the Davy family, led the attack on nonconformists in the Crediton Corporation in 1663. Both were newcomers in 1660.[118]

The ages and educational experiences of the JPs of the two decades were broadly similar. There were four men over seventy in 1652 and only one a decade later but in general age was not a significant disqualification from office since premature death was an ever-present possibility. In 1669 the constables of the hundreds of North Tawton, Winkleigh and Witheridge in mid-Devon petitioned the justices at Exeter for replacements for 'the late...Sir John Chichester, Colonel Jefford [Gifford], Mr [John] Pollard and Mr [John] Bury'.[119] Gifford was sixty-three when he died but Chichester was only forty-four. Death had removed a justiciary presence in mid-Devon and seventeenth-century mortality rates suggest that such an accident would have been not unheard of. At the other end of the age-spectrum there were around ten JPs in each of our samples under thirty-five.

The educational background of both revolutionary justices and the avenging royalists were almost identical. Over half went to an inn of court or university, but nearly all of these followed the well-beaten path to

Exeter College, Oxford. Despite the wider life of the university and town which Devon students could not have avoided, west country undergraduates preferred the clubbable fellowship of their neighbours to more adventurous choices. It is interesting that only two or three in each decade had been to Cambridge but that among them were the most eminent Devonians of their day: Attorney-General Edmund Prideaux and General George Monck.

It used to be argued that the magistrates of the 'Puritan Revolution' dealt more brusquely with the problem of poverty than did their predecessors. The idea of a 'new medicine for poverty', compounded of self-help and bourgeois thrift has largely been replaced by a view of the Interregnum justices as either notably imaginative or at least diligent in the field of social policy. On the other hand, as this study will show, there was undeniably an attack during the 1660s on public provision for the poor. A study of those wills of Devon magistrates which have survived the destruction in World War Two of the Devon probate registry[120] suggests that in the private disposition of wealth to relieve the poor the JPs of the 1650s and 1660s shared common assumptions.

The charitable bequests of fifty magistrates may be ascertained from their wills. Those who were in office during the Interregnum gave an average of £19.66 in doles, those who succeeded them an average of £23.44, but these bald and probably not very helpful generalities conceal a wide variety of sums and stipulations. They range from the single pound left by Edmund Fowell to the poor of Calstock, and the £2 legacies of Samuel Trelawney and John Hore to the poor of Plymouth and Chagford respectively, to the £50 (to be invested) left by Sir John Northcote to the poor of Newton St. Cyres and Crediton. The lawyer John Doddridge left the exceptional sum of £115 to the poor of Barnstaple, Ilfracombe, Fremington and South Molton, as well as £40 to the corporation of Bristol for a piece of plate to be inscribed 'ex dono Johannis Doddridge recordatoris civitatis Bristoll'. (He could well afford to leave these sums, for his other each bequests amounted to over £1,700.[121]) Most were simple unconditional doles to be distributed among the poor of the donor's parish, but the gentry tended to stipulate that the larger sums should be invested for the annual distribution of the interest.[122]

The problem of complex bequests fatally undermines these average sums. Just as land was devised in trusts and did not usually appear in wills except in incidentals, so more complicated bequests to the poor were established in trusts and separately administered. Those whose wills did not mention the poor cannot be dismissed as careless of their social obligations. The reports of the Charity Commissioners offer something of a corrective to the one-sided view of gentry philanthropy offered by the wills alone. Published between 1815 and 1839 the reports for Devon dealt, parish by parish, with the history of all bequests remembered in the villages and their compilers sought out the parish elders of whatever social station in an effort to be as comprehensive as possible.[123] Moreover they studied the wills of the more eminent benefactors to compare the terms of the original bequests with their subsequent history. Sir Thomas Putt left an annual rent-charge of £10 for a school in Gittisham, though no mention of it was found in his will; extra-testamentary benefaction was common. Sir William Morrice left land for the erection of an almshouse at Sutcombe by an indenture, and in the same way Hugh Stafford established an annual rent-charge payable to the poor of Dowland. In 1682 Bartholomew Gidley conveyed half an acre at Winkleigh to Richard Dunning on behalf of Winkleigh parish, for the use of poor women.[124] The commissioners' reports are invaluable as a partial compensation for the loss of the Devon wills, even though the extinction of certain charities, over the interval of one hundred and thirty years since they were established, makes quantification misleading. In Jordan's words, those who devised trusts were 'men whose aspirations were clearly and quite specifically defined and who possessed the knowledge and the resources wherewith to ensure that their wishes would be carried out in perpetuity'. His studies of *all* charitable giving demonstrate how unusual a group the JPs were. The average amount they gave was much above that of all donors, and they were, in crude numerical terms, a minority; fifty-six per cent of Somerset donations were given by husbandmen and yeomen, in Devon a group whose philanthropic intentions are now lost to us because of the destruction of their wills.[125] The commissioners' reports partly redress this; of the hundred-odd local officeholders whose names they recorded, only about a quarter sat on the Devon Bench in the 1650s or 1660s.

The effects of successive land transactions on Devon administrators deserve some attention. The financial straits of the parliamentary and then the republican government were the motive for the successive sales of the bishops', deans' and chapters' and crown lands, rather than the creation of any dependent administrative class. By the act of November 1646 for the sale of bishops' lands, the governors of the county benefitted not at all. The bishop's lands of Exeter diocese produced £14,120.3*s*.1*d*. at sale and most of these lands fell into the hands of Exeter merchants and outsiders. The Bishop's Palace was conveyed for £450 to Simon Snowe, the presbyterian MP for Exeter secluded in Pride's Purge, but he seems to have bought it on behalf of the mayor and commonalty of Exeter, who undertook all repairs to it.[126] The other properties, with the exception of Bishop's Nymet manor, were messuages in Exeter and were sold between 1647 and 1651. The names of the same purchasers recur in the evidence for the sale of capitular lands, authorised by the act of 30 April, 1649.[127] It is apparent that a substantial re-sale trade developed in the Exeter properties[128] and that it involved local merchants like Henry Gandy and William Hamm, and agents like Zachary Trescott, who was awarded a £10 annuity by the City of Exeter for his diligence on their behalf.

A few local officials were involved in the traffic in capitular lands. Richard Clapp of Sidbury, sequestration official, sold a tenement in Branscombe to Richard Huse of that parish, and another Branscombe man, Ellis Bartlett (assessment commissioner from 1657) bought a tenement there in 1650 from two carpet-bagging Londoners who had been the first purchasers from the trustees. Giles Inglett, the deputy clerk of the peace, bought property in East Teignmouth for the mayor and burgesses

of Exeter. Among direct purchasers were Thomas Boone and Gregory
Clement, revolutionary MPs who bought Membury manor from the Dean
and Chapter of Windsor, and Combe Pasford manor from the Exeter
capitular estate. Most church land purchasers, however, were not local
men at all but prominent politicians like the Vanes (who bought, or were
awarded by Parliament, Dawlish, Sidbury and Culmstock manors, with
some premises in Topsham) and John Lambert (who acquired the manor
of Braunton Dean) with London merchants and syndics like John
Herrick, Giles Sumpter and Richard Alford.[129] The pickings were rich
enough to tempt home those who had left Devon for places of easier
prosperity. George Walter, a Devonian by birth, wrote to the royalist
delinquent, Sir Francis Fulford, from London. Walter was interested in
some capitular lands in Braunton, of which Fulford was the sitting tenant.
By the legislation of April 1649 such tenants on long leases were to have
the first option of purchase, and Walter offered either to help Fulford
pursue his claim, through his contacts with the trustees, or to give him a
consideration if he would, in any case, declare an interest in the estate, to
discourage competitors. By this subterfuge Walter hoped to recover
£1,000 laid out for the use of Parliament by buying with 'doubled' bills. In
the event the plans seem to have misfired since the Close Rolls record John
Lambert as the grantee.[130]

The sources for the sales of church lands are scattered and by no means
comprehensive. The sales of crown lands, by contrast, are more fully
documented, and it was in these sales, made under the legislation of July
1649 that the Devon revolutionary group made its greatest profits. The
properties and their purchasers with sums paid, are given in Table 5.
Devon was not among counties with very extensive crown property; the
total sale value of £25,560 was not a quarter of that sold in
Northamptonshire, for example, where the total value was £103,788.[131]
Indeed, 76.36 per cent of Devon sale values represented Bradninch
manor, although these are sale *values*, not sums raised, as Sir John
Habakkuk has pertinently pointed out.[132] The act of sale established that
crown lands were to be sold at the capital value of thirteen years purchase,
the highest value of all confiscated estates, so that the *annual* value of a
property like Lydford Castle, for example, was really quite small. The
sale of Bradninch manor distorts the stake held in the land
market by Devonians; Thomas Saunders's interest in the property swells
the proportion of crown lands bought by local men to nearly eighty per
cent. In fact, of the twelve purchasers, five were Devonians and the other
seven were two Cornishmen and five complete outsiders. Among the
purchasers were two corporations. The Plymouth Orphans' Hospital
acquired Sutton Pool in the port through the good offices of Edmund
Fowell, a Plymouth barrister, JP and MP for Tavistock in 1650, and
Eustace Budgell acted as agent for the Corporation of Dartmouth in
buying the office of water-bailiff there. Budgell, too, was a lawyer and of a
family of lawyers.[133] These properties, with the manor of West Ashford,
were the only Devon crown possessions to be bought by immediate
tenants.[134]

Table 5 The Sales of Devon Crown Property

Property	Purchaser	Date	Price	Post-1660 tenant, (where known)
Bradford manor	John Warr	19 June 1650	£893 12s.3d.	–
Bradninch manor	Thomas Saunders, John Gorges	8 January 1650	£19,517 11s.10¼d.	John Ashburnham
Dartmouth water-bailiwick	Dartmouth Corporation	4 November 1650	£213 6s.8d.	–
Exeter Castle Ditches	John Rooke et al.	14 April 1650	£2,335	John Owen, Andrew Raddon
Lydford manor	William Menheir	10 December 1658	£178 14s.	William Menheir (court profits)
Lydford Castle	William Braddon	23 September 1650	£97 17s.10d.	–
Okehampton/ Plympton honour	Anthony Rous	11 July 1655	£346 1s.8d.	–
Sidmouth Mills	Edmund Prideaux	26 February 1650	£429 6s.8d.	–
South Teign manor	William Braddon	11 December 1650	£250 2s.6d.	–
Sutton Pool, Plymouth	Plymouth Hospital Trustees	30 October 1650	£230	Richard Arundel
West Ashford manor	John Collymore, William Phillips	9 December 1650	£353 16s.4½d.	–

Budgell and Fowell acted as agents for purchasers. More prominent as intermediaries were those who bought on behalf of others in something of a professional capacity. John Warr, the chaplain of Colonel Edward Prichard of Llancaiach in Glamorgan, was typical. Among the properties he bought were Lydford manor (for Thomas Menheir of London) and Bradford manor (for the soldiers of a regiment).[135] John Aubrey of Reading bought lands in the precincts of Exeter Castle for £960 but it is not clear whether these were personal purchases with bought debentures, or were for the soldiers of Colonel Robert Blake's regiment. Certainly purchases of his elsewhere were later re-sold.[136]

William Braddon, a Cornish foot captain, lawyer and MP, supposedly worth £150 a year, was one of the few who were sympathetic towards Quakers. It may have been these sympathies which helped him to a place on the Devon Bench, at a time when Cromwell was actively concerned to moderate the aggressive instincts of most Devon JPs. As a crown land buyer, however, he became a local landowner overnight, and could thus justify his appointment as a JP without reference to his military career or his political participation in central government.[137] Land could assist men to county eminence. Like Braddon, Thomas Saunders first acquired land on behalf of soldiers but ended up the principal beneficiary with his partner, John Gorges of Pounsford, Somerset, the man 'but of yesterday'. He sold at least half his land to local soldiers, lawyers and to his brother, the presbyterian minister, Lawrence Saunders, but retained enough at Bradninch to leave to his cousins, the Lands of Silverton.[138]

The trimming justices at sessions, upon whom county government depended, did not profit greatly by crown land sales. The beneficiaries were soldiers and government officials, and they bought outside the county as well as within it. Among them were John Blackmore, Richard Burthogg, Henry Hatsell, Sampson Larke and Thomas Saunders.

Edmund Fowell bought Harewood in Calstock, on the Cornish border, for £555; Nathaniel Byfield, minister of Silverton, bought land as far afield as Berkshire.[139]

The sale of fee farm rents in which fixed sums as rent-charges changed hands, rather than real estate, was arguably less of an irrevocable step, and tempted the more cautious of Devonians. The fee farm rents were sold by legislation of March 1650, with later amendments. The ambiguous nature of the sales, with purchasers continually in strife with tenants of the properties, proved the most burdensome of sales to the government.[140] S.J. Madge, the most meticulous historian which the topic of crown lands has attracted (or is likely to attract) concludes that 'it is quite impossible ... to state how many thousands of little rents of tenants and fee-farmers were exposed to sale between 1649 and 1659'.[141] Nevertheless, the order books, accounts and contracts of the trustees for the sale of fee farm rents[142] may be studied to discover who were most active purchasers. The most extensive transactions in Devon were doubtless made by Thomas Boone, Rump MP and later Cromwell's ambassador to the Baltic, whose name is not to be found among the purchasers of crown lands, but who bought fee farm rents in Devon, Somerset and Yorkshire to the value of £7,183.1s.6d.[143] Among the rent charges he acquired were those of Tavistock Abbey, Ashburton manor and the City of Exeter. The list of rents was large but the uncertainties of rent collection could hardly constitute the basis of his very considerable fortune, which he retained after the Restoration.[144] Edmund Prideaux, the Attorney-General, bought the fee farm rents of properties which he already owned, including those of Ottery St Mary manor and the site of Forde Abbey where he was building a palatial residence, for £1,539.10s.3d.,[145] to add to his purchase of the crown property of Sidmouth Mills. John Searle, the sequestration agent, assisted by Sampson Larke, bought the rents of Dunkeswell manor and Lee Deep Grange for not less than £110. These men enjoyed strong links with central government but among the gentry purchasers without such easy access to the trustees for the sales, and who bought to consolidate ancestral estates, were Richard Duke, Thomas Reynell, John Drake and John Land.[146] Fee farm rents were incumbrances on estates, so it was natural that immediate tenants should take advantage of opportunities offered them to purchase without competition in the thirty days from 1 April 1650, or in most cases at later dates.[147]

Minor gentry and yeomen bought fee farm rents. William Phelips of Thorncombe, constable of Axminster hundred from 1657 to 1660, and grand juror throughout the 1660s, bought the fee farm rent of Holditch manor, in partnership, for £292.17s.0½d., but seems to have been the only participant in the minor offices of local government to take such opportunities. Thomas Scoble, Humphrey Atweek and George Foxcroft bought rents but there is nothing to associate them with county administration.[148]

The net effect of the land sales of the Interregnum was to benefit interloping speculators and merchants, confirm the status of military men in the county and develop the wealth of the few who held civilian office in successive governments. They bought little material gain to most JPs and touched lesser gentry, who served as constables and jurors, hardly at all. Had the land-holdings been larger the sales would probably have confirmed existing social tendencies;[149] as it was they were merely a share-out among the more actively partisan. They drove a wedge between central and local government, since the most prominent purchasers were inevitably identified with the former.

All former crown lands reverted to the monarchy after 1660. In some cases death had already intervened to rob some purchasers of the enjoyment of their property. Thomas Saunders, who bought Bradninch, died in 1660; Edmund Prideaux, who added Sidmouth Mills to his estate, in 1659. (Prideaux's heir, in any case, hung on to his father's most valued possession, Forde.) In other cases the Crown was sympathetic to purchasers. Exeter Castle Ditches were a detached part of the manor of Bradninch and were bought by John Aubrey of Caversham, Oxfordshire, for over £2,000 in 1650, supposedly for the soldiers of the regiment of Col. Robert Blake.[150] It is clear that this was not a military purchase, however, and that Aubrey sold off the tenements in the property piecemeal to local people. Among the buyers was Andrew Raddon (possibly the brother of the clerk of the peace and postmaster under the Protectorate, Edward Raddon) and John Owen. Other purchasers were Francis Childe and John Rooke. In 1660 the pre-sale tenants recovered rights to their leases, and among them was one Margaret Biglestone who seemed set to recover her interest. Raddon and Owen petitioned, however, and an investigation and survey were ordered. It was revealed that John Rooke had managed to force other occupants of the tenements to acknowledge his lordship of the area, but the situation remained so confused that the surveyor, Sir Charles Harbord, suggested that the mayor and aldermen of Exeter should arbitrate. They reported that before Raddon and Owen bought the Ditches they had 'layn waste many yeares and were worth about 20s. p.a.';[151] after development by Raddon and Owen the property was worth £20 at least. The developers were confirmed in their title as was Francis Childe. It was realised that Rooke's lease of the entire property should be stopped, if 'his Majestie doe give this to any servant'.[152] This was diligence rewarded, a pragmatic solution and support for the judgements of the Exeter mayor and aldermen.

There was no general policy of support for the interests of urban corporations in these disputes, however. The governors of Plymouth Orphans' Hospital—the corporation in another guise—had acquired the vital harbour of Sutton Pool in 1650 for £230.[153] In 1660 Richard Arundel requested a lease of the pool—which would give him an immensely powerful lever against the merchant princes of Plymouth, who traded from the quay—on the grounds that his family had served Charles I in 'the worst of times'. A survey was undertaken by Harbord, and he reported that the Plymouth Corporation, the former owners, were quiet: 'I have not heard of any peticion or address by them ... for a further estate therein'.[154] By December 1660 an improved value had been put on the property, as a result of new buildings erected during the 1650s. On this occasion the improvements did not become the reward of the improvers, however, and Arundel was granted his lease. The earlier silence of the mayor and aldermanic body proved to have been a calm before the storm.[155] Plymouth claimed possession of the pool by an act of 1440, and a dispute dragged on until 1664. The Plymouth claimants ransacked local archives in an effort to prove their case. They contacted Nicholas Rowe, the clerk of the peace for Devon during the Commonwealth, then living in retirement at Lamerton, to go through the papers of his late father-in-law, the presbyterian Thomas Gewen of Bradridge. Whether he was stirred by memories of the 'Good Old Cause' or by a simple desire to help old friends, Rowe wrote back a detailed letter to suggest where legal ammunition against Arundel could be found.

The case of the King against the mayor and commonalty of Plymouth was heard in the Exchequer. A jury was drawn from the Devon gentry who were to be selected, lest undue influence be allowed to prejudice the case, from 'out of the hundreds of the east of Exon'. Each side had a right to reject twelve out of forty-eight of these freeholders.[156] This came two years after Plymouth was visited by the county gentry commissioners for regulating corporations, when eighteen common councillors and magistrates were dismissed.[157] They remained as freemen and as influential merchants, however, and the course of the struggle against Arundel proved that the city was no more amenable to Crown control after 1662—indeed, was probably less so. The appearance on the list of jurors to judge their case of men like Sir Peter Prideaux, John Pollard of Langley and John Gifford of Brightley (all of whom had been commissioners for corporations in 1662) must have served only to revive resentments against the intrusive county gentry. For the other side, the names of Henry Walter of Ashbury (JP 1650 to 1652) and Thomas Beare of Huntsham (committeeman, 1644) must have been almost equally unwelcome. The final jury was a well-balanced group of neutrals like Robert Fortescue of Filleigh, John Garland of Marwood, moderate Cavaliers like Richard Cabell and a few who had served in local government at the fag-end of the Protectorate, like Samuel Tanner and Edmund Walrond. In view of the political climate it was a reasonable selection, but Plymouth lost its case and paid Arundel £550 in costs.[158] The rights of the Crown had been upheld but its relations with Plymouth had been poisoned. When Count Magalotti of Tuscany visited the town in 1669 he repeated the current view that the massive citadel, then still being built, was designed to keep the citizens of Plymouth in check.[159]

In most cases, the recovery of crown lands was less spectacular and was conducted in something of a spirit of give-and-take. The cofferer of the Royal Household, John Ashburnham, acquired tenements in Bradninch which, as part of the Duchy of Cornwall, was under the stewardship of the Earl of Bath, steward of the Duchy and Warden of the Stannaries. Sir George Carteret received the lease of Leeham manor.[160] On the other hand Major John Blackmore hung on to tenements in Windsor Great Park and in Cornwall the heirs of Thomas Gewen held Bradridge.[161] Requests by Interregnum purchasers for arrears of fee farm rents outstanding after the

Restoration had recovered them for the Crown were invariably met, although they were not highly prized by the monarchy and were sold off from 1670.[162] The recovery of the lands was marked by a spirit of moderation and did not merely serve to speed up further the headlong rush for place and patronage in the 1660s. On the whole it seemed aimed at minimising tensions in a society in which land was the key to status and prosperity. If the policy of compromise was designed to win over Interregnum purchasers to the monarchy, on the other hand, it failed spectacularly. John Blackmore and Andrew Raddon, purchasers who retained a stake in their properties after 1660, were involved in local disaffection; Raddon later became a Rye House plotter.[163]

The enthusiasm of the royalist gentry for the re-established church has been well described elsewhere.[164] Ecclesiastical administration in the diocese of Exeter has long since found its historian,[165] but there still remains the question of whether, given that there was a *rapprochement* of peculiar warmth between the gentry and the Anglican church, there was an economic basis for that *rapport*. In other words, did the 'natural rulers' in Devon have a greater financial stake in the regime of the 1660s than had their predecessors of a decade earlier? The Laudian practice of frowning on leases to laymen expired with Laud himself. Canon John Bury was the only member of the post-Restoration chapter to espouse such views and he was 'in almost constant disagreement with his colleagues on the subject of leases'[166] He proposed to rack-rent as a response to 'the calamity of the times'. The surviving dean and chapter leases for lives were continued despite him. The recovery of capitular property from the purchasers of the 1640s and 1650s in Devon, as elsewhere, proceeded smoothly. A list of tenants of the cathedral from 1641 has survived,[167] and although it is incomplete, if offers overwhelming evidence of the recovery, with fourteen of the seventeen properties it mentions back in chapter hands in the 1660s. Colyton manor was sold to Daniel Marwood of Lyon's Inn, Middlesex, for £983.17s.4¾d. by the commissioners for the sale of church lands in 1649. Marwood seems to have acquired the property from the tenant, his relation, John Marwood, a constable and grand juror, but in 1660 the dean and chapter let Colyton to John Marwood again on a twenty-one-year lease. The Marwoods were not so fortunate with another property bought by Daniel in 1650; tenements in Hennock passed to Thomas Washer in 1660.[168] Tenants compliant in 1660 could plead *force majeur*, surrender their title deeds and hope to retain their tenancies on terms comparable to those enjoyed before the sales of the late 1640s, and it seems probable that this occurred in a large number of cases.

It is not always clear whether sitting tenants were restored to properties in 1660 or merely suffered a change of landlord. Ide manor was before the civil war in the hands of the Gandy family but in 1650 it was sold to a London merchant, Henry Sealy, and was quickly re-sold by him to William Lee of Heavitree and Richard White of Exeter. In 1661 John and Henry Gandy were again the tenants, but as John Gandy had not been averse to buying property in St. Stephen's parish, Exeter, in 1650 as well as other property in Ide in 1654, one wonders whether or not the family had actually been dispossessed of Ide during the Interregnum.[169] The question of possession during the 1650s modifies the contrast between the lists of purchasers of capitular lands enrolled on the Close Rolls and the lists of tenants before and after the civil war and Interregnum.[170] The impression gained is that the 1650s intruders from outside the county were ousted in 1660 by the pre-war tenants among whom were leading royalist delinquents. For example, Richard Duck was the immediate tenant of Ide rectory, was succeeded by the purchaser, William Hamm, an Exeter merchant, and acquired his lands again in 1660. Sebastian Isaac leased Thorverton manor before the war; it passed to William Barton in 1649, and in 1661 the manor was leased jointly to four people, among them Nicholas Isaac.[171] Peter Sainthill was replaced by Sir Henry Vane in Dawlish manor, and although Sainthill may have failed to recover it in 1660, it had been rented by another royalist, Sir Peter Ball, by 1676.[172] Of the thirteen families named on the list of tenants from 1641 to 1661, no fewer than ten provided JPs and commissioners in the 1660s and six were families of erstwhile delinquents. The Marwoods, the Trosses and the Luxtons of Winkleigh frequently sent grand jurors to Exeter and served as high constables.

The dean and chapter surveys and leases of the 1660s reveal that at least twenty-seven participants in local government benefited from the long-lease policies of the Exeter dean and chapter from the early 1660s and that by far the greater number of these were of JP and tax commissioner status. John Ashburnham acquired the lease of Staverton manor in 1666 for three lives, even though the dean and chapter had been ordered not to lease to him in 1662. (He was expelled from the House of Commons in 1667.) Eustace Budgell, who had been agent for purchasers of crown lands in the 1650s and an undersheriff in 1654, found the past no obstacle in his scramble for favourable leases, and rented the sheaf of Upottery and, in partnership, the rectory and tithes of Braunton.[173] The chapter, far from following Canon John Bury's lead, seemed anxious to cement an alliance with the county gentry and restore their fortunes by way of the rising tide of royalism. The capitular leases of the 1660s strengthened the ties between the ruling class and the church, and hence between the gentry and the central government, certainly in the euphoric 'honeymoon' of 1660 to 1662, although after that period it becomes a difficult concept to test.

None of the Devon MPs was an important tenant of the church and those who rented any land from her were presbyterians. Sir John Northcote, who thought the contribution of deans and chapters amounted to eating, drinking and getting up to piss, rented a small parcel of land in Newton St Cyres, and Sir Walter Young and Sir John Davy, suspected by Bishop Ward of trying to undermine the church settlement, acquired the tithes of Sidbury. In the mid-1670s, Sir Thomas Putt, the son of the Puritan merchant, William Putt of Gittisham, was leased Stoke Canon manor.[174] But these men and others were all in the commission of the peace, and in this sense the effect of dean and chapter leases was to confirm their status as 'natural rulers' in Devonshire rather than as

'Church and King' votaries at Westminster—to exemplify further the frequency with which land distribution confirms social change.

NOTES

1. Godfrey Davies: *The Restoration of Charles II* (1955), pp. 6-7.
2. *The Humble Petition of many well-affected Persons of Somerset, Wiltshire and some parts of Devon* (1659); *C.J.*, VII, p.683; Barry Reay: 'The Quakers, 1659 and the Restoration of the Monarchy', *History*, LXIII (1978), p. 195 for a corrective to the notion of early Quaker passivity.
3. Mary Coate (ed.): *The Letter Book of John Viscount Mordaunt* (Camden, 3rd series, LXIX, 1945), pp. 58, 66; Coate: *Cornwall*, p. 306.
4. C.H. Firth, G. Davies: *The Regimental History of Cromwell's Army*, p. 688; C.H. Firth (ed.): *The Clarke Papers*, IV (Camden, new series, LXII, 1901), p. 216; Bodl. Clarendon MS 68 f 100 v. There is a most detailed narrative of the part played by men of Devon and Cornwall in the Restoration in Coate: *Cornwall*, Ch. 14, pp. 298-321, idem: 'Sir William Morrice and the Restoration', *English Historical Review*, XXXIII (1918), pp. 367-77.
5. QS Order Book; *A Letter from Exeter* (1660); *A Declaration of the Gentry of the County of Devon* (1660); White Kennet: *A Register and Chronicle Ecclesiastical and Civil* (1728), p.20; Coate: *Letter Book*, p. 160; *CSPD 1659-60*, pp. 349, 363, 366, 368. The Rump had re-assembled on 26 December, 1659.
6. 'If we look westward we shall find most of [Monck's] kindred and allyes engaged in the Devonshire Declaration', Clarendon MS 68 f 181, 69 ff 9-10. Thomas Clifford was involved in this declaration: J.J. Sutherland Shaw: 'A Biography of Thomas Clifford, First Lord Clifford of Chudleigh' (Glasgow PhD, 1935), p. 13; C.H. Hartmann: *Clifford of the Cabal* (1937), p. 24.
7. Son of Sir Samuel Rolle (for whom *vide* Underdown: *Pride's Purge*); MP for Devon 1654, Colonel of foot 1650, all assessments etc. 1647 to 1660; JP 1647 to 1659 but never prominent on the Bench. Died 1660. *T.D.A.*, XLVIII, p. 335, XXXVI, pp. 299-300; Vivian: *Devon*, p. 655; F & R; DQSOB; PRO PROB 11/303/30.
8. *Old Parliamentary History*, XXII, pp. 68-70; *Clarke Papers*, IV, pp. 258-59, 260.
9. Coate: *Cornwall*, p. 311; even in mid-January 1660 he was 'Black Monck' to the royalist Mordaunt. Maurice Ashley's view of Monck as a royalist from August 1659 is not generally shared: *General Monck* (1977), pp. 163-64.
10. Cf. Thomas Bampfield, 1657: 'We all agree that till violence was offered to the Parliament [in 1648] the laws ought to be confirmed, but for what was done since I cannot in conscience consent to some of them'. *Burton's Diary*, II, pp. 88-89.
11. *A Letter to General Monck in answer to his of the 23rd of January directed to Mr Rolle* ... (1 Feb., 1660).
12. *Animadversion Upon Generall Monck's Letter to the Gentry of Devon* (3 Feb., 1660).
13. *A Letter*; *Animadversion*; both these pamphlets have been attributed to William Morrice (James Davidson: *Bibliotheca Devoniensis* (1852), pp. 89-90) but the styles of the two works are very different. Morrice's rather turgid theological works are more akin to the style of *A Letter*.
14. *The Fair Dealer, or a modest answer to the sober letter of his Excellency* (4 Feb., 1660).
15. Clarendon MS 69 ff 9-10.
16. *Ibid.* 69 f 179, 70 f 110; C 66/2939/24.
17. *The Parliamentary Intelligencer*, XXI (1660) (14-21 May), pp. 351-53.
18. *A Declaration of Parliament that all Sheriffs, Justices of the Peace and Constables that were in office ... shall be continued.*
19. *The Continuation of the Life of Edward, Earl of Clarendon* (1759), pp. 8-9; Everitt: *Community of Kent*, pp. 320-21. Clarendon noted the 'indecency and incongruity' of this.
20. *CSPD 1660-61*, e.g. pp. 84, 88, 89, 94, 120, 135, 136, 192, 248, 303, 365.

21. Prince: *Worthies of Devon*, p. 37; Wilts. R.O. Duke of Somerset's MSS Box 55, J. Kellond to Edward Seymour; *H.M.C. 15th Report Appendix VII* (Duke of Somerset's MSS), p. 93; PRO PC 2/55/520, SP 29/62/1.
22. *CSPD 1660-61*, pp. 82, 461; PC 2/55/340.
23. *CSPD 1660-61*, p. 88, (SP 29/6/51); *TDA*, IX, pp. 336-349; Andriette: *Devon and Exeter in the Civil War*, p. 169.
24. PRO C 82/2269; *Somers Tracts*, VII, pp. 423-25; SP 29/22/113. Roberts had served under Prince Maurice in the West of England.
25. *CSPD 1660-61*, pp. 383-88; S.K. Roberts: 'Alehouses and Government Under the Early Stuarts', *Southern History*, II (1980) pp. 45-71; T.G. Barnes: *Somerset 1625-1640*, esp. Ch. 7; M.J. Hawkins: 'The Government' in C. Russell (ed.): *The Origins of the English Civil War* (1973), esp. pp. 51-59. Contrast Edward Raddon's opposition to the proposed farm of the Post Office in 1653: BL Add. 22546 f 123.
26. G.E. Aylmer: *The State's Servants*, p. 100; SP 29/21/125; *CSPD 1660-61*, pp. 365, 433; PRO C 66/2933/14, 2939/24, 2944/29, 2945/30, 2957/2, 2999/40, 3035/4. The stewardship of the Duchy of Cornwall and borough of Bradninch, before the civil war in the hands of feodary Gewen, was, in 1660, separated from the office of feodary and given to Sir John Grenville, through Monck's good offices: PRO E 317/10/6/6; *CSPD 1660-61*, p. 73.
27. *CSPD 1660-61*, p. 82; *CCC*, p. 1391; *CCAM*, p. 471; QS grand jury lists; SRO DD/WO Box 56, W. Young to J. Willoughby, 13/12/60.
28. *CSPD 1666-67*, pp. 434, 538, (Browning's correspondent was James Hickes, Post Office clerk: J.C. Hemmeon: *The History of the British Post Office* (1912), pp. 24, 26-27); PRO PC 2/62/427; DQSOB., Midsummer 1662; Rowe and Jackson: *Exeter Freemen*, pp. 147, 163; W.B. Stephens: *Seventeenth Century Exeter* (1958), pp. 90-91.
29. SP 29/190/6; Vivian: *Cornwall*, p. 577; Llywellynn Jewitt: *A History of Plymouth* (1873), pp. 267-69, 271-72; Cambridge Univ. Lib. DD 8/30/5 f 23 v; PRO E 317/10/16; E 121/2/2; West Devon R.O. Plymouth City MSS W 459; *CTB*, I, p. 35. See pp. 163-64 above.
30. Prideaux Place, Padstow, Misc. MSS, Morrice to Prideaux 9/2/61; *CTB*, I, pp. 4, 190-91; PRO E 190/953/4, 5; Clarendon: *Continuation*, p. 46. In Clarendon's view, Morrice was a countryman who failed to understand government: *Continuation*, p. 368. Cf. F.M.G. Evans: *The Principal Secretary of State* (1923).
31. *CTB*, I, p. 17; *CSPD 1660-61*, p. 280; C 66/3038/7.
32. Vivian: *Devon*, p. 658; *TDA*, XVII, p. 217; PROB 11/369/23; *Statutes of the Realm*, V, p. 330; F & R, II; QS jury lists.
33. C 66/3038/7; *CTB*, I, pp. 600, 611; Stephens: *Seventeenth Century Exeter*, p. 90; *DCNQ*, XV, p. 168.
34. *CTB*, I, p. 7; E 190/954/4; Vivian, p. 722; *CCC*, p. 1256. Sir Thomas Stucley was M.P. for Tiverton from 1661 until his death in 1663.
35. *CTB*, I, p. 4; Vivian: *Cornwall*, p. 349; PRO C 5/429/14. Opie was reported as an excise defrauder in 1652: SP 18/24/122.
36. *CTB*, I, p. 413; Vivian: *Cornwall*, p. 346. Noy was in office by 1670 but was out by 1675: E 190/954/13; PRO CUST 18/1A.
37. *CSPD 1668-69*, pp. 598, 651; SP 29/270/97; Vivian: *Devon*, p. 20, *Cornwall*, p. 577.
38. E 122/222/66; *CSPD 1652-53*, p. 584; *TDA*, XLIV, p. 668; Aylmer: 'Checklist of Central Officeholders'; F & R II, p. 660.
39. *CSPD 1649-50*, p. 76, *1652-53*, p. 584; E 190/953/1. Aylmer: *State's Servants*, pp. 266-67 for Blackborne, a native of Plymouth.
40. E 190/952/3; E 122/232/21; *CSPD 1659-60*, pp. 24, 100, 252; SP 25/98/26; Aylmer: 'Checklist'; F & R II, p. 1245.
41. *CSPD 1650*, p. 511, *1653-54*, p. 60.
42. *CSPD 1650*, pp. 504, 507; F & R II, pp. 463-64, 660-61, 1065-66, 1366; DRO Commissions of the peace 1659; *CTB*, I, p. 634.
43. SP 29/449/90. Pierce's will was proved in 1688 in Exeter, and Rolle's in 1686 ('Of Holsworthy'). Fry: *Calendar of Wills ... in Principal Registry*.
44. E 190/952/2; Rowe and Jackson: *Exeter Freemen*, p. 141; *TDA*, XVII, p. 217; *Lists of Sheriffs*. Deeble was an Exeter assessment commissioner from 1657 to 1660: F & R II, pp. 1066, 1323, 1366-67.

45. *Burton's Diary*, IV, pp. 383, 394-401, 415-21; *CJ*, VII, pp. 634, 635, 637; *CSPD 1657-58*, p. 159; *CCC*, p. 3246.
46. Chandaman: *English Public Revenue*, pp. 42-44, 52-55.
47. *CTB*, I, p. 425, Vivian, p. 174; *TDA*, LXXII, p. 262; *Official Returns of Members of Parliament*; *CCAM*, p. 641; *CCC*, p. 1652; *Burke's Peerage* (1850), p. 912.
48. *CTB*, I, p. 639; Chandaman, *op. cit.*, pp. 54-56. For Colleton (another Exeter merchant): G.E.C.: *Complete Baronetage*, III, p. 161; *CCC*, p. 1356.
49. *CSPD 1667-63*, p. 109; *CTB*, I, p. 390; Vivian: *Cornwall*, p. 192; Chandaman, *op. cit.*, pp. 58-59. Grenville was MP for Liskeard and an underkeeper in St James's Palace: J.R. Jones: 'Court Dependents in 1664', *Bulletin of the Institute of Historical Research*, XXXIV (1961), pp. 81-91.
50. C 66/3022/20, 2946/31, 2933/18, 3000/44.
51. Chandaman, *op. cit.*, p. 52.
52. 'Customer' and 'collector' were different terms for the same official: Hubert Hall: *A History of the Custom Revenue* (1885, 2 vols.), II, p. 44.
53. Although the army officials of the 1650s disappeared at the Restoration there was no thorough purge of government offices; in 1661 it was noted that in the Post Office there were some who 'nothwithstanding his Majesties most gratious act of indempnitye still darre to utter there dislike of the present government in sordid and ungrateful expressions': SP 9/209/82.
54. Chandaman, *op. cit.*, p. 22; Hartmann: *Clifford of the Cabal*, p. 24; Sutherland Shaw thesis cit. pp. 13-15; Stephens: *Seventeenth Century Exeter*, pp. 89-92.
55. PRO CUST 18/1, 2; *DCNQ*, XV, pp. 161-69. I am grateful to Dr Colin Brooks for the Customs House reference.
56. Northam parish registers of baptisms, marriages and burials (transcripts in care of Devon and Cornwall Record Society, originals in DRO); DRO Northam PW 131: places in Northam church, 1672.
57. Stephens: *Seventeenth Century Exeter*, pp. 89-90; Topsham Parish Registers (transcripts held by Devon and Cornwall Record Society, originals in DRO); *CTB*, I, p. 470; Chandaman, *op. cit.*, pp. 43, 54-55. Peter Hagedot's will was proved in Exeter in 1679 and he was described as 'of Exeter', as was Zachary Dashwood, waiter and searcher, whose will was proved in 1693: Fry: *Calendars of Wills*. Hagedot was sheriff of Exeter, 1666, mayor 1670: *CSPD 1670*, p. 224.
58. CUST 18/1, 2; *DCNQ*, XV, pp. 161-69; H.C. Tomlinson: 'Place and Profit: An Examination of the Ordnance Office 1660-1714', *Transactions, Royal Historical Society*, 5th series, XXV (1975), pp. 55-75. The Topsham principal boatman, Marmaduke Robins (d. 1680) was exceptional. He had an annual salary of £26 and had a house in Topsham with three hearths, the norm for a juror or constable: E 179/245/17/22.
59. Arlington was postmaster-general from 1667: *CSPD 1665-66*, p. 573. The candidate of the Duke of Albemarle, Sir John Colleton, excise farmer, was supported by the Exeter agent for wine licences: SP 29/188/98.
60. Roope was described in 1664 as surrendering his patent but must have recovered it: *CSPD 1663-64*, p. 262, *DCNQ*, XV, pp. 165, 168; SP 29/188/48.
61. SP 29/190/6, 192/119; C.A.J. Skeel: 'The Canary Company', *EHR*, XXXI (1916), pp. 529-44; Clarendon: *Continuation*, pp. 485, 493, 495-98. Edward Seymour implicated Clarendon in the Canary patent in the drive to remove him. W.C. Abbott: 'The Long Parliament of Charles II', *EHR*, XXI (1906), p. 42n.
62. The Duke of York unsuccessfully backed Albemarle's candidate, Colleton, in the Dartmouth election and this was not the first rebuff he suffered in attempting to sway Devon elections. He wrote to the corporation of Exeter in 1661 requesting their support for Sir Richard Ford in the forthcoming general election: 'As the good opinion the king hath of him will render your choosing him acceptable to his Majestie, soe his generall abilities and particular experience in merchants affaires ... will render it advantageous to yourselves'. Ford, like Colleton, was a Devon man who settled in London as a merchant. He was a governor of the Merchant Adventurers, and a contractor to the Navy, in which capacity he must have come to the notice of the Lord High Admiral. He was defeated at Exeter by a large freeman vote for John Maynard: DRO DD 71796A; *CJ*, VIII, p. 55; *TDA*, LXI, pp. 196, 212; *CSPD 1660-61*, pp. 153, 331, 372, *1661-62*, *passim*; *CTB*, I, *passim*.

63. CRO DD/T (Tremayne MSS) 1662.
64. G.F.T. Jones: 'The Composition and Leadership of the Presbyterian Party in the Convention', *EHR*, LXXIX (1964), pp. 334-35, 354 and *passim*; Lady Elliott-Drake: *The Family and Heirs of Sir Francis Drake*, I. *passim*; *TDA*, VII, p. 364; PROB 11/307/48 (Drake was on close terms with his 'kinsman', Maynard); *DNB* (William Russell); Clarendon MS 72 ff 59-60; J.R. Jones: 'Political Groups and Tactics in the Convention of 1660', *Historical Journal*, VI (1963), pp. 159-77.
65. Padstow 'Misc. MSS': Morrice to Prideaux 20/8/60. The views of Clarendon and Burnet on the common sense of the act in Joan Thirsk: *The Restoration* (1976), pp. 5-8.
66. Morrice to Prideaux, *ibid.*
67. 'In pride and undutifulness he every day makes a further progress', Seymour to Lady Seymour March 1661: WRO 1332 (Duke of Somerset's MSS) Box 55; cf. same to same March 1662, Box 50.
68. BL Add 11314 f 17; *CJ*, VIII, pp. 272-73 (Clifford was a teller with Seymour for the yeas); R.W. Clayton: 'The Political Career of Edward Seymour 1661-1704' (York DPhil, 1976), pp. 9-10.
69. Clarendon: *Continuation*, pp. 42-43.
70. David Ogg: *England in the Reign of Charles II* (1956, 2 vols.), II, p. 474.
71. Prideaux Place, Padstow, 'Misc. MSS': Morrice to Prideaux 7/7/61, 2/9/62.
72. The earliest commissions for the 1660s are PRO C 220/9/4 (1660-1662) and BL Egerton 2557, Add. 36781 f 42 (1661), the last two not to be found in the list given by T.G. Barnes and A.H. Smith in *Bulletin of the Institute of Historical Research*, XXXII (1959), pp. 221-42.
73. *DCNQ*, XXI, p. 284.
74. K.M. Beck: 'Recusancy and Nonconformity in Devon and Somerset, 1660-1714' (Bristol MA, 1961), p. 101; *TDA*, XCVIII, p. 212.
75. A.H.A. Hamilton: *The Note Book of Sir John Northcote*, p. xl; J.R. Jones: 'Political Groups and Tactics', p. 167.
76. Beck thesis cit., p. 94, *Calamy Revised* for Francis Sourton, Courtenay's relation by marriage.
77. *CCC, CCAM, passim.*
78. *CCC*, p. 1221, 1161, 1808; Vivian, pp. 4, 7, 94-95, 262-63. 1640 tax commission lists may be found attached to statutes 16 Charles I c. 2, c. 32, c. 44. (*Statutes of the Realm*, V).
79. *CCC*, pp. 1126, 1228. He *was* rewarded with the recordership of the City of Exeter.
80. QS Order Books marginalia.
81. Vivian, p. 480; PROB 11/376/76.
82. PRO C 231/7 (formerly IND, 4214), p. 322; PROB 11/342/71; Lysons, p. 479.
83. C 231/7, p. 259. Vivian, p. 645; *Somers Tracts*, VII, pp. 586-615 esp. pp. 588-89.
84. Lists of JPs for the 1660s: PRO C.220/9/4; C 193/12/3; C 66/2986, 3022, 3074 (amendments in C 231/7); BL Egerton 2557; Add. 36781 f 42.
85. Dodd: *Studies in Stuart Wales*, Ch. 4; Barnes: *Somerset 1625-40*, p. 161 for a brief discussion of the subsidy commissioners of the 1620s; they were apparently 'with very few exceptions' justices: Richard Cust: 'A List of Commissioners for the Forced Loan of 1626-27', *Bulletin of the Institute of Historical Research*, LI (1978), pp. 199-206 discusses regional variations.
86. *Statutes of the Realm*, V: 12 Charles II, c. 9; c.27, c. 28, c. 29; 13 Charles II c. 3, 14 Charles II c. 8; 15 Charles II c. 9; 16, 17 Charles II c. 1; 18, 19 Charles II c.1. 1670s: 25 Charles II c. 1; 29 Charles II c. 1, 31 Charles II c. 1.
87. Ellis Bartlett, William Kelly, Richard Lee, John and Samuel Tanner, William Williams.
88. *DNB*; Vivian, pp. 526, 688; Witcombe: *Charles II and the Cavalier House of Commons*, pp. 73, 198.
89. *CCC*, p. 1511; *Burke's Commoners* (1836), p. 198; Vivian, p. 707; Witcombe, p. 204.
90. Lysons, p. cix; Vivian, pp. 107, 582; PROB 11/327/72; Ashley: *General Monck, passim*, for references to Christopher Monck; *DNB*
91. Men like John Bragg, John Davy of Ruxford, Nicholas Dennis of Orleigh, (lawyer, and 'pleb.' at Pembroke College Oxford), John Hawkins of Slapton. Among merchants of

considerable wealth were James Rodd, Jonathan Sparke, and at a lesser level, the Roopes of Dartmouth.

92. Western: *The English Militia*, pp. 11-16; John Miller: 'The Later Stuart Monarchy' in J.R. Jones (ed.): *The Restored Monarchy 1660-1688* (1979), p. 30.

93. I.M. Green: *The Re-establishment of the Church of England*, pp. 4-5, 180-84.

94. SP 29/11/157; Duke of Somerset's MSS Box 55; QS Box 74 (Easter 1669); accounts of Richard Yolden.

95. *Mercurius Publicus*, XXI (23-30 May 1661), pp. 325-28; Green, *op. cit.*, pp. 182-83.

96. The solidarity was powerful enough to comprehend Gabriel Barnes, foot captain in 1650, assessment commissioner, postmaster and friend of Thomas Larkham, as well as JPs from the 1650s such as John Drake and John Quick. They must have taken the Oaths of Supremacy and Allegiance.

97. SP 29/8/188-89.

98. SP 29/11/157. Smith may already have been singled out for other duties; in Epiphany 1661 the Devon Bench certified that he was suitable as an excise farmer. DQSOB.

99. SP 29/42/63, *CCC*, pp. 1329, 1361, 1689; Coate: *Cornwall*.

100. *DCNQ*, XXI, pp. 225-26, 282-85; Clarendon: *Continuation*, pp. 42-43.

101. BL. Add. 11314 f 27.

102. SP 29/83/8. For Fowell's labours for Williamson at Dartmouth see pp. 144, 220-21 above.

103. Miller: 'The Later Stuart Monarchy', pp. 30-31; Chandaman: *English Public Revenue*, p. 262 *et seq.*

104. Add. 11314 f 27. Calmady was an assessment commissioner through the 1660s and 1670s; it may have been his earlier association with the Commonwealth which cost him a place on the Restoration Bench.

105. SP 29/5/11; *CCC*, pp. 1361-63; (for 'Bottomless' Bagg see H.R. Trevor-Roper: *Archbishop Laud* (1940), pp. 224-25); Howard: *Devon Protestation Returns*, I, p. 231 ('Bale' should be 'Bagg'); Vivian, p. 34; C 54/24/22; W. Devon R.O. Plymouth City MSS 'Black Book' ff 16-17 v, 317; W 73 A; QS Box 72 (Easter 1667) examinations before N. Horsman; SP 29/88/60, 449/90; *CSPD 1663-64*, p. 170 for George Carteret's interests in Plympton (The source of the assertion in the National Trust guide to Saltram that Carteret lived there after 1660 is unknown.)

106. SP 29/88/60, 99/169, 449/90; *CSPD 1660-61*, p. 375.

107. See my note in *BIHR* liii (1980), pp. 258-65. Principal sources are SP 29/420/35, 36; T.B. Howell: *State Trials*, VI, pp. 233, 235, 238; C.H. Firth (ed.): *The Memoirs of Edmund Ludlow* (1894, 2 vols.), II, pp. 341-42; Kennet: *A Register and Chronicle, Ecclesiastical and Civill*, pp. 839, 845; C 82/2346a.

108. W.G. Johnson: 'Post-Restoration Nonconfirmity and Plotting' (Manchester MA, 1967), pp. 185, 190-92, 202.

109. *CSPD 1654*, p. 585, *1655*, pp. 253, 446, 542, *1656-57*, pp. 445, 448, 558; E 121/2/2; PROB 11/302/274; DQSOB Michaelmas 1661, gaol calendars 1661 to 1670; Peter Earle: *Monmouth's Rebels: The Road to Sedgemoor 1685* (1977), pp. 35, 150, 175.

110. Coate: *Cornwall*, pp. 316-18; B.S. Capp: *The Fifth Monarchy Men* (1972) *passim* but esp. p. 244; Ludlow: *Memoirs*, II, pp. 305-06, 308-09, 315-16.

111. *TDA*, LXXII, p. 261; *A Narrative of the Late Parliament* in *Harleian Miscellany*, VI, p. 467; Firth and Davies: *Regimental History of Cromwell's Army*, pp. 193, 195; *CSPD 1659-60*, pp. 8, 24; Vivian, pp. 228, 232; *CCC*, p. 2948; Hoskins: *Devon*, pp. 372, 392, 484; SP 25/77/867, 890; QS Box 57: Easter 1650 recognizances. Vivian confuses two generations of Coplestones.

112. BL Add. 21, 947 ff 121, 141; A. Browning: 'Parties and Party Organization in the Reign of Charles II', *Transactions, Royal Historical Soc.*, 4th series, XXX (1948), p. 30. In a letter to Richmond, Coplestone spoke of a visit by his son [? in-law], 'Poulett, to Hinton' to suggest that a daughter married one of the Pauletts of Hinton St. George, Somerset. Although no complete pedigree of that family seems to be in print, Coplestone was certainly related to the Lacey family of Stogumber: F. Brown: *Abstracts of Somersetshire Wills*, 4th series, (1889), p. 72. It may well have been this Coplestone who intended to stand for James II in Plymouth in 1688; Sir George Duckett: *Penal Laws and the Test Act* (1882-83, 2 vols), II, pp. 230-33.

113. Hoskins: 'Ownership and Occupation of Land in Devonshire', p. 23.
114. Cf. Gregory King on the 1682 to 1683 Warwickshire Visitation: 'I believe there is not above a third part if so many that are really gentlemen'. P. Styles: *Studies in Seventeenth Century West Midlands History* (1978), p. 115. In Devon 'Mr, seems to have been an ambiguous designation for those of gentleman-bordering-esquire rank: e.g., DRO Chudleigh PO 1, PW 1; Cullompton PO 1.
115. *CCC*, pp. 97-98; K.M. Beck: 'Recusancy and Nonconformity in Devon and Somerset' (Bristol MA, 1961), p. 50; Hoskins: *Devon*, pp. 236-37; Prince: *Worthies*, p. 711; Pearse Chope: *Early Tours*, pp. 106, 110. Pace Hoskins there is no evidence that the Courtenays were still Catholics. Thomas Clifford, later Lord Clifford, was the first of his family to espouse Catholicism.
116. Recusant rolls sampled: PRO E 377/49/17, 61/5, 63/11.
117. The distribution of the ranks of gentry affects our perception of the charitable giving of the gentry and the fashion for house-building in the later seventeenth century; *vide* N. Pevsner: *The Buildings of England: North Devon* and *South Devon*. Cf. Underdown: *Pride's Purge*, p. 355.
118. *DCNQ*, XXII, p. 48, DRO 1660A/265.
119. QS Box 74 (Midsummer 1669): Petition of hundred constables dated 8/5/69.
120. PROB 11; DRO 96 M (Rolle), 21/44 (Tuckfield); West Country Studies Library, Exeter: Transcripts by O. Moger of local wills; PRO C 108/93 (Chancery Master's Exhibits).
121. PROB 11/329/54, 320/89, 376/76, 352/155; DRO 96 M/Box 15/6B.
122. E.g., the wills of Josias Calmady, John Fowell: PROB 11/374/148, 355/136.
123. *Reports of the Commissioners ... Concerning Charities and Education of the Poor* (Devon reports bound 1815 to 1839 in 2 vols.).
124. Ibid., I, part 2, p. 35, II, part 5, pp. 29, 171-72.
125. W.K. Jordan: *The Forming of the Charitable Institutions of the West of England* (Transactions, American Philosphical Soc., new series, L, part 8, 1960), pp. 45, 78.
126. F & R I, pp. 879-910, 910-11, 1114-16, 1121-23; 'An Account of the sale of bishops' lands between the years 1647 and 1651', *Collectanea Topographica et Genealogica* (1834), pp. 1-8, 122-27, 284-92. (I owe this reference to Dr. I.J. Gentles); D.R.O. City of Exeter Act Book, IX, 1647-55, f 41; *TDA*, LXI, p. 211; Keeler: *The Long Parliament*, pp. 344-45; W. Cotton: H. Wollocombe: *Gleanings of Exeter (1877)*, pp. 174–75.
127. F & R II, pp. 81-104, 140-42, 152-56, 200-05. E.g. the purchase of Philip Starkey, a London cook: 'An Account of the Sale of Bishops' Lands', *op. cit.*; Exeter Cathedral Library Dean and Chapter MSS 576, 579, 638; QS bundles. I owe many of the Cathedral Library references to the archivist, Mrs Audrey Erskine.
128. Palmer's Index (PRO IND 17355) to C 54 (Close Rolls); Exeter Dean and Chapter MSS 375, 574-80. 638, 674, 689-91, 1004-05.
129. Herrick bought Bishop's Nymet manor, Alford the manors of Halberton Dean, Woodbury and Stoke Canon.
130. Bodl. Tanner MS 56/260. F & R II, pp. 83-84 *et seq.*; IND 17355. *CCC*, p. 1311; *TDA*, LXXII, pp. 261-62.
131. F & R II, pp. 168-191, discussed in Ian Gentles: 'The Sales of Crown Lands during the English Revolution'. *Economic History Review*, 2nd series, XXVI (1973), pp. 614-35; idem: 'The Purchasers of Northamptonshire Crown Lands 1649-60', *Midland History*, III (1976), p. 206.
132. H.J. Habakkuk: 'Public Finance and the Sale of Confiscated Property during the Interregnum', *Economic History Review*, 2nd series, XV (1962-63), pp. 72-73.
133. PRO E 121/2/2; Ian Gentles: 'The Debentures Market and Military Purchases of Crown Land, 1649-60' (London PhD, 1969), p. 247; Madge: *Domesday of Crown Lands*, p. 389 ('Badgell' should be 'Budgell'). Budgell's father was agent for the Champernown family; Eustace was undersheriff in 1654: Bodl. Tanner MS 287 f 117; DRO Z 12/25/2, 9/2, Z1/10/292; Carew and Martin MSS DD 56621; Rowe and Jackson: *Exeter Freemen*, p. 132.
134. Cambridge University Library DD 8/30/5/23 v, 25 v.
135. *Ibid.*, DD 8/30/4/22 v; E 121/2/2; Gentles: 'Sales of Crown Lands', pp. 624-26. For

Warr: C. Hill: *The World Turned Upside Down* (1975), pp. 272-76, *idem: Puritanism and Revolution* (1968 ed.), pp. 83, 85.

136. E 121/2/2; Cambridge Univ. Lib.: DD 8/30/4/60 v; Gentles thesis cit., p. 246.

137. DD 8/30/4/36, 48 v; Gentles thesis cit., p. 257; E 121/2/2; Madge, *op. cit.*, 224, 384, 386; Prince: *Worthies*, p. 413; BL Add. 18, 448 f. 24 v; *West Answering to North*, pp. 39-40; PRO C 193/13/6 (*liber pacis* where Braddon's name is erased, to suggest recent inclusion).

138. E 121/2/2; DD 8/30/4/50 v; Gentles thesis pp. 249, 266, 331, 351; PROB 11/302/274; Underdown: 'Settlement' in Aylmer (ed.), *The Interregnum*, pp. 173, 180; idem: *Somerset in the Civil War and Interregnum*, pp. 167-68.

139. Gentles: thesis cit., pp. 254, 261-62, 283, 293, 306, 331.

140. F & R II, pp. 358-62, 412-19, 498-500. The fee farm rents and their sale are discussed exhaustively in Madge *op. cit.*, pp. 96-101, 231-38.

141. Madge, *op.cit.*, p. 233.

142, PRO E 315/139, 140, 141, 142, 173, 174. Particulars of Devon sales are in E 315/138.

143. E 315/139/57-58, 128, 131, 178; E 315/140/45, 74; E 315/141/10, 11, 19.

144. PROB 11/363/71: he left over £17,000 in bequests alone.

145. E 315/139/75, 120, 178; E 315/140/45.

146. E 315/139/72.

147. E 315/139/86, 95, 103; E 315/140/17, 27, 56, 70; E 315/141/3; E 315/144 unpaginated end of volume. F & R II, p. 360. Reynell seems to have been the only Devon tenant to purchase within the time specified by the act, but there was never much competition for fee farm rents, hence the introduction of 'doubling' in an effort to clear remaining rents and boost government funds: Madge, pp. 99-100.

148. E 315/139/16, 35, 155, 167, E 315/140/26, 68, 69, E 315/144/14.

149. Gentles: 'Sales of Crown Lands', pp. 614-15.

150. E 121/2/2; DD 8/30/4/60 v, 30/6/15 v.

151. PRO CRES 6/2/482-84.

152. SP 29/66/63. Also CRES 6/1/45-46, 6/2/481-84, 489.

153. E 121/2/2; DD 8/30/5/23 v.

154. CRES 6/2/64,65.

155. *Ibid.*, 261-62, 288-89; C 66/2964/9.

156. The papers in the case are collected in W. Devon R.O. Plymouth City MSS W 459 parts 1 and 2.

157. Plymouth City MSS 'Black Book' ff 16-17.

158. R.N. Worth: *Calendar of Plymouth Municipal Records* (1893), p. 209.

159. Pearse Chope: *Early Tours*, p. 101.

160. CRES 6/2/228, 601.

161. *Ibid.*, 6/1/29; W 459 part 2: Letter Nich. Rowe to Wm. Warren 3/6/64.

162. E.g., CRES 6/1/236, 238, 250, 116, 255, 102; 6/2/287; PRO IND 17347.

163. Johnson: 'Post-Restoration Nonconformity and Plotting', pp. 316, 463.

164. I.M. Green: *The Re-establishment of the Church of England*, pp. 4, 180-83 modifies orthodoxy. Less original is R.A. Beddard: 'The Restoration Church' in Jones (ed.) *The Restored Monarchy*, pp. 161-166. Beddard ignores Green's major contribution.

165. Whiteman: 'The Episcopate of Dr Seth Ward ...' (Oxford DPhil, 1951).

166. *Ibid.*, pp. 70-71; Prince: *Worthies*, p. 153.

167. Bodl. Rawlinson MS D 1138 ff 1-11; Whiteman: thesis cit., p. 69.

168. Rawl. D 1138 ff 1-11; Exeter Dean and Chapter MS 6056/1, 6047/1/1; DRO QS bundles.

169. Rawl. D 1138 ff 1-11; Dean and Chapter MSS 6024/1,4,5,6,7, 6025/1/1, 3/2; PRO IND 17355.

170. PRO C54 is known to be incomplete (Madge, pp. 71, 101); the Dean and Chapter MSS are also.

171. Rawl. D 1138 f 1-11; IND 17355, Dean and Chapter MSS 580, 4030, 6055.

172. Dean and Chapter MS 6050/2/6; *CJ*, VI, p. 440; Violet Rowe: *Sir Henry Vane the Younger* (1970), pp. 169-71.

173. Dean and Chapter MSS 4030, 6042/13 a.

174. Hamilton: *Note Book*, p. xl; Dean and Chapter MSS 6026/3, 6051/6, 6040/1. Bishop Ward thought little of Sir Walter Young, but Young's connections with William

Morrice obtained Sidbury for him over Ward's head: *DCNQ*, XXI, pp. 284, 366. Ward was not the only observer to detect a Presbyterian/Independent amity (or conspiracy) which had certainly not prevailed before 1660: SP 29/44/69, 83/8.

Chapter Seven

Administrative Patterns 1649-1670

Patterns of participation have been explored in a chronological context, and the sub-structure of local government has been outlined. The exits and entrances in the commission of the peace could be extensive but no contraction of its claim on the local communities of Devon followed. The authority of the Bench remained undimmed and the range of its activities did not narrow. Its supervision was so far-reaching and pervasive that a general survey here would founder in the wealth of quarter sessions evidence. Attempts to abstract the work of the magistrates in statistical form, to eviscerate the complexity of judicial and administrative forces and the subject matter on which they acted, have conveyed a misleading impression of simplicity. In this chapter, three topics which claimed much of the energy of magistrates and their subordinates have been chosen as a focus for detailed study: the development of petty sessions and the role of clerks, the treatment of poverty at county level, and the way in which the magistrates supported one of the legislative pillars of the 'reformation of manners'.

Clerks and the Development of Petty Sessions in the 1660s

Quarter sessions meetings underscored the power of magistrates but the machinery of business conducted there was under the vigilant gaze of a group of lesser gentlemen, the assistant clerks of the peace. At their head was the clerk of the peace, appointed by (or at least acceptable to) the *custos rotulorum*. In Devon this accountability counted as an aspect of the local patronage structure, if not as a feature of administrative routine. The connection between *custos* and clerk was strong enough to ensure that in 1649 Nicholas Rowe, the nominee of *custos* Edmund Prideaux, prevailed in the clerkship over Charles Vaughan, the presbyterian MP, who claimed a grant of the office from the House of Commons. It was strong enough to produce Rowe's resignation when Prideaux relinquished the position of *custos* and to secure Edward Raddon, John Disbrowe's local secretary, as his successor, when Disbrowe became *custos* in 1653. At the Restoration Monck was made *custos*, and it followed that the son of a fellow presbyterian, Sir John Northcote, should benefit from his patronage, and that when Monck died in 1670, John Northcote junior should resign his place.[1]

The clerk in Somerset was 'a pivotal figure' in local government, who 'possessed the eyes and ears of magistracy', wielding 'complete authority' over subordinates.[2] The Devon clerk was no longer able to exercise such complete power. Subordinate clerks stayed while the titular clerks of the peace came and went. The career of Giles Inglett illustrates this continuity. The Ingletts were from Lamerton near Tavistock and ancestral roots probably secured Giles his position in the office of the clerk of the peace. Charles Vaughan, nominally clerk from 1642 to 1649, had been the Tavistock estate steward of the fourth Earl of Bedford, and Nicholas Rowe, clerk from 1649 to 1653, came, like Inglett, from Lamerton, which suggests that the Bedford dynasty retained a residual measure of official patronage after the eclipse caused by the death of the earl in 1641.[3] Inglett was a deputy clerk by July 1641 and later became a deputy treasurer for the sequestration of royalists. He assumed responsibility for the clerkship during the dispute between Vaughan and Rowe but he stayed on as a deputy or assistant clerk throughout the 1650s and 1660s. In 1662 he was responsible for paying fees owed by the Devon quarter sessions to the court of King's Bench for despatching indictments there.[4] By the early 1640s Inglett had moved to Chudleigh, nine miles from Exeter, where he became a prominent parishioner. He was one of the 'Seven Men' of the parish on several occasions and in 1657 was the principal agent in attracting Stephen Bloy of Oxford to be vicar of Chudleigh. Bloy was described in the year of his appointment as an 'orthodox ... minister' and he was moderate enough to survive the St Bartholomew's Day ejections in 1662.[5] Giles Inglett was steward of the Mallock estates at Cockington and thus served the gentry in both a public and a private capacity although he himself was known in Chudleigh as 'Mr' Inglett. He died in 1682 but his son Giles became an attorney and resigned the town clerkship of Totnes in 1688.[8]

Henry Fitzwilliam was another clerk whose association with the governments of the Commonwealth and Protectorate proved no obstacle to later success. Fitzwilliam kept courts for the county sequestration committee in 1651, and was town clerk at Tiverton by 1654. He organised the unsuccessful campaign to secure Major John Blackmore as MP for Tiverton in the first Protectorate Parliament. (Blackmore was the government candidate.[7]) Fitzwilliam was a Tiverton man but his promotion to a deputy clerkship of the court of quarter sessions brought with it residence in Trinity parish, Exeter. He took the clerkship when Edward Raddon resigned, possibly because Disbrowe may have relinquished the title of *custos* when Oliver Cromwell died in September 1658. In 1660 he was replaced by John Northcote but he kept a place in the county establishment. He was given the task of examining the taxation accounts of petty sessional meetings and the following year, in 1661, he was made treasurer for the county gaol money, and re-elected yearly through the decade. In the summer of 1665 his diligence was recognized in his appointment as overall county treasurer at an annual salary of £20 plus 2s.6d. in the pound for all rate arrears handled by him.[8] This salary distinguished Fitzwilliam's tenure from that of the last treasurer, Edward Jones, who had died in 1639.[9] He must have accumulated substantial wealth; he held two houses in Exeter, of seven and three hearths each, and he left £20 as a bequest to the wardens of Tiverton for the use of the poor there. He died in 1689 or 1690. Like Inglett, Fitzwilliam took the opportunity to serve as an estate steward, in his case to Lord Mohun of Okehampton, who had in the 1640s and 1650s been a sequestered royalist when Fitzwilliam was doing nicely as an estate steward for the government.[10]

The continuity in the service of deputy clerks balanced changes in the clerkship itself. The clerk of the peace was in no position to dictate to his subordinates. Barnes makes great play on the power of the clerk, on his capacity to appoint and dismiss at will, but the Devon clerks co-operated amicably partly, no doubt, because of the long service of deputies. The signature of the clerk of the peace is as prevalent as an official stamp among the sessions papers but it concealed the limits of his power. One cannot assume that men like Nicholas Rowe and John Northcote wielded as much power as their ubiquitous signatures suggest; sheriffs, too, signed a rich variety of documents but their real power was small. Some clerks of the peace were virtual absentees. Charles Vaughan, clerk from 1642 to 1649 did not take office until 1646 because of the disruption of the war years. Edward Raddon was a senior under-officer in the inland letter office and had little time to exercise his local authority. Moreover, the deputies enjoyed much initiative in their own right and corresponded with JPs and their clerks for a mutually convenient arrangement of the court's business. Sometimes letters from the JPs or their clerks took the form of covering notes when recognizances were despatched with requests or hints for justiciary action in sessions. Thus John Wood, Sir William Morrice's clerk at Werrington, wrote to John Edy at his office in the Half Moon Inn, Exeter High Street, to enclose some recognizances for bastardy. He requested another warrant against some elusive malefactors and complained that 'Matthias Henry of Lifton and Peter Standon of Holsworthy have not paid me for their recognizances and therefore I shall desire they may not be discharged without paying my fees'.[11] Thomas Dyer, the clerk of Arthur Perryman of Plympton, a JP from 1649 to 1654, warned a fornicator and his sureties of the court's displeasure and reported to Giles Inglett that he had 'spoken with each of them face to face; the said Butler told me that hee would appeare this sessions to answer ... the bastard as I understand is dead'.[12]

Clerks or even private individuals would write to postpone or to cancel any planned judicial procedure. John Salkeild, high constable of Bampton hundred, wrote to Fitzwilliam to tell him that the threatened estreat over the repair of a bridge was now unnecessary: 'Now we are agreed for what is past and that Arthur Steevens hath undertaken to repaire the bridge before witnes and hath tymber delivered him for the worke'.[13] Thomas Bromfield wrote similarly to John Edy that indictments framed against two men for a forcible entry could now be dropped: 'For wee are agreed and doe not intend to goe any further in it'.[14]

Correspondence was conducted between officials of the hundreds, justices' clerks and the clerks of the court of quarter sessions which could have pre-disposed the outcome of a judicial decision. There is, however, no positive evidence to suggest that the poor were unscrupulously oppressed. Only when there was a *prima facie* case to answer, most commonly in cases of bastardy, did the clerks speak openly of their suspects as criminals. In other examples, an impartial detachment could be maintained. Paul Orchard wrote to Edy in 1663 of a man bound to appear in court: 'All that I shall desire is that you would gett him to be called and lett him cleere himself as well as he can'.[15] It was not, however, unknown for favours to be sought of clerks and probably no more uncommon that such favours should be granted. Daniel Condy, the Tavistock gaoler, wrote to Nicholas Rowe, clerk of the peace, in 1651, on behalf of the town magistrates. Their petition was offered 'in my behalfe for which I shalbe thankfull unto you and shalbe ready at any time to perform any office of curtesie for you'.[16] Mere politeness was transcended in a letter which Richard Tregeare, another clerk in the service of William Morrice, wrote to John Edy in 1667:

> I did by the importunity of severall of Holsworthy as by the espetiall desire of John Beaford a very poor man whose certificates are enclosed promise to use my utmost for his discharge. It was for bastardy; he hath twice appeared, and since, an order is made and obayed as the inclosed declares. He is a miserable poor man, hath sent his fee and desires your kindness to get him discharged. I will make it also my request in his behalfe ... I was also desired by a hundred constable to excuse his not appearing this tyme. He is at present indisposed but a very honest man and one who noe way will fayle in his duty. If you will excuse him I will be your debtor a bottle of sacke next season or half a crown—at your election.[17]

At least this was an 'abuse' of justice in favour of those least able to defend themselves, a moderation of *droit administratif*. As for the Holsworthy transgressor, his instructions from Exeter had been obeyed, and Tregeare was merely speeding up due process of law.

Between sessions, correspondence between the court and its magistrates arrived at and was despatched from the offices of the clerks in the Rose and Crown in Castle Lane, Exeter, and the Half Moon Inn along the High Street. The clerks enjoyed fees which had long since been established. When Charles Vaughan, clerk from 1612 to 1641 and uncle of his namesake who served from 1646 to 1649, wrote an account to the royal commissioners on fees in 1628 he described how when he had entered the clerk's office in 1606 he was instructed in the fees by a retired clerk whose teaching was based on what had been practised in the 1570s.[18] The clerk of the peace 'controlled his subordinates' remuneration' and although Inglett, Edy, Fitzwilliam and Oliver Portingall never complained, so far as it is possible to know, the 1649 order establishing Inglett as clerk, while Vaughan and Rowe fought for the disputed office, provided that the *locum tenens* 'should have the fees', as if the Devon clerk were used to complete control over these perquisites. Every stage of a progress through the local legal system attracted a fee. For a man accused of a misdemeanour a recognizance to appear at the sessions would cost two shillings, the drawing of the indictment one shilling, engrossing information against the defendant one shilling per sheet and entering his appearance and the verdict six pence and two shillings respectively. A case might cost a defendant 7s.6d. in fees; Barnes has calculated that such costs would amount to twice the sum payable as a fine,[19] even though the likelihood of extracting the fees varied according to the social rank of the criminal. In 1650 alone, at least two hundred and thirty recognizances were drawn up and the fees could not have amounted to less than £100, with accretions from administrative writing. The JPs made *ex gratia* awards to the clerks after hectic sessions. Edward Raddon was given forty-five shillings for his work on a new statute book. In 1664 Giles Inglett junior was paid thirty-five shillings for writing thirty-four hearth tax warrants. At Easter 1665 Inglett and John Edy shared fifty shillings for writing ninety-nine orders.[20] The Devon clerks may best be considered not as a body of factious squabblers over the spoils of office, but as a group of discreet attorneys and administrators who made themselves comfortable by their privileged occupation. Inglett had a seven-hearthed house in Chudleigh, Fitzwilliam had one the same size in Exeter. Eustace Budgell, a crown land trader, was an undersheriff with much the same kind of duties as the clerks; he, too, had a seven-hearthed residence at St Thomas, the Exeter suburb.[21] Inglett and Fitzwilliam moved from more distant areas to parishes near their administrative work; they were committed to their lucrative but responsible duties. An Exeter-based administration was developing into a standing bureaucracy; local residence (rather than the migratory trips four times yearly, undertaken by magistrates) was evidence of this. So were the shift towards salaries for officials and the emergence of the petty jury as a readily-summonable sub-structure raised in the Exeter area under the direction of the clerks, their bosses in an embryonic administrative hierarchy.

Yet it would be perverse to overstress these developments in the internal workings of the court of quarter sessions; away from the minutiae of cameral procedure the magistrates held sway over the machine. The grist to the administrative and judicial mill came almost entirely from the JPs, processed in correspondence and orders by their clerks. Examples have been quoted of their prejudices and dispositions but their power depended utterly on that of their employers and on their diligence or lassitude as justices. Unlike the clerks of the court of quarter sessions, magistrates' clerks were their employees and could be dismissed at will. They are elusive figures. Although they drew up recognizances and fair-copied examinations conducted by their masters, their names never appear on the parchment and paper of the official record. Even the most obscure justices employed clerks. Arthur Perryman's clerk, Thomas Dyer, wrote 'an iustio' after his master's name on his letters because Perryman had only risen to magisterial status in 1649 when servants of the Commonwealth were cautious and few—there might be doubts about his identity.[22] When the former yeoman, Thomas Saunders, journeyed around the West Country taking bail-bonds as a commissioner for Major-General Disbrowe in 1655 and 1656 he had with him a clerk, Joseph Coombe,[23] but Saunders, despite peasant gentry origins, had, after all, been military governor of Exeter. Some upstart magistrates were of virtually the same social background as the clerks they employed but one can only speculate on the consequences of this affinity for the quality of administration.

The individual contributions made by the clerks to the judicial work of their employers cannot be underestimated, and in many cases their influence ran wider. Most of the clerks have left behind them only the anonymous bulk of their masters' official papers, now filed in the quarter sessions bundles. We know the names of a few. Richard Tregeare and John Wood, clerks to the Morrices of Werrington, Thomas Dyer, clerk of Arthur Perryman, Giles Barrell, that of Sir Courtenay Pole, Mr Southcott the factotum of Christopher Wood, Thomas Mogridge, clerk of Josias Calmady[24]—and Thomas Cole, the clerk of William Martin of Netherexe, for whom most evidence has survived and who was typical of his class.

Thomas Cole was born in Crowan, near Camborne in Cornwall in about 1630.[25] His father, John Cole, served the Mohun family at their seat in Trewenna. A marriage alliance between the daughter of Sir Reginald Mohun and Sir Henry Carew of Bickleigh near Tiverton brought Thomas Cole into the service first of the Carews and then into that of the Martins of Oxton and Heavitree through a connection between the Martins and the St Aubyn family whose seat was at Crowan.[26] Sir Nicholas Martin was the son of a recorder of Exeter who was knighted in 1624 and who participated in the defence of Exeter against the royalists in 1643. Nicholas sat as a recruiter MP for Exeter from 1646 to Pride's Purge, after which he retired from politics until his death in 1653.[27] After the Restoration his eldest son, William, (by this time installed at Netherexe Barton in the Exe Valley), was included in the commission of the peace, and Thomas Cole became his clerk.[28] Martin only went to four quarter sessions meetings, before his death in 1662.[29] Cole then spent most of the 1660s as steward of the Martin estates for William Martin's widow, who moved to Heavitree, and her sons William and Nicholas. In the 1670s he worked for the Carews at Bickleigh until his death in about 1686.

In his first period as a justice's clerk, Cole undertook the widest variety of administrative business, including the writing of militia orders for a negligent cousin of his master's and settling a structural disaster which had befallen a cesspit in Thorverton. (Cole was assisted in this by the minister, John Preston, who 'ended the Jakes-businesse knowing the shiring thereof would be stinking and noysome to the court'.[30]) Just as the clerks of the peace and their assistants were pressed by justices' clerks for mercy or for speedy action on behalf of those they favoured, so the justices' clerks were likely to be importuned by those in trouble. Cole was asked to postpone a demand for a debt to be paid, and was petitioned by a husbandman whose little property was liable to confiscation. In the 1680s Cole was asked to judge between the conflicting claims of quarrelling tradesmen.[31] These were examples of how Cole's position as a clerk merged with his duties as estate steward. These interests blended with sinister implications when Nicholas Martin made Cole a gamekeeper in 1676 with power, under the Game Laws, to seize guns and the spoils of poachers.[32] Cole's integrity seemed beyond reproach, however; when William Barton, one of a Silverton family which had provided a recorder of Bradninch in 1650 and a

JP in 1648, had a horse stolen in 1669, it was to Cole rather than to his master he wrote for action:

> I had a horse stollen on May day last, the theefe is apprehended and in gaoll, I doe suspect John Bayly of his parish to be an accessory wherfor pray lett me have a warrant for him and for those under-written to appear as witnesses ...[33]

The trust placed in Cole may be gauged by the request of a head constable that he should settle his accounts for the mustermaster,[34] and by his work for the repair of Thorverton bridge in 1678. This matter indicates how new methods were being introduced into one of the major responsibilities of local government. The procedure in cases of decayed bridges had, time out of mind, been *ad hoc*. A presented bridge would be referred to the scrutiny of some neighbouring magistrates who by consulting older inhabitants would decide whether the bridge had in the past been a county charge or whether repair was the duty of private landowners. Bridge treasurers were appointed to collect for a specific repair but they were usually yeomen and minor gentry who had served as constables. Cole's appointment reflected the developing omnicompetence of the magistrates; he could be controlled much more closely than any constable. New financial techniques were employed, also. In the past no provision had been made for the maintenance of bridges, only for their repair. £400 had been agreed by sessions to be sufficient to restore the bridge but an offer was received from Nicholas Thomas, a local yeoman, to maintain the bridge for ten years afterwards for the fixed sum of £300. His tender was accepted and articles of covenant were signed by Thomas and the four magistrates originally required to inspect the decayed bridge. Cole witnessed the agreement. The administrative cost of repairing the bridge—the allowance to Cole and three other justices' clerks—was fourteen per cent of the whole.[35] From 1650 to 1653 the total administrative cost of the excise had been under nine per cent; according to Mary Coate 12.2 per cent of the receipts from Cornish sequestered royalist estates was dissipated in the salaries of functionaries.[36] Not much can be made of these isolated examples but it would seem that administration was getting costlier, and was cheaper in London than in the provinces.

Cole steadily acquired greater responsibilities in the running of the Martin and Carew estates in the 1650s and 1680s. He was consulted about the felling of trees, and we discover him arranging the export of peas from Topsham.[37] He handled correspondence arising from the changes of incumbents at Netherexe parish.[38] He acted *in loco parentis* for young Nicholas Martin in the early 1670s. Martin had gone up to Oxford, and in 1669 wrote Cole an account of his friends and adventures at Trinity College. The following year came an ominous request for money despite an acknowledgement of Cole's 'love and good counsel'. By 1672 Martin had moved to London and Cole tried to curtail what he saw, with some alarm, as a rake's progress:

I never thought I should heare such reports of you as lately I have, how you are
given to gameing, cursing, drinking and swearing and are growen so careless of
the good of your selfe as you have threatened to kill such as have advised you for
your good ... there must be a day of reckoning come at last and then what will
that be to eternity?[39]

Their relationship survived this crisis; by the late 1670s Nicholas
Martin, now enjoying his inheritance, was offering to make Cole a
commissioner for affidavits in Devon: 'If you will accept of the place to
bee one I suppose it may be worth £20 p. annum ... It's a place that will
bee of very little difficultie and paines'.[40]

Thomas Cole had extended his influence into the family affairs of his
employers; Nicholas Martin was godfather to Cole's son and the overseer
of his will. But when Cole wrote his will he described himself as
'yeoman'; the house he occupied in Netherexe only had two hearths,
typical for those of husbandman/yeoman status. He had accumulated
land in Farringdon near Exeter, and tenements in Exeter, Upexe and
Tiverton. He left cash bequests of over £200 to his daughters
and others, but his will was a solemn reminder of how much
he owed his advancement to his peculiarly privileged position with the
Carew and Martin families.[41]

Cole's career reveals something of how, of all the groups of officials who
served the magistrates, the justices' clerks enjoyed the most power and
initiative, even though their tenure of office was the least independent of
all. The dormant juries and the harrassed constables not only served
quarter sessions apathetically or unquestioningly but also did little to
further their own interests, as a group, to the Bench. The petition of the
constables for foot-post allowances, composed in a period of intense
pressure on local time and resources, was exceptional. The jury system
included a fully-developed procedure for presenting the views of jurors
but it had fallen into parochial self-interest and desuetude. Indeed, there is
small reason to believe that constables and jurors regarded themselves as
specific interest groups at all. The clerks did, however, doubtless because
of their dependence on fees. Barnes has described how the justices' clerks
and the officials in the office of the clerk of the peace conspired to ensure
that fees were paid; for example, the clerk of the peace would refuse to
discharge a recognizance unless all fees were settled.[42] As court business
increased in volume, so did the receipts from fees, though not without
added obligations for the clerks. In 1665 and 1668 the magistrates and the
clerk of the peace made the clerks responsible for bringing in their
recognizances to the court by the Tuesday of the sessions week in
order to hasten business. There was to be a forfeit of ten shillings
for each late recognizance. A clerk could lose his fees by decree of the
court or by collusion of other clerks;[43] to relieve this insecurity and to
induce co-operation between the clerks for their mutual benefit the
following agreement was reached in 1678 by the clerks of the Exe Valley
justices:

> It was ... mutually agreed upon by and between we whose names are subscribed that at any tyme thereafter at any publique meeting of the justices of peace if it shall happen that by reason of sickness or in a journey or otherwise occasionally hindered either of our masters shall be absent if his clarke be present or master present and the clarke absent that the clarke in such case shall have his equall proporcion of fees as fully as if his master and clarkes were present provided his absence be not wilfull and on purpose to excuse himselfe from the travell and paines that must be performed by other clarkes.[44]

The magistrates' clerks appear after 1660 as a confident group of administrators but Barnes noted such confidence among the clerks of Somerset in the period before 1642; is it not simply that the Devon record is substantially fuller for the post-war decades? Barnes shows how the clerk 'was ... merely a pawn in the games of clashing interests and desire played out at the sessions'.[45] Associating with others to protect one's interests is not the behaviour of a pawn.[46] The Exe Valley agreement was reached among clerks who met frequently in petty sessions; their enhanced self-confidence seems linked with the revival of these meetings after 1660. Petty sessions were convened by the clerks of the magistrates concerned in them and were based on no institutional structure. Their only connection with quarter sessions came when records of their proceedings in criminal matters, with informal accounts by justices of administrative business delegated to them by quarter sessions, were sent to the clerk of the peace.

Privy sessions were held in towns, and in rural areas for the licensing of alehouses, in early seventeenth century Devon.[47] Licensing was undertaken mostly out of quarter sessions by groups of justices working in areas corresponding loosely with the hundreds. From this limited task meetings were developed in the 1630s as a response to Privy Council pressure in social policy. The Book of Orders of 1631 was a re-issue of a 1586 edition with influence from contemporary practice in Northamptonshire.[48] It enjoyed the compilation and despatch to the Privy Council reports on the number of licensed alehouses, vagrants, apprentices bound, absentees from church, in a comprehensive effort to stave off the effects of an appalling dearth of corn. Through this stimulus provided by the Privy Council and sustained by the assize judges petty sessions developed from meetings with one specific task in hand—the licensing of alehousekeepers, for example—to bodies with wider administrative functions. The civil war halted this development and disrupted quarter sessions. Individual magistrates and 'select vestries' managed as best they could.

Quarter sessions were refurbished by 1647 but the revival of petty sessions seems to have been confined to alehouse licensing and to meetings in the larger towns. Honiton, for example, although it did not enjoy a charter of incorporation, had sessional meetings in the 1650s[49] and the Protestation Return for Tavistock, a parliamentary borough but without a charter, noted the presence of seven 'magistrates', although they were presumably town governors responsible for enforcing local licensing laws promulgated by manorial and hundred courts. 'Privy' or *ad hoc* meetings were used by the commissioners for the major-generals in 1655 and 1656; Martin Blake, the vicar of Barnstaple, was haled before one such 'in full body at the New Inne in Exon where Major Blackmore had the chaire'.[50] Attacks on Quakers were proof that individual justiciary action flourished in Devon. The Friends' counter-attack on the Bench as a 'new authority', a criticism of the independent vigour it displayed, was misplaced;[51] the energy derived strictly from the zeal of a few individuals not from a collective ethos. But properly defined, 'petty sessions' were more than the one or two justices meeting to deal with offences which Lambarde and Dalton had described. By Elizabethan and Jacobean statutes, two JPs could punish mothers of bastard children, gaol recusants, close unlicensed alehouses and imprison poachers. It is possible to describe meetings organised to deal with at least several of them cases together as petty sessions; they required planning and the co-operation of three or four magistrates. It is the element of management which distinguishes petty sessions from the meetings held in the 1650s.

The Interregnum was not a period of administrative change in the localities. Successive governments were not goaded by the spur of dearth. The Commonwealth tackled social problems by enacting legislation, by attempting to manage its executive problems *in* Parliament rather than by supervision of the provinces. The Protectorate resorted to intensive management of local administration briefly, during the rule of the major-generals, and although co-operation achieved more during this campaign than attacks on local privilege, the political repercussions of the intrusion brought the experiment to an abrupt end early in 1657.

The Interregnum assize judges were not burdened with the direction of local government. They arbitrated in contentious issues which the magistrates had failed to settle. Repairing bridges and settling individuals on particular parishes were therefore the most numerous tasks referred to assizes in the 1650s and 1660s, but the entry 'noe orders' was frequently made in western circuit meetings.[52] The decline of assizes as a means of social control continued into the 1660s. J.S. Cockburn argues that this was because assizes had become tarred with the brush of early Stuart absolutism and were henceforth of limited acceptability in the provinces, but the reticence of assize judges may be considered as an aspect of a general faltering by central government in the field of social policy, of a failure to re-adopt 'Thorough'. Even when the legislation collectively if erroneously known as the 'Clarendon Code' was enacted, the assize judges remained silent. Only during the early 1660s when quarter sessions called desperately for the payment of local rate and national tax arrears did the assize clerk record the support of the judges for the campaign of retrenchment.[53]

What of the Privy Council, which had provided much of the stimulus for the policy of 'Thorough' during the 1630s and whose *Acts* and *Registers* are crammed full of orders dealing with the minutiae of directives and reports? There was some continuity between the vigour of the 1630s and the developments of the Restoration decade. The common brewhouse in Exeter, established in the later 1630s, was a cause of complaint for the

Exeter Brewers' Company both when it opened and in 1660, but the Restoration Privy Council acted as its Laudian predecessor would have done, and referred the contested monopoly to the nearest JPs.[54] The Council was prepared to intercede when economic interests were threatened, in more egregious cases. Tobacco-growing was once more prohibited, an enquiry was launched into proposed demolition work on Plymouth quay, and the eternal squabbles between excise officials and brewers were conscientiously examined.[55] The Council merely responded to pressure on these matters, however, and no particular direction was being followed. Thus, the Privy Council acceded to the request of the House of Commons in 1662 that a proclamation be prepared in order to counter the only dearth which blighted food distribution in the 1660s, and it supported the initiative of the Middlesex magistrates in making alehousekeepers remove their signs from the streets to their walls, to relieve congested thoroughfares.[56] Intervention was sporadic. The only local issue which exercised the Privy Council regularly and consistently was the supervision of the re-established militia. There were repeated exhortations to zeal against those of 'unreclaimable mutinous spirit', detailed instructions about the keeping of accurate muster-rolls, the reimbursement of serving militiamen, and the preparation of accounts which were to be despatched to Whitehall.[57]

The neat, continuous orders in the Privy Council registers obscure important differences in the role of the Council before and after 1660. E.R. Turner's thesis of 'Cabinet government' effectively developing in this period is now discredited, but his view that the Privy Council was no longer a body in which differences of opinion could be submerged in the forceful vision of a Laud or a Strafford may be confirmed. The Council had become as large and unwieldy as local assessment committees, and for much the same reason. As a result of the explosion in patronage several Privy Council committees were created to deal separately with foreign policy, military and trade matters, and with the petitions of various interest groups in the country at large.[58]

Privy Council and assizes, which had spearheaded social policy in the 1630s, had by the 1660s adapted to a less contentious role, forced on them by changes in the patronage structure in 1660, by less need for action to remedy social dislocation and by the psychological inheritance of the traumas of the civil war to which they, during the Personal Rule, had allegedly contributed. Neither was able to influence administrative developments in the localities. Petty sessions revived in the 1660s but it was not because of central supervision of local affairs. Evidence for petty sessions meeetings in Devon is not to be found in the quarter sessions bundles (except in reports on matters referred from the Bench to the parishes[59]), nor in the State Papers Domestic (monthly reports from the JPs to the Privy Council had lapsed by 1640). One must resort to the private papers of the men who made the local government system work, and for Devon there is no better source than the thirteen volumes of papers relating to the Carew and Martin families, and particularly to William Martin (1626–1662) and Sir Henry Carew of Bickleigh

(1599–1681).[60] The papers include the miscellaneous warrants and orders drafted by these two Exe Valley magistrates in the 1660s and 1670s.

The papers afford an impression of continuity in local procedures, developed during the personal rule of Charles I, which survived in attenuated form for twenty years to break forth again after 1660. Licensing sessions were still being held, even though central government now insisted that would-be licensees should produce certificates from the local excise office. Writs were issued in order to settle local matters in the name of the assize judges, though with no great frequency. Substantial fines of thirty-nine shillings each were levied on defaulting *petty* constables for not attending with presentments. The making of presentments by petty and hundred constables to petty sessions confirm, above all, that a pre-war pattern of local government, at a level most sensitive to parochial needs and parochial distinctions, continued as before. In warrants directed from the JPs, who convened the meetings, to petty constables, tithingmen and other minor officials the range of presentable offences was recited in as full a list as any under Charles I. The delinquents to be apprehended included unlicensed alesellers, bakers and butchers, drunkards, swearers, masterless men, unbound apprentices and those who failed to attend church. (The last two groups were to be apprehended by overseers of the poor and churchwardens.) Among other delinquents who were to be included were unlawful gamers, those illegally married and (even before the Game Act of 1671) those who with an income less than £100 kept 'gunnes or other engines that do kill or destroy any deeres, fowle, hares etc.'.[61] Not only were petty constables to attend, however, but they were enjoined to produce written accounts of their service,[62] a refinement of the oral accounting which would seem to have been common in the 1630s meetings.[63] The development of sessions went further than this. The selection of overseers and surveyors, once conducted in each parish by the great man and the democratic vestry or 'six men' (as they were known in some parishes) was in the Cullompton area at least being reserved to the petty sessions and the magistrates who attended. The constables of Bampton, a parish ten miles from Cullompton, were summoned to Henry Skinner's house to be given the names of their parish officials for the coming year.[64] Petty sessions could be a 'court' of appeal for cases such as that vexing the Holsworthy constables: 'There is money given for the benefitt of the poore of our parishe ... which the overseers will not give an account of but only for the increase of the money'.[65] Parochial disputes over taxation were forestalled by the holding of meetings to confirm or adjust the rates for assessments made by parish assessors, nominated by the JPs holding the petty sessions. Several parishes could be dealt with in one meeting.[66]

The petty sessions of the 1660s and later speak loudly of the self-confidence and power of the magistrates, enhanced at the Restoration as the county gentry came back in force. Regulating taxation, controlling parish officials and bringing the recalcitrant to heel were all dealt with by the JPs themselves, without interference by juries or other bodies. Were the Exe Valley justices conspicuously busy men, inclined to communal effort in the 1660s because of a special commitment to making the Restoration work? Were they a group of Cavaliers or zealous Anglicans?

John Bluett, Thomas Beare, Samuel Sainthill and William Walrond, who met frequently in the 1670s, were all newcomers to government in 1660. Sainthill was an ex-Cavalier; Walrond had been nominated as an assessment commissioner during the Protectorate. Beare was commended by Bishop Ward as performing 'service beyond expectation' for the Church of England in 1671; Walrond was a presbyterian who evaded the Conventicle Acts by building a private chapel at his house in Uffculme.[67] Walrond also served in petty sessions with Sir Henry Carew and Francis Drewe, both ex-royalists.[68] At Chulmleigh in the early 1660s John Bury of Colleton, Sir John Chichester of Raleigh, John Gifford of Brightley and John Pollard of Langley met monthly 'to dispatch his majestie's businesse as well as the affaires of the country'. Gifford and Chichester were royalists (the latter was MP for Barnstaple from 1661), Bury and Pollard were neutrals in the civil war, but whereas Bury left a bequest to the Anglican minister of Ashreigny, Pollard counted John Champneys as a 'loving friend' and Champneys was the Interregnum recorder of Torrington, a persecutor of Quakers and a presbyterian Cromwellian.[69] Petty sessions were operable despite religious and political differences.

The flexible, adaptable quality of petty sessions extended to their geographical coverage. Licensing sessions had been based only loosely on the hundreds, as lists of recognizances show; the parishes covered were frequently determined by personal factors such as the extent of JPs' territorial influence or the nearness of a parish to their homes. The same priorities were evinced in the summoning of sessions. The Hayridge JPs extended their administration as far as Bampton, and the Chulmleigh meeting dealt with the hundreds of North Tawton, Witheridge and Winkleigh but not all the hundreds of the North Grand Division of the county (by this time a partition relevant only in the summoning of the militia forces of Devon).

Petty sessions therefore thrived in Restoration Devon but not because of pressure from government at assizes or in Privy Council. One might seek the inspiration for the sessions in parochial developments. The collapse of quarter sessions government across the country in the 1640s undoubtedly forced parishes to their own resources in maintaining order. J.S. Morrill suggests that this process continued profoundly enough to bring about enhanced political awareness in the parishes from the late 1640s, and it is certainly a feature of administration in Devon at this time that certificates of good character attested by ministers and others were a preliminary to securing alehouse licences.[70] After 1650, improved harvests relieved the alehouses from the criticism of their wasteful consumption of barley, and the development of the excise tax gave central government good reason to limit attacks on alehouses rather than to limit alehouses themselves.[71]

The value of alehousekeeping as a means of poor relief was recognized more openly in the parish than in Whitehall. The principal inhabitants of a parish could suffer some anxiety that an alehouse should remain open. Walter Downe of Lewtrenchard, suppressed on the evidence of an informer, William Beare ('one who is well knowne to your worshipps what he is') was relicensed by local JPs but remained afraid to open again 'by reason of that his grand enemy'. Local supporters, among them minor gentry, wrote to quarter sessions in 1655 that Downe could be trusted to accommodate travellers (including 'persons of quality') and stable horses, and they recited his troubles on his behalf.[72] Self-interest was doubtless the motive; the local economy would have suffered if 'persons of quality' *en route* from Okehampton to Launceston did not stop, a 'blind' alehouse which served no useful purpose might attract an unwelcome visit from the major-general, and the former alehousekeeper, without employment, would have burdened the poor rates.[73] A Silverton officer, Thomas Were, wrote an impassioned letter to Thomas Cole to avert the fate of an unlicensed aleseller:

> I have been often a sollicitor to you on the behalfe of some poore of our parish, but I will assure you I neither trouble you nor my selfe in their matters unlesse I thinke their condition pittiful. There is one Mary Clarke (I thinke a trespasser to the lawe) that brewes a bushell or two once in a moneth, who is this day summoned before Sir Henry [Carew] for selling drinke unlicensed. Pray sir represent her poverty to Sir Henry and I question not but that she she may be remitted ... I hope when her fault is putt into one ballance and her miserable distressed case into the other the latter will waye downe the former and soe become an object rather of misery than justice.[74]

Certificates from 'principal inhabitants' of parishes, including the incumbents, to the fitness of would-be alehousekeepers, continued through the 1650s, 1660s and 1670s. Licences were requested for those who 'hath a great charge of children', 'for it is poverty which is the mayne cas that wee intrete your wishipes faver' and who had the additional qualification of deference, of social passivity which recommended a Bampton applicant who 'demeaned himself very sivill'.[75]

These examples all come from the Exe Valley where the dealings of petty sessions are well-documented, but the parochial independence they suggest was not viewed as an extension of petty sessional authority. In Silverton there was a monthly meeting of the rector and the wardens and overseer, of quite a different order from those of courts leet and other feudal relics. No magistrates attended. It was a 'select vestry', in essence, and its convenors strove, with some annoyance, to educate its traducers into accepting its administrative integrity. They wrote to Sir Henry Carew:

> The officers have made complaint to us that they have ever and anon the trouble created them to waite on your worship to satisfy the unreasonable and impertinent clamours of some persons who have now lesse reason then ordinary to trouble any neighbour justices by seeking reliefe, in regard we have instituted a monthly meeting within our parish where cognizance is taken of such objects of charity as we (that are best acquainted with their wants) know fitt to be relieved: wee therefore humbly and unanimously crave that favour at your hands that you would upon that score save yourselfe and us the trouble of creditting every complaint thats brought against us, and we shall gratefully acknowledge it as a special favour...[76]

A Jacobean administrator considered that grand jurors were 'better acquainted with the comon grievance of the countrie then justices';[77] in the 1660s a select vestry could claim to be 'best acquainted with [the] wants' of the poor; here are two examples of thought which claimed to limit the sovereignty of 'natural rulers'. The initiatives in the parishes after the civil war did not benefit ultimately the JPs, but stimulated a shift from courts leet towards the more oligarchical but more effective select vestries. The development of petty sessions in the 1660s seems only to confirm the self-confidence with which the county gentry swept back into power at the Restoration; the enthusiasm for privy sessions in the Exe Valley can be explained, after all, by the convenience of the meetings for gentry who by co-operation could evade attendance at quarter sessions whose dates and duration were inflexible.

Magisterial self-confidence expressed itself naturally at quarter sessions. It lay behind the almost obsessive delving into past accounts which the justices undertook repeatedly during the 1660s. A muster-master whose service had ended fifteen years previously was in 1661 ordered to have arrears of fees. The accounts of treasurers for local rates back to 1642 were ordered to be produced. Henry Fitzwilliam, the county treasurer, was congratulated on having wrung £661 of desperate arrears from former officials. The magistrates reminded themselves that such arrears were not to be written off under the terms of the Act of Indemnity, and parishioners were subtly encouraged to root out former constables who had hidden money:

> Constables of the hundreds and their executors are uppon requiry of the payment of any arrears to shewe their bookes of accompt unto the parishioners if by any parishe they shalbe thereunto required and in case of refusall the next justice of peace is desired to binde them over to the next sessions.[78]

In a further display of corporate assertiveness the justices declared that because of 'a very great charge of all uppon the county' constables were no longer to make presentments to assizes but to sessions only.[79] The abdication by assizes of social control was thus by the mutual agreement of central and local government, and resolved a conflict between assizes and sessions which had smouldered during the reign of Charles I. During Lord Keeper Coventry's reforms in the 1620s it was ordered that all presentments should be made at assizes, and the Devon JPs responded with an appeal that this 'grievaunce of the countrey' be remedied, that 'the presentments be transferred to them as formerlie'.[80] The assize order was repeated in 1629, however; the constables did not have to present offences at, or even attend, quarter sessions, and the judges were adamant: 'This order to be final, without innovation'.[81] The gentry had to wait until their ascendancy in the county was unchallenged in order to reverse this *diktat*; their opportunity came in the 1660s and not before.

Much financial retrenchment undertaken in the Restoration period sprang, of course, from the demands made upon local administration by maimed soldiers, demands which fell most heavily on the head constables. The new militia also attracted careful husbanding of resources. But the

JPs went beyond common prudence; they were concerned to assert their authority and its retrospective extension (in demands that accounts be cleared) and to confirm, by written orders, the application of procedures which had developed in the Interregnum and earlier. The appointment of treasurers in the Easter sessions of each year was common in the 1630s, though the number appointed varied. By the 1650s a treasurer for each of the funds for maimed soldiers, hospitals and gaols was being appointed annually at the Easter sessions, but the Restoration justices felt it necessary to bestow upon this practice an enhanced legal status by writing it up 'that soe the said accompts maie not any more for the future be brought into confusion as formerly they have bine thereby'.[82] This is a 'bureaucratic' characteristic, in the Weberian sense, but whether the more business-like techniques of the 1660s and after were produced by the vigour of a self-confident Bench or whether these techniques created confidence among magistrates seems impossible to resolve. The JPs of 1660 were aggressive, and were confronted by social dislocation in the guise of an apparent army of maimed soldiers seeking relief from the magistrates. The erstwhile military commanders had to become charity administrators. Theirs was a tendentious view of the past fostered by absence from government for over a decade in some cases and by complete inexperience in others. The local administration of the 1650s was not marked by 'confusion', although the early years of the Rump had seen some effectiveness through muddle, and it may have been the inclusive concept of government, the fluidity of functions among the reliable, to which the hierarchy of 1660 objected most.[83] A pressing social problem, a confidence in authority and in the justice of the Restoration settlement, an exaggerated impression of the enemy's shortcomings—it was natural that the oligarchy should issue a torrent of orders and warrants to its subordinates in government and yet maintain continuity in government while declaiming the rectitude of its methods to its immediate posterity.[84] The written order as public justification has been encountered before,[85] and goes some considerable way to account for 'bureaucracy', for 'administrative innovation' in the 1660s. The legacy of the Interregnum was more considerable than Cavaliers would allow. Two case studies of procedure at quarter sessions, one from the administrative, one from the criminal side of the court's business, will examine this continuity.

The Poor and the Prisons 1649-1670

The most recent work on the history of poor relief has demonstrated that the theory of early socialist historians that charitable giving collapsed during the Interregnum was unsubstantiated.[86] Research has shifted towards quantification, but A.L. Beier and J.S. Morrill have been more concerned to assess the temper of poor law administration than to explore the attitude which prompted the orders. It is not intended here to construct a defence for the Interregnum JPs against charges of inadequacy or inhumanity. The competence and diligence of the magistrates have already been vindicated. What follows is a narrative account of the problems faced in the administration of the Devon prisons and county poor relief, where the two converged, to highlight continuity, to expose the limitations of early modern bureaucracy and to throw into relief the limitations of action this bureaucracy imposed on justices trying to make it work in the periods of both 'Puritan' and 'Cavalier' ascendancy.

Bridewells, or houses of correction, were established by statutes of 1576 and 1598, consolidated in 1601 and 1610, which embodied the distinctions between the poor who sought work but could not find it, the able-bodied vagabonds and the old, sick and otherwise unable to work. Setting the poor on work was the avowed intent of legislators, and houses of correction were intended to provide schemes for employment. In practice, from the early seventeenth century onwards, the distinction between the unable and the unwilling to work was not sustained. Inadequate understanding of economic forces and a powerful association in the minds of the ruling classes between poverty and disaffection[87] produced, from the appearance in the early years of the century of houses of correction at Newton Abbot, Tavistock, Chulmleigh and Honiton,[88] orders despatching petty criminals as well as the indigent poor there.[89] Not only did this perversion of the declared purpose of bridewells—the appearance of which the Webbs surely post-date[90]—spring from prevailing notions of the status of the poor, but also from the administrative structure of poor relief which was, from the mid-sixteenth century, essentially parochial. Bridewells were never more than the last resort of this system; it was but a short step from a desperate problem to 'desperate rogues and vagabonds'. By the 1630s there were houses of correction at Tavistock and Newton Abbot, with smaller and less closely-regulated establishments at Torrington and Honiton. The Newton Abbot house was not the property of the county; during our period Thomas Reynell of East Ogwell, JP, drew arrears of rent owed him for the site. The 1631 Book of Orders provided that houses of correction were to be moved near to common gaols and stipulated that gaolers were henceforth to be governors. The association of the poor and the criminal was elevated to government policy, and administration of the houses was placed in the hands of fee-taking gaolers in an effort to rid the county of a burdensome responsibility.[91] In local terms this order launched efforts to find a suitable site in Exeter, near the common gaol at Rougement Castle, for a new house of correction. A site at St Thomas, 'near Exebridge', was bought in 1635 from the trustees of the estate of the late Sir John Whiddon (among them John Maynard) for £600. At much the same time Edward Jones was appointed sole county treasurer because his temporary predecessors had 'used to substitute their servaunts and others of inferiour condition to execute their places'. Jones set about repairing the grand jury chamber at Exeter Castle and began to spend money in advance of its receipt from high constables—by exploiting credit from Exeter merchants, perhaps. The establishment of the St Thomas bridewell was thus part of a period of retrenchment and reform from 1635 to Jones's death in 1639.[92]

Magistrates appointed the keepers of the bridewells. For most of the 1650s Daniel Condy was keeper or governor at Tavistock, John Morgan at St Thomas and there are references to the service of Thomas Coleman at

Honiton and Richard Vann at Torrington. Thomas Sheeres was governor at Newton Abbot until 1655 when he was succeeded by Thomas Bright. The intention of the Book of Orders had not been implemented: unlike common gaolers the governors were paid salaries. Five pounds each quarter was the fixed sum through the Fifties and Sixties, although the salaries were never regularly paid because of the inadequacy of the rate collection on which they were drawn. By the summer of 1650 John Morgan was a year in arrears and since governors paid for repairs on their own initiative and from their own funds it was not surprising that by 1651 necessary repairs to the house of correction were expected to cost £20.[93] Arrears of salary and repairs to, rather than maintenance of, the houses were constant problems of the Interregnum, and arose from the fiscal handicaps of local government rather than from lack of interest by the JPs. Salaries were payable not by the annual treasurer for gaols but, in accordance with the precedent of the 1630s, by the manager of the county stock, Edward Anthony, an Exeter goldsmith who had been treasurer of the defence fund in Exeter against the royalists in 1643.[94]

Dissatisfaction with Anthony's failure to clear the arrears grew, however. In 1652, when it seemed that he was detaining funds raised in the eastern division of the county and which had been allocated to Thomas Coleman, the governor at the Honiton house of correction, his accounts were inspected by John Disbrowe. A year later, Sir John Davy, JP, was managing the stock and paying the expenses of both the governor of Newton Abbot bridewell and the agent of the Committee for the Army who had been sent to Devon to examine the accounts of a former receiver-general of assessments in the county.[95] Anthony was still paying in money in 1655 and recovered some status in 1656 and it may be suspected that his demotion in 1653 owed something to the fall of the Rump and Disbrowe's enhanced control of county patronage; Sir John Davy was certainly a favourite of the Major-General.[96] Davy's elevation did little to improve the quality of poor relief. Edward Jones had been appointed in the Thirties because treasurers were inclined to abdicate control to servants, less accountable to the Bench than their masters. By 1655 Davy had run true to form, and his servant, Richard Rowe, was compiling accounts and chasing up defaulting constables. At the next sessions his own accounts were scrutinized in a purge on defaulters which went back to 1641[97] but it was a further measure of the indecision of the justices that the Newton Abbot bridewell was reported to be in decay.

The first six years of the Interregnum were marked by a failure to achieve adequate control over subordinate treasurers and to establish working rules for the management of the county stock. There was no commitment to the notion of a single treasurer as an advance on earlier waywardness, and what appeared to be the reservation of fiscal control to the JPs themselves was really devolution to minor private servants not appointed by sessions at all. This administrative weakness did not imply a lack of interest by the JPs in plans for the relief of the poor and for the punishment of rogues. John Morgan at St Thomas spoke of promises that he should receive a further stock from the county. A new bridewell at

Ottery St Mary was ordered, with stock and implements 'for the keeping, correcting and setting on work of such rogues, vagabonds, sturdy beggars and such other idle and disorderly persons as shalbe from tyme to tyme there committed'—an initiative which betrayed the fears of the gentry that the poor were necessarily idle. In 1658, while watches and wards were resumed against vagrants, it was ordered that four bridewells should have new stocks of up to £200 each because they were proving to be inadequate to set on work those committed by the court and those willing but unable to find employment. In 1658 an inquiry was undertaken into the future of the lazar house at Torrington (Taddiport) after its occupants had petitioned the Bench that its funds were no longer being provided. It was concluded that the house should be continued even though it sheltered only three inmates and they were promised sixteen pounds a year with the possibility of funds from their parishes of settlement. In 1659 a new house of correction was opened at Honiton.[98]

Most of the effort directed by the Interregnum JPs in their social policy involved the St Thomas house of correction. Since its construction twenty years earlier it had struggled along, as had the other houses, in arrears and without regular funds. In 1653, probably on the very day that Cromwell expelled the Rump Parliament, it was noted in the sessions minutes that accounts had 'been neglected for many yeares together' and the JPs declared their intention to discover 'how the £900 and odd moneyes given by John Maynard Esq. to this county was bestowed and where the same doth now remaine and of theire whole proceedings'.[99] The '£900 and odd' derived from the will of Eliseus Hele, who was buried at Bovey Tracey in 1632. Maynard had been a trustee of the Whiddon property which had originally funded St Thomas and as a rising lawyer of gentry eminence it was unremarkable that he should be appointed a trustee of another Devon gentleman's will. Hele left his property to endow several local charities, including a workhouse at Exeter, but such was his charitable piety that he failed to leave anything to his posterity: in the 1650s a grand-daughter, Joan, the wife of Captain Lister.[100] Maynard had failed to pay out the money the Devon JPs had expected because of a protracted dispute over the terms of Hele's will. During the first session of the second Protectorate Parliament the issue was brought before the House in the same spirit of self-conscious omnicompetence which had summoned James Nayler there. The Treasury was unable or unwilling to settle the affair but the parliamentary debate ranged over the usual claims and interests. West Country MPs were 'unsatisfied that anything should be taken from these uses and settlements in their country' and Thomas Bampfield made a vigorous speech impugning the integrity of the claimants, Hele's heirs-at-law.[101] £980 had already been laid out on the St Thomas building but the work had been interrupted by war and, it seemed, scarcely resumed since. It was finally resolved that the charitable uses bequeathed by Hele should remain but that the balance of the estate should descend to Joan Lister. The sympathy of most MPs had not extended to the poor at St Thomas, however, nor even to Mrs Lister, as much as to the late Eliseus Hele, whose own emotions had been stirred by the psalmist; not at his metaphor of man as vanity but at the outrage of 'getting goods and cannot tell who shall the same enjoy'.[102]

By an indenture of 1658 it was agreed that St Thomas should receive £1,000 raised by entry fines on Hele's lands, and that 'the workhouse for the gaol' should be first priority for the revenue thus raised.[103] The parliamentary debates had confirmed the funding for the workhouse but before this the JPs had made their own plans for centralizing the sheriff's prison at Stoke Canon under their own control.

The Webbs distinguished between houses of correction and common gaols. The common gaol at Exeter Castle was run by John Richards for whatever fees he could extract from the prisoners.[104] Victuals and beer were provided, by outside contract, for the inmates who had even to buy their own sustenance.[105] The gaol, at Exeter Castle, was for detention before trial and, in some cases when security for future good behaviour could or would not be given, after judgement. Just as Richards, the gaoler, lived by fees, so he owed his position to him who held the right of keeping the gaol, a heritable right which was rented for forty shillings a year from Sir John Rolle by Thomas Drake of Winscombe until his death in 1661, and thereafter, by his son. Dennis Drake must have appointed John Gill, Richards's successor, in 1669.[106]

North of the City of Exeter, at the village of Stoke Canon, stood another prison: the debtors' gaol of the sheriff of Devon which housed poor prisoners, victims of adverse judgments in the sheriff's tourn, 'men of straw' whose debts could not be paid by distraint of their goods. Poor prisoners were haled to Stoke Canon by the sheriff's bailiffs. Stoke Canon gaol or the 'ward house' was, with the land in which it stood, the property of the dean and chapter of Exeter Cathedral. It was sold with other capitular lands, and was acquired by Richard Alford who leased it to the gaoler there, Walter Kellond, at an entry fine of eighty shillings and a yearly rent of 26s.8d. By 1661 the dean and chapter had acquired the ward house again and leased it with the manor of Stoke Canon itself to Thomas Drewe and Nicholas Mitchell. The prison was large enough to accommodate forty poor prisoners in 1665 under Walter Kellond's charge,[107] but during the 1650s the numbers there dropped sufficiently to justify the scheme of the JPs that all debtors should 'upon bargain and contract with the sheriff' be transferred to St Thomas where they would, of course, be mixed with the indigent poor under the control of the magistrates themselves. Stoke Canon was private property; St Thomas had the advantage of being owned by the county of Devon. Moreover, Stoke Canon ward house had fallen into disrepair since its confiscation from the dean and chapter. The government might have been expected to approve the magistrates' initiative; the decline of the Stoke Canon gaol was almost certainly the result of legislation to relieve poor debtors.[108] In fact, the reaction from Whitehall was very different. Interregnum governments, like that of Charles I, had discovered the usefulness and pliability of sheriffs. To close down the sheriff's ward would be to accede to a dangerous degree of magisterial hegemony in the county. Sheriff John Coplestone met the JPs in the jury chamber at Exeter Castle to discuss the plan, but nothing came of their talks. In 1658 an uncompromising assize order insisted on the removal of poor prisoners, then at St Thomas, back to Stoke Canon (or even somewhere else) within three months.[109]

One result of this decision was that the Hele or Maynard scheme was protected. The St Thomas workhouse was damaged by flooding in 1659 and a dispute arose over the governorship. It was referred 'out of respects to Sir John Maynard and his benevolence to the said house' to Hele's trustee, and Maynard selected John Stripling of Chudleigh, a maimed ex-royalist soldier on a county pension, to be keeper.[110] As partisans of the royalist cause could be protected by the dispensation of minor offices,[111] so those of the opposite persuasion could expect scant sympathy. Richard Vann, the governor of Torrington bridewell, 'behaved himselfe as a man disaffected to his Majestie' and was accordingly dismissed. Daniel Condy was petitioned against by the inhabitants of Tavistock because of his Independent sympathies and his solid support for Thomas Larkham. There was an inquiry into affairs at the house of correction but Condy vindicated himself. He lost the constableship but retained his post as governor in a remarkable piece of magisterial inconsistency. Condy's merits spoke louder than his detractors; certainly the sessions order books record regular payments to him of expenses laid out on the bridewell. Condy was a man of means; most other governors were insubstantial. John Stripling was to all intents on poor relief, and his successor, David Hart, was nearly carried off to Stoke Canon by two sheriff's bailiffs.[112]

The Restoration justices dealt with houses of correction more decisively and more confidently than their predecessors had a decade earlier, partly out of self-righteousness or concern to be seen to differ from the Interregnum JPs. Thus Walter Kellond was ordered to hand over the keys of St Thomas to John Stripling in a firm repudiation of the plan to merge bridewell and debtors' gaol. Thus lists of prisoners who had been in the house of correction were required, and thus those who had provided food at the common gaol fourteen years before were now rewarded. The administration of the prisons was scrutinized by Henry Fitzwilliam in a survey of rates arrears, and the county stocks at five bridewells were mentioned in a report in which he estimated the sum recoverable to be £2,100.[113] It was Maynard's charity, constructed in detail during the Interregnum, which preserved the county bridewells from sequestration. As it was, poor relief was included in a drive towards bureaucratic rectitude, and orders were agreed for the disposal of £2,000, half provided by Maynard, half by the county, for charitable purposes. The assumptions about poverty and disorder were well-illustrated in the general description of 'setting on work of idle and poore persons'. 'Undertakers' (projectors) were to manage the bridewells on payment to the county of a fixed sum from the profits of the employed stock. What was new in these proposals was that the machinery of inspection and accounting by the 'persons of quality' on the Bench was established in writing. A committee comprising Maynard and the county MPs (chosen because of their easy access to Maynard in London) with Henry Ford and Thomas Carew, JPs living near Exeter, was appointed. St Thomas bridewell was to be the showpiece of the Hele-Maynard gift but bounty overflowed sufficiently to fatten the other stocks as well. The St Thomas premises were repaired, on this occasion to the tune of over £40, under the supervision of an assistant clerk of the peace. Maynard seemed reluctant to pay over his share, however; by the summer of 1665 letters were sent by the JPs to request his £1,000, and to the assize judges requesting that the prison population in the common gaol should be relieved: a hint that St Thomas would make a suitable overflow. At the same time the other bridewells were examined. Fearing a heavier commitment than the rates income could bear, the magistrates inquired into the securities offered by the bridewell governors against economic disaster, and turned Torrington bridewell off county maintenance and back on to the provision of the ten hundreds of the north division.[114]

The development of the county's charitable resources, implied in Maynard's £1,000, seemed to run counter to a more prevalent mood of retrenchment, of limiting Devon's commitments to meet the demands made of it. Ominously, St Thomas was occupied by Dutch sailors (prisoners of war) in 1666. The want of necessary implements to set the poor on work there had been noted six months earlier. The governor, Maynard's choice, turned out to be a contentious character who provoked two petitions to sessions, and when he died the justices allowed his daughter to collect the 'one long rack' he had built at St Thomas for the cloth-making process.[115] This may have provided outdoor relief for Anne Stripling but it boded ill for the able-bodied poor in the workhouse. Stripling's successor was another poor man, David Hart, who ended a brief governorship in prison by January 1669, and by then it seemed that St Thomas was being included in the doubts about the value of 'setting the poor on work'.

The complaint to the assize judges that there were too many in the common gaol seemed to be bearing fruit, however. Maynard's parliamentary influence also came to bear on a successful bill (18 and 19 Charles II c. 9) for enforcing existing legislation. It recited the need to relieve the excesive numbers of those in gaol and enshrined the details of the St Thomas plan in the act, a piece of combined public and private legislation. A messuage was to be purchased in order to supply funds for the 'common gaol and workhouse'. An overseer and deputy were to have annual salaries of £50 and £10 each, and a minister was to officiate there for £30 a year. The scheme was now a response to a failure in the fees system of the common gaol at the Castle; many prisoners could no longer maintain themselves there. St Thomas had begun as a workhouse for the poor, had been described in 1665 as a house for 'setting on work idle and poore persons' and four years later it had become a gaol and a workhouse. Whether this more closely matched the needs of the county, as the JPs saw them, or whether the legislative authority provided a useful fillip to local administration, the details of the plan were executed smartly by the JPs. In the summer of 1668 Daniel Condy, the Tavistock governor, a substantial merchant, an Independent who had opposed the Restoration with a display of para-military force in Tavistock, was appointed governor at St Thomas, with the approval of a committee which included a zealous Anglican, and at least two ex-Cavaliers. Fitzwilliam was to give Condy £400 for materials. By October 1668, John Hornabrook was appointed deputy and John Reynolds, incumbent of St Thomas parish, minister.[116]

At the same time negotiations commenced between the justices and Mrs. Frances Pollard 'concerning the purchasing of her estate called Burgett' although at Easter 1669 it was noted that no convenient estate had yet been found.[117] Meetings were arranged between Maynard and the JPs to agree temporary employment of the funds but from the summer of 1669 St Thomas began to take its quota as an overflow from the common gaol. From that date separate gaol calendars for St Thomas appear in the order books, and prisoners were sent there in increasing numbers. At Michaelmas 1669 there were fifteen, in the summer of 1670 there were twenty-seven prisoners remanded, whipped and ordered to be transported.[118] The house of correction was in every way merely an annexe or overflow for the common gaol and such harshness was a perversion of the spirit of Hele's bequest. At the Epiphany sessions of 1670, when Albermarle's death was announced, and on the eve of the second Conventicle Act and—further evidence of gentry hegemony—'a period in which Parliament's fundamental prejudices were respected',[119] the full intent of recent developments was laid bare. Those of St Thomas who were 'idle, dissolute and disorderly' or insane were, if they could not support themselves, to be maintained by the parishes whence they came. Felons 'usually committed formerly to the gaol' were to be relieved by the county. Setting on work was not even mentioned as a possibility, and it was agreed that the bridewells of Honiton, Newton Abbot and Torrington should 'cease from being bridewells for the county of Devon at midsummer next'.[120] If neighbouring hundreds wanted to assume responsibility, it was their look-out.

The shift towards parochial self-help, triggered by the Act of Settlement of 1662 but extended into the realm of practical poor relief, occurred ironically at a time when administration in the county was better able to cope with demands made of it than it had been for about thirty years.[121] The Hele charity of 1634 came to fruition thirty-five years later in an atmosphere not of charitable piety but of defensive vigour against the poor. The St Thomas building was intended as a workhouse, but its germination had passed through an ambiguous phase as a bridewell for the poor and idle and it was commissioned in 1669 as a prison with no commitment at all to setting the poor on work. The Restoration justices acted decisively but the bridewell simply offered them an expedient to end overcrowding in gaol. Had the bequest never been made, it is difficult to avoid the conclusion that county government would have moved in a more muddled way, but just as surely, towards a system based on punishment rather than relief. In 1669 St Thomas became a central prison administered closely by the JPs, who served notice on workhouses more distant from Exeter. In its funding, its location and its purpose, St Thomas bridewell accorded well with the aspirations of the Devon county gentry.

Fornication and Bastardy 1649-1670

A recent essay by Keith Thomas on the origins and later history of one of the most distinctively 'Puritan' measures of the Rump, the act for 'suppressing ... incest, adultery and fornication', consolidates work of wider scope on the 'Puritan Reformation of Manners'. Keith Wrightson has admirably quantified the volume of offences against the spirit of such a reformation[122] but here it is hoped to examine in more detail the cases brought under the 1650 act and to trace the spirit of this legislation where it persisted after 1660. Evidence for the criminal side of western circuit assize business is lacking, so the source must be the quarter sessions records of Devon: the series of gaol calendars in the order books, bundles of examinations and indictments. The punishment for fornication under the 1650 act, three months' imprisonment and an obligation to be of good behaviour for a year,[123] implied detention from the end of one sessions to the beginning of the next, and the clerk entered the marginal note 'for fornication' against the names of such offenders. The number of fornication cases can thus be compared with the volume of prosecutions as a whole (figure 1).

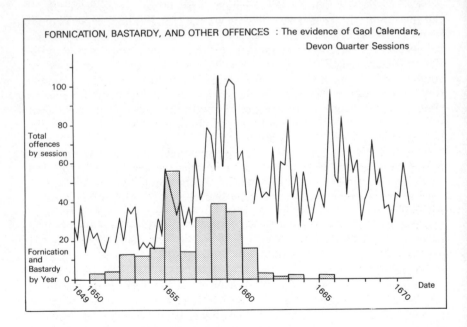

Gaol calendar entries[124] are a reliable source for prosecutions. Unlike examinations, indictments or true bills they are an accurate measure of convictions. True bills could be rejected by a trial jury, except where they were confessions. It is not clear how Dr Wrightson undertook his 'reconstitution' of quarter sessions prosecutions in Essex and Lancashire; 'prosecutions' cannot be calculated by adding together the numbers of any single document. Sometimes Dr Wrightson seems to equate 'prosecutions' with true bills; sometimes not.[125] This criticism does not, however, reduce the force of the contrast between Essex and Lancashire and Devon, in this aspect of moral regulation. The 1650 act hardly made an impact on the former two counties; in Devon it was enforced with some vigour. On the other hand, aleselling convictions soared in Wrightson's counties during the Interregnum, but played only a very minor role in the volume of Devon convictions.[126]

There could be no clear distinction between bastardy as an offence, and fornication, because such a distinction had not been clearly made before 1650. Fornication had not been an indictable offence in statute law. It was prosecuted in church courts, manorial courts and in common law courts as a breach of the peace. He who sought to prosecute the parents of a base child was on firmer ground. Elizabethan legislation sought to minimise parochial obligations in these cases, and provided that unmarried mothers could be whipped and sent to bridewell.[127] These statutes were not repealed when the 1650 act was passed; they remained as a sort of alternative to it. Discrepancies in descriptions of offenders between entries in order books and in gaol calendars confirm this; 'for bastardy' or 'for fornication' could be interchangeable. Most of those found guilty of fornication were unmarried and pregnant. To conflate bastardy and fornication cases for graphic purposes is to follow contemporary practice.

The comparatively few prosecutions in the early 1650s reflect the magisterial reticence described in Chapter Two. The 1650 act applied from 24 June and must have been welcome because from late 1651 the number of prosecutions brought under it never fell below double figures until it lapsed. By 1653 sexual offences comprised thirteen per cent of the total; by 1655 over thirty per cent. During 1655 and 1656 the institutions of local government were shaken. Disbrowe returned with commissioners. The jury was overhauled. Civil and clerical 'Triers' were instituted and the moderately presbyterian 'Devon Association' was established. But the fifty-six cases dealt with in 1655 did not usher in a godly golden age. The pace of reform faltered the following year and when it recovered it was easily dwarfed by the volume of other prosecutions. 1655 was a freakish exception to the pattern of a steady increase in fornication and bastardy prosecutions through the decade to 1659. The volume was maintained during 1659 itself, a year of 'appalling political chaos' or of 'the collapse of order', but the Restoration was disastrous for those who had viewed fornication as a crime, not a moral lapse, and bastardy as an indictable offence rather than as a problem for the parish.[128]

What impact did Disbrowe exercise on the drive against fornication in 1655? At the end of the Epiphany sessions of that year, thirteen were in houses of correction for fornication, including seven from an earlier commital. There were no new convictions at the Easter meeting. In the summer, however, reformation was pursued with a startling vigour. Two men were gaoled as fathers of bastards, for not fulfilling previous court orders, a woman was gaoled as a bastard-bearer, and twenty-two people (only one of whom was male) were imprisoned for fornication. At

Michaelmas only another twelve were prosecuted, so the key to the 1655 peak lies in the summer sessions, which had opened on 12 July. By that time the Penruddock trials had been concluded and Disbrowe was executing Council of State directives on the militia. By mid-June the difficulties attending this work had made Disbrowe 'weary' of Devonshire.[129] The midsummer sessions should thus be set in a context of heavy policing in the county and of military intervention. When Disbrowe, Hatsell and Blackmore turned up at Exeter Castle on 10 July they presided over a selection of cases chosen partly to convince them of the loyalty of the Devon Bench. Among the other cases treated on that occasion were the first two prosecutions of Quakers in Devon and a case of contemptuous words spoken of the Lord Protector.[130]

Yet if Disbrowe was hailed as a peripatetic Solomon it is possible that his presence tempered the rigours of the law. On this occasion the twenty-two fornicators were gaoled briefly for the duration of the sessions. 'Committed for fornication—now bailed' is the calendar entry, and it is unlikely that it refers to a previous sentence since earlier totals of offences are low. The Quakers got off lightly, too, each with a £5 fine after repudiating the authority of the court. The man who spoke disparagingly of Cromwell was fined the same. These sentences were not typical. At the Easter sessions a common barrator, or slanderer, was fined £100 and a prisoner who had the previous year spoken ill of the Protector was languishing in prison unable to pay a £500 fine. It seems unlikely that JPs would bring in a large number of fornication cases to sessions and then dismiss them with sentences lighter than those prescribed in legislation. Their unusual action surely has something to do with Disbrowe's unusual presence.

Central government had no general policy to restrain the merciless diligence of its local supporters, however; indeed there was no lack of legislative support for those determined to impose Puritan ethics on the community by force. By attaching the death sentence to adultery and making it an offence determinable at quarter sessions, the Rump act offered local governors the power to reverse a trend, long-discernible at sessions, towards binding over capital felonies to assizes.[131] But was adultery prosecuted, in fact, by the Devon magistrates?

F.A. Inderwick's study of the administration of the 1650 act was published as long ago as 1891[132] but is of particular relevance here because his enquiry was based on West Country sources. He noted few adultery cases. An adultress whose offence was committed 'with a priest' was convicted at Taunton in 1650. There was a case at Exeter City sessions and three others at Devon assizes in 1654, 1655 and 1660. For none of these cases is the sentence recorded. These isolated examples may be augmented. At the Easter sessions of 1651 a man was gaoled for adultery and at Michaelmas 1655 another was imprisoned on suspicion of the offence. A series of separate gaol calendars in the sessions rolls mention a couple remaining in prison awaiting trial for incest in 1652, and in 1655 and 1656 Thomas Saunders committed a further three people for adultery. Incest was a capital offence under the 1650 act; brothel-keepers, two of which were imprisoned by Rowland Whiddon (brother-in-law of sheriff John Coplestone) were punished by whipping, branding and three years in a house of correction. Recidivists were hanged.

These calendars were compiled by the keeper of the common gaol and conflated assize and quarter sessions cases but the pattern of punishment indicates that fornication was treated as a misdemeanour at sessions and the less frequent offences of adultery, incest and brothel-keeping were regarded as felonies to be referred to assizes. The 1650 act was quickly assimilated into an established judicial pattern. Except in an oblique reference during the Easter quarter sessions of 1654 to the execution of a woman at the previous assizes for adultery there is no proof, because of the paucity of evidence relating to assize cases, that adulterers were executed. It is not possible to aver that death was not the fate of adulterers; only that when on rare occasions adultery cases were judged in sessions lesser punishments were usually meted.

To discover more about sexual offenders and their backgrounds it is necessary to resort to the examinations of suspects undertaken in the parishes by the JPs. Copies were delivered to quarter sessions to form the basis of prosecution. Over 250 examinations of cases in which fornication was an element have survived; only twenty-five to thirty were of men. The typical male examinee vehemently denied the charges brought against him, however improbable the denial. Before the Easter sessions of 1656 Edmund Arscot, JP, examined a couple from the West Devon parish of Germansweek whose child had been born only four months of their marriage. The wife confessed to fornication, the husband denied it. No more details are given—it could be that the husband felt aggrieved enough to bring the prosecution—fornication and bastardy examinations tended to follow a fixed pattern, just as magistrates tended to follow a routine in their inquiries. In most instances denial was easily made and could not be gainsaid. The Plymouth merchant, Philip Francis, questioned a Plymstock man in January 1657 about an alleged sexual encounter a year before; the man denied it and with no more evidence the case expired. To be prosecuted successfully most fornication and bastardy cases depended on confessions, since such a private offence was rarely reliably witnessed by third parties. Complex personal relationships lay behind statements to magistrates. At Easter 1654, Robert Duke of Otterton examined a Newton Poppleford couple. The woman confessed to fornication but in mitigation claimed that she had been promised marriage by her partner. He vehemently denied everything but did insist that he had been long pestered by the woman in question and implied that her infatuation for him lay behind the charge.[133]

Confessions from men were rare. Henry Hatsell, a major-general's commissioner, secured a confession in the summer of 1655 from a Plymstock man who admitted both fornication and responsibility for a pregnancy. Hatsell's achievement may not have been unconnected with an aggressive campaign by the commissioners against moral laxity. More commonly the absence of corroborating evidence prompted denials, and the 1650 act, so savage in its scale of penalties, reflected the concern of its drafters that there should be legal safeguards against abuse by the sexually jealous or otherwise mischievous: 'No parties confession shall be taken as evidence within this act against any other but only against such party so confessing'. For the pregnant woman, deserted by her partner in the face of retributive magistratic enquiry, even her naming the father of her unborn child had no legal status as evidence.[134]

The stage of pregnancy at which female suspects came before the justices could be significant. It might offer some insight into whether there was an organised campaign against the unmarried sexually active or whether premarital pregnancies were ignored until physical appearances made delay impossible for those whose diligence was being monitored by central government. In some fifty-eight cases the stage of pregnancy at which accused women were examined is beyond reasonable doubt. Women were invariably asked when sexual intercourse first took place, and on how many occasions thereafter, so it is possible to estimate a maximum length of pregnancy, provided that the testimony of examinees is accepted as accurate.[135] Most confessions thus obtained were given when the women were six months with child, according to their own statements, suggesting that many women were examined when their pregnancy was all too visible and when they could hardly deny their condition. If an extra-marital pregnancy could not be concealed there would be little purpose in distorting the circumstances of a sexual relationship which caused it, except in the forlorn hope that judgment would be less severe on fornication which rested on a brief encounter rather than on a regular liaison.

The number of examinations at later stages of child-carrying decreases steadily after the total of twenty examined at six months. There were eight cases at seven months, five at eight and four during the terminal month. In fact the second largest group of examinations occurred when suspects were, on their own confessions, three months pregnant. The number of cases at four and five months together come to a total of nine, the number at three months. At three months of pregnancy the condition is becoming apparent, certainly to the expectant mother, and frequently to others. In short, it seems that pregnancy came to the attention of magistrates at fairly climacteric times during its course; when it was first detectable to the women concerned and to their immediate family or 'extended family' circle, and again when it was becoming clearly and publicly visible to a wider social group.

Nevertheless there were exceptions to the pattern of apprehension of illicitly pregnant women at later months in their conceptions. An Awliscombe woman claimed before the zealous Interregnum careerist magistrate, John Tyrling, of that parish, that she was pregnant and that she had first had sex six weeks before.[136] Before the summer and Michaelmas sessions of 1660, John Champneys and John Wollocombe, two of the most vigorous hounders of fornicators and bastard-bearers that the Interregnum had produced, were examining the last cases, in view of discussions then proceeding in the Convention Parliament, which could be prosecuted under the 1650 act. Wollocombe remained in commission until his death in 1663 but Champneys was dismissed in 1661. Both probably felt, with Thomas Larkham, that the events of the Restoration were a 'blasphemy against the gospel', and both made no concessions to political change in London; they continued to act out of sessions energetically and unfalteringly. Wollacombe examined a woman from Lapford in mid-Devon and Champneys a north-Devonian woman from Combe Martin—their cases were heard in a separate sessions, it should be noted—who both claimed to be twelve days pregnant.[137] They were examined as likely producers of bastards, not simply as fornicators, but a bastardy case could hardly be successfully prosecuted at such an early stage. The answer is that local JPs realised that the 1650 act, like all Interregnum legislation, was open to question at the King's return. Champneys and Wollocombe were sure that an offence had been committed but were uncertain whether the 1650 legislation any longer supported their actions. A confession of pregnancy would ensure a prosecution based, without fear of contradiction, on Elizabethan and Jacobean law. Ironically, the confused state of high politics forced JPs to be more precise than they had been when old and new legislation ran parallel, in making clear upon which statutes their action was founded.

There were prosecutions after base children had been born: on average about three in each sessions between 1649 and 1660. Post-natal questioning accorded with the spirit of earlier legislation: parish liability for keeping an illegitimate child was the criterion of action. (The high infant mortality rate and the possibility that parental circumstances could alter during pregnancy suggested that in examining women at early stages of child-carrying the justices were adhering to different criteria.) The 1650 act made no mention of bastardy *per se*. Although bastards had to be provided for nonetheless, there was a streak of vindictive zeal running through the pragmatism of the 1650s. At Easter 1654, William Putt, another diligent JP, a merchant and an opponent of alehousekeeping, examined an Ottery St Mary couple whose only offence was to have had a child less than nine months after marriage. In January 1656 Christopher Savery, a jury reformer, interviewed a Revelstoke married woman whose husband she declared not to be the father of her child. John Blackmore, career soldier and Cromwellian knight, inquired into the circumstances by which a Stokeinteignhead wife had a child three months *before* her marriage, at Easter 1657. Before the Easter sessions of 1653, Thomas Reynell, a young barrister, examined two married women, one from Dawlish, the other from Newton Abbot. One had allegedly had sexual intercourse six months before marriage, the other had been delivered of a child four months after her wedding. Such people were hardly guilty of 'abominable and crying sins' in the sense of persistent crime conveyed by the 1650 act. The absence of supplementary testimonies from hostile witnesses suggests that they were not the victims of the elders, or other inhabitants, of their parishes.[138]

Confessions were a means of evading the jury system. A confessor would be indicted on a true bill, and her case could proceed immediately to judgement. A bundle of ninety-six true bills, almost all the fornication cases recorded from 1655 to 1660, has survived.[139] Only about half of these cases proceeded to trial by jury, and the sympathy of juries towards the suspects is evident. Three were judged guilty, twenty-seven were acquitted. Two cases of adultery were acquitted, and two were traversed: postponed or sent to assizes. With only a ten per cent success rate at trial, and with what may have been a jury reluctance to deal with adultery cases at all, the 'reformation of manners' in this aspect, at least, could not be said to have been endorsed by the yeomanry which comprised the sessions petty jury. There is very little evidence for grand jury interest. At Easter 1659 two Sidmouth people were presented as 'lewd and scandalous liveing people' but the postscript 'see the ministers presentment heere annexed' makes it clear where the initiative lay on that occasion.[140]

Those who made up the sub-structure of government played little or no part in the prosecution of sexual offences. Some insight into parochial perceptions of wayward behaviour may be gained by considering the cases where third parties did offer evidence. In 1637, John Quick of Newton St Cyres heard the evidence of two ostlers who claimed to have witnessed fornication at a Topsham lodgings-house. An Ashton servant described how a man lay with three girls in the same bed but neither she nor a fellow-servant could admit that they had seen any improper behaviour. At Newton Abbot the landlady of a lodgings-house watched over Nicholas Hayes, who was apparently ill. At 11.00 p.m. a serving-girl came into the room and while Mrs. Webber was out, got into bed with the 'sick' man. In the morning Mrs. Webber went to report the couple for fornication. Under examination, however, she had to admit first, that she had been in the room with them until five in the morning, and then that she had not actually witnessed any sexual activity.[141] A powerful element of personal, sexual jealousy could be inflamed by the mutual antagonisms of communal, but not family, life. Jealousies could be probed and found to be the tap-root of false testimony. In January 1656 John Searle questioned two women in connection with rumours of fornication at an Ottery St Mary lodgings-house. Something about their evidence failed to convince Searle, even though he was an aggressive persecutor of royalists and of scandalous ministers. He summoned Justinian Harris and Richard Hull, the constables, who told him that the chief informant had actually denied her own allegations to them. All she had seen, apparently, was a woman's 'naked thigh'. The informant's next-door-neighbour gave a garbled account of how the woman lived next to him 'in the tyme of the troubles, and ... hath had a bastard, that in the tyme of the troubles there was very base order, a notorious whore living then there who is now rotting of the pox'. For all of them, the woman's allegations were merely the regrettable reminder of a time in the recent past when law and order in Ottery left much to be desired. They were more interested in preserving social harmony than in allegations of sexual misconduct.[142]

Testimonies could be tainted by revenge and by malicious snooping. A Bittadon woman alleged she heard another woman declare that a third woman was pregnant; an East Down man led a constable to a barn where they discovered a couple *in flagrante delicto* even though, on his own evidence, before he ran for the constable, they were merely strolling through the village. Class tensions lurked in some instances. A Yealmpton husbandman swore that he saw the village schoolmaster and his servant copulating in the window of his house. John Heywood of Chittlehampton, a servant to Colonel John Rolle, a presbyterian JP, confused marital with professional responsibilities when alleging that he had been cuckolded by one who, in his view, compounded the offence by abusing his master.[143]

It is not possible to separate fully the motives of informers. A rare example of genuine outrage against a sin is to be found in an examination from 1666, after the 1650 act had lapsed, and outrage mingles 'Puritan' mores with social tensions and the wilful pursuit of those suspected to have broken social convention. In the middle of October, 1666, Katherine Haydon, the wife of a Crediton labourer, was standing on her doorstep when Symion Ballamy, a man she recognized as a Drewsteignton yeoman, rode up to the house next door and, without dismounting, kissed and spoke affectionately to Mary Frost, who had run out to greet him. Mrs Haydon heard them agree to meet in a fortnight's time outside Crediton, 'in order', as she put it, 'to the satisfaction of their beastly lusts'. Mrs Haydon managed to keep her own counsel until her husband, Augustine, returned that evening. He said nothing until the fortnight elapsed and then he asked James Langaman, the husbandman for whom he worked, to go with him to the furse brake where the couple were to meet, 'to see what the effect would bee'. On the fateful day Langaman and Haydon concealed themselves in the furse brake and waited. After a while the couple appeared, embraced, and then, in Haydon's words:

> stept backe in the edge of the brake out of sight of this informant but nearer to ... Langaman who stood heard by in the hedge and came nearer to see the issue and further upon his oath constantly affirmeth that he found the said Mary layeing upon her back with her coates up to her midle and the said Symion layeing upon her body with his breeches aboute his heeles with his foot against a furse stub ... thereupon the ... spoke to the said Symion asking him whether an old man with one foot in the grave might not be ashamed of such wickednesse and thereuppon the said Symion being astonished suddenly turned off her body soe as he, this informant saw both there wickidnesse and saw his virile member come out of the body of the said Mary in a most bestiall and shamefull manner and further said that the said Symion did proffer to give them ... twenty shillings to conceale his wickidnesse.[144]

The examining magistrate was no adherent to the 1650 act; Francis Fulford, of a county family from Dunsford, had come afresh to government in 1661 without experience of war, sequestration or of the Interregnum bench. Whether the language of the deposition was that of the witnesses or of Fulford or his clerk, it is apparent that 'Puritan' perceptions were not confined to the 1650s. But were there any magistrates who specialised in these offences, who returned a particularly high number of examinations to sessions? In many cases diligence in this kind of prosecution was matched by conscientious attendance at quarter sessions. Thomas Reynell, who came to three-quarters of all meetings between 1649 and 1660, examined twenty fornicators. William Putt attended all but three meetings between 1652 and 1660 and inquired into ten such incidents. John Champneys came to nineteen sessions and examined sixteen cases. Christopher Wood came to twelve and examined thirteen. The evidence of crude numbers indicates that JPs were more likely to attend a sessions meeting than they were to examine a sexual case. The champion specialist was John Wollocombe, who went to a dozen meetings but examined thirty-one cases. Wollocombe was typical of the supporters of the 1650 act; he was a presbyterian of the second rank of county gentry. Unlike most of them (Reynell was the other exception) Wollocombe survived in the commission of the peace in 1660.

In Essex and Lancashire the JPs were supported by a clerical ministry of 'unprecedented size and quality';[145] the reformation of manners was to be enforced by proselytization as well as by social control. Keith Thomas has shown how the 1650 act was the expression of a durable strand of opinion at Westminster. There was a strong tradition of moral severity in Exeter. John Hooker, of the late fifteenth century, had found a spiritual heir in Ignatius Jourdain, the scourge of the unrighteous and the friend of the poor in Exeter before the civil war. Jourdain's hagiographer, Ferdinando Nicholls, was himself rector of St Mary Arches parish, Exeter, from 1631 until 1662, and supported Jourdain's moral crusade without question. Nicholls was typical of the Devon presbyterian clergy.[146]

The parishes where large numbers of examinations were conducted have been compared with the lists of clergy ejected in 1662 in order to discover any possible link between Puritanism and severe treatment of fornicators.[147] No pattern emerges and more examinations were likely to be held in parishes where there were more people rather than where there were Puritan clergy.[148] There were six cases in Ashburton where the moderate Joshua Bowden was incumbent, and five in Tavistock, whose vicar, Thomas Larkham, was more 'antinomian' in his conduct than 'Puritan'. The influence of godly ministers on magistrates was more subtle and more intellectual than practical.

After 1660 the patterns of examinations remained much as before with most cases involving confessions of pregnancy. There were also confessions of fornication without pregnancy and the gamut of allegations of sexual misbehaviour, including some adultery cases.[149] But after the Restoration sentences to the common gaol were no longer permissible.[150] The gaol calendar entries demonstrate this change. In the sixteen-fifties the JPs could despatch convicts to the house of correction (for bastardy) or to the common gaol (for offences under the 1650 act). There was less scope for choice after 1660. In January 1656 Robert Duke questioned a pregnant Sidmouth woman. On the examination sent to the court, Henry Fitzwilliam, deputy clerk of the peace, wrote: 'Mr Dukes clerk informs that his master will send her to Bridewell therefore no bill [of indictment] to be drawne'.[151] She went directly to the house of correction at St Thomas without even appearing in court. This procedure had remained open to JPs throughout the 1650s, even though law reformers disapproved.[152]

With an average number of twenty to thirty each year gaoled under the 1650 act it may seem surprising that magistrates preferred a more public course of action, however more laborious, to swift and summary despatch to bridewell. The preference for public action accords well with seventeenth-century notions of social control; godliness had to be seen to be preferred.[153] Collective action also created a spirit of unity among Devon magistrates which doubtless helped to preserve a measure of unanimity during a time of rapid political change. In the early 1650s collective justice mirrored insecurity. The lapse of the 1650 act contributed to the development of extra-sessional justice by reverting the treatment of offenders to the justices singly or in pairs, a reversion which accorded well with the general drift towards petty sessions government.

Forty-four Devon justices examined two hundred and fifty-five cases between 1649 and 1660, and the same number inquired into one hundred and forty-two cases between 1661 and 1670. Because of deficiencies in the Interregnum record, the estimate for the 1650s is a minimum; the Restoration bench examined only fifty-five to fifty-seven per cent of the Interregnum caseload and this estimate is a maximum.

After 1660 no JPs were specialists. Sir John Davy, Sir John Chichester, baronets, and William Bogan were the most zealous persecutors; each had eleven or twelve cases to his credit. Davy was a presbyterian, Bogan an Anglican and Chichester was certainly a royalist.[154] Only service on the Bench was a common characteristic among them. The two most implacable Puritan prosecutors of the Fifties, Wollocombe and Reynell, failed to maintain an interest in these offences. Wollocombe's total after 1660 was two, Reynell's one. At lesser levels William Fry (nine cases 1649 to 1660, four cases 1661 to 1670) and Robert Duke (four cases 1649 to 1660, five 1661 to 1670) maintained some continuity in performance. For Wollocombe and Reynell a moral code had been the outward sign of a political commitment; the Restoration made enforcement of this code no longer practicable since conspicuous zeal in this area would have singled them out as unrepentant partisans of a disgraced regime. The confidence of their erstwhile preoccupations was irrevocably lost and their energies were diverted elsewhere rather than into an effort to adapt their moral vision to the prevailing legislative order.

To summarise briefly. The 1650 act offered magistrates a more public method of dealing with sexual offences than had early Stuart legislation. During the ten year life of the act prosecutions brought under it proceeded in much the same way as they had done under older laws, until they reached open court, and even then the old legislation continued while the act was in force, and outlived it. Most cases in the 1650s and 1660s involved confessing pregnant women and comparatively rarely was evidence reliably wrung from third parties. Bastardy was never clearly distinguished from fornication. There was no general campaign against the unmarried sexually active although one or two Puritan JPs may be considered specialists. The magistrates took notice of the visibly pregnant whose plight was common knowledge. There is no evidence to suggest any interest in the enforcement of sexual morality among those who formed the sub-structure of county government, nor can the influence of clergymen be regarded as decisive. In the 1650s the JPs acted diligently in the public mode of quarter sessions rather than in the less laborious, more private realms of petty sessions and personal initiative; a preference which was partly an aspect of the reformation of manners but partly a reflection of a lack of confidence among the Interregnum justices. The distinction between action at sessions and outside it accounts for the reduced sessions caseload after 1660 and is probably a more decisive difference between the Fifties and Sixties than the influence of the 1650 act. Legislation aimed at intruding into semi-autonomous local communities was assimilated into patterns of local development, was swallowed up by local administrative procedures which proved hardier than centralist *ukase*.

NOTES

1. P.27 above; Stephens: *Clerks of the Counties*, pp. 77-79; DQSOB Epiphany 1670. Raddon's career is traced in my note in *BIHR* 1980.
2. T.G. Barnes: *The Clerk of the Peace in Caroline Somerset*, pp. 5, 23, 28.
3. Vivian, pp. 500, 662; *TDA*, LXVI, pp. 260-61, XLII, p. 266. The local office-holding Russells of the 1660s were Col. John Russell (?1618-?1687) and William Russell, third son of the fifth earl, who was executed for his part in the Rye House Plot (*DNB*). Some Inglett wills may be found in West Country Studies Library, Exeter: Moger Abstracts XII, p. 7901, Oswyn Murray collection XIX, 8/36.
4. DRO DD 55874; SP 28/128 (Devon) Pt. 1/24 v; SP 28/208 (list of sequestration agents); DQSOB Michaelmas 1662; DRO QS box of unsorted MSS marked 'feedback' (information from Mr M.G. Dickinson, to whom I am grateful).
5. DRO Chudleigh churchwardens' book PW1, pp. 609-11, 613-14, 646, 647, 680, 682, 685, 689, 693, 709, 713, 715, 721, 724. Inglett's son, Richard, was at Oxford when Bloy was recruited: Foster: *Alumni*.
6. DRO 48/13/2/2/7; Chudleigh churchwardens' a/cs PW3; *TDA*, XXXIII, p. 543.
7. Pp. 41, 81-82 above for this.
8. DQSOB 1660 to 1670 *passim* but esp. Michaelmas 1660, Epiphany 1662 (when he was county treasurer in all but name), Misummer 1663, Midsummer 1665, Epiphany 1669.
9. QS Order Book 1/7 (1633 to 1640): Easter 1635, Epiphany 1636, Easter 1639, Michaelmas 1639, Epiphany 1669.
10. W. Harding: *The History of Tiverton*, II, p. 209; Hoskins: *Exeter in the Seventeenth Century* (1957), pp. 65-66; BL Add. 11314 f 50; PRO PROB 11/398/5.
11. DRO QS Box 68 loose (letter dated 10 January, 1679).
12. QS Box 56: bundle Epiphany 1648-1649 (letter dated 6/1/1649).
13. *Ibid.* Box 63: bundle Epiphany 1659-1660 (undated letter).
14. *Ibid.* Box 72: bundle Michaelmas 1667 (letter dated 9/7/67).
15. *Ibid.* Box 69: bundle Easter 1664 (note dated 15/1/64).
16. *Ibid.* Box 58: bundle Michaelmas 1651 (letter dated 29/9/51).
17. B.L. Add. 11314 f 41; DRO DD 55952 for a similar bribe by Tregeare in 1665.
18. PRO E 215/1102, reproduced in Barnes: *Clerk of the Peace*, p. 39, because Vaughan's list 'differs little from those extant from other counties'; J.S. Cockburn: 'Seventeenth Century Clerks of Assize—Some Anonymous Members of the Legal Profession', *American Journal of Legal History*, XIII (1969), p. 319.
19. *Clerk of the Peace*, p.40.
20. DQSOB Midsummer 1658, Epiphany 1664, Easter 1665. In 1663 new fees were agreed: DQSOB Epiphany 1663.
21. DRO Q/RTR Hearth Tax 1/6; PRO E 179/102/534; Hoskins: *Exeter in the Seventeenth Century*, pp. 65-66.
22. Perryman's nine-hearthed house in Plympton put him around the level of minor gentlemen, including the clerks of the court.

23. SRO DD/WO Box 53 (loose).
24. BL Add. 11314 f 41; DRO QS Box 68 (loose); Box 56 Epiphany 1648-1649 (presentments and petitions); Box 58 Michaelmas 1651; DD 56171.
25. DRO Consistory Court of the Bishop of Exeter, Deposition Book 869 (unpaginated).
26. BL Add. 11314 ff 7-11; Vivian, p. 136, *Cornwall*, p. 438; W.G.W. Watson: *The House of Martin* (1906), p. 128.
27. Prince: *Worthies*, pp. 576-79; Underdown: *Pride's Purge*, Appendix.
28. PRO C 220/9/4, C 193/12/3. The occupiers of Netherexe Barton paid a quarter of the parish poor rates: C 108/93/2.
29. DQSOB marginalia; will proved Principal Registry, Bishop of Exeter 1662 (Fry: *Calendar*).
30. BL Add. 11314 ff 31, 35.
31. DRO DD 56787; PRO C 108/93/4 (letter of 11/10/62, Thomas Mapowder to Cole); Add. 11314 f 62.
32. DD 55999, 56012; Kenyon: *Stuart Constitution*, pp. 503-05.
33. DD 55848. John Barton's will: PROB 11/304/66. Evidence of his appointment as recorder of Bradninch is in QS Box 58/Michaelmas 1651 recognizances.
34. DD 56580 v.
35. PRO C 108/93/3,7.
36. Aylmer: *State's Servants*, p. 29 and note 18; Coate: *Cornwall*, p. 222.
37. DD 56311, 56577, 56775.
38. *Ibid.* 56100, 56309; Add. 11314 f 48.
39. Add. 11314 f 43; DD 55978, 55889.
40. DD 56394; *Statutes of the Realm*, V, p. 846: 'An Act for taking ... Affidavits'.
41. C 108/93/5, DD 55978; E 179/245/17/12; Margaret Spufford: *Contrasting Communities*, pp. 39-40; idem: 'The Significance of the Cambridge Hearth Tax', *Proceedings, Cambridge Antiquarian Soc.*, LV (1962), p. 56.
42. Barnes: *Clerk of the Peace*, p. 24. In 1660 Cole write to the deputy clerks concerning a man bound by recognizance for bastardy. He was found innocent and Cole requested his discharge, 'payinge his fees, to be cleerd'. QS Box 64/Michaelmas 1660 (undated letter).
43. DQSOB Epiphany 1665, Easter 1668.
44. DD 56429. Five clerks, including Cole, signed the agreement.
45. Barnes, *op. cit.*, pp. 32-33. The Webbs considered the clerks ineffective: *The Parish and the County*, pp. 348-49.
46. Concern for justice thinly disguised self-interest in a 1667 petition by the clerks of the peace to the Privy Council that some recognizances were not being returned to sessions. (The more recognizances filed, the greater the fees.) PRO PC 2/59/317.
47. There is a reference to 'privie sessions' (presumably at Honiton) in Kilmington churchwardens' a/cs in 1626: DRO Kilmington PW 2. (I am grateful to Mr T.J. Falla for this reference); Hamilton: *Quarter Sessions*, pp. 50-51, 67-71.
48. Silcock: 'County Government in Worcestershire', p. 105.
49. SRO DD/WO Box 57 (Mallock): John Mallock to John Willoughby, 1650: 'I have promised my uncle to meet him Satterday at Honyton where meete foure justices'. Cf. Holsworthy in 1651: DQSOB Michaelmas 1651.
50. Bodl. MS J. Walker c 4 f 181; Chanter: *Life and Times of Martin Blake*.
51. *West Answering to the North*, p. 90.
52. PRO ASSI 24/21,22.
53. Cockburn: *A History of English Assizes*, pp. 186-87; ASSI 24/22/96.
54. PRO PC 2/55/52; S.K. Roberts: 'Alehouses and Government under the Early Stuarts', *Southern History*, II (1980) *op. cit.*
55. PC 2/55/146, 17, 38; PC 2/56/241, 409; Joan Thirsk: 'New Crops and their diffusion' in C.W. Chalklin, M.A. Havinden (eds.): *Rural Change and Urban Growth 1500-1800*, pp. 94, 95.
56. PC 2/55/523, 56/520. Hoskins: 'Harvest Fluctuations and English Economic History', *Agric. Hist. Rev.*, XVI (1968), pp. 21, 29.
57. PC 2/55/63, 340, 530, 2/56/53-58, 498-99, 2/59/438, 442, 447, 471.
58. E.R. Turner: *The Privy Council in the Seventeenth and Eighteenth Centuries* (1927-1928,

2 vols.), I, pp. 380-81, 410; Jones: *The Restored Monarchy*, p. 12, Tomlinson: 'Financial and Administrative Developments', in ibid, 105-10; Ogg: *England in the Reign of Charles II*, pp. 190-91.

59. And in notes by hundred constables that presentments had been made to petty sessions.
60. DRO DD 55770-56831.
61. DD 56408, 56491, 56607, 55988, 56183.
62. DD 55948. This was as early as 1663.
63. The emphasis in these had been the acknowledgment by JPs that they had *supervised* the constables: SP 16.
64. DD 55653, 55847.
65. DD 56183.
66. DD 55990, 56006.
67. Vivian, pp. 60, 94, 663, 769; *CCC*, p. 1391; *DCNQ*, XXII, p. 48, XXI, p. 284; Charlotte Walrond: *The Walrond Papers* (1913), p. 42.
68. *CCC*, pp. 1517, 1689; *CCAM*, pp. 668, 1103, 1127, 1371, 1412-13.
69. QS Box 74/Midsummer 1669, petition May 1669; DQSOB Michaelmas 1669, *CCC*, p. 1237, *CCAM*, pp. 641, 720; *TDA*, LXXII, p. 262; PROB 11/324/17, 326/22; E 377/63/11; *West Answering to North*; F & R II.
70. Morrill: *Cheshire 1630-1660*, pp. 230, 239; *idem: Cheshire Grand Jury*, pp. 36-37; S.K. Roberts: 'Alehouses and Government', (Exeter MA), pp. 74-76 and sources cited there.
71. *Thurloe State Papers*, IV, p. 451; for the later seventeenth century see C. Brooks: 'Taxation, Finance and Public Opinion 1688-1714' (Cambridge PhD, 1972), Chapter 5.
72. QS Box 60/Michaelmas 1655, undated petition.
73. Central government may have tolerated alehouses for revenue, but defaulters in excise payments were fined heavily. In 1663 Devon quarter sessions arbitrated in a dispute over a Tormohun aleseller's fine of £18.5s. The JPs reduced it to forty-five shillings, perhaps with the alehouse as poor relief in mind: DQSOB Midsummer 1663 (cf. *ibid.* Midsummer 1662).
74. DD 56696.
75. *Ibid.* 55950, 55978, 55979, 55986, 55994, 56355, 56803. In 1666 quarter sessions advised JPs in Exmouth to 'have respect unto the certificate of the minsters and officers of the said parishes in licensing persons to sell beer', DQSOB Epiphany 1666.
76. DD 55962.
77. Morrill: *Cheshire Grand Jury*, pp. 5, 45-47.
78. DQSOB, Easter 1661, Midsummer 1661, Midsummer 1663, Michaelmas 1663, Epiphany 1662.
79. *Ibid.* Epiphany, Michaelmas 1661.
80. *Ibid.* Epiphany 1623.
81. PRO ASSI 24/19/1/1.
82. DQSOB Epiphany 1662. The county treasurers deserve more attention. They were minor gentlemen but were not chosen because of earlier service as constables or jurors. Many had not served at all outside their parishes. Order Book marginalia indicate that they were selected by the JPs because they were *personally* reliable.
83. Morrill: *Revolt of the Provinces*, p. 118; pp. 38-39, 66-68 above.
84. Alexander Hamilton's comment on the public behaviour of warring states may be appropriate; to recover superiority the lesser will 'quickly resort to means similar to those by which it had been effected, to reinstate themselves in their lost pre-eminence'. *The Federalist*, essay 8 (Dent ed., 1911), p. 33. I am grateful to Dr. Colin Brooks for suggesting this source.
85. E.g. p. 57 above. In 1662 William Jennings, mayor of Plymouth, defaced the Plymouth Black Book, the 'official history' of the town, in a blatant attempt to alter the record of the opening of the new church there in 1657. The 1657 chronicler had remarked on 'some disturbance by a paltry pretended churchwarden'—Jennings. W. Devon R.O., Plymouth Black Book f 15 v.
86. Sidney and Beatrice Webb: *English Local Government: English Poor Law History Part I: The Old Poor Law* (1927), p. 98; E.M. Leonard: *The Early History of English Poor Relief* (1900), p. 277; J.S. Morrill: *Cheshire 1630-1660*, Chapter 6, esp. pp. 247-52; A.L. Beier: 'Poor Relief in Warwickshire 1630-1660', *Past and Present*, XXXV (1966), pp. 77-100.

87. Best expressed in the preambles to Tudor and early Stuart legislation. The purpose in providing a county stock was in 18 Elizabeth c. 3 declared to be that young people should be used to work, that rogues should have no excuse for idleness and that those willing to work should have the opportunity: J.R. Tanner: *Tudor Constitutional Documents* (1922), p. 482.
88. George Oliver: *Ecclesiastical Antiquities*, I, p. 202; *TDA*, C, p. 67.
89. Although Professor Pearl has demonstrated how in Interregnum London, bridewells and workhouses were separate institutions: D. Pennington and K. Thomas (eds.): *Puritans and Revolutionaries: Essays in Seventeenth Century History*, pp. 206-32.
90. S. and B. Webb: *English Prisons Under Local Government* (1922), p. 14.
91. DQSOB *passim* but e.g. Easter 1652, Midsummer 1661; C. Hill: *Society and Puritanism in Pre-Revolutionary England* (1969 ed.), p. 261; Kenyon: *Stuart Constitution*, p. 501. Presumably felons were meant to pay the fees of the poor.
92. DQSOB 1/7 (1633-1640) Michaelmas 1637—a direct response to 'printed orders'; *ibid*. Easter 1635, Epiphany 1636, Midsummer 1639, Michaelmas 1639, Epiphany 1640.
93. *Ibid*. Michaelmas 1651, Epiphany 1649, Michaelmas 1657, Michaelmas 1650, Easter 1658, Easter 1649, Epiphany 1655; *ibid*. Midsummer 1650; QS Box 57 bundle Easter 1651: 'Charges about St. Thomas house of correction'.
94. CRO Vivian MSS 22M/BO/33/20; *DCNQ*, XVIII, p. 343.
95. DQSOB Michaelmas 1652, Michaelmas 1653, Epiphany 1654, Michaelmas 1654.
96. *Ibid*. Midsummer 1655, Epiphany 1656; *Thurloe State Papers*, IV, p. 413. (Disbrowe was *custos* from 1653).
97. DQSOB Epiphany 1655 (2 orders), Easter 1655.
98. *Ibid*. Easter 1652, Michaelmas 1655, Epiphany 1656, Easter 1658 (3 orders), Midsummer 1658, Michaelmas 1658, Epiphany 1659.
99. *Ibid*. Easter 1653. The sessions opened on 19 April but subsequent daily sittings are only rarely dated in the order books. They were usually never less than three days long.
100. Hoskins: *Devon*, p. 341; *Burton's Diary*, II, pp. 183-89; *C.J.*, VII, pp. 548-49; Hamilton: *Quarter Sessions*, pp. 215-17.
101. Lislebone Long's warning: 'I like not your meddling with your legislation in private men's estates' went unheeded: *Burton's Diary*, II, pp. 187-89.
102. *Ibid*. II, pp. 183-84; Psalm 39.
103. *Reports of the Commissioners ... concerning Charities and Education (Devon)*, Pt. 4, p. 68.
104. Sporadic attempts were made to control him by making him write up gaol calendars. S. and B. Webbs: *English Prisons*, pp. 4, 5 *et seq*.
105. DQSOB Epiphany 1662 for a retrospective payment to a baker; *ibid*. Midsummer 1665.
106. PROB 11/305/137. Thomas Drake was a cousin of Sir John Drake of Ash and should not be confused with the brother of Sir Francis Drake of Buckland.
107. Exeter Dean and Chapter MSS 6040/3, 4030; SRO DD/WO Box 19/3, 4.
108. DQSOB Epiphany 1655; F & R II, pp. 240-41, 321-24, 378-79, 582, 754-64, 860-61, 888-89, 897, 911-15, 943-45.
109. DQSOB Michaelmas 1657; ASSI 24/22/62 v.
110. DQSOB Michaelmas 1659, Easter 1661, Midsummer 1661, Michaelmas 1661; Epiphany 1661 for lists of maimed soldiers.
111. In 1667 another Chudleigh man whose house had been burnt down requested of the JPs 'a licence to collect some moneys in certaine places'. He was supported by thirty parishioners: QS Box 72/ Michaelmas 1667 Petitions.
112. DQSOB Michaelmas 1662; QS Box 73/Michaelmas 1668 Petitions; pp. 176-77 above.
113. DQSOB Easter 1663, Midsummer 1662, Epiphany 1662, Midsummer 1663.
114. *Ibid*. Easter 1663, Midsummer 1665.
115. *Ibid*. Easter 1666, Michaelmas 1667, Michaelmas 1665, Midsummer 1665, Michaelmas 1666, Easter 1667; J.C.A. Whetter: 'The Economic History of Cornwall in the Seventeenth Century' (London PhD, 1965), pp. 165-66. At Easter 1670 David Hart, another ex-governor, requested compensation for a 'settling house'.
116. DQSOB Midsummer, Michaelmas 1668. G. Oliver: *Ecclesiastical Antiquities*, I, p. 58. Reynolds had been appointed after his predecessor had been ejected in 1662, and one can only imagine what his relations were with Condy. The appointment of godly ministers at prisons had been an aim of Commonwealth law reformers: G.B. Nourse:

'Law Reform under the Commonwealth and Protectorate', *Law Quarterly Review*, LXXV (1959), p. 522.

117. The sale of fee farm rents eventually provided the wherewithal: Hamilton: *Quarter Sessions*, pp. 215-17.
118. DQSOB Easter 1669, Midsummer 1669 *et seq.* for St Thomas gaol calendars.
119. D.T. Witcombe: *Charles II and the Cavalier House of Commons 1663-74*, p. 181 (cf. W.C. Abbott: 'The Long Parliament of Charles II', *English Historical Review*, XXI (1906), p. 56).
120. DQSOB Epiphany 1670.
121. See P. Styles: 'The Evolution of the Law of Settlement', *Birmingham Historical Journal*, IX (1963-64), pp. 33-63. The great debate on the poor from 1660, which inspired grand juror and constable Richard Dunning to write *A Plain and Easy Method showing how the office of Overseer of the Poor may be managed* (1685), had no practical effect in Devon. See also Dunning's *Bread for the Poor* (1698).
122. K. Thomas: 'The Puritans and Adultery: The Act of 1650 re-considered' in Pennington and Thomas (eds.): *Puritans and Revolutionaries*, pp. 257-82; K. Wrightson: 'The Puritan Reformation of Manners' (thesis cit.).
123. F & R II, pp. 387-89.
124. DQSOB at the end of the entries for each sessions.
125. Wrightson, pp. 136-37, 142-45.
126. *Ibid.* pp. 143, 144, 146, 148. Wrightson omits prosecutions of bastardy from his tables; had they been included, his totals may have been higher. His point that aleselling offences could be dealt with by summary jurisdiction may explain their absence from the Devon sessions: *ibid.* pp. 163-67
127. 18 Elizabeth c. 3, 7 Jac. 1 c. 4, s. 7 (*Statutes of the Realm*, IV, Pt. 2); Dalton: *Countrey Justice* (1635 ed.), pp. 37-39.
128. J.P. Kenyon: *Stuart England* (1978), p. 178; A.H. Woolrych: 'Last Quests for a Settlement' in Aylmer (ed.): *The Interregnum*, p. 201; F & R III, pp. xxxi-xxxiii.
129. *CSPD 1655*, pp. 192, 241; SP 25/76/112; *Thurloe State Papers*, III, pp. 556-57.
130. Midsummer sessions preceded a proclamation of August 1655 enjoining 'speedy and due execution' of the 1650 act, a symptom of the government's conversion to intervention in local government: Thomas *op. cit.*, p. 279.
131. Barnes: *Somerset*, pp. 50-54; H.C. Johnson (ed.): *Minutes of Proceedings in [Wiltshire] sessions*, p. xiii; DQSOB gaol calendars (for the rarity of the death penalty).
132. F.A. Inderwick: *The Interregnum* (1891), pp. 34-39.
133. QS Box 61, bundle Easter 1656 examinations, bundle Epiphany 1657 examinations; Box 60, bundle Easter 1654 examinations.
134. Box 60, bundle summer 1655 examinations (*ibid.* for another example from Axminster, and cf. Box 64 bundle Michaelmas 1660 examinations); F & R II, p. 389.
135. When the time of the first recalled act of sexual intercourse is given as over nine months before the date of interrogation the case has been abandoned in these calculations.
136. QS Box 60 bundle Easter 1654 examinations.
137. B.L. Loan 29 f 50 v; QS Box 64, Midsummer and Michaelmas examinations, 1660.
138. Box 60 bundle Easter 1654 examinations, Epiphany 1656 examinations; Box 64 bundle Michaelmas 1660 examinations; Box 59 misplaced Easter 1657 examinations; Box 59 bundle Easter 1653 examinations.
139. QS Box 63, loose bundle of indictments 1653 to 1660.
140. Box 67, bundle Easter 1662: misplaced presentment of April 1659. Constables in Somerset did not interest themselves much in private morality: G.R. Quaife: *Wanton Wenches and Wayward Wives* (1979), p. 50, *et seq.*
141. Box 61 bundle Epiphany 1657 examinations; Box 62 bundle Midsummer 1658 examinations. Similar cases, all involving servants, can be found in the examinations for Midsummer 1652, 1653 (Box 59); Easter 1657 (misplaced), Michaelmas 1659 (Box 64).
142. QS Box 60 bundle Epiphany 1656 examinations.
143. QS Box 60 examinations in bundles Epiphany 1654, Epiphany 1656, Easter 1654; Box 59 bundle Midsummer 1652 examinations.
144. Box 71 bundle Epiphany 1667 examinations.
145. Wrightson: 'Reformation of Manners', pp. 225, 227, 261; Chapter 11 *passim*.

146. Thomas, *op. cit.*, pp. 266-69, 272-73, 276-78; Worden: *The Rump Parliament*, pp. 232-34; *TDA*, XXIX, pp. 350-77; Hoskins and Finberg: *Devonshire Studies*, p. 369; F. Nicolls: *The Life and Death of Ignatius Jourdain* (1654), pp. 44, 49, 73 77-80.
147. Information on ejections from Matthews: *Calamy Revised*, Calamy: *Nonconformists' Memorial* (Palmer, ed.); Calamy: *Continuation*.
148. E.g., Ashburton (six cases), Tavistock (five cases), Ottery St. Mary (five cases), Honiton (three cases). The general prevalence of examinations in sexual cases has to be squared with the demographic evidence to suggest an astonishing drop in the number of registered illegitimate births during the 1650s: P. Laslett, K. Oosterveen: 'Long Term Trends in Bastardy in England', *Population Studies*, XXVII (1973), pp. 255-86, esp. pp. 260, 268. More work needs to be done on parish registers as a source for parish attitudes and behaviour, but Quaife suggests a connection between low bastardy rates and high levels of pre-nuptial pregnancy: *Wanton Wenches*, pp. 247-48 and sources cited there.
149. In QS Box 70 bundle Midsummer 1665 examinations; Box 69 bundle Epiphany 1664 (x 2) examinations.
150. Except for males refusing to obey maintenance orders in cases of bastardy.
151. QS Box 60 bundle Epiphany 1656 examinations.
152. *CJ*, VII, p. 433; Thomas, *op. cit.*, pp. 279-80.
153. Cf. K. Wrightson, J. Walter: 'Dearth and the Social Order in Early Modern England', *Past and Present*, LXXI (1976), p. 41. The major-generals were keen to ensure public interest in what they did; James Berry was pleased that his rough treatment of some Monmouth alesellers 'made a great noise with us': *Thurloe State Papers*, IV, p. 545. Interest in market-places may be partly explained thus: *ibid* IV, pp. 278, 686.
154. *DCNQ*, XXI, p. 284 (Gowers: Exeter MA, 1970, p. 219 is a wrong identification: see Vivian, p. 272, DRO 1660 A/262-65 for Davy of Ruxford); Vivian, pp. 99, 174; *TDA*, LXXII, p. 262; PROB 11/365/16 (Bogan), 363/114 (Chichester); *CCAM*, p. 641.

Conclusion

The 'local government system' was not like William Paley's watch, a self-regulating mechanical contrivance set in motion by the unseen hand of a Tudor watchmaker. Like the 'county community', another suspect artefact, 'local administration' is something of a shorthand term that does not bear the closest scrutiny. In this study we have been concerned to demonstrate the relationships at local level which conditioned the performance of local administrative tasks and which shaped the pattern of participation. The relationship between participation and performance is rich and complex and cannot be understood simply by exploring the mechanics of government—even though it has been contended here that administrative change does have a momentum of its own.

Individual components of the 'system' were perceived differently by different external agencies. Thus the jury system, although cherished by legal pundits and Leveller polemicists, was harrassed by magistrates and central authority (if somewhat fitfully) and was reviled by the Diggers. To the yeomanry of Devon, if the pattern of involvement is a reliable guide, it no longer had much to offer and was certainly not seen as a first resort for political activists. The jury was not the mediator of class relations it once may have been but it was a useful indicator of the state of those relations: quiescent juries reflected the eclipse of the yeomanry. Reform drives marked in the 1650s the ascendancy of radical lawyers and administrators, in the 1660s the apotheosis of a newly-rampant landed royalism.

The sub-structure of government provided a degree of continuity in performance which changes in the commission of the peace and militia commissions have concealed. There was a definite, recognized hierarchy in the structure. Accountability, always a theoretical consideration, intruded more and more into the lives of constables and bailiffs. The amount of paper and parchment consumed by the administrative machine was increasing, and the importance of sound, thorough record-keeping was becoming generally appreciated. The weaknesses in the system were specific but profound. Particularly at its lower levels, seventeenth-century local government lacked definitions of aims and limits of power. Authority for action was not in dispute but the methods of enforcing that authority were. Most of the concern by justices of the peace at inadequate local revenues derived not from the refusal of ratepayers to pay but from failure by constables to hand over the sums collected and from their tendency to disappear into the hundreds and parishes, beyond official control. The growth of accounting procedures and the role of the petty jury as an Exeter-based *posse comitatus* compensated for this to some extent.

Local administrators under the Commonwealth strove against the inheritance of a county government machine which had, in the Forties, been squeezed by the demands of parishes on the one hand, and by Parliament on the other. Unrest in the parishes had been provoked by the natural disasters of plague and famine; an unprecedented level of military taxation was a further aggravation. Parliament was forced to Fabian slowness in meeting the failures of tax-collection: deadlock over paying the army its arrears ruled out reform. There was a delicate balance of interests between the Army and Parliament in which watchful eyes were kept on levels of tolerance shown by the public. Changes in the commission of the peace, the militia and assessment commissions were all undertaken in the context of national political change; even the abortive 1648 militia scheme, although it was aimed at county autonomy, would have been an act of centralization, a direct result of the disposition of parliamentary power. Factions froze and paralyzed reform; indifference smothered the demand by the Plymouth committee that all the well-affected should be invited to participate in county administration.

After 1649 there were more genuinely county initiatives, if fewer overt expressions of parochial grievances, than before. As Devonian strength at Westminster was enfeebled by Pride's Purge so there was less central restraint on local ways of making the system work in an inclusive concept of government. The commissions of the peace were no measure of commitment; real power was exercised by the militia officers and even by those outside central nomination. Local views on filling blank military commissions triumphed, and even aspects of policy which were genuinely centralizing ran into trouble. Sequestration reforms foundered between pressure from the centre and localism; officials could not convince Goldsmiths' Hall that the strengths of regional practice were adequate reasons for failure.

A flexible division of labour among the well-affected arose from the rarity of complete commitment in Devonshire. It was a feature peculiar to the late 1640s and the early years of the Rump. During the 1660s the commission of the peace resumed its role as an index of local support. A hierarchy of prestige and function in local officeholding was reconstructed, and flexibility, never more than an expedient, was abandoned.

From the mid-Fifties local opinions were forwarded with some force. Administrative confidence is itself a useful notion with which to test differing official responses in the period. As local assertiveness flourished faction again had to be accommodated if political settlement were to be secured. Parliament was one safety-valve, local committees were another. The unruly parliaments of the Protectorate were the expression of local tensions (submerged at home in county solidarity) as well as the battle-ground for a clash of political ideologies. After the disaster of the major-generals, relations between the counties and central government were poisoned. There was a sourness towards the Protectorate, whose declared intentions of healing and settling were so blatantly contradicted by a policy of literal adherence to Clause XXXVII of the Instrument of Government in order to protect Quakers. On a local view, settlement would have been achieved by total surrender to county pressures.

Tax commissions grew in size during the 1650s not simply as successive regimes sought to broaden their support, but also as a result of developing intra-county faction. The 1657 commission was not so much a return to normality as a means of defusing tension harmlessly by providing a focus for the aspirations of competing political groups. After 1660 faction was subdued in common recognition of the monarchy but there was no 'depoliticization', 'party politics' was replaced by the politics of social prestige, and assessment commissions became an overspill, a 'waiting list' for those whose county standing entitled them to a share in government.

The confidence of local government can be measured by the degree of administrative muscle-flexing practised by its representatives. In the mid-1650s control of the jury system seemed the key to political security, even though the presentments system had atrophied. Quarter sessions juries had abandoned the roles created for them by Tudor legislation, and the capacity of the Bench to control them became simply a test of strength with no other practical purpose. In the 1660s it was the turn of the constables to become the victims of the drive towards magisterial hegemony; although during this decade the test of strength produced tangible benefits in improved accounting procedures.

Turning from the general attributes of local government to the details of its performance, it has become apparent that more work needs to be done on the relations between quarter sessions and the parishes. The pursuit of fornicators in the 1650s attacked parochial preferences for harmony and minimising tension:[1] the act of settlement of 1662 elevated the parish to a significance in local government which had been continuously eroded since Elizabethan statutes on social policy. Was there a general shift in attitude towards parochial initiatives?

Sampling the parish records of Devon certainly confirms the findings of others that there was a full measure of popular participation in local institutions.[2] There was a rich tangle of manorial courts, hundred courts and parish meetings in which manorial tenants and villagers not only made decisions but also held office regularly and democratically. Participation in voting was the reasonable implication of widespread communal responsibilities. Office-holding itself was regarded as such a responsibility and among the others were typically the burdens of road repairs, property maintenance and water supply preservation. The poor rate and other local and central taxes were burdens on the pockets, rather than on the time, of parishioners. Rights and responsibilities were never equally balanced, of course, and the mid-seventeenth century was a period of increasingly oligarchic parochial government. In Chudleigh, parish meetings, held twice a year, were attended by fifteen to twenty of the most prominent socially exalted inhabitants. They elected the Seven Men, a 'select vestry' which changed annually but which would frequently hand over executive power in the parish to two or three named individuals. In Tavistock parish there were 'Twelve Men', in Hartland, 'Twenty Four Governors'. Even though Crediton had no charter and was therefore not a borough its twelve governors were powerful enough to attract the attention of the county gentry commissioners appointed by the terms of the Corporation Act. The separation of parish meetings and their managements was a restriction on popular involvement. The county institutions and the social hierarchy which reinforced them curtailed what at first glance appears as the quasi-autonomy of the parishes. Town meetings and their officers had to produce their accounts of poor relief for the inspection and counter-signatures of JPs. This was not a mere paternalistic commendation by local squires. In both decades the signatures on poor books include those of magistrates who lived far distant from those whose accounts they approved.

Parish accounts were taken in bundles by the hundred constables to Exeter, where they were examined by the justices at sessions. The changes in the commission of the peace from 1649 to 1670 were arbitrary in their effects on this supervision. Some parishes may have benefited from the scrutiny of JPs who lived nearby. In the 1650s Bere Ferrers accounted to magistrates from adjacent Plymouth; in the 1660s to county gentry who lived further afield. Cullompton accounts were internally audited by Robert Cockeram during the Interregnum but by JPs from the next (rural) parishes after the Restoration. In the case of Chudleigh, however, the distribution of magistrates favoured the town in the Sixties. The influence of the JPs could extend further into the financial affairs of the parish; in 1654 the churchwardens of Bere Ferrers recorded payments to justices' clerks 'to make our rate'. Even in a parish of two hundred and forty-eight adult males administrative skills were at a premium.

Thus 'the extensive participation of nearly every adult male in local affairs'[3] was hedged about by qualifications imposed by the wider social and institutional structure in the county. Further up in the county hierarchy, decision-making and initiative by those of parochial gentleman or yeoman status deteriorated into the mere bullying of their subordinate officials. Head constables did as they were bid by the justices. Grand jurors, robbed of their presenting function by Marian legislation, confined themselves to the parish pump problems vexing each of them separately. This parochial narrowness only reflected where the interests of minor gentlemen and yeomen lay; in a sense the 'county hierarchy' was an artificial construction based on a 'conspiracy' between central government and the justices of the peace in which lesser men could serve diligently and worthily but without any real power. Lower down the pyramid of local government the picture was bleaker still. The entire jury system rested on the efforts of bailiffs, who owed their places to the complexities of the local patronage machine. The frequently exalted sources of their authority did nothing to disguise their own obscurity. Petty jurors were becoming an oligarchy of have-nots whose principal qualification was residential proximity to Exeter.

During these decades patterns of participation among the minor officials varied hardly at all. No more of them served, neither did the quality of those in service improve or deteriorate. The structure of the jury system and the pattern of hundredal participation persisted unaltered through these troubled decades to prevent a collapse in the performance of local government, and therein lay the contribution of the officials below the level of magistrate.

The numbers of those in the commission of the peace remained fairly constant with perhaps something of an increase in the 1660s, but on a longer view it was in the tax commissions that participation developed from the trusted oligarchy of the county committees of sixty or so in the Forties towards a two hundred-strong reservoir. That so few traces of the activities of assessment and subsidy commissioners have survived can suggest only that either their work was uncontentious and informal or, more likely, that it was scarcely noticeable because of the commissioners' failure to function as a group. In either case tax administration was surrendered to local pressures during the Restoration period and pre-figured the operation of the 'acceptable and accepted' land tax.[4]

The stability of the commission of the peace in the 1660s is to be contrasted with changes of bewildering frequency in the previous decade, and corresponds to changing patterns of central-local government relations. The 'centralizing' policies of the Interregnum have been exaggerated; both the experiment of the major-generals and the sequestration reforms of 1650 foundered because no rules for administrative behaviour had been provided and reforming energy was dissipated in establishing them. Local procedures held up well even during the intrusion of the major-generals. The aim of government in the earlier 1650s was to create a dependable cadre of supporters in the commissions. Only in the later years was there evidence of a return to broader concepts of 'representativeness' and even then it may be guessed that a wider spectrum of social status was the aim rather than a consensus of political opinion. Nayler's case and the history of the second Protectorate Parliament as a whole offer evidence of a revival in the 'country' and by implication in the 'county' ethos. The Restoration was a surrender to the county gentry and the apotheosis of a local squire like William Morrice who grew progressively more active in local affairs during the 1650s might have been the history of magistracy itself in these two decades. Changes in the commissions after 1660 were aimed not at achieving support but at a more sophisticated concept of 'balance'. Once the office-holders of the Interregnum had been eliminated from the local political consciousness, the changes were few until the 1670s and the reappearance of party conflict.

Perhaps the most decisive measure of the effectiveness of a regime, when attitudes and the various facets of participation have been examined, is the quality and volume of its performance. The abstention and exclusion of the royalist gentry from local government had surprisingly few effects. Despite attacks on the Bench in the earlier years of the decade enough county gentlemen remained to endow the Devon magistracy with adequate kudos. The competence of new men cannot be doubted and although J.S. Morrill's view of the Cheshire magistrates as notably humane and enlightened is not reflected in this study, the Devon JPs met the severe problems confronting them in the late 1640s and early Commonwealth period squarely if not particularly imaginatively. The new participants introduced no changes in the performance of government tasks but devoted some energy to the problem of controlling the structure.

The Sixties were more innovative but only insofar as the interests of JPs and county gentry and local government itself were co-extensive. Attitudes to the poor, the resumption of petty sessions development, the endless stream of posturing directives to subordinate officials, the Corporation Act, the Game Laws—all indicate the extent of the surrender to the gentry in 1660. Even the militia was transformed from the scourge of the localistic into the county community itself in martial guise. The range of local government activity was not extended but the improvements in fiscal methods, the drive towards greater accountability of officials to the JPs, produced more readily available funds to relieve maimed soldiers, the most urgent demand made of the Bench after the Restoration. The harrying of yeomen constables enhanced the dignity of the harriers, and the maimed soldiers themselves were but a group of dependents wounded in the cause of Charles I, a cause viewed ironically, with small justification, as the cause of the county community. Mr Hinton's dictum that government was 'granted in response to a demand'[5] remained broadly true at local level but the enforcement of the 1650 fornication and adultery act by a section of the magistracy against the wishes of parish leaders revealed how, in order to be successful, 'centralization' had to strike a chord in the localities even if it could, in so doing, transcend institutional boundaries.

The government of 1649 began its work with no illusions that it could claim more than minimal consent. The Restoration regime, more confident, more effective, certainly more popular, rejected realism at its inauguration in favour of disingenuous posturing, always a useful expedient for magistrates, which bordered on self-deception. It was the response of the Bench to an almost unwelcome degree of continuity. Such continuity in performance had to be maintained but the government responsible for that performance had to be execrated. It was much like Clarendon's unconvincing attempt to praise Cromwell while insisting that 'he had all the wickednesses ... for which Hell fyre is prepared'.[6]

NOTES

1. K. Wrightson, D. Levine: *Poverty and Piety in an English Village: Terling 1525-1700* (1979), pp. 134-41.
2. DRO: Bere Ferrers PO 20, PS 1, PW 56, 43-47; Broadclyst PW 10/2, PO 1, 40, 44, 57, 131 OF/A/1-2; Chudleigh PW1, PO1; Crediton 1660 A/262-289; Cullompton PO 1, PW 2, PV 1; Hartland 1201 A/PW 2 A; Hennock PO 2; Tawstock PW 2, PW 11; Warkleigh PO 1.
3. Carl Bridenbaugh: *Vexed and Troubled Englishmen 1590-1642* (1968), p. 242 quoted by K. Thomas: 'The Levellers and the Franchise' in Aylmer (ed.): *The Interregnum*, p. 61.
4. C. Brooks: 'Public Finance and Political Stability: The Administration of the Land Tax 1688-1720'. *Historical Journal*, XVII (1974), pp. 281-300.
5. R.W.K. Hinton: 'The Decline of Parliamentary Government under Elizabeth I and the Early Stuarts', *Cambridge Historical Journal*, XIII (1957), p. 127.
6. Clarendon: *History* (Macray ed.), VI, p. 97.

Index

221